THE POEMS
OF
AIMERIC DE PEGUILHAN

Edited and translated with introduction and commentary

BY

WILLIAM P. SHEPARD

(late of Hamilton College)

AND

FRANK M. CHAMBERS

(Northwestern University)

NORTHWESTERN UNIVERSITY PRESS
EVANSTON, ILLINOIS
1950

NORTHWESTERN UNIVERSITY STUDIES

VIRGIL B. HELTZEL, *Editor*

Humanities Series Number Twenty-four

Open access edition funded by the National Endowment for the Humanities/Andrew W. Mellon Foundation Humanities Open Book Program.

William P. Shepard, Frank M. Chambers. The Poems of Aimeric De Peguilhan. Evanston, Ill.: Northwestern University Press, 1950.

ISBN 978-0-8101-3868-1 (paper)
ISBN 978-0-8101-3869-8 (ebook)

PREFACE

This edition of the poems of Aimeric de Peguilhan was begun a number of years ago by the late Mr. Shepard (died 19 November 1948). He had established critical texts and made translations of all the poems, and had written notes for the first nineteen. Then, increasing ill-health compelled him to give up the idea of ever completing the edition, and he turned his material over to me for that purpose. Unfortunately, in the process of transfer, everything connected with the poems numbered fourteen through nineteen was lost. I had, therefore, to reestablish the text of these poems, to translate them, and to write notes for them as well as for poems twenty to fifty-two. Since, however, Mr. Shepard had already published separate editions of a few of the later poems, I drew freely on these for the notes. For the Introduction, the text of the *Vida,* the list of proper names, the glossary, and the work of assembling the edition, I alone am responsible. Furthermore, since Mr. Shepard's texts were not actually ready for the printer, I had to copy and check all that he had done, including the texts and all the variant readings. In doing so, I occasionally took the liberty of introducing readings closer to those of the MSS, which Mr. Shepard had altered. For example, where he had given the text of one MS in the orthography of another, I uniformly adhered to the orthography of the MS used as a base. This seemed to me far less arbitrary than an attempt to regularize the spelling, which was not carried out consistently in any case. In a very few lines, I have ventured to differ with Mr. Shepard's interpretation, but never, I think, without giving due consideration to his opinion, for which I have learned to feel the greatest respect. It is likely that he himself, on revising his work, would have made a good many of the changes that I introduced.

The task of proving that poem 31 was not written by Aimeric was largely mine; and the rejection of poem 53 is wholly my work (see the section on attributions).

The edition is, however, to some extent the result of a real collaboration. Mr. Shepard and I spent a few days together one summer discussing the edition, and we exchanged numerous letters concerning it. His health permitted him to read the first draft of that part of the Introduction which deals with the life of the poet, and he suggested a few changes and additions. Some ideas later incorporated into other sections of the Introduction, and into the notes that I wrote for the individual poems, likewise came in the first place from him. And, on the other hand, he repeatedly asked my opinion concerning the work he had already done.

I should perhaps say here, once and for all, that I am not entirely responsible for the rather extensive changes made in the text and notes of certain poems that Mr. Shepard had published separately. He introduced many of them himself into the texts that he turned over to me. But here also I carried out the principle enunciated above of adhering as closely as possible to the readings and orthography of the MS serving as base.

Our readings are taken from the printed diplomatic editions of the MSS designated $ABD^{e}FaGHLOPQSUa^{1}c$ (see Pillet-Carstens, *Bibliographie der Troubadours*, Halle, 1933), though in some cases Mr. Shepard checked these editions with the MSS themselves. For the others, Mr. Shepard made copies directly from the MSS. In addition, I have checked these latter readings from photostats made for Mr. Shepard (and given by him to the Hamilton College Library), from microfilms of the Modern Language Association of America series deposited in the Library of Congress, or directly from the manuscripts.

The poems are arranged in this edition according to the numbering of Pillet-Carstens, based on that of Bartsch (see the Bibliography). This seemed more satisfactory and less confusing than an attempt to rearrange the poems according to a systematic classification by genres or by dates.

The bibliographical material given for each poem includes only critical editions and such other editions as are not listed in Pillet-Carstens.

The variants are meant to be fairly complete, apart from merely orthographical differences. I believe that no variant which seriously affects the meaning has been omitted.

I should like to express my thanks to the librarians of the Hamilton College library, the Library of Congress, and the J. P. Morgan Library of New York (owner of MS. *N*), for their kindness in lending me photostats and microfilms and in supplying information. I wish also to thank the Modern Language Association of America (and particularly Mr. W. T. Pattison, of the Committee on Photographic Reproductions) for arranging to have some of these microfilms made, at my request; and Miss Mary Hilton and Miss Virginia Casey, of the Deering Library of Northwestern University, for securing various interlibrary loans. I am indebted to the Committee on Research of the Northwestern University Graduate School for a grant which enabled me to purchase certain microfilms. And I wish to thank my wife for patient and invaluable help in preparing the manuscript for the printer.

FRANK M. CHAMBERS

TABLE OF CONTENTS

[1] The first lines are given as they appear in Pillet-Carstens.

INTRODUCTION

LIFE

Aimeric de Peguilhan was one of the last of the great Provençal poets. In his time, the Albigensian persecutions brought to an end the carefree life of many Southern courts, and ended likewise their generous patronage of literature. In Spain and in northern Italy the Provençal lyric found a haven for a while; Aimeric himself enjoyed the hospitality of both these countries. But a literature cannot hope to survive for long on foreign soil, and when the great poets died, none took their place. At length only the arid productions of the *puis* remained as an epitaph to this shortest-lived of all significant literatures. The soul of the Provençal lyric was gone; it had passed into Italian and French poems, and thence has pervaded most of the love poetry that the western world has produced.

At his best, Aimeric almost rivals Bernart de Ventadorn in his graceful and unusually sincere tenderness. But even his most violent partisan could hardly assign him a rank beside Bernart, for his moments of genius are all too rare, and the mass of his work provides abundant evidence of the monotony and triteness of Provençal poetry. Even when he is not distinguished, however, he has certain merits. For the most part, he avoids the wilful obscurity that mars the work of some of the best troubadours; his poems are simple and clear, his expression direct, his images apt and unstrained. His songs reveal a high-minded man of taste and discrimination, and in his *tensos* he usually defends the more idealistic alternative. It is also true that he never descends to the cynicism and the crudity which are common even in the more respectable troubadours. Aimeric's poems are consistently noble in thought, if sometimes pedestrian in expression.

In the absence of any historical records, there are two main sources for the facts of Aimeric's life: the Provençal *Vida* (the text of which immediately precedes the poems in this edition), and his own verses. The *Vida* supplies a vague and not too reliable framework for a biography; but at least it is not derived entirely from the poems themselves (as is often true), and so has, in a sense, the authority of an independent source. From the allusions in the poems to historical personages and events, one can piece together the probable course of the author's life; but here too the references are distressingly vague, and the people in many cases cannot be identified with certainty, either because the names are not explicit (Count, Lady), or because the persons themselves are unknown (Saladon). Nevertheless, a fair number of great names are found in the poems and in the envois, and make it possible to supplement and correct the *Vida* with more specific information, and to set approximate dates for the main events of Aimeric's career.

His family must have come originally from the village of Péguilhan, in the department of Haute-Garonne, near Saint-Gaudens; but Aimeric himself, according to the *Vida*, was born in Toulouse. A certain Pons de Peguilhan was consul of Toulouse in 1202;[1] we have no other historical records of the family. The date of Aimeric's birth we may fix, for reasons which I shall give in a moment, not later than 1175. The *Vida*, from which alone we know something of his early life, says that his father was a cloth-merchant. "And he learned songs and *sirventes*; but he sang very badly. And he fell in love with a townswoman, his neighbor, and that love showed him how to compose, and he made about her many good songs. But her husband picked a quarrel with him and did him dishonor; Aimeric avenged himself by wounding him in the head with a sword; wherefore he had to leave Toulouse and go into exile." There are two possible echoes of this in the extant poems. In one (34), Aimeric deplores the fact that love is no longer what it was in the days before he was exiled. And Guillem de Berguedan may be alluding to this adventure in the final thrust of his *partimen* with Aimeric: "Valiant Sir Aimeric, don't try to brag! For if you loved as much as you boast (that you do), you would not have come so far away from Toulouse."

Aimeric addresses a poem (7) to a Count of Toulouse, who in all probability is Raymond VI (born 1156, ruled 1194–1222). Another poem (51), addressed simply to a "Count," may also be meant for Raymond. And some MSS (which we follow in our texts) address two poems (21, 46) to the "Queen of Toulouse"—Eleanor, wife of Raymond, who was so called by the troubadours because she was the daughter of a king, Alfonso II of Aragon. It was not unusual, in speaking of ladies who married men of lesser rank than themselves, to give them the title which they might have claimed by right of birth. If these envois are authentic, then Aimeric dedicated three and possibly four poems to the Count and the "Queen" of Toulouse. When did he know these people? In the first place, it is not necessary to suppose that he met Eleanor in Toulouse, for she was the sister of one of Aimeric's Spanish patrons, Peter II of Aragon, and she did not marry Raymond until 1200, when she was still extremely young. So it is quite possible that Aimeric came to know her in Spain, after he had left Toulouse. This is indeed likely, for her name is joined in these envois with those of the king and prince of Castile. As for Raymond, nothing tells us whether Aimeric knew him before he left Toulouse, or whether he met him later. In any case, both the envoi that is certainly meant for Raymond and the one that may be for him indicate that the poems were *sent* to the Count (perhaps from Spain), not delivered in person. We may therefore assume that if Aimeric knew Raymond before going to Spain, it was only briefly.

On leaving Toulouse, then, according to the *Vida*, Aimeric "went to

[1] Chabaneau, *Biographies*, page 282, note 1.

Catalonia; Guillem de Berguedan received him, and helped him and his poetry, and gave him his palfrey and his garments, and presented him to King Alfonso of Castile, who advanced him in arms and in honor. And he stayed in those regions a long time."

The only monument we have to the friendship between Aimeric and Guillem is the *partimen* (19) between the two on the subject: Whether it is better to love without return, or to be loved without being in love oneself. The cynical Guillem chooses the second alternative, as promising greater reward, and Aimeric defends the first.

Guillem de Berguedan was from Bergá, near Barcelona, and is the author of some twenty *sirventes* and a few other poems, often very obscure and very indecent—not at all the sort of thing one would expect Aimeric to like. But we may be grateful to him for helping our poet with his horse and his cast-off clothing (fairly common gifts to troubadours), and especially for introducing him to the King of Castile. Throughout his life, Aimeric was singularly fortunate in securing the good-will of the great. Whether through Guillem or in some other way, he came into the good graces not only of Alfonso of Castile, but also of Peter II of Aragon; and he undoubtedly spent some time in both courts, for he addresses a total of eleven poems to these kings and their families.

His stay in Spain, more than anything else, helps to fix the date of Aimeric's birth. His encounter with Guillem de Berguedan tells us that he must have come to Spain before 1200, since Guillem seems to have died about that time.[2] His envois to the king of Aragon provide a further limitation.

Aimeric directs seven poems (14, 20, 27, 38, 42, 43, 49), by envois, to a King of Aragon, not otherwise designated. But in the poem *En aquelh temps* (26), he laments the death of several patrons, among them King Peter of Aragon, who can only be Peter II (1196–1213). It seems natural, therefore, to assume that all these other poems were also meant for Peter. Jeanroy[3] attributes two of them to Peter's son James, and supposes that Aimeric made at least two trips to Spain. This seems to be a purely gratuitous assumption, and on the whole a rather improbable one, since Aimeric was in Italy shortly before James's accession (1213), and nothing indicates that he ever left that country again. The two envois that Jeanroy would claim for James (14, 42) contain these words: "King of Aragon, whoever sees your joyous countenance may well say, 'From a good father comes a good child' " (14), and "To the good King, son of a good father, go your way, Song, into Aragon" (42). These expressions imply that the king had only recently come to the throne, at the death of his father; but I see no objection to applying them to the early years of Peter, whose rule began in 1196. Aimeric

---

[2] Jeanroy, *Poésie lyrique*, I, 377.

[3] *Op. cit.*, I, 196.

may or may not have known Peter's father, Alfonso II; but at least Alfonso left a good reputation behind him, which Peter himself did not, having died at the battle of Muret, fighting against the Christian army of the Albigensian crusaders. And since Aimeric actually names only one King of Aragon in his poems, I think we are safe in giving all these envois to that one—Peter II.

We have seen, however, that at least two of Aimeric's poems were addressed to that king in the early years of his reign, which would mean shortly after 1196. This, of course, fits in perfectly with the date we have given above for Aimeric's encounter with Guillem de Berguedan. Working back from this, and remembering that Aimeric had had amorous adventures and had composed poems before coming to Spain, we must place his birth at least as far back as 1175.[4]

Three poems of Aimeric are addressed to Alfonso VIII, King of Castile (1158–1214). In one (21), his name and kingdom are expressly stated; in another (50),[5] he is called only "King of Castile"; the third (24) is addressed only to "King Alfonso." But there is little doubt that the second and third, as well as the first, refer to Alfonso VIII. "King Alfonso" also stands in the list of lately deceased patrons in *En aquelh temps* (26), along with "his fair son"; although not otherwise identified, this is undoubtedly the Infante Ferdinand, who died in 1211, around the age of twenty-two. Another poem (46), addressed to the "Infante of Castile," is meant for the same prince.

We have already mentioned two envois to the "Queen of Toulouse." But other MSS give one (21) to "the well-taught Queen," and the other (46), to "peerless Queen Eleanor." If these envois occurred alone, these variants would call for no comment here; but in both, this lady shares the honors with a member of the royal family of Castile—with Alfonso in one and the Infante in the other. Now, Alfonso's wife was named Eleanor (as was the "Queen of Toulouse"); and if we followed these MSS, we should normally think that the poet had the Queen of Castile in mind, in view of the company she keeps. The identification is not absolutely certain; but it seems to us that the reading "Queen of Toulouse" would be more liable to modification by scribes than the other forms we have quoted, and we take it for the original name.

Several other persons share these Spanish envois. The name of a certain "Countess of Sobeiratz" is linked with that of Alfonso (24). This is presumably Elvira de Sobiratz, wife of Ermengaud VIII (1183–1208), the last Count of Urgel; she is praised by both the other Aimerics (de Sarlat and de Belenoi), as well as by our poet.[6]

---

[4] Bergert's date of 1180 (*Damen*, p. 78) is a little late.

[5] Certain MSS give this envoi to "Tiriaca"; this would be a *senhal* designating some unidentifiable person.

[6] Bergert, *Damen*, p. 43.

The name of Gaston VI of Béarn occurs twice (42, 49); on both occasions, his partner in honor is Peter of Aragon. Gaston ruled over a considerable region around Pau. From the eleventh century on, most of the Viscounts of Béarn had acknowledged allegiance to no sovereign; but the kings of Aragon claimed them as vassals, and Gaston was quick to appeal to Peter II when his land was invaded by the crusaders. Neither poem was written at the court of Aragon, for in the other envois Aimeric bids them both to go into Aragon. It is quite possible, then, that Aimeric was visiting Gaston when he wrote the poems, although the *Vida* says nothing of such a visit.

The Count of Comminges is praised in an envoi (27), likewise in the company of Peter II. The County of Comminges lay not far to the southwest of Toulouse; its seat, Muret, was the scene of a great battle during the Albigensian Crusade. Like Béarn, Comminges owed some sort of allegiance to Aragon; it is natural, therefore, that the ruler of Comminges should be connected in this envoi with the King of Aragon. The Count at this time was Bernard IV (1181–1226).[7]

This Bernard of Comminges married Mary of Montpellier in 1197, and divorced her in 1204.[8] Now, one MS (*C*) joins the name of the Countess of Comminges with that of Peter II. The poem in question (14) is one that we have already dated early in Peter's reign, so the time would fit perfectly; and I am inclined to believe that the envoi to the Countess is genuine, even though the other MSS omit it. If it is authentic, then Aimeric was something of a prophet, for he linked thus the names of a future husband and wife: in the same year that Mary was divorced from Bernard, she married Peter of Aragon.[9] Another poem (43), addressed to Peter, to a Countess Mary (who may be Mary of Montpellier-Comminges), and to the Marquis of Montferrat, causes very serious difficulties. It will be discussed among the Italian poems.

In addition to the envois, the list of patrons in *En aquelh temps* (26) presents four Spanish names. Three we have already mentioned. The fourth is "En Dieguo," who is to be identified with Diego López de Haro, a lord of Vizcaya.

This completes the list of Aimeric's Spanish and semi-Spanish patrons, and, incidentally, the list of his poems that we know to have been composed in Spain or near it. They are all *chansos*, addressed, apart from the envois, to unnamed ladies, to Love, and the like. Not one of them refers to any historical event or to any identifiable person. Not a word in any of them helps to define Aimeric's relations with his noble patrons. The poem *En aquelh*

---

[7] Bergert, *Damen*, p. 33.

[8] Bergert, *Damen*, pp. 32–34.

[9] Mario Equicola obtained, perhaps from a now lost *Vida*, the information that Aimeric "amò Donna Maria di Ragona, et ingannato da lei, amò Donna Endia de Lisle, sorella del Conte di Tolosa." Indie, sister of Raymond VI, married Raymond de l'Isle-Jourdain in 1206 (Chabaneau, *Biographies*, p. 283). This, of course, is to be taken with a grain of salt.

temps makes it clear that some of them *were* his patrons (a fact which we should have taken for granted anyway), but nothing more than that. We cannot know whether the poet went first to the court of Aragon or to that of Castile, how long he stayed in either kingdom, what he did while he was there, whether he actually visited the little courts of southern France, and many other interesting things. Diez[10] arranges several of the poems into a *Liebesroman*, in which Aimeric's real or pretended amorous adventures are put into a logical sequence; but I fear the sequence is somewhat arbitrary. One can group together certain poems on similar themes—for example, 46 and 14 (the poet begins to see the faithlessness of one lady and the kindness of another, whom he had neglected for the first); 20, 42, 51 (he dares not reveal his love, because of his lady's high rank). But how is one to connect these two groups, or to fit in number 7, which refers to a new love which has severed him from an old one; but here the new lady does not love him, while in 14 she loved him before he loved her? I am afraid that ingenuity finds little reward in such endeavors, which can lead at best only to more or less plausible hypotheses.

It is certain, however, that after spending several years in Spain, Aimeric left there and went to Italy. One MS of the *Vida* (*R*) says that he stopped at Toulouse, in the guise of a sick relative of the King of Castile, to see his first love, whose husband was away on a pilgrimage to Santiago; but this little tale is probably apochryphal. It is likely, however, that one and perhaps two of Aimeric's *partimens* are to be dated between his departure from Spain and his arrival in Italy.

Robert Meyer, in his study on Gaucelm Faidit, dates the *partimen* in which Aimeric engaged with the poet (28) "after 1207";[11] he thinks that it was composed in southern France, perhaps at the court of Raimon d'Agout. The poets choose Raymond Roger of Foix (ruled 1188–1223) for their arbiter in this debate, a fact which would certainly place the poem before the Albigensian Crusade, in which the Count of Foix suffered much, and would have had other things on his mind than judging such trifles. We are probably safe in placing the poem in the year 1208. It is likely, furthermore, that the *partimen* with Elias d'Ussel (37) was written at about the same time, possibly in the same place; for Elias and Gaucelm had literary relations with each other,[12] and we have nothing else to go by in placing this poem.

Aimeric may also have stopped at Aups (in Provence) to make the acquaintance of Blacatz, to whom he sends a *chanso* (8) by this envoi "Song, go and tell Sir Blacatz in Provence that he gives worth to worthiness and

---

[10] *Leben und Werke*, pp. 345–346.

[11] *Das Leben des Trobadors Gaucelm Faidit*, p. 57.

[12] See Audiau, *Poésies des quatre troubadours d'Ussel*, pp. 13–14, and Chabaneau, *Biographies*, p. 247.

repute to the reputable, for one cannot, praising him, overpraise him; his worth is so worthy and so true."

I see no reason to discredit the statement of the *Vida* that Aimeric went immediately to Montferrat upon reaching Italy. The Marquisate of Montferrat lay near to France (in Piedmont, around Casale), and the lords of Montferrat had shown themselves liberal patrons of the poetry of Provence. Precisely when Aimeric arrived there is another matter. Assuming that he went to Spain around 1197, that he stayed there eight or ten years ("a long time," says the *Vida*), and that he took a year or two to reach Italy (and these are only guesses), then he would have come to Montferrat around 1208 or 1209. These dates fit what we have said above about the *partimen* with Gaucelm Faidit, and also suit the time of his arrival at the court of Este, which we can fix somewhat more accurately.[13]

Peire Vidal and Raimbaut de Vaqueiras had preceded Aimeric at the court of Montferrat, and Raimbaut especially had won the esteem and friendship of Marquis Boniface I (1192–1207). Boniface had made him a knight and had taken him along on the Fourth Crusade. Both lord and poet died in the East, presumably in Boniface's kingdom of Thessalonica. This kingdom was given to Boniface during the Crusade, to console him for not having been chosen emperor. At his death, he left it to his younger son Demetrius, while his older son William IV took charge of the lands in Italy. Demetrius was driven out in 1222 by the Prince of Epirus. In 1224, William organized an army to reinstate his brother in Thessalonica, but died (1225) before he could start out.[14]

If our dates are correct, it was William IV (1207–1225) whom Aimeric met at Casale or at Moncalvo ("Moncal"), and to whom he addressed two poems. One is that, already mentioned (43), sent by three envois to the King of Aragon, to a "Countess Mary," and to the Marquis of Montferrat. Here are the three envois: "King of Aragon, every day your noble deeds grow more abundant, because you know how to season them so nicely with friendliness and good manners.—I should hardly believe myself that I once saw the lordly marquis (*lo marques emperial*) at Montferrat or at Moncal, if I should not see him there another time.—The Countess Mary is so good that, as God help me, I know no lady with more good qualities and with fewer bad ones, unless one should wrong her." This is rather puzzling. Were it not for the second envoi, which can be meant only for the Marquis of Montferrat, we could refer the last to Mary of Comminges; but it seems unlikely that Aimeric had been at the court of Montferrat in 1204, when

[13] Cavedoni (*Accoglienze*, p. 284) dates Aimeric's arrival around the turn of the century; but our chronology up to this point is well enough established to permit us to reject this date.

[14] This is taken largely from Jeanroy, *Poésie lyrique*, I, 231, and from Schultz-Gora, *Briefe*, pp. 111 ff.

Mary ceased to be Countess of Comminges. Bergert[15] takes the "imperial marquis" literally, and refers it to Boniface of Montferrat at the time of the capture of Constantinople (April 12, 1204), when there was talk of making him emperor. Mary's marriage to Peter II was celebrated on June 15 of that year, and Aimeric might not have heard of her separation from Bernard when he wrote the poem. Schultz-Gora[16] thinks, as I do, that to Aimeric the "Marquis of Montferrat" is always William IV, and that the poem was written later than 1204. He identifies "Countess Mary" as Mary of Auramala. Bergert objects that the title does not fit her, and that Aimeric is accurate in his use of titles. I think the Countess Mary must remain a problem; but even if we leave her out of account, it is strange that Aimeric should have directed his poem to patrons as far removed from each other as the King of Aragon and the Marquis of Montferrat. And, incidentally, although the envois imply that the poem was not written at Montferrat, they do not imply that it was written away from the court of Aragon; this is a further complication. There is the possibility that Aimeric used the same poem more than once, merely taking off an old envoi and adding a new one; then the copyists, finding several envois attached to the same poem, simply copied them all into their anthologies. That may be what happened here. If so, then the Countess Mary is in all likelihood Mary of Comminges, and the poem in its original form belongs to Aimeric's Spanish sojourn. The envoi to the Marquis of Montferrat was then added and the poem sent back to him after Aimeric had left his domains.

The other poem addressed to William of Montferrat is a crusade song (11). In it, Aimeric pleads with the Marquis to take the cross, and praises William of Malaspina for having already done so; he also recalls the glorious deeds of earlier lords of Montferrat: "Marquis of Montferrat, your forbears held the glory and honor of Syria; and may you, Lord, wish to have it too. In God's name, put on the holy sign and pass over yonder, for that will give you fame and honor in this world, and salvation in God." Lewent[17] places the poem in the spring of 1213, when Innocent III began to urge a new crusade to accomplish what the Fourth had been turned aside from doing: namely, to reconquer the Holy Sepulcher. In 1213, Philip Augustus and Frederick II were hostile to John of England and Otto IV, and are doubtless the "kings and emperors" blamed in the poem for not making peace among themselves. The crusade was to be discussed in the Lateran Council of 1215; meanwhile, many took the cross, but few showed any inclination to

[15] *Damen*, pp. 33–34. De Bartholomaeis (*Poesie storiche*, II, 32) would date the poem (or the envoi to the Marquis of Montferrat) in 1220, after the coronation of Frederick II, and explain the *marques emperial* on the ground that William was a cousin of Frederick.

[16] *Briefe*, p. 144.

[17] *Kreuzlied*, pp. 28–30. See also Luchaire, *Innocent III—la question d'Orient*, pp. 281–299. Diez (*Leben und Werke*, p. 351) dates the poem in 1215, which does not fit quite so well.

depart for the East. The Marquis of Montferrat did not take the cross, and eventually, because of the apathy of the Christian rulers, the whole plan was abandoned, or rather postponed.

Since none of the poems of Aimeric can be assigned definitely to his stay in Montferrat, we may conclude either that the poems he wrote there have been lost, or that he remained only a short while.[18] If he arrived around 1209, as we think, then the latter conclusion is probably the correct one, as we shall see.

Although the Marquis of Montferrat is the only Italian patron named in the *Vida*, the extant poems show that he held a far less important position in Aimeric's life than did the families of Este and Malaspina. It is to them that Aimeric must have gone on leaving Montferrat, and probably first to the court of Este. He was there in 1212, and he was at the court of Malaspina in 1220. It is a comfort to find a few easily determinable fixed points in Aimeric's career, which up to now has been so vague; 1212 is actually the very first date of his life that we know with certainty. In general, the Italian poems of Aimeric contain a comparative abundance of historical and personal allusions, which allow us to place them with some accuracy. Unlike those written in Spain, they are not exclusively concerned with the poet's real or imagined loves (though these are by no means neglected), and the patrons are not always relegated to a brief envoi. In addition to a number of *chansos*, there are four funeral laments composed in Italy, and several *tensos*, *coblas*, and *sirventes*.

Azzo VI of Este (1196–1212), whose marquisate lay around Ferrara and Verona, ruled the latter city jointly with the Count of San Bonifazio from 1207 to 1212. In 1212, both men died within a short time of each other, in the month of November.[19] Since Aimeric was at the court of Este, it was only natural that he should couple the names of the two nobles in the *planh*, or funeral song, that he wrote for the occasion. Actually, he composed two *planhs*, in both of which both names appear.[20] It may be that he was dissatisfied with the first poem, and wrote another. One (48) is preserved in only two MSS, and may be the rejected first poem, though the second (30) is by no means a reworking of it. Or Aimeric may have felt that two deaths called for two poems, lest it be thought that he was economizing his effort. Whatever the reason for the duplication, it is evident that

---

[18] The reason for his short stay may well have been William's lack of generosity, to which both Folquet de Romans and Falconet allude in no uncertain terms (Jeanroy, *Poésie lyrique*, I, 236). In this respect, William was quite unlike his father, Boniface I, who was more than generous.

[19] See Cavedoni, *Accoglienze*, p. 274, and De Bartholomaeis, *Poesie storiche*, I, 182. According to the chronicles quoted there, the Count died November 10, and Azzo November 15.

[20] Kolsen, in *Zeitschrift*, XLI, 541–542, attributes 48 to Folquet de Romans, against the testimony of the two MSS, and in a rather arbitrary fashion. This and other questions of authorship will be discussed in a later section.

the main subject of both poems is the Marquis of Este, and that the Count of San Bonifazio is added because of his association with Azzo and because of the coincidence of their deaths.

Azzo's virtues were those dear to the troubadours: generosity first of all, and then courtesy, kindness, and the ability to recognize and reward merit. Perhaps because he died shortly after Aimeric came to Este, Azzo appears in Aimeric's poems only as a dear memory, rather than as a living friend. He is named in that goodly company of patrons whom Aimeric calls over, sadly and lovingly, at the beginning of the famous invocation to Frederick II (26), to which we have referred several times: Alfonso of Castile and his son; Peter of Aragon; Diego; the Marquis of Este; Saladon . . . they are all dead; who remains? Aimeric addresses no poems to Azzo, but his extreme gratitude argues more than a passing acquaintance in the Marquis's last days. I think we must set his arrival at the court of Este not later than 1210.[21]

The family of Este was one of the oldest and most distinguished of the Italian noble houses. In the thirteenth century, they gained quite a reputation as patrons of Provençal poetry; but it appears that Aimeric was among the first to profit from their hospitality.[22] Bertoni is, I think, exaggerating when he says that Azzo VI was for Aimeric what Boniface of Montferrat was for Raimbaut de Vaqueiras;[23] I should like to reserve that place for William Malaspina, since Aimeric's acquaintance with Azzo cannot have lasted very long; but it is clear that Azzo welcomed him kindly and hospitably.

Azzo had two sons, Aldobrandino and Azzo, and at least two daughters, Beatrice and Costanza. Aldobrandino succeeded his father in 1212, but died three years later, leaving only a daughter, Beatrice. Azzo VII, therefore, succeeded his brother in 1215. We can probably put in that year a *tenso* (35) which Aimeric wrote with Guillem Raimon. This poem has to do with a young marquis who has just come into the title, and with whom the poets are not very well pleased. The grievances are vague, but among other things Guillem expresses the hope that the young man may resemble his father or his brother; Aimeric replies that he is the son of his mother. The mention of the father and brother would point to Azzo VII, whose father and brother had preceded him in the marquisate. The verses occur in only one MS (*H*), which attributes them to Guillem Raimon and "N'Aimeric"; thus it is not absolutely certain that they are the work of Aimeric de Peguilhan. If he wrote them, and if he had in mind Azzo VII, even though the verses may have been written jestingly, they show a certain lack of taste

---

[21] Cf. Casini, in *Propugnatore*, XII², 96 ("Rambertino Buvalelli").

[22] Casini, in *Propugnatore*, XII², 94–95; Cavedoni, *Accoglienze*, p. 269.

[23] Bertoni, *Duecento*, p. 20.

not elsewhere apparent in the works of Aimeric. At all events, the poet must not have liked Azzo VII as well as his father, for he mentions him nowhere else in his poems, though he asks Azzo's wife to judge a question of amorous casuistry.

There is, however, one other member of the Este family to whom Aimeric sings with evident admiration and gratitude: Beatrice. Beatrice took an interest in Aimeric, and was repaid with the paternal adoration and jocose love-making of the poet. So, I think, we must interpret the poems in which Aimeric professes to be languishing for love of the beautiful young Beatrice, who will have none of his love. Perhaps I should make it clear, however, that Aimeric nowhere makes love to "Beatrice of Este." He addresses poems to her by envois, often joining her name with that of William Malaspina; but the full name never occurs in the body of his poems. He makes love (particularly in the *descort*, 45) to "Lady Beatrice," who also figures in two envois, once in the company of the same William Malaspina. To complicate matters, he wrote a *planh* at the death of a "Countess Beatrice." Are these all the same lady? And who was she, or who were they?

Beatrice, daughter of Azzo VI (born 1191),[24] was, according to contemporary accounts, a girl of great beauty and virtue, who spent her youth "amid the pomp and favors of the world, amid ornaments and vanities of divers kinds, as is the custom of noble women of society."[25] But before the age of thirty, she wearied of this worldly life and entered a nunnery, probably between 1218 and 1220. She founded the Convent of San Giambattista at Gemmola, where she died in 1226, in the odor of sanctity.[26]

This Beatrice's niece, the daughter of Aldobrandino, was born around 1215. In 1234 she became the third wife of Andrew II of Hungary, but on the death of her husband she was so persecuted by her step-son Bela IV that she escaped in men's clothing and returned to Italy. Like her aunt, she retired to the convent of Gemmola, where she died in 1245.[27]

A third Beatrice of Este, another niece of the first, and daughter of Azzo VII, was born not before 1222, and died, likewise in a nunnery (that of San Antonio di Ferrara), before 1264.[28]

Aimeric is not alone in singing the praises of Beatrice of Este: Rambertino Buvalelli also addressed several poems to her.[29] Now, Rambertino died in 1221,[30] and could have written only for the daughter of Azzo VI. I see no reason whatever to doubt that she is also Aimeric's Beatrice. True, Bar-

[24] Bergert, *Damen*, p. 81.

[25] *Ibid.*, pp. 81–82.

[26] *Ibid.*, p. 82; Muratori, *Antichità estensi*, I, 404–405.

[27] Bergert, *Damen*, p. 82; Muratori, *Antichità estensi*, I, 419.

[28] Bergert, *Damen*, p. 82; Muratori, *Antichità estensi*, II, 20–21.

[29] Bertoni, *Rambertino Buvalelli*, pp. 3–6.

[30] *Ibid.*, p. 9.

bieri[31] and Diez[32] prefer the daughter of Aldobrandino; but in their day, because of some poems wrongly ascribed to Aimeric, it was thought that he lived far into the thirteenth century, and this identification seemed the more likely of the two.

Some have thought that so saintly a maiden as Azzo VI's daughter could not have inspired the purely secular praises of our poet; but if Rambertino wrote poems for her, why not Aimeric? Besides, she lived at the court until the age of twenty-seven or twenty-eight, presumably without declaring her intention of becoming a nun, and had plenty of time to receive the homage of our two poets. It is true that the troubadours generally sang for married ladies, but nothing compelled them to do so always; Raimbaut de Vaqueiras wrote for another unmarried Beatrice, the daughter of Boniface of Montferrat. And, finally, a conclusive argument in favor of the daughter of Azzo VI is that Aimeric often couples her name with that of William Malaspina, who died in 1220; at that time, the second Beatrice was five years old, and the third not yet born.

Beatrice of Este appears alone in the envoi of one song (16), and she is named three times (33, 34, 41) with William Malaspina, though I must admit that not all these envois appear in all the MSS. In addition, Aimeric chooses her for arbitress in a *partimen* (3) with Albert de Sestaron; Albert appeals to Emilia da Ravenna, the wife of Pietro Traversara.

Now, what about "Lady Beatrice," who figures in two envois (2, 12)? Is she Beatrice of Este? Since her name is joined in one of these poems (12) with that of William Malaspina, the constant partner of Beatrice of Este in the other poems, I think we can be certain that she is the same lady.

So far, we have met Beatrice only in envois, clearly in the guise of a patroness. But in the poem *Qui la vi en ditz* (45), Aimeric makes love to a "Lady Beatrice." Would this have been quite fitting, since marriage was normally required to let down the bars to love? I invite the reader to turn to the poem itself and form his own opinion. Personally, I see no real difficulty. In this poem, Beatrice is a noble lady, above Aimeric in rank, and from whom he expects no love in return for his affection, which he describes as *ses enjan* "without guile." All he asks is that she listen to his prayer to her; if she will listen, he wants no other favor from any lady. Is it not possible to regard this as the playful expression of the half paternal affection that Aimeric felt for Beatrice, mingled with the conventional love of the troubadour for every lady to whom he wrote a poem?

One other problem remains in connection with Beatrice of Este. Is it she whose death Aimeric laments in the *planh* (22) for "Countess Beatrice," perhaps the most touching of his funeral songs? That would certainly be the natural assumption. We are sure that Aimeric had a sincere regard for

---

[31] *Origini*, p. 112.

[32] *Leben und Werke*, p. 354.

Beatrice of Este, and we have no indication that he even knew any other Beatrice. But two apparently insuperable obstacles stand in the way of this identification. In the first place, Beatrice of Este was not a countess; in the second, she died a nun, and that fact is not mentioned in the poem. This lament, I suspect, has given rise to more research and more hypotheses than any other of Aimeric's poems except *Li fol e·il put* (32). Every Beatrice at all contemporary with him has been passed in review and accepted by one critic, only to be rejected by another. Diez[33] suggests Beatrice of Provence, wife of Charles of Anjou; but she died in 1269, when Aimeric would have been a very old man; and we have no evidence that he was ever at the court of Provence. Éméric-David[34] supposes a Beatrice who married William of Malaspina; since his wife's name was Este, she would then be the Beatrice of Este of the poems; unfortunately, her first name is unknown,[35] and this can only be a hypothesis. If it were true, it would solve nearly all our difficulties, and also answer a question I have avoided raising: Why does Aimeric so often link the names of Beatrice and William? Accepting Azzo VI's daughter as our Beatrice of Este, we are forced back on the rather lame explanation that the coupling of their names was a coincidence: that Aimeric simply wished to honor both of them.

Zingarelli[36] and Bergert[37] review these and other nominations for the rôle of Countess Beatrice: Papon, Galvani, and Desimoni favor the daughter of Thomas I of Savoy, wife of Raymond Bérenguer I of Provence, and mother of Diez's Countess Beatrice; but she also died very late for Aimeric (1266). Cavedoni[38] suggests the wife of Thomas I of Savoy; the date of her death is not known, but nothing indicates that Aimeric knew her or her court. Gröber[39] suggests the second Beatrice of Este, Aldobrandino's daughter; but, as we have seen, she was not a countess but the daughter of a marquis and the widow of a king, and she too died in a convent. Torraca[40] proposes Beatrice of Mangona, who married Count Paolo Traversara in 1216. This Beatrice died young, before February 9, 1225.[41] She was the daughter of a count, the sister of counts, and the wife of a count. Both her title and the date of her death fit perfectly. It is even likely that Aimeric knew her. He addresses a poem (47) to "Lady Emilia," presumably Emilia da Ravenna, who was the second wife of Pietro Traversara, and consequently in touch with the wife of his son Paolo. This Emilia, the reader may

---

[33] *Leben und Werke*, p. 357.

[34] In the *Histoire littéraire de la France*, XVIII, 690–693.

[35] Bergert, *Damen*, p. 79.

[36] *Due trovatori*, pp. 38–46.

[37] *Damen*, pp. 77–79.

[38] *Accoglienze*, p. 287.

[39] In *Romanische Studien*, II, 371 (see Zingarelli, *Due trovatori*, p. 46).

[40] *Donne italiane*, p. 52.

[41] *Ibid.*, p. 49.

remember, was chosen for judge by Albert de Sestaron in his *partimen* (3) with Aimeric.

Bergert[42] half-heartedly follows Torraca in making Beatrice of Mangona the Countess Beatrice of the *planh*. He also agrees that it may be to her that the "Lady Beatrice" poems are addressed. I have already expressed my conviction that these latter poems are meant for Beatrice of Este. As for the *planh*, it does seem unlikely that it was written for the daughter of Azzo VI, and Beatrice of Mangona is the most promising substitute yet put forward. But I am reluctant, even in the face of all this evidence, to believe that the Beatrice of the *planh* is other than the Beatrice of Este of the *chansos*. The matter, to my mind, is not settled; perhaps it never will be.

Torraca was led to his discussion of the *planh* by his study of another Provençal poem, the famous *treva* (236, 5a) of Guillem de la Tor, which he dates[43] shortly before 1220. In this poem, the two sisters Selvaggia and Beatrice of Auramala are quarreling because of the *mesclança e batailla* that a poem of one Aimeric had raised between them; each is afraid that the other's virtues may be praised above her own. Various ladies come to see them in order to effect a truce (*treva*), which they do apparently by simply suggesting it. The poet certainly does not tax his ingenuity to think of any solution of the difficulty; the poem's only value lies in the list of names of which it mainly consists. First of all comes Beatrice of Este:

> Na Biatritz i ven d'Est cui fins prez capdella,
> del marqueset d'Est *sor*, on valors renovella;
> e de Ravena i ven n'Esmilla cui apella
> fis prez, e de Magon na Biatritz la bella . . . [44]

In these lines, *sor* is Torraca's emendation for *moiller*, which is one syllable too long, and which also makes trouble because none of the Estes at that time had a wife named Beatrice. Torraca takes this Beatrice of Este to be the daughter of Azzo VI, sister of Azzo VII, the "marqueset." This gives some support to our conclusion that this is Aimeric's Beatrice of Este. She was well known in her day, appearing *first* in this group of ladies, and has nothing of the future nun about her. It will be noticed that Beatrice of Mangona also figures here. But the reference to Aimeric is even more interesting. Torraca[45] seems to believe that it was Aimeric de Peguilhan who brought about the strife between Selvaggia and her sister. Bergert,[46] however, points out that none of our Aimeric's extant poems mention Selvaggia or Beatrice of Auramala, whereas Aimeric de Belenoi does (9, 21). But it must be noted that Aimeric probably knew the sisters, as they were daugh-

---

[42] *Damen*, p. 79.

[43] *Donne italiane*, p. 51.

[44] Quoted from Torraca's text, *Donne italiane*, p. 57.

[45] *Op. cit.*, pp. 16, 41–42.

[46] *Damen*, p. 86, n. 1.

ters of Conrad of Malaspina, the brother of Aimeric's William Malaspina; certain MSS even give to Conrad one poem (25) that others attribute to William. I think we must admit that either Aimeric could have caused the dissension.

Beatrice and Azzo VI were not the only members of the Este family to receive Aimeric's homage. One MS (*O*) contains an envoi to Johanna, who married Azzo VII in 1221 and died in 1233. Zingarelli,[47] who quotes the envoi, admits that *O* is not a reliable source, and that it garbles the text of the poem in question (15). I think we may dismiss the envoi as spurious possibly imitated from that of another poem by Aimeric (2). But Aimeric definitely calls on this Johanna in one envoi (17): "Because Lady Johanna is most worthy and knows and perceives and understands, I wish her to decide justly which one should say of Love, good things or bad." Finally, some have thought Johanna the "lady baptized on Saint John's day":

> Una domna leyal
> Sai ieu qu'es de Plazensa,
> Mas estai en Valensa . . .
> E ten Guarda e Verona mandan,
> E·s bateget lo jorn de sant Johan (40).

Zingarelli,[48] whom we follow in our interpretation, takes the whole stanza as a series of plays on words: Piacenza, pleasing; Valenza, worthy; Garda, prudence; Verona, sincerity; the last line would then mean that she was joyful (*Johan, joia*), or that she had virtues normally ascribed to Saint John. He attributes the stanza to Beatrice of Este. This he thinks more likely, since William Malaspina is mentioned in the envoi, which follows immediately; and Aimeric delights in putting Beatrice and William together.

William, Marquis of Malaspina and Massa (1194–1220),[49] was the nephew of Albert of Malaspina, who joined in a *tenso* with Raimbaut de Vaqueiras (15, 1). William's interest in Provençal poetry was therefore no new thing in the family. About his life, our information is very scanty. The lands of the Malaspinas lay in Lunigiana (the region between Genoa and Tuscany, centering around Massa), but it is not clear which of these territories belonged to William and which to other branches of the family.[50] Aimeric expresses his opinion of William and defines their relations very succinctly: "The worthy William Malaspina upholds generosity and lady-service and courtesy and me" (41). In addition to the four envois already mentioned above, in which William's name is paired with that of Beatrice, William appears in four other poems, which add something to our knowledge of the man. One is the crusade poem addressed to the Marquis of

---

[47] *Due trovatori*, pp. 30–31.

[48] *Op cit.*, p. 36.

[49] See, among others, Jeanroy, *Poésie lyrique*, I, 240.

[50] Schultz, *Zeitschrift für r. Ph.*, VII, pp. 190, 193; also Jeanroy, *loc. cit.*

Montferrat, in which Aimeric praises William Malaspina for having already taken the cross (11). Since the crusade of 1213 was abandoned, it is unlikely that William ever went to the Holy Land. The second poem (40), (containing the reference to the lady baptized on Saint John's day), has this envoi: "However much others may bestir themselves or oppose him, Malaspina stands firm and upright." The third is the rather difficult *Li fol e·il put e·il filhol* (32).[51] In this, certain shameless and undeserving minstrels are shown thronging to Malaspina: "Now you will see the band and the troop coming towards Malaspina, of which they have the flesh and the hide." While this is obscure, it seems to imply that Malaspina was a place much frequented by *jongleurs* (and poets), the bad as well as the good.

The fourth poem calls for a somewhat longer discussion. It is the famous *planh* for William (10), which we can date in 1220. Aimeric praises William for the qualities dear to the troubadours, and compares his patron to Alexander, to Gawain,[52] to Yvain, and to Tristan. After these conventional eulogies, Aimeric adds this stanza, which seems sincere: "Fair, dear, and worthy Lord, what shall I do now? How can I remain here alive longer without you? You treated me so well in words and deeds that all other favors I scorn, in comparison with yours. Certain men, on your account, were wont to honor and welcome me, who now will be like strangers whom I have never seen. I shall never, at any time, find one to take your place nor who will make amends for your loss. I do not believe that anyone can do that." There can be little doubt that William Malaspina befriended Aimeric more than any other great lord whom he met in Italy, and that Aimeric repaid his beneficence with a very genuine affection. The *planh* and the other poems give abundant proof of the high esteem in which the poet held him.[53] We may assume that Aimeric spent a considerable time with the Marquis, and, from one phrase in the *planh* ("how can I remain *here* alive longer without you?"), we might infer that he was present when William died. In any case, it is reasonable to believe that the bulk of his stay at Malaspina came after the death of Azzo VI (1212), though he may have known William earlier.

Five MSS (*ADIKS*) of one poem (25) name Conrad of Malaspina in an envoi where the majority have William. Jeanroy,[54] under the impression that there are only two such MSS, thinks that "Conrad" is a scribal error for "William." I am not entirely convinced that this is true, even though

---

[51] Probably written around 1220: De Bartholomaeis, in *Studj romanzi*, VII, 1–59 and 287–342; Bertoni, *Duecento*, p. 23. The first writer places it after the death of William Malaspina.

[52] Or, according to other MSS, to William (of Orange?).

[53] De Bartholomaeis (*Poesie storiche*, I, 247) thinks that the *Salados* (otherwise unknown) of *En aquelh temps* refers to William. It is strange that William's name does not appear there, but I doubt that Aimeric would have called the Marquis by his proper name everywhere else, and then used a nickname here, particularly since the list contains no other *senhals*.

[54] *Poésie lyrique*, I, 240, n. 4.

the name does appear in company with that of Beatrice of Este. Indeed, I should say that for this very reason the scribes, having already come across William sharing the honors of the envois with Beatrice, would be inclined to substitute his name for that of Conrad, not the other way around. In our text, therefore, we read "Conrad," realizing that we may be mistaken. Aimeric, of course, could easily have known Conrad through William.

This concludes the list of Aimeric's known patrons, but not that of the Italian nobles to whom he refers. In the poem *Li fol e·il put* (32), he deplores the overrunning of the court of Saluzzo by disgusting and ill-spoken minstrels; this may indicate a first-hand acquaintance with conditions there. But since this is uncertain, I see no reason to go into the history of Saluzzo here.

There is, however, one politically important figure yet to be considered: the Emperor Frederick II. Frederick was born in Sicily, and spent much of his life there, surrounded by a court in which sprang up (somewhat later) a school of Italian poetry. Some have assumed that Frederick was also a patron of Provençal poetry; but this does not seem to be true. The Provençal poems addressed to him reflect, I believe, rather a political than a personal feeling of the authors. This appears to be the opinion of most scholars now.[55]

One of Aimeric's poems to Frederick is pretty obviously the result of hearsay, not of personal acquaintance; this is *En aquelh temps* (26), to which I have referred time and time again because of the enumeration of Aimeric's patrons which begins it. The poet continues in this vein: I was about to give up song, because I thought Worth and Largess dead; but now both are restored, for God has sent a great physician to heal them of their mortal illness—he is Frederick; Medicine, bid him make haste in doctoring. Diez[56] dates the poem shortly after Otto's death (1218), when Frederick was generally recognized as King of the Romans. De Bartholomaeis[57] places it between September 3 and October 31, 1220. It was surely composed before Frederick's coronation (November 22, 1220), since Aimeric does not call him "Emperor." I think, furthermore, that it was written before the death of William Malaspina, whom Aimeric could hardly have failed to mention if he, like the poet's other patrons, had been dead at the time.[58] In any case,

---

[55] Jeanroy, *Poésie lyrique*, I, 257: "Le fait est qu'aucun autre troubadour ne nous est connu pour avoir résidé à la cour de l'empereur." (He has just said that Guillem Figueira tried to win Frederick's favor, but in vain.) Augier Novella (39, 2) declares that Frederick is more generous in words than in deeds. Nothing seems to justify Anglade's assertion (*Littérature méridionale*, p. 92) that Aimeric was the protégé of Frederick.

[56] *Leben und Werke*, p. 352.

[57] *Poesie storiche*, I, 246 (between Frederick's return to Italy and All Saints' Day, mentioned in no. 13, which also refers to this poem). But I am not quite certain that we must take *sai* to mean "to Italy"; it might mean "to us on earth."

[58] We have already spoken of De Bartholomaeis's theory that *Salados* is William Malaspina, which seems not too likely.

this is apparently Aimeric's first poem to Frederick in point of time. In writing it, he may have been hoping for gifts and hospitality.

Aimeric addressed love-lyrics to Frederick by these envois: "Because he knows more than the others and upholds wisdom and knowledge and everything good, the Emperor, who is worthy over the worthy, will know whether I speak well or ill" (52); and "Song, go, in my name and in Love's, to the good, the fair, the valiant, the worthy man whom Latins and Germans serve and to whom they bow as to a good emperor. He has so much superiority over the highest, generosity and worth, honor and courtesy, sense and knowledge, judgment and discernment, (he who is) rich in riches to conquer rich worth" (15). These were written after Frederick's coronation, and might imply that Aimeric had actually made his acquaintance; but I think we can hardly take it for granted, on the strength of these poems, that Aimeric ever lived at Frederick's court. He may have been angling for an invitation that never came; or these poems may be a return for some trifling gift. There is, by the way, a possibility that Aimeric was favorably inclined toward the Emperor because the houses of Montferrat and Este were at first his partisans.

The rest of Aimeric's poems written in Italy are mostly *coblas* and *tensos* with various poets, although there is also a poem which the author calls a *fablel*, with an envoi to Sordello. The other poets whom Aimeric met in Italy were Guillem Raimon, Albert de Sestaron, Bertram d'Aurel, Guillem Figueira, and a certain Lambert. With the exception of Sordello and possibly Bertram and Lambert, these men were all natives of southern France, who found hospitality in Italy.

Aimeric exchanges three sets of *coblas* with Guillem Figueira, who had come to Italy some time before 1220.[59] Guillem was apparently a boorish individual who prided himself on having little to do with members of polite society. These *coblas*, at any rate, are written in no lofty vein, but consist largely of insults hurled back and forth, or allusions to obscure brawls in which acquaintances of the two poets took part. Two of the sets of *coblas* (9, 36) belong to the second category, and call for no comment here.

The third (13) is more interesting. Guillem begins with this *cobla*: "Bertram d'Aurel, if Sir Aimeric should die before the Feast of Martyrs (All Saints' Day), say: To whom would he leave his possessions and his riches which he won in Lombardy suffering cold and pain? The inn-keepers tell us that. But he made the medicine well and spoke great praise of the King (provided he considers *that* an honor)." The last sentence alludes clearly to Aimeric's poem *En aquelh temps*, with its conceit of Frederick II as the physician come to heal Worth and Largess; De Bartholomaeis has used this fact and the allusion to All Saints' Day to date *En aquelh temps*, as we have already seen. As for the rest of the *cobla*, it may be true that Aimeric had

[59] Levy, *Guilhem Figueira*, p. 2.

amassed a considerable fortune (a relative matter, of course) at the homes of the rich; there is no doubt that he knew how to ingratiate himself with noble families.[60] Guillem implies that he did so with some sacrifice of personal comfort, perhaps at the cost of self-respect (so I interpret the lines); I am not able to refute the charge, but I hardly see that we are obliged to accept it as gospel truth, since insults are commonly based on exaggerations or on deliberate lies. However that may be, Aimeric gives as good as he received, inquiring of Bertram to whom Guillem would leave his false and treacherous heart, and who, at Guillem's death, would conduct harlots and be the lord of tramps and topers.

Bertram says nothing about Aimeric's wealth, but has a number of suggestions concerning the disposal of Guillem's various qualities and possessions. Among other heirs, he names Sir Lambert as the fitting recipient of Guillem's lechery. Lambert closes the series by expressing his satisfaction at the choice, and his perfect willingness to accept the legacy. I mention all this only because some have thought that this "Lambert" (otherwise unknown) was Rambertino Buvalelli, whose name is often written with an L. This identification has in its favor the fact that Rambertino was undeniably at the court of Este, and probably knew Aimeric there; but Bertoni, in his edition of Rambertino, indignantly rejects the attribution of these coarse lines to his poet.[61] Bertram d'Aurel, the remaining participant, is completely unknown, save for a mention in another *cobla* (36), as having taken part in a fight with "Guillem del Dui-Fraire," described as "the teacher of Sordello."[62]

Sordello also exchanged *coblas* with Aimeric (7a). Aimeric hurls the first stone with a scornful mention of Sordello's meek acceptance of a blow over the head with a bottle. Sordello replies in kind: "I do not believe that a man ever saw a fellow so greedy as that old contemptible beggar Sir Aimeric with his doleful face. He who sees him is worse than dead; and although his body is twisted and thin and dried up and old and limp and halt, a thousand times as much he said . . .[63] as he ever did." This confirms the accusation made by Guillem that Aimeric had put by a tidy sum, and encourages us to believe that the "cold and pain" mentioned by Guillem mean that Aimeric got his money by enduring the caprices of his patrons. Some of the poems (those to Frederick II, for example) may justify the "beggar"; like many of his fellow poets, Aimeric was not slow in hinting for money. He praised several patrons for their generosity; but never, I think, in any of his extant poems, does Aimeric descend to means of begging that

[60] Jeanroy (*Poésie lyrique*, I, 257) thinks these lines ironic: Aimeric tried his best to get money from various persons, but failed; and this is quite acceptable also.

[61] Bertoni, *Rambertino Buvalelli*, p. 68. Jeanroy (*Poésie lyrique*, I, 393) identifies Lambert from this, his only poem, as a "clerc défroqué devenu jongleur."

[62] Levy (*Guilhem Figueira*, p. 100) thinks this may be Guillem de la Tor.

[63] Two syllables are missing here, and the sense is not quite clear.

might be called "contemptible." Sordello, however, may be referring to tactics that Aimeric used in person. Even more interesting than this characterization is the description of Aimeric's physical appearance; it is particularly valuable since we have no other. One must remember, reading it, that Aimeric was at this time about fifty years old.[64] Apparently, with all his accumulated wealth, he had not taken on flesh. Whether we should accept literally the reference to his lameness and his twisted body, I cannot say.

In a poem (44) addressed to Sordello, Aimeric says that his lady thinks him too old to be a lover. He defends himself against the charge by alleging his aptitude for battle and by calling attention (somewhat complacently) to his cleverness and his discerning heart. He ends thus: "Messenger, bear my *fablel* [or *flabel*] into the Marches, to Sir Sordello, who will make a new and loyal judgment of it, as he is wont to do, so that I may be freed of blame." This would seem to have been written before the *coblas* just quoted, for Aimeric hopes here that Sordello will clear him of the charge that Sordello himself makes in his *cobla*.[65] Uc de Saint-Circ likewise calls Aimeric old and unfit for love.[66]

We have already mentioned the *coblas* (35) with Guillem Raimon concerning the "young marquis," and the *partimen* (3) with Albert de Sestaron, in which Beatrice of Este and Emilia of Ravenna are selected for judges. Aimeric also made a *tenso* (6) with the latter poet, on the subject "Nothing at all."[67] This is simply a play of wits, and not a very good one. The place and date of composition of the poems with Albert de Sestaron may be fixed within certain limits because of the judges chosen for one of them (3): Emilia (a member of the Guidi family) did not marry Pietro Traversara, and thereby become Emilia of Ravenna, until 1216; and in 1220 Beatrice of Este was already a nun. So this poem lies between these two dates; the other (6) probably belongs to the same period, though, in

---

[64] Schultz (*Zeitschrift für r. Ph.*, VII, 204) dates these *coblas* around 1225, which may be correct. Sordello's *floruit* is commonly given as 1225–1270; cf. Jeanroy, *Poésie lyrique*, I, 429.

[65] Presumably both were written very early in Sordello's career (around 1225); for Sordello was in Provence in 1229, after having been in Castile and Portugal. See Jeanroy, *Poésie lyrique*, I, 429.

[66] "Sir Aimeric once wrote *coblas* about a prostitute, and had joy of her; now I hear that he has put his heart and all his hope in a washerwoman; that is what happens to a man who is too old: all his affairs go from bad to worse when old age breaks him and casts him down. No girl will ever welcome him with words of flattery or honor; or if she does so, it will be because she is destitute and wretched; and she must needs lack bread, wine, and lodging who would lie down with him or kiss his wrinkled, rancid skin" (457, 5; Jeanroy and Salverda de Grave, *Uc de Saint-Circ*, pp. 91–92). The editors date this at about the same time as Sordello's *cobla*.

[67] Suggested by the *Farai un vers* (183, 7) of William IX and the *Escoutatz, mas no sai que's es* (389, 28) of Raïmbaut d'Aurenga.

view of the somewhat less formal tone, we may assume it to have been written second. As for the place, the best guess is Ferrara, at the Este court.[68]

One of Aimeric's *chansos* (4), dealing with the poet's unfortunate experience in changing a bad love for a worse, has this envoi: "I make known to Sir Rainier of the Courtly Vale (*Rainier de Val Cortes*) this: I do not hope for any help from my cutting words." I am not able to identify this Rainier, either as a real name or as a *senhal*. Since the poet does not praise him, he probably was not a patron, but that is about all that one can say.

I have indicated the clear references to Aimeric that have come to my attention in the works of other poets. They are confined mostly to *coblas* and *tensos* which Aimeric provokes or answers. Jeanroy[69] has this note on a certain Fortunier: "Deux coblas adressées à Gasquet, qui parait être un jongleur au service d'un Aimeric, lequel pourrait être Aimeric de Péguilhan." Since this is only a possibility based on a probability, and since we have no further information about this Gasquet, we may content ourselves with this mention.

The date of Aimeric's death is not known. The two *planhs* on the deaths of Count Raymond Bérenguer IV of Provence and the famous Manfred, once attributed to Aimeric,[70] would have meant that he was alive in 1245 and 1266; but scholars are now generally agreed that he wrote neither of these pieces. Diez's *floruit* of 1205–1270 was based on an identification of the Countess Beatrice of the *planh* (22) which is now generally rejected, as we have seen above. None of the poems that we can date even approximately seem much later than 1225. Naturally, this does not prove that Aimeric died then: many of his poems may be lost; we may be misreading others; and some of those without envois or datable allusions may belong to a later period. But, on the other hand, nothing compels us to believe that Aimeric lived beyond 1230.[71] He would have been around fifty-five years old then, a reasonably advanced age for the thirteenth century, and I am inclined to follow Jeanroy[72] in putting his death not far from that year.

Jean de Nostredame's account of Aimeric's life is based largely on the Provençal *Vida*, with a few additions from the poems. It contains many details that are surely false; nevertheless, it is worth quoting for a few interesting observations. Here are the two versions:[73]

---

[68] J. Boutière, *Poésies du troubadour Albertet*, pp. 16–17.

[69] *Poésie lyrique*, *I*, *368*.

[70] The question of the authenticity of several poems is discussed in a separate section of this introduction.

[71] De Bartholomaeis (*Poesie storiche*, II, 167) says that Aimeric died before 1242; I do not know his reasons for the assertion.

[72] *Poésie lyrique*, I, 331–332.

[73] Chabaneau-Anglade, *Jehan de Nostredame*, pp. 69–70.

Aymeric de Pyngulan, gentilhomme thoulousain, fut bon poète en rithme provensalle, et mesmes a mesdire, s'enamoura d'une bourgeoise de la ville, contre laquelle ayant faict quelque chanson satirique, fut frappé griefvement sur la teste par un parent de la damoyselle, pour occasion duquel fut contraint se retirer à Guilhem de Bergedam en Cathalongne, duquel il fut honnorablement receu, et apres l'avoir faict guerir de la blessure, chanta de belles chansons à sa louange; pour raison desquelles il luy bailla de beaux presens, et luy fist avoir entree et cognoissance avec le roy Alphons de Cathalongne, avec lequel se tint un long temps; et ayant faict une satyre contre Gaucelme, maistre d'hostel du roy, par laquelle on pouvoit facilement entendre qu'il avoit desrobbé la couppe d'or où le roy beuvoit, fut contraint se retirer en Provence, chez la princesse Beatrix, heritiere de Provence, fille de Remond, comte de Provence, avant qu'elle espousast Charles, comte d'Anjou, frere de sainct Loys, roy de France; avec laquelle il fust le bienvenu, aymé et prisé, pour les bonnes et plaisantes inventions qu'il avait en la poesie, dont il estoit le vray maistre. Il en feist une, et la chanta souvent en la presence de la princesse, en laquelle il recitoit qu'il n'y ha tant d'animaux parmi la terre, ne tant d'oyseaux parmi le boys, ne tant d'estoylles au ciel qu'il ha de facheux pensemens chaque nuict dans son coeur. Peu de temps apres se retira en Lombardie avec l'une des marquises de Malespyne, à la louange de laquelle feist de fort belles et doctes chansons; estoit grand compaignon de Guy d'Uzez, de Peyre Vidal et des deux Rambauds. Trespassa au service de la dicte marquise environ l'an 1260, de laquelle il avoit esté amoureux, ainsi que l'ont escript le Monge des Isles d'Or et Saint Cezari, dont il en feist ce traicté intitulé *Las Angueyssas d'Amour*. Le Monge de Montmajour mesdit de cestuy ce qu'il en a voulu dire. Petrarque l'a imité et suyvi en plusieurs passages et en faict mention en son Triomphe d'Amour.

Aymeric de Pingulan, de Thoulouse, fut fils d'ung marchand de draps, bon poëte en rithme provensalle et mesmes a mesdire. S'enamoura d'une bourgeoise de la ville, pour laquelle ayant faict quelque chanson satyrique, fut frappé par quelqu'un de ses parents sur la teste et fut contrainct se retirer de Thoulouse, et s'en alla en Cathalogne, chez Guilhem de Bergedan, duquel il fut fort honorablement receu, et prenant plaisir à sa poesie, luy feit de moult beaux et profitables présens, et luy bailha entrée avec le roy Alphonx de Cathalogne, avec lequel se tint un long temps. Mays, ayant luy faict une satyre contre Gaucelm, maistre d'hostel du roy, par laquelle l'on entendoit facilement qu'il avoit desrobé la coupe d'or où le roy beuvoit, fut contrainct s'oster de là et se retirer chez le comte Berenguier, du temps que ses quatre filhes estoient en prix et en bruit, et sur toutes feit plusieurs chansons qu'il adressa à Beatrix. En une de ses chansons il dict "qu'ainsin que le cerf est pris, je suis son home lige, et jamais home qui ayme ne fut plustost conquis que je fus, quand elle tira son gant et que je luy baysay sa blanche main, laquelle baysant m'entra tant vivement l'amour dans mon corps que je demeuray sans vie." Pétrarque, prenant argument sur ceste chanson, en a faict ung sonnet qui se commence

Nostredame failed to say how the sonnet begins, and I have not been able to find it; the poem of Aimeric is *Qui sofrir s'en pogues* (46), lines 29–36. Contrariwise, the comparisons which Nostredame attributes to Aimeric in the first version are in none of the extant poems, but may be found in Petrarch's *sestina*, number 237 of the *Canzoniere*:

> Non ha tanti animali il mar fra l'onde,
> Nè lassù, sopra 'l cerchio de la luna,
> Vide mai tante stelle alcuna notte,
> Nè tanti augelli albergan per li boschi,
> Nè tant' erbe ebbe mai campo nè piaggia,
> Quant' ha 'l mio cor pensier' ciascuna sera.

Nostredame did not follow the *Vida* exactly, and may have had before him another version, now lost. His identification of Beatrice as the daughter of

Raymond Bérenguer undoubtedly influenced Diez and other scholars, who were then obliged to follow him in putting Aimeric's death late in the thirteenth century. It is unlikely that Aimeric was a "grand compaignon" of Gui d'Ussel, Peire Vidal, Raïmbaut d'Aurenga, and Raïmbaut de Vaqueiras; but, since he composed a *partimen* (37) with Elias d'Ussel, he may have known Gui as well. None of the extant poems of Aimeric refer to the maître d'hôtel Gaucelm and the king's golden goblet, mentioned in both versions of Nostredame.

ATTRIBUTIONS

We have already mentioned that Kolsen[1] would deny *S'eu anc chantei* (48) to Aimeric. His reasons are, briefly: (1) Aimeric would not have written two *planhs* on the same subject; (2) the attributions of *CR* (which alone contain this poem) are often wrong, as, for example, when they attribute poem 29 also to Aimeric (for this, see below); (3) Folquet de Romans may have been in Italy in 1212, when the poem was written, and he certainly knew the Estes; (4) this poem resembles those of Folquet stylistically; (5) the poems of Aimeric and Folquet are intermixed in *R*. From this, Kolsen concludes that Aimeric did not write the poem, and that Folquet probably did. I consider this hypothesis as far from proved. In my discussion of Azzo VI, above, I gave my reasons for thinking that Aimeric might have written two poems on the same two deaths. The attributions of *R* are often wrong, as Kolsen says; but those of *C* are much more often correct; as for the falseness of their attribution of poem 29, that is, to say the least, doubtful, and should not be used to prove anything about the reliability of the MSS. It is possible that Folquet de Romans was in Italy in 1212; but so were dozens of other troubadours. The stylistic resemblances that Kolsen points out are slight, and one could find just as many to link the poem with other works of Aimeric. As for the order of poems in *R*, one could probably prove almost anything on that basis, for the MS is chaotic. On the whole, I see no reason whatever to doubt the testimony of the two MSS, that the poem belongs to Aimeric.

Some nine other poems, which we likewise accept as genuine, appear with divergent attributions in certain MSS. *Sg*, for example, gives 25 to Raïmbaut de Vaqueiras, 49 to Giraut de Bornelh. But no one, as far as I know, has taken these isolated ascriptions seriously; all the other (and better) MSS give both poems to Aimeric.

P attributes 14 to Jausbert de Poicibot, 33 to Blacasset. But *P*, not an exceedingly reliable source, is unsupported here by any other MS; so we do not question Aimeric's right to these two poems.

In *R*, poem 27 appears twice, once under the name of Aimeric de Belenoi, and once under that of Peire Vidal. Since this MS is notorious for its blunders, we may dismiss these attributions without further ado. All the other MSS give the poem to Aimeric.

The second-rate source *g* would deny to Aimeric what is p.)bably his most famous poem (50), the one for which Dante praises him, and which

---

[1] *Zeitschrift*, XLI, 541.

all the other MSS (except *O*, where it is anonymous) ascribe to Aimeric. It is certainly his.

The index of *C* (called *CReg* by Pillet-Carstens) lists 18 under Uc de Pena; but the poem appears under Aimeric's name in the body of the MS. It is anonymous in *IK*, but is attributed to Aimeric by the other six MSS. I do not hesitate to accept it.

Concerning two poems, the evidence of the MSS is not so conclusive. *Anc mais de joi ni de chan* (8) appears ten times under the name of Aimeric, four times (plus *CReg*) under that of Guillem Figueira, and once (*P*) under that of Giraut de Bornelh. Emil Levy, in his edition of Guillem, denies it to his poet on stylistic grounds, and thinks it to be the work of Aimeric. This seems likely, as its tone and substance are not unlike those of several other poems of Aimeric.

Hom ditz que gaugz non es senes amor (29) appears among the poems of Aimeric in *COR*, but is attributed in *Tc* to Arnaut de Maroill. Friedmann[2] and Kolsen[3] would give the poem to Arnaut. But Stronski[4] explains why he thinks the poem was (wrongly) attributed by the copyists to Arnaut: it contains these words, *Qu'ilh* (my eyes) *en ploran quasqun jorn ses duptansa*, which suggested what the Monge de Montaudon said about Arnaut in his satire on contemporary poets (305, 16): *Qu'ades clamon merce sei oill, On plus chanta l'aig' en deissen*. I am inclined to accept this explanation, and claim the poem for Aimeric, particularly because it appears that *Tc* had one common original, and so do not present two really independent testimonies. Furthermore, they belong to the same family as *O*, which puts this poem definitely among the poems of Aimeric, as do *CR*, belonging to a different family. And, finally, it is worth noticing that in both *T* and *c* the poem in question is the last of the series ascribed to Arnaut, always a weak position when questions of attribution are being discussed.

Several scholars[5] have thought that Aimeric wrote the *planh* for Manfred (461, 234), which appears in *IK* (the only MSS which preserve it) after the poems of Aimeric de Peguilhan. But we have seen above that Aimeric was probably dead long before 1266, when Manfred died, and we may reject this attribution, especially since it is only a guess in the first place.

The same MSS (*IK*) do ascribe to Aimeric another poem, *Ab marrimens angoissos et ab plor*, which Bartsch accepted, and called number 1 of Aimeric's poems, but which is rejected by Pillet-Carstens, who follow the attribution of *a*[1] (to Peire Bremon Ricas Novas: 330, 1a). It is likewise a *planh*, for Raymond Bérenguer IV of Provence, who died in 1245. Even

---

[2] *Einleitung zu einer kritischen Ausgabe . . . Arnaut de Mareuil*, p. 35.

[3] *Zeitschrift*, XLI, 542.

[4] *Folquet de Marseille*, p. 124*.

[5] See the references in Pillet-Carstens, p. 15.

before the discovery of a^1, which was unknown to Bartsch, Zingarelli[6] expressed grave doubts of Aimeric's authorship, largely on stylistic grounds. His reasons are sound, and are supported by what we have said above concerning the chronology of Aimeric; nothing whatever persuades us that he was still alive in 1245. We therefore follow Zingarelli and Pillet-Carstens in denying this poem to Aimeric.

A third poem, *Lanqan chanton li auzeil en primier* (31) is almost certainly not the work of Aimeric. We have already given a critical edition of this poem, and explained why we consider it impossible that Aimeric should have written it.[7] As Pillet-Carstens had already expressed doubts concerning Aimeric's authorship of the poem, our rejection of it will not come as a surprise to anyone. Here are our reasons for denying it to Aimeric: (1) it begins with a picture of spring, which leads the poet's heart to love; this was common in the twelfth century, but occurs nowhere in the authentic poems of Aimeric; (2) the vocabulary of the poem contains a great many words which Aimeric never uses; (3) this poem is full of the beauties of nature; Aimeric never mentions them; (4) Aimeric does not use the forms *carnau*, *aitau*, etc., which appear here in the rime; (5) the envoi calls on Peire Rogier, who, as nearly as we can tell, died when Aimeric was a child. We feel certain, therefore, that Aimeric did not write this poem. One MS (*D*) attributes it to Guillem Rainol d'At. This attribution also offers some difficulties, but, as we show in the article referred to above, they are not so serious as those against the authorship of Aimeric; we are inclined to give the poem to him.

It has long been known that the *cobla* from *H* which Bartsch numbered 5 among Aimeric's compositions was in reality one stanza of poem 49. But I only recently stumbled across the fact that poem 53 is likewise part of another poem.[8] In this case, however, the poem is not by Aimeric. The stanzas which Bartsch and Pillet-Carstens ascribe to Aimeric appear in *CR*; but a fuller version of the poem appears in twelve MSS under the name of Daude de Pradas: *Be·n aj' amors, car anc me fetz cauzir* (124, 6). There is no doubt that the poem belongs to Daude. I am at a loss to know why *CR* (both of which contain the full version, under Daude's name) give this shortened form to Aimeric.

Other poems attributed to Aimeric in isolated MSS, against the decisive agreement of the other MSS, are:
Aimeric de Belenoi, *Meravill me* (9, 12; *CRegR*).
Jausbert de Poicibot, *Partit de joi* (173, 8; *CReg*).

[6] *Due trovatori*, p. 39.

[7] Shepard and Chambers, "Lanqan chanton li auzeil en primier," in *Romance Philology*, II, 83 (August, 1948).

[8] F. M. Chambers, "Us jois novels, complitz de grans beutatz," in *Modern Language Notes*, May, 1949, p. 333. Mr. Schutz had not come across this false attribution when he prepared his edition of Daude (see Bibliography).

Guiraut de Salaignac, *Aissi com cel* (249, 1; *C*).
Pons de Capdoill, *L'adregz solatz* (375, 12; a^1).
Raimbaut de Vaqueiras, *Ara pot hom* (392, 3; *N*).
Richart de Tarasco, *Ab tan de sen* (422, 1; *c*).
Sordello, *Qui be·s membra* (437, 29; *IK*).
Most of these have been discussed in the editions of the poets concerned, and the attributions to Aimeric have been universally rejected. I see no grounds for claiming any of them for Aimeric.

VERSIFICATION

Over half of Aimeric's poems are *chansos:* 30, to be exact, out of the 50 that seem definitely his. The others are: four *planhs* (10, 22, 30, 48), one crusade song (11), two *sirventes* (26, 32), one *descort* (45), one poem which he calls a '*fablel*' (44), one fictitious *tenso* (23), seven genuine *tensos* (3, 6, 19, 28, 35, 36, 37), and three sets of *coblas* (7a, 9, 13).

Aimeric's versification is comparatively simple and uniform. He generally limits himself to one type of verse for each poem; that of ten syllables is by far the commonest, occurring in over half of the *chansos*, as well as in many of the other poems. There are ordinarily (in a *chanso*) five stanzas of eight lines each, and one or two envois, whose length varies somewhat. Feminine rimes are rarer than masculine, and do not appear at all in about half of the poems. The same rimes are usually kept throughout a given composition, nor does their order often vary. But in nine poems the rimes change from stanza to stanza (or every two stanzas), either through rearrangement or through the introduction of new rimes; in the latter case, the rime is sometimes derivative (*prims*, *prima*, etc.). Internal rime is found in only four poems, two of which are *tensos*. Aimeric's most ambitious attempt in this style is the highly artificial *Ses mon apleich* (47), in which one internal rime occurs eight times in the first stanza, another in the second, and so on. It is noteworthy that this and all the other poems containing internal and derivative rimes belong to Aimeric's later, Italian, period. Such trifling evidently did not appeal to him at first. Isolated rimes (riming only with their counterparts in the other stanzas) are very rare. The only rime-scheme used more than twice is *abbaccdd*, which occurs thirteen times.

Here is a more complete description of Aimeric's versification, arranged by rime-schemes. Feminine rimes are indicated by italics; a* means that the line contains an internal rime which is identical with the end-rime; a** means that the line contains an internal rime different from the end-rime. The syllable-count is for masculine lines; feminine lines contain one more syllable. In the first column are given the numbers designating the rime-schemes in Maus, *Peire Cardenals Strophenbau*.

12 aaaaaaaa 23, 26 (all lines 10 syllables)
29 aaaa_b*b_ 35 (a, 11 syllables; b, 13)
33 aaaa_bbbb_ 25 (all lines 10 syllables; derivative rimes)
— aaaabbccddee_ff_ 46 (all lines 6 syllables)
— aaa_b*b_ 36 (a, 11 syllables; b, 13)
132 aabba_cc_dd 4 (a, b, c, 7 syllables; d, 10)
148 aabb_c_bb_c_ 16 (last line 5 syllables; all others 7)
159 aabbccdd 52 (all lines 10 syllables)

183 aab*cc*bdd — 39 (all lines 10 syllables)
188 aa*b*ccdd — 38 (all lines 10 syllables)
208 ababaacc — 17 (all lines 8 syllables)
— ab*ab*ab*ab*c*d*c*dc*d*c*de*f*e*f*e*f*e*f* 45 (all lines without internal rimes, 5 syllables; e, 7; the rest, 6)
249 a**b**a**b**a**b**b**a** 47 (all lines 10 syllables; derivative rimes)
251 *a*b*a*b*a*bb*a*bb — 13 (all lines 7 syllables)
308 a*b*a*bb*cc — 29 (all lines 10 syllables)
359 ababccdd — 33 (all lines 10 syllables)
a*b*a*bcc*dd — 20 (all lines 10 syllables)
366 ababccddee — 11 (all lines 10 syllables)
393 *a*b*a*bc*d*cee — 42 (all lines 7 syllables)
402 a*b*a*b*c*dd*cee — 21 (all lines 10 syllables)
444 *a*bb*aa*bb*a* — 43 (a, 7 syllables, b, 8)
463 abbaacc — 27 (all lines 10 syllables)
471 abbaaccdd — 37 (all lines 8 syllables)
abbaa*cc*dd — 48 (all lines 10 syllables)
481 abbaa*c*dd*c* — 8 (a, b, 7 syllables; c, d, 10)
509 *a*bb*a*cc*a* — 14 (first four lines, 7 syllables; last three, 10)
515 abba*cc*add — 10 (all lines 10 syllables)
528 abbacccdd — 30 (all lines 10 syllables)
535 abbaccdd — 7, 18, 22, 28 (all lines 10 syllables)
24 (all lines 7 syllables)
34 (a, b, c, 7 syllables; d, 10)
abbacc*dd* — 3 (a, b, c, 8 syllables; d, 10)
abba*cc*dd — 12, 15 (all lines 10 syllables)
41 (a, b, 8 syllables; c, 7; d, 10)
*a*bb*a*ccdd — 7a, 9 (second line, 5; last line, 10; others, 7)
*a*bb*a*cc*dd* — 2 (all lines 7 syllables)
546 abbaccdde — 6 (all lines 8 syllables)
554 abbaccddeeff — 49 (all lines 6 syllables)
579 abbacddc — 50 (all lines 10 syllables)
606 abbac*d*effe*d* — 51 (last line 10 syllables; others 6)
660 abbccdd — 19 (all lines 10 syllables)
669 abbccdd*e* — 32 (all lines 7 syllables)
709 abbcddeeff — 40 (a, b, c, d, e, 6 syllables; f, 10)

A few deviations from Maus's classification need to be noted. Evidently because of the internal rimes, Maus lists poem 47 under scheme 12; it belongs under 249. I cannot find 46 in his list at all, and there is no number to correspond to its rime-scheme. Maus puts 36 under scheme 61, counting the internal rime in the fourth line as a separate line, although the similar poem 35 is not so treated; he has no number for 36 as we print it. Likewise, in 45, Maus counts the final echo-rimes as separate lines, and lists the poem under

487; there is no number for the rime-scheme as we have it. Maus puts 44 under 78 (aaabcccbdddb); actually, the poem seems to be without stanzaic structure; the MSS do not divide it up.

Change of rimes, not indicated in the above list, occurs necessarily in the poems (23, 26) that have only one rime for each stanza. Number 45, which has very long stanzas, simply introduces a whole new set of rimes (in the same pattern) for each new stanza. Number 42 alternates all its rimes but one from stanza to stanza: so *a* of stanzas one and three becomes *d* of stanzas two and four, *d* becomes *a*, *c* becomes *e*, *e* becomes *c*, while *b* remains constant. In 50, rimes *c* and *d* of each stanza become *a* and *b* of the following stanza, and two new rimes are introduced. In 16, *a* and *c* remain constant, while *b* changes with every two stanzas. Derivative rimes (25, 47) change from stanza to stanza.

No other poems have the same rime-schemes as 36, 42, 46, 51. The combination of rime-scheme and meter is unique in 8, 10, 14, 21, 30, 35, 38, 49.

Several poems of Aimeric have the same metrical system as poems by other troubadours, combined with the same rimes in the same order. Number 32 agrees in this way with Peire Vidal, 25, and Bertran de Born, 28. Since Peire's poem is a *chanso*, while Aimeric's and Bertran's are *sirventes*, we may assume that Peire invented the pattern, and that the other two poets copied it from him.[1]

Maus (*Peire Cardenals Strophenbau*, p. 60) points out a similar agreement between Aimeric, 15, and four other poems: Peire Cardenal, 4; Sordello, 6; Perdigo, 1; and 461 (anonymous), 231. The last two have *-ors* instead of *-or* for the first rime, but all (except P. Cardenal, 4) have *amor*(*s*) as a rime-refrain in the first line of each stanza. Since Peire Cardenal wrote only after 1220, the probable date of Aimeric's poem, and since the other three poems are no more than fragments or single *coblas*, while Aimeric's is a complete *chanso*, I think we can agree with Maus (p. 61) that Aimeric probably invented the pattern, and the others imitated him.

Lanfranc Cigala imitated Aimeric's poem 34 in his religious song 18. Meter and rimes are the same; but Lanfranc introduced a rime-refrain (*marritz*) in the first line of each stanza. In this case, the dates tell us which way the imitation went.

Similarly, when we find the meter and rimes of Aimeric's number 25 in Guillem Anelier 4, we know from the dates of the two poets that Guillem Anelier imitated Aimeric. These poems are based on derivative rimes, which change from stanza to stanza; but all the rimes appear in the same order in both poems.

The series of *coblas* to which Aimeric's number 13 belongs shares its meter and rimes with several other pieces: a *pastourelle* (13) of Gui d'Ussel, an exchange of *coblas* between Uc de Saint Circ (30) and Guillem del Baus

[1] Aimeric probably indirectly, through Bertran. See the notes on the poem.

(3), and another exchange of *coblas*, between Gui de Cavaillo (5) and the Count of Toulouse (1). I do not know that it is possible to determine who invented the form, but Gui d'Ussel is the most likely.

Peirol, in his crusade-*sirventes* (28), has taken the meter and rimes of Aimeric's number 27, which is definitely earlier.

The *chanso* number 4 has the same meter and rimes as two other poems: Gaucelm Faidit, 62, and Guillem Figueira, 5. Since Guillem's poem is a *sirventes*, and the other two are *chansos*, one may assume that Guillem imitated one or the other of them. This is the opinion of Levy in his edition of Guillem Figueira, p. 24. But Levy does not venture to decide whether Aimeric imitated Gaucelm, or the other way around. Robert Meyer (*Das Leben des Trobadors Gaucelm Faidit*, p. 39) dates Gaucelm's poem in a perfunctory and unconvincing fashion between 1199 and 1201. If this is accurate, then it is very likely that Aimeric is the imitator, for those years are close to the beginning of his career. A few pages later (p. 57), Meyer dates the *tenso* (28) between Aimeric and Gaucelm "after 1207"; he thinks it was composed in southern France, perhaps at the court of Raimon d'Agout. This fits nicely into the chronology that we have worked out in our Introduction; we assume there that Aimeric left Spain around 1208 and went to Italy through southern France. Quite likely, at the time of this meeting, one of the two poets paid the other the honor of copying a metrical pattern of his inventing. Whether or not Meyer's date for Gaucelm's poem is correct, it would be natural for Aimeric, the younger man, to pay this tribute to Gaucelm; and we suspect that this was the case. Then, when Aimeric met Guillem Figueira in Italy, the latter imitated his imitation; for, as Levy says (*loc. cit.*), we have no knowledge that Guillem and Gaucelm ever met each other.

Finally, the author of the anonymous *sirventes* 461, 6 adopted the meter and rimes of Aimeric's *chanso* number 17, and the late poet Joan Esteve used the rimes and complicated structure of the *descort* (45) as the framework of a religious song (266, 8).

List of rimes:

ada: 9
ai: 10, 25, 44
aia: 25
aire: 21, 35, 36, 41, 42, 45; internal rime: 35, 36, 45
ais: 3, 45, 46, 47; internal rime: 45
aiser: 47
al: 11, 23, 40, 43, 52
als: 17, 28, 38, 42
an: 8, 14, 15, 16, 25, 26, 27, 32, 37, 40, 42, 44, 45, 46, 50; internal rime: 45
anc: 7a, 9
anda: 25
anh: 25

ọnher: 47
ọr: 3, 4, 6, 7, 11, 12, 13, 15, 18, 19, 29, 32, 33, 38, 40, 48, 49, 50; internal rime: 47
ọrn: 44
ọrs: 16, 17, 27, 30, 39, 45, 52
ọrt: 7a, 9, 23, 45; internal rime: 45
ọs: 7, 11, 19, 20, 21, 24, 26, 45; internal rime: 45
uelh: 33
ur: 37, 49
ura: 48
us: 44
utz: 22, 44

Caesura. In the ten-syllable line, Aimeric most frequently places the caesura after the fourth syllable, which is generally stressed:

> De tot en tot / es er de mi partitz
> Aquelh eys joys / que m'era remazutz. (22, 1–2)

But this fourth syllable is fairly often unstressed ('feminine caesura'), as in the second of these lines:

> Que·l sieus solatz era guays e chauzitz . . .
> E·l respondres / plazens ez abelhitz. (22, 17, 20)

And the caesura is not uncommonly after the sixth or some other syllable:

> E·il pro qe·il dan son plus, / e·il ris qe·il plor. (15, 12)
> Senher, que folhs faitz, / qu'ieu grat no·us en sen. (16, 2)

In lines under ten syllables, there is no fixed place for the caesura, and it is frequently lacking.

Elision and hiatus. Aimeric always elides the final vowel of unstressed *me*, *te*, *se*, *ma*, *ta*, *sa*, *lo*, *la*, *li* (the definite article), *de* before another vowel.[2] The final vowel of *que*, *se* or *si* ('if'), *li* (indirect object pronoun) is generally elided, and so is the final unstressed *-e* or *-a* of all words of more than one syllable. Hiatus occurs some twenty times after unstressed *-a* of verbs and nouns: *Tolosa, al* (7, 53), *anava e* (10, 24), *devria esser* (11, 21), *largueza e* (48, 32) etc. Here is a fairly complete list of all other exceptional cases of hiatus:

1) *si*, *se* ('if'): *si a* (11, 58), *se a* (44, 57), *si eu* (51, 18).
2) *que*: *qe a* (16, 38), *que es* (38, 36), *que hier* (50, 42); cf. *quez a* (39, 32).
3) *li* (indirect object): *li o* (18, 36), *li enans* (38, 8).
4) final *-e* of words of more than one syllable: *penre e* (19, 18), *allegre e* (23, 8), *perdre e* (50, 19).

Aimeric does not avoid hiatus after a stressed or unelidable vowel: *va ab* (29, 13), *e me e se* (18, 38), *aisso es* (30, 4), *qui aisso* (37, 25), etc.

---

[2] Several of these words likewise lose their syllabic quality *after* another vowel (*no·m*, *no·l*, etc.); where they occur between two vowels, we have uniformly joined them with the following vowel: *no m'es parven*, not *no·m es parven*.

We have not tried to be more consistent than the manuscripts in indicating the elision of final vowels. Where such a non-syllabic vowel is written in the MS we were following, we have left it in the text. The meter will tell whether two vowels are to be pronounced separately or in one syllable; and to eliminate all the non-syllabic ones seemed to us an unwarranted tampering with the text. Perhaps in some regions it was customary to slur the vowels together, as in Italian or Spanish verse, rather than to do away with the first one.

Aimeric's theory of composition and versification must be derived largely from its results; but in a couple of poems he expresses his ideas in words. Three stanzas of one *chanso* (34) are devoted to the distinction between *vers* and *chanso*. For our comment, see the notes to the poem. He designates another poem (44) a "*fablel*" or "*flabel*" (a name apparently of his own invention). In contents, it does not differ markedly from a kind of personal *sirventes*. But the form is rather distinctive, in that the stanzaic structure is tenuous: the rime-scheme is *aaab*, with *a* changing and *b* remaining through out; and the thought is often carried over from one quatrain to the next. The MSS do not divide the poem into stanzas; and we follow them in this.

In our discussion of figures of speech (below), we shall have occasion to comment on these lines (47): "I do not go about without my plane and my file, with which I fabricate words and plane and file them, for I see no subtle or delicate work of any sort subtler or more delicate (than mine), nor a more skillful worker in precious rimes, nor one who breaks up his words more (*ni plus pesseich sos digz*), nor who rimes them better (than I.)" By "breaking up his words," he means apparently that he dissects or analyzes them; but even that is none too clear. The rest indicates that he had a high opinion of his own ability, and knew that his success came from hard work. This poem, incidentally, is one of the most elaborate metrically, with internal rimes and derivative end-rimes.

STYLE, METAPHORS, IDEAS

Aimeric avoids the obscurity of the *trobar clus*. Most of his poems are quite clear; they seem positively crystalline to the reader who has struggled through a few verses of Raïmbaut d'Aurenga or Arnaut Daniel. The difficulties that one encounters in Aimeric are mostly in personal allusions that escape us, and in spots where the MS readings are confused or lacking. His vocabulary does not differ notably from that of the other Provençal poets of his day. For this reason, it has seemed unnecessary to draw up a complete glossary for this edition; there is, however, at the end of the volume, a list of words not found, or found only with other meanings, in Levy's *Petit dictionnaire provençal-français*.

Among the proper names found in the poems (of which there is a special table preceding the one just mentioned), the names of patrons and poets call for no comment here, since they have already been discussed. The others show a nodding acquaintance with ancient history and literature (Alexander, Hector, Tydeus), a normal interest in religious matters (Jesus, St. Matthew, St. Andrew), and a pretty thorough familiarity with the *romans bretons* (Yvain, Arthur, Tristan, André de France, and probably Gawain). There are only a few allusions to the *chansons de geste*: Gui de Nanteuil and possibly William of Orange (who would replace Gawain in 10). Among the geographical and historical names (Pope Innocent, the Turks, Syria, Mount Tabor), it is interesting to find references to the Assassins and the Old Man of the Mountain, which we shall discuss below, under metaphors. Most of the other names come from literary sources, and show something of Aimeric's taste in reading. It is not clear from the references, however, that Aimeric knew either French or Latin. He may well have obtained his acquaintance with these heroes orally or in Provençal translations.

Senhals designating either ladies or patrons or friends are infrequent in Aimeric. Excluding the *Salomos* of poem 31, which we deny to Aimeric (see above, under Attributions), there are six possible *senhals*, each of which occurs only once: Rainier de Val Cortes (4), Tiriaca (50, *var.*), Salado (26), Na Gentils-Cors (12), Belhs Perago (41), and Miehls-de-be (24). In the last three cases, furthermore, it is possible to take the designation otherwise than as a *senhal* (see the notes to the poems in question). If they are really *senhals*, the persons they refer to are unknown.

Several scholars have noticed Aimeric's effective use of metaphors; so Diez,[1] speaking of the comparisons in *Si com l'arbres* (50), adds: "Der

[1] *Leben und Werke*, p. 347.

Troubadour liebt diese Redeblumen . . . doch verschwendet er sie nicht; auch sind sie nie verbraucht und stets wohlgewählt." This is a fairly accurate appraisal, but it requires some amplification. In the first place, less than half of the poems contain any similes other than the most prosaic and obvious: "Distressed, afflicted, unloved, loving, like the lover who weeps and is sad, I crave your mercy" (21). This type we may disregard. The more elaborate ones fall into several categories:

(1) One person is compared to another specific person: Aimeric or his patrons are likened to various characters of history or fiction—Tristan, Yvain, Gawain, Alexander, etc. Considerably more original and more striking is the comparison, which occurs twice (24, 42) of himself (or his heart) to an Assassin, and his Lady to the ruler of the sect, the Old Man of the Mountain.[2]

(2) One person is compared to some type-character: Aimeric compares himself to a serf (46), a pilgrim, faithfully pushing on toward his goal (49), a money-changer who changes bad for worse (4), a gambler, who gets in deeper than he thought he would (12), a timid fencer who is afraid to try to get in a blow (38). Love is like a bully who fights a defenseless person (7), a servant who is so eager to serve others that he neglects those whom he should serve (7), a bad master who mistreats his servants (49). Frederick II is compared throughout a whole poem (26) to a physician who has come to heal the virtues dear to the troubadours of wounds they had received when various patrons died.

(3) The comparison is based on some fact or legend of external nature: Love draws the poet toward his Lady like a magnet (12, 24). His Lady thinks she will make him kill himself like the bustard, which exposes itself to the attack of the hawk (18). The poet has worked toward his own destruction, like the stag at bay (18). Like a captured bird, he still sings bravely (41). Like an overloaded tree, the poet has lost his Lady and himself, through loving too much (50). As the basilisc dies when he sees himself in a mirror, so Aimeric will die because he looked upon his Lady (50). And, finally, this rather homely comparison: As salt preserves meat, so Gaston preserves Gascony (42).

(4) A few others are not easily classifiable: Like a toy given to a child and then taken away is a coquettish pretense of love (50). Love is compared at some length to an investment; Aimeric has greatly increased the capital

---

[2] As far as I can discover, the Assassins and their leader are mentioned only about four more times in all Old Provençal literature: by Giraut de Bornelh (242, 45), by Bertran de Born (80, 8), by Bernart de Bondeilhs (59, 1), and in the anonymous love-letter beginnng *Bona domna, pros ez onrada* (published by Suchier in *Denkmäler prov. Lit. und Spr.*, I, 311). The comparison with the Assassins led Suchier to think that Aimeric might have written the love-letter; but of course this is only a guess. On this matter of the Assassins in Provençal, see my article "The Troubadours and the Assassins," in *Modern Language Notes*, April, 1949, pp. 245–251, and a complementary note scheduled to appear in the same journal in 1950.

of sighs which came to him from his Lady (43). Writing verse is compared to planing and filing (47); this may come indirectly from Horace (*Ars Poetica*, 291) or other Latin writers. Apparently based on a proverb is the comparison of useless effort to baptizing a donkey (4).

These are the types (and most of the actual metaphors and similes). Now, it will be apparent from an examination of these that not one is based on the beauties of nature—sound, sight, or smell. Of these things, Aimeric apparently had no perception. He never says that one thing looks or sounds like another, but rather that one thing (or person) behaves like another. Some of the similes present a vivid picture—the stag at bay, the overloaded tree—but the main force of the best ones is dramatic, not pictorial. In a few lines, Aimeric sketches a little scene from life (the gambler, the captive bird, the child and the toy) and makes effective use of it to drive home his point. This ability is one of his greatest claims to distinction as a poet.[3]

Aimeric's conception of love and *domnei* do not differ much from those commonly accepted by other poets of his day. He proclaims himself the vassal of his Lady (38), even her slave: "I am yours more truly than the slave who is bought and sold" (42). In his *tensos*, he generally champions faithfulness in love, and a more ideal conception of love than some of his opponents; but he is not above deserting one lady who has betrayed him for another who seems more worthy (7). Through it all, he keeps his faith in love itself, although it brings sufferings, for even these are good (15, 52, 23, etc.).

It will be apparent to one who compares the *chansos* written in Spain with those written in Italy that the latter are more philosophical (discussions of Love's power and virtues), while the former are more personal, and relate specifically to the lady whom the poet loves at the moment. This may be due simply to increasing age, which brings a tendency to moralize; it may also mean that in Spain Aimeric was really in love, while in Italy he was only pretending, and so had recourse to generalities. The last poems that are approximately datable are not *chansos* at all, but *tensos* and *coblas*; love, apparently, had ceased to play a very important part in Aimeric's life (compare the accusations that Sordello and Uc de Saint-Circ made, that he was too old for love).

---

[3] Many of the comparisons are borrowed from earlier troubadours, as one can see from the notes to the poems. Cf. also W. P. Shepard, in *S.udies for William A. Read*, p. 181.

CONTEMPORARY JUDGMENTS

The most valuable (not to say the only) ancient testimony of Aimeric's high rank as a poet is that of Dante.[1] In the *De vulgari eloquentia*,[2] Dante gives a list of poems on the level of composition that is "et sapidus et venustus etiam et excelsus, qui est dictatorum illustrium." He names one poem by each of the following writers: Giraut de Bornelh, Folquet de Marseille, Arnaut Daniel, Aimeric de Belenoi, and Aimeric de Peguilhan[3] in Provençal; Thibaut of Champagne in French; and in Italian Guido Guinizelli, Guido delle Colonne, Guido Cavalcanti, Cino da Pistoia, and Dante himself. I have copied the whole list in order to show in what company Dante places Aimeric—the "illustrious poets" of Provence, France, and Italy. In judging Aimeric, we might do well to bear in mind the opinion of this great critic and poet.

The MSS themselves bear witness to Aimeric's popularity. Not one of the significant chansonniers fails to include at least a few of his poems, the average number being between fifteen and twenty. And some of his poems (7, 12, 14, 15, 25, 27, 40, 41, 50, 52) were so well liked that they appear in almost all the MSS.

The number of quotations from Aimeric in the works of other writers provides a further indication of the esteem in which he was held. In his *Breviari d'amor*, Matfre Ermengaud quotes no less than twenty-three passages, from thirteen poems (2, 7, 8, 12, 15, 17, 23, 24, 27, 33, 40, 41, 43). Jaufre de Foixa, the Catalan grammarian, quotes from two poems (25, 34), and Berenguier de Noya from four (7, 16, 18, 41). Giammaria Barbieri likewise cites four poems (9, 33, 41, 50), and gives a brief account of Aimeric's life, drawn largely from the Provençal *Vida*. And, finally, in commenting on the Italian verse Egli è quel che rinfresca in te la vita, Francesco da Barberino adds this note:[4]

> Et Naumerich de pegulian provincialis in lingua sua dicit: Amor tenuit in senetute me iuvenem, et iuventus quam michi contulit fecit in iuventute me senem. Pueri etiam qui moventur instinctum solo nature hoc sepe loquuntur quod lictera testus facit.

This does not occur in any of Aimeric's extant poems.

---

[1] Petrarch's bare mention of "Amerigo" in the *Trionfo d'Amore* (line 55) is neither so flattering nor so sure.

[2] Book II, chapter vi.

[3] The poem named is *Si cum l'arbres que, per sobrecargar* (50).

[4] *Documenti d'amore* (ed. Egidi), pp. 32, 36.

ORDER OF POEMS IN THE MANUSCRIPTS

Those MSS having more than two poems together have them in this order:[1]

A: 46 41 27 33 7 15 12 50 20 38 42 34 21 49 18 40 24 14 43 2 26 47 25 10 52 4 31 / 37 19 / 32
B: 46 41 15 12 50 21 40 26 10 52
C: 25 43 15 7 46 27 34 50 18 40 47 (249, 1) 14 12 41 33 42 21 17 20 23 38 24 45 10 22 11 49 2 26 52 8 30 48 32 4 29 51 53 39 / 28 / 19
D: 46 41 27 33 7 52 4 11 24 14 43 2 26 47 25 45 10 23 21 50 15 49 18 38 40 12 20 30 44 / 32 / 19 / (8) / (31)
D[a]: 42 34 22 17 31 8 / 28 3
D[c]: 27 46 7 49 2 41 24 40 15 52 17 14 18 28 3
E: 17 20 10 22 11 49 26 8 30 45 42 14 40 2 24 7 12 18 38 / 3
Fa: 41 46 27 33 12 38 50 52 25 7 40
G: 52 27 14 15 41 25 50 12 7 40 8 / 28 / 3
IK: 20 23 38 42 24 21 50 14 7 49 43 27 46 2 41 47 33 12 25 34 45 15 52 17 40 31 8 / 19 28 3 / (8) / 32 / 10 22 30 / 26
J: 46 14 2 15 50 25 24 34 17
L: 12 / 8 / 23
M: 40 4 14 27 43 12 7 18 41 42 46 33 50 21 25 15 / (45) / 28 / 6 / (23) / 19
N: 15 52 33 4 20 23 38 42 24 21 50 14 27 46 26 47 12 25 40 7 (392, 3) 43 41 / (45) / (8) / 28
O: 50 29 39 27 15 / 52 17 / 33 / 6
P: 14 41 17 50 12 27 15 / (33) / (8) / (46) / (7a) / (47)
Q: 52 27 14 15 41 25 50 12 7 40 8 34 46 47 45 / 19 / 28
R: 4 / 23 / 17 20 38 10 22 2 26 33 8 30 48 32 / 19 / (8) / 25 45 51 43 46 53 34 12 24 41 14 11 52 42 49 40 50 21 7 47 29 39 / (27) / (27) / 6
S: 50 20 25 12 27 15
T: 40 / (29) / 42 7 14 18
U: 40 15 8 52 12 47 14 25 7 34 21 27 44
a[1]: (375, 12) 43 27 10 26 45 50 / 6 / 28 19 3
c: 50 27 34 21 7 12 20 15 47 14 43 39 41 16 46 25 52 (422, 1) 8 40 / (29)
f: 12 7 15 / 21 4 23 20 25 50 27 52 2 33

Certain similarities of arrangement are obvious. The order in *G* is the same as that of the first eleven poems in *Q*; these MSS surely have a common source. The first eight poems in *IK* appear in the same order in *N*. The first five in *A* and *D* are identical. Likewise, the order of poems would

[1] A diagonal line separates poems that are not contiguous.

indicate a kinship (which is confirmed by the variants) between certain parts of *CEMR*; and there are still other similarities. The order of poems in *IK* is especially noteworthy, since there the poems whose envois show them to have been written in Spain are kept entirely separate from those written in Italy. In both series, there are one or two poems without envois. We have not ventured to assert, on the strength of their position in these MSS, that they were written in Spain or in Italy, respectively; but in the absence of any further indications, that might be a good guess.

BIBLIOGRAPHY

Works to which reference is made by abbreviated titles, and two editions too recent for inclusion in Pillet-Carstens.

Albertet (de Sestaron): *Les poésies du troubadour Albertet*, p. p. J. Boutière (estratto da *Studi Medievali*), Torino, 1940.

Carl Appel, *Provenzalische Inedita aus Pariser Handschriften* (Altfranzösische Bibliothek, XIII), Leipzig, 1892.

Karl Bartsch, *Grundriss zur Geschichte der provenzalischen Literatur*, Elberfeld, 1872. (Bartsch, *Grundriss*)

Fritz Bergert, *Die von den Trobadors genannten oder gefeierten Damen* (Beiheft 46, *Zeitschrift für romanische Philologie*), Halle, 1913. (Bergert, *Damen*)

C. Cavedoni, "Delle accoglienze e degli onori ch'ebbero i trovatori provenzali alla corte dei Marchesi d'Este," in *Memorie della Reale Accademia di Modena*, II (1858), 260. (Cavedoni, *Accoglienze*)

Camille Chabaneau, *Biographies des troubadours*, in *Histoire générale de Languedoc*, X, 208–409. (Chabaneau, *Biographies*)

Eugen Cnyrim, *Sprichwörter, sprichwörtliche Redensarten und Sentenzen bei den provenzalischen Lyrikern* (Ausgaben und Abhandlungen, 71), Marburg, 1888. (Cnyrim, *Sprichwörter*)

Daude de Pradas: *Poésies de Daude de Pradas*, p. p. A. H. Schutz (Bibliothèque Méridionale, 1, XXII), Paris-Toulouse, 1933.

Vincenzo De Bartholomaeis, *Poesie provenzali storiche relative all' Italia* (2 vols.), Roma, 1931. (De Bartholomaeis, *Poesie storiche*)

Friedrich Diez, *Leben und Werke der Troubadours*. Zweite vermehrte Auflage, von Karl Bartsch, Leipzig, 1882. (*Leben und Werke*)

Lucien Foulet, *Petite syntaxe de l'ancien français* (Classiques français du moyen âge), 3e édition, Paris, 1930.

Alfred Jeanroy, *La poésie lyrique des troubadours* (2 vols.), Toulouse-Paris, 1934. (Jeanroy, *Poésie lyrique*)

Emil Levy, *Petit dictionnaire provençal-français*, 2e édition, Heidelberg, 1923. (Levy, *PD*)

Emil Levy, *Provenzalisches Supplement-Wörterbuch* (8 vols.), Leipzig, 1894–1924. (Levy, *SW*)

Matfre Ermengaud, *Le breviari d'amor*, publié par Gabriel Azaïs (2 vols.), Béziers-Paris, n.d. (*Breviari d'amor*)

F. W. Maus, *Peire Cardenals Strophenbau in seinem Verhältnis zu dem anderer Trobadors* (Stengel's Ausgaben und Abhandlungen), Marburg, 1884. (Maus)

Alfred Pillet-Henry Carstens, *Bibliographie der Troubadours*, Halle, 1933. (Pillet-Carstens)

François-Just-Marie Raynouard, *Lexique roman* (6 vols.), Paris, 1836–1844. (Raynouard)

Oscar Schultz-Gora, *Die Briefe des Trobadors Raimbaut de Vaqueiras an Bonifaz I, Markgrafen von Monferrat*, Halle, 1893. (Schultz-Gora, *Briefe*)

Franz Semrau, *Würfel und Würfelspiel im alten Frankreich* (Beiheft 23 zur *Zeitung für romanische Philologie*), Halle, 1910.

Francesco Torraca, *Le donne italiane nella poesia provenzale* and *Su la "Treva" di G. de la Tor*, Firenze, 1901. (Torraca, *Donne*)

Eduard Wechssler, *Das Kulturproblem des Minnesangs*, Halle, 1909. (Wechssler, *Kulturproblem*)

Nicola Zingarelli, *Intorno a due trovatori in Italia*, Firenze, 1899. (Zingarelli, *Due trovatori*)

VIDA AND POEMS

Vida

N'Aimerics de Peguillan si fon de Toloza, (2) fils d'un borges qu'era mercadiers (3) que tenia draps a vendre; (4) et apres chansos e sirventes, (5) mas molt mal cantava. (6) Et enamoret se d'una borgeza sa vezina, (7) et aquela amors li mostret trobar; (8) e si fes de leis maintas bonas chansos. (9) Mas si se mesclet ab lui lo maritz d'ela (10) e fes li dezonor. (11) E N'Aimericx si s'en venguet, (12) qu'el lo ferit d'un' espaza per la testa; (13) per que·l covenc az issir de Toloza (14) e faidir. (15) Et anet s'en en Cataluenha, (16) e·N Guilems de Bergueda si l'acuillit (17) et enanset lui e son trobar, (18) e det li son palafre e sos vestirs (19) e prezentet lo al rei N'Anfos de Castela, (20) que·l crec d'armas e d'onor. (21) Et estet en aquelas encontradas lonc tems. (22) Pueis s'en venc en Lombardia, (23) on tug li bon home li feiron gran honor; (24) et en Lombardia definet, (25) en eretgia, segon c'om ditz.

Notes and Variants

This text is substantially that of *E*. The *Vida* also occurs in *ABIKPR*. The numbers in the text, designed to facilitate reference for the variants which follow, are placed where the MS has periods.

1. Naimeric *EP*, Aymeric *R;* peguilla *E*, piguillan *AIK*, piguignan *B*, pegulla *R*, pepugnan P.

2. filh *R;* mercadier *IK*.

3. *for this whole clause, R has only:* de draps; (que) e *P*.

4. et *lacking IK;* et apres tensos e c. e s. *A;* e sirventes *lacking P*.

6. borgeza sa vezina *lacking P;* sa vezina *lacking R*.

7. *lacking P;* trobars *R*.

8. si *lacking ABIKPR*.

9. Mas lo m. dela se m. ab luy *PR*, E mesclet se cum lui lo marritz de la domna *IK*, E mescle se ab lo marit della *AB;* (lui) leis *E*.

11. Naimeric *P*, Neymeric *R;* si *lacking R*.

12. qe lo f. *P*, quel f. *R*, en tal guisa qez el lo f. *B;* en la testa *AB*, per mieg lo cap *R*.

13. couenc issir *B;* (issir) fayzir *R*.

14. *lacking R*.

16. An g. de bergedan que lacuilhi *R*, An Guillem de berguedan en guillems (si l'acuillit *lacking*) *A;* En Guillem *B*, Es en Guillelm *P;* si *lacking P*.

17. et *lacking A;* (enanset) lenanset *AR*, sauet sen *P;* lui e *lacking R;* en son t. *IKP*. *After this, ABIK add:* en la premiera canson quel auia faita (qel fetz *A*), *and IK add further:* e fetz lo ioglar.

18. quel li det (donet *A*) son p. *AIK*, tant qel li donet son p. *B;* li *lacking P;* (son p. e sos v.) mot *R;* son uestir *AB*.

19. e presentollo *P*, el presentet *B;* al bon rei *AB;* (N'Anfos) Anfos *BIK*.

20. (que·l crec) lo qals lo crec dauer e *B;* (d'armas) darnes *ABIK*.
21. e lay estet lonc temps *R*.
22. e puois *AP;* uenc sen *R*, sen anet *P;* lorbardia *E*.
23. ou *P;* li ualen home *P;* gran *lacking R; A adds:* e gran plazer.
24. e lay definet *R*, e fenic en lombardia *A;* (definet) fenic *AB*, se finet *P*.
25. *only in E*. Cavedoni attributes it to a confusion with the heretic Almaricus of Chartres (see Chabaneau, *Biographies*, p. 282).

In addition to the above, there is the following, which is found only in *R*; we give the text of that MS without emendation:

E fon aventura que·l marit de la dona guery de la nafra e anet a San Jacmè. E N'Eymeric saup o e ac volontat d'intrar en Toloza; e venc s'en al rey e dis li que si li plazia volria anar vezer lo marques de Monferrat. E·l rey si·l det bando d'anar, e mes lo ben en arnes de totas res. E N'Aymeric dis al rey que passar volia per (?) Toloza, mas regart avia de so qu'el sabia; que·l rey sabia tot lo fag, e vi que la amor de sa dona lo tyrava. E det li companha tro Monpeslier; et el det as entendre als companhos tot lo fag, e qu'els li aiudesso, qu'el volia vezer sa dona en forma de malaute. Et els responderon qu'els feran tot so que comandaria. E can foron a Tholoza, los copans demanderon l'alberc del borzes, e fon lur ensenhatz, e troberon la dona e disseron li que un cozi del rey de Castela era malautes, que anava en pelerinage, e que·l plagues que lains pogues venir. Ela respos que layns seria servitz e onratz. E N'Eymeric venc de nueg e·ls copanhos colgueron lo en un bel lieg. E l'endema N'Eymeric mandet per la dona, e la dona venc en la cambra e conoc N'Eymeric, e det se grans meravilhas, e demandet li com era pogut intrar en Tholoza. Et el dis que per s'amor, e comtet li tot lo fag. E la dona fes parvent que·l cubris dels draps, e bayzet lo. D'aqui enant no say co fo, mas tan que cinc jorns lay estec N'Eymeric per occayso d'esser malautes. E cant s'en parti d'aqui, anet s'en al marques, e fon ben aculhit.[1]

---

[1] Chabaneau (*Biographies*, pp. 282–283) printed both versions of the *Vida*. But his edition gives no variants, and he occasionally makes what seem to us unjustifiable alterations in the text of the MSS. We have, therefore, made a completely new edition of the entire text. The edition of the *vidas* by A. H. Schutz and J. Boutière, which will supersede Chabaneau, was still in the press when we sent this book to the printer.

1

"AB MARRIMENS ANGOISSOS ET AB PLOR"

The poem numbered I by Bartsch (*Grundriss*) is rejected by Pillet-Carstens on the basis of objections raised by Zingarelli and others, and of a divergent attribution in a MS unknown to Bartsch. It is certainly not the work of Aimeric. See the section of the Introduction on attributions. Critical edition by Zingarelli, in *Due trovatori*, p. 41.

2

I. Ades vol de l'aondansa
Del cor la boca parlar;
Doncs, pus tan parli d'amar,
Be pot creire ses duptansa
Ma don', al mieu parlamen,
Qu'ieu am de cor finamen;
Mas ges hieu lieys no·n creiria
Per dig, si plus no·n fazia.

II. Quar no sap, a ma semblansa,
Domna miels Amor lauzar
Que tan pauc en vuelh' obrar.
Mout m'ac bella comensansa
Ves que·m pagua de nien.
Siey huelh m'an emblat mon sen
Ab tan belha maestria
Que·m fa plazer ma folhia.

III. Mas anc no vi fin' amansa
Ses alques de follejar,
Ni joy d'amor ses pezar,
Ni ses maltrag gran honransa;
E quar al menhs d'onramen
Ses plus son miei pessamen,
Sueffre plus leu tota via
L'afan doblat quascun dia.

IV. Et ieu dobli la balansa,
Que·l doble tenc lieis plus car.
Totz jorns qu'aissi sai doblar
Doblamen ma malanansa;
Mas assatz doblet plus gen
Tristans quan bec lo pimen,
Quar el guazanhet s'amia,
Per so per qu'ieu pert la mia.

V. Soven mi dona pezansa,
Ves que·m fa tart alegrar;
E fora·m greu ad honrar;
Mas l'onors e l'esperansa
Mi tenon alques jauzen.
Tot vuelh si' a son talen,
Qu'eyssamen si so seria
Si tot hieu no m'o volia.

VI. Na Biatritz, no·us sabria
Lauzar tan quo·us covenria.

VARIANTS

I. 4. Be puesc dire *J*. 5. (don' al) donau *R*. 6. (de) del *D*. 7. (hieu) en *ADEIJK;* (lieys) lors *D;* (no·n) nom *ADEJ*. 8. diz *D*, digz *AEIJKf;* (no·n) nom *AJ*.

II. 10. amors *R*. 12. (m'ac) mauc *IK*. 13. quẽ *C;* pago *D*. 14. (emblat) camiat *C;* (mon) lo *DEIJKR*. 16. Quen *J;* fai *ADE*, fan *J*.

III. 17. Manc non vi *J*. 18. (alques) aquels *IK*. 19. (pezar) preiar *DEJ*, pensar *f*. 21. (al) ab *J*. 22. *lacking f;* (son) soi D^c*;* (miei) miein *D*. 24. doblar *EJ*.

IV. 25. (ieu) en DD^c. 26. Que dobles tenc lieis per car *A;* Ca doble *EJ*, Cal doble *f*. 27. jorn D. 28. ma benanansa *CR*. 29. doblat *D*. 30. (bec lo) pec del *f*. 32. Per aisso quieu *AE*, Per aquo quieu *J*, Per so queu *D;* (qu'ieu) qen D^c.

V. 34. Neys *C;* (tart) trar *IK*. 35. fora *ADEIKRf;* (honrar) durar *AJ*. 36. (l'onors) lamors *EJ;* lasperanza *DIK*. 37. (tenon) ten *EJ*. 39. (si so) si o *E*, sis *J;* si soria *f;* seriã *D*. 40. hieu *lacking EJ;* (m'o) lo *IK*, o *R*.

VI. 41. sabia *R*. 42. Tant lauzar *AEJ;* coueria *D*.

TRANSLATION

I. Always out of the abundance of the heart the mouth speaketh. Therefore, since I speak so much of loving, my Lady may well believe without any doubt, from my words, that I love from my heart, faithfully. But I should not believe her about it at all, for mere words, unless she did something more.

II. In my opinion, no lady knows how to praise Love better than she, who so little wishes to practice it. It (my love) had a very fair beginning, but now it pays me nothing (gives me no satisfaction). Her eyes have stolen all my sense, with such lovely mastery that it makes me rejoice in my own folly.

III. Yet I never saw a faithful love that did not have some folly in it, nor joy of love without sorrow, nor great honor without trouble; and since my thoughts are at least about honor and nothing else, I suffer ever more easily the torment which is doubled every day.

IV. And I double the scales, for I hold her doubly dear. Almost every day I can double my ill fortune doubly. Tristan, when he drank the love potion, doubled in a finer way, for he won his lady by the means by which I lose mine.

V. She gives me heart-heaviness often, while she is slow in making me rejoice. (And it would be difficult to honor me.) Yet Honor and Hope keep me a little joyous. Let it all be as she will; for, even though I did not wish it, it would be so anyhow.

VI. Lady Beatrice, I could not praise you as highly as would be fitting for you.

NOTES

Ten MSS: *ACDD^{c}EIJKRf*, of which D^c contains only lines 17–32. Stanzas II and III are quoted in the *Breviari d'amor*, lines 30425 and 28661, respectively (variants: 23. *(leu) l'en.* 24. *dobla*). Stanzas I and VI are printed in De Bartholomaeis, *Poesie provenzali storiche*, I, 229, according to *A*. Stemma:

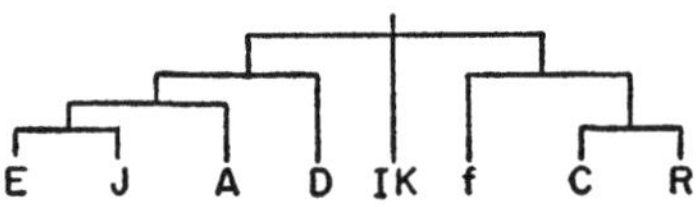

ADEJ: 7 (nom), 19 (-*A*) — *CRf:* 7 (hieu)
AEJ: 32, 42 — *CR:* 28
EJ: 24, 26, 36, 37, 40 — *IK:* 12, 18, 34, 40

This stemma raises a few difficulties, but I think not insuperable ones. We can assume that *A* corrected a wrong reading in 19 (not too difficult a correction). As for 35, *E*'s *onrar* looks so much like *durar* (a much more likely word) that one can understand how easy the confusion was; it is not too hard to believe that the same mistake could be made independently by *A* and *J*. *IK* seem to stand apart from both of the other groups. The position of D^c cannot be determined, since so little of the poem appears in that MS. As *C*'s readings appear to be generally better, we have chosen it as base.

This song is a good example of the inability of the troubadours to compose what Jeanroy (*La poésie lyrique des troubadours*, II, 113) calls "un tout logiquement agencé." Here, one strophe has no evident connection with the preceding. The thought is vague, more incoherent than usual.

1–2. A reference to the well-known scriptural saying, found in Matthew, XII, 24.

3. *parli*. This late and analogical form is rather common in Aimeric's poems; cf. *dobli*, v. 25.

14. That the eyes "steal" either the heart or the senses is a truism with the troubadours. See especially Wechssler, *Das Kulturproblem des Minnesangs*, 383–384. *C*'s reading *camiat* is isolated and does not suit the thought.

17–24. No love without folly or suffering is again a commonplace with the troubadours. See Wechssler, *op. cit.*, 190ff.

25–32. Folquet de Marseille, whom Aimeric often imitates, is found of "doubling" his woes or his desires. Cf. Stronski's edition, III, 47; IV, 38; etc.

28. The reading of *ADEIJKf* is more in keeping with the rest of the piece than that of *CR*.

30–32. The troubadours often allude to the Tristan legend. See Aimeric's poem 10, line 16 and the editions of Bernart de Ventadorn, Folquet de Marseille, Pons de Capdueil, etc. It is not possible to determine which version of the story Aimeric had in mind here.

34. The reading of *C* (*Neys*) is isolated, and seems less good than that of the other MSS.

3

I. N'Albertz, chausetz al vostre sen
D'un amic qu'enquier per amor
Doas domnas d'una valor;
E l'un' ama lui e·ill cosen
Lo plus, ab que de l'autra·s lais
Qu'el ama·l doble meillz e mais,
Et aquella no·l vol amar ni·l deigna.
Digatz ab cal d'ambas l'es mielz que·s teingna.

II. N'Aimerics, pauc a d'ensien
Qui no·n sap triar lo meillor.
A guissa de fin amador
Voill amar celei coralmen
De cui anc mos cors no s'estrais;
E vos voill c'amez en biais,
Qu'eu non ai cor que fals guizardon preingna,
Anz voill servir tan c'al ric joi aveingna.

III. N'Albertz, ben sai que·l conoissen
Tendran e·l bon entendedor
Vostra rason per sordeior,
C'ab mej' amor sai qu'es plus gen
C'om baizan jazen sia gais
C'ab tota sospir e pantais.
Mais pretz lo frug on ab las mans ateingna
C'aisel qu'es autz, on lansar mi coveingna.

IV. N'Aimerics, ges no m'es parven
Que·us entendatz en gran honor;
E no s'eschai a preguador
C'aissi s'an camjan ni volven,
Anz deu esser fis e verais.
E no voill c'aitals frugs m'engrais;
Mas voill esser totz temps secs plus que leingna
Que manje frug de que talanz no·m veingna.

V. N'Albertz, quan son comunalmen
D'engal beutat e de lausor,
Fas a lei de bon partidor
Que·ls mals vos las e·ls bens eu pren.
Qu'als bes taing c'om s'afraingn' e·s bais
E fuia·ls mals a grant eslais;
Qu'anz que s'arda ni que trop s'escompreingna
Deu om gardar del foc ab que l'esteingna.

VI. N'Aimerics, li galiamen
Que fan li fals e·il trichador
An tornat domnei en error;
Et a vos non es d'avinen
Que·us dejatz cargar de tal fais,
Qu'anc fis amics sidonz no trais;
Et eu sui sel cui fin' Amors enseingna
Que leialmen ves ma domna·m capteingna.

VII. N'Albertz, car es de beutat rais
Na Biatritz d'Est, on pretz nais,
Voill d'aquest plaig juge so que·s coveingna;
Mas eu cre ben que ma rason manteingna.

VIII. N'Aimerics, a N'Emilla lais
De Ravena, c'ades val mais
En tot bon fag c'a pro domna coveingna,
Lo jujamen, e c'ab lo dreg s'en teingna.

VARIANTS

I. 1. Nalbert *D*^{a}*a*^{1} (*and so throughout*), Nalbertetz *IK*, Albert *E*, Albertet *G*. 2. Dunc amic qui *G*. 3. (d'una) de gran *a*^{1}. 6. (ama·l) ama e *G*. 7. no lama ni nol d. *G*, no lama nil d. *E;* (ni·l) ni *a*^{1}. 8. d'ambas *lacking E;* (que·s) que *a*^{1}.

II. 9. essien *D*^{a}*EGa*^{1}. 12. (Voill amar) Amarai *EG;* amar *lacking D*^{a}. 13. mon cor *E*. 14. veill *E;* came *IK*. 15. cors *G*. 16. quel ricx iois *E*, qel ric ioi *G*.

III. 17. Nalbertet *EG* (*and so in the rest of the poem; see above*, 1); sa *D*^{a}*;* que·l *lacking E*, qill *G*. 20. Ab *E*, Car *a*^{1}. 21. Com ia se (iaisen *G*) baisan s. g. *EG*, Com iauzenz si e g. *a*^{1}. 22. Cab totz ans *a*^{1}, Cab totas *D*^{a}*EIK*. 23. (pretz) am *D*^{a}, an *D*^{c}*;* (ab las) a la *G*, ambas *a*^{1}. 24. Que sel *D*^{c}*EG*, Quaisses *a*^{1}.

IV. 25. Naimerit *G*. 26. Qeu *Ga*^{1}*;* granz h. *G*. 27. pregardor *I*. 30. (m'engrais) me atrais *D*^{a}*IK*. 31. estar *D*^{c}*;* (secs plus) plus secs *D*^{a}*EGa*^{1}, plus sos *D*^{c}. 32. Qeu *D*^{c}*;* manges *G*, mainiar *a*^{1}*;* (que) qel *G;* (veingna) preignha *a*^{1}.

V. 33. Nalbertetz *IK* (*see above*, 1 *and* 17); (quan son) fason D^a, car son EGa^1. 34. beltaz *G*, beutatz *I*. 35. *lacking* D^a; Faitz *E*, Faç *G*, Fait a^1. 36. Qel mal *G;* (e·ls) el *G;* (eu) en Ia^1. 37. Cal bes D^aIK, Cal ben *EG;* (e·s) e Ga^1. 38. fuial mal *E*, fugal mal Ga^1; grans *EG*. 39. Qan a^1; sardi *G;* ni que *lacking E;* que *lacking* D^a. 40. om *lacking IK;* sesteingna D^a.

VI. *lacking G*. 42. e·il *lacking IK*, oill a^1. 45. Quens *I;* (cargar) gardar a^1; daital D^aE, daitals a^1.

VII. *lacking G*. 49. (*see above*, 1 *and* 17). 51. Voill iutge daqest p. a^1. 52. que *lacking* a^1.

VIII. 53. nesmilla *G*, namille a^1. 55. En toz bos (bes *G*) faitz $GIKa^1$; pros Ga^1; domnas a^1. 56. se t. Ga^1.

TRANSLATION

I. Sir Albert, choose, according to your mind: a lover woos two ladies of equal worth. One loves him and grants him the utmost, provided that he abandon the other, whom he loves doubly more dearly. But she will not love him nor condescend to him. Say now with which one of the two it is better that he abide.

II. Sir Aimeric, he has little wit who cannot choose the better. Like a faithful lover, I will love truly her from whom my heart never departs; and I will that you love like a double-faced wretch. I have no desire to take a false guerdon,—rather will I serve till I attain a precious love-joy.

III. Sir Albert, I know well that the wise and the efficient lovers will hold your choice the worse. I know too that it is more pleasing to be gay with a half-love, kissing and lying, than to sigh and dream for a whole love. I prefer the fruit that one can reach with his hands to the one that hangs high and at which one must hurl something to get it.

IV. Sir Aimeric, it does not seem to me that you make love in an honorable way, because it is not fitting that a wooer should keep changing and turning. Rather should he be faithful and true. And I do not wish that any such fruit should fatten me. I would rather always be thinner than a stick of wood than eat a fruit for which I had no liking.

V. Sir Albert, since they (these ladies) are of equal beauty and worth, I act like a good debater when I leave to you the bad and take the good. It is fitting that a man should bow and stoop before the good and should flee the bad in all haste; for, before it flame up or be kindled too much, one should have the means to put out the fire.

VI. Sir Aimeric, the deceits of the false lovers and the tricksters have led lady-service astray; and it is not gracious of you to assume such a burden, for a faithful lover never betrays his lady. And I am a man taught by true Love, so that I bear myself loyally toward my lady.

VII. Sir Albert, I wish the Lady Beatrice of Este to judge this debate, as to what is right, for she is a ray of beauty, and Worth is born in her. I believe that she will uphold my cause.

VIII. Sir Aimeric, I leave the decision to the Lady Emilia of Ravenna, for she is more famed for all good traits that pertain to a lady; and may she abide by the right!

NOTES

Seven MSS: $D^aD^cEGIKa^1$. Only vv. 23–24 and 31–32 appear in D^c. Critical editions: W. P. Shepard, in *Modern Philology*, XXIII, 18–23; Jean Boutière, in *Les poésies du troubadour*

Albertet, pp. 81–84 (both based on *I*). Our text (base also *I*) differs only slightly from Mr. Shepard's earlier text, chiefly in a closer adherence to the base MS. Stemma:

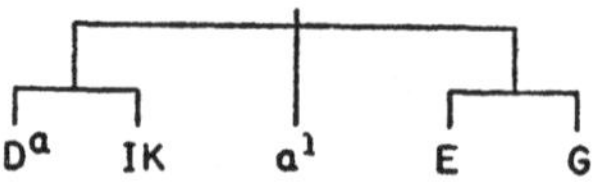

DªIK: 30, 37 *EG:* 12, 16, 17, 21, 37, 38
IK: 1, 14, 31, etc.
*a*¹ does not agree consistently with either group, and has many independent variants of its own (3, 20, 21, 22, 23, etc.); we therefore assume it to be descended in another line.

1. The measure proves that the correct form of this troubadour's name is Albert, not Albertet. Boutière makes no pronouncement on this matter.

5. For the locution *se laissar de*, "give up, forsake," see Levy, *SW*, IV, 311.

6. Zingarelli (*Intorno a due trovatori in Italia*, p. 30), referring to this *tenso*, states as its subject: "decidere si sia a preferire una donna che vi accordi i suoi piaceri senza amarvi, od una che non vi dia nulla, ma vi ami." To understand it thus, Zingarelli, who does not give the text, must have read v. 6 as *Que l'ama*. This interpretation is excluded by vv. 4 and 7, as well as by the general tenor of the debate.

6. Examples of the adverbial accusative *lo doble*, "doubly," have not been observed elsewhere in Provençal, as far as we know.

14. In this verse, it is evident that *DªEGa*¹ have a reading preferable to that of *IK*. We suspect that the original had: *E volez qu'eu am en biais;* but we have not ventured to introduce this conjecture into the text.

20. The *mej' amor* "half love" that the poet feels for the first lady is contrasted with the *tota* "whole love" that he has for the second. Boutière: *totas* (line 22, with the majority of the MSS); he translates: "que de soupirer et de rêver auprès de toutes." This interpretation seems to us less good than the one we suggest.

21. *baizan jazen*. This asyndetic pairing of participles is common in Provençal and in Aimeric. Cf. Peire d'Alvernhe (ed. Zenker), XII, 85–86:

> Lo vers fo faitz als enflabotz
> A Puoich-vert tot jogan rizen,

and several examples in Aimeric's *tenso* with Elias d'Ussel (no. 37). See Schultz-Gora, in *Zeitschrift für romanische Philologie*, XVI, 514.

23–24. Cnyrim, *Sprichwörter*, no. 688.

30. Boutière: *me atrais*. We prefer the reading of *EGa*¹.

32. *Que*. This use of one *que* for two ("than that") is common enough in Provençal and Old French. Cf. Folquet de Marseille (ed. Stronski), X, 23–24:

> Anceis voill mais mon dan sofrir jasse
> Que·ls vostres tortz adreitures claman.

For Old French, see Foulet, *Petite syntaxe de l'ancien français*, p. 336.

39–40. This also looks like a proverb. It is not cited by Cnyrim.

55. Boutière: *en totz bons faitz*. We read *en tot bon fag* (with *DªE*) because the following verb is singular.

4

I. A ley de folh camjador
Ai camjat mal per pejor,
E so son doas foldatz.
Pero si son tan cenatz
Que ben conosc ma folor.
Si mos sens no m'en castia
E sec ades ma folhia,
No m'en deu hom planher, anz deu plazer
Mos dans, pois tan ponh en mi deschazer.

II. Quar s'ieu falhi al major,
Pus ai falhit al menor;
Per que·l falhirs es doblatz,
O c'es endreg Dieu peccatz,
E blasmes endreg lauzor,
E crims endreg cortezia,
E vergonha endreg d'amia
E dans endreg recebr' autruy aver:
Doncs si deu selh guardar que deu valer.

III. E doncs diguatz mi, senhor!
Que falh vers un trobador
Qu'es conogutz e prezatz
E pels melhors enansatz,
S'ilh l'aunis ni·l contracor?
D'autr' afar quo·s portaria?
Leu devinar o faria:
Qu'aisselh' honra so que deu vil tener
E so ten vil qu'onrar deu e temer.

IV. Be farai castic forsor,
Si non cre castiador;
Mas si bendig non amatz
Ni vergonha no duptatz,
Cum conoisseretz honor,
Ni castiars que valria?
Aitan me mescabaria,
Quar sa cresma pert qui·lh met e·l lezer
Qui filh d'aze bateja jorn ni ser.

V. Aissi mezeis, non alhor,
M'en rancur en fatz d'amor,
Que lo vils a croys mercatz
M'en vensera miels assatz,
Que·m fassa tal dezonor,
Qu'ieu ges no m'en venjaria
Tan fort, neys s'ieu l'aucizia.
Vida·l don Dieus e·l cresca son saber!
E no·l pot om piegz orar ni voler.

VI. A'N Rainier fas de Val Cortes saber
Socors non es que de mos tratz esper.

VARIANTS

I. 1. (de) del *N*. 3. Aisso *ADf*, Aco *MNR*; son *lacking f*. 6. E si mo cen nom castia *C*, Si mo cen no mo c. *R*, Doncs pueis conosc ma follia *M*, Donx pus aiss ma mort follia *f*; (m'en) me *N*. 7. *lacking N*; No men deu hom planher mia *CR*, Si mos sens no men (me *M*) chastia *Mf* (=6). 8. Ans deu quascus mon dampnatge plazer *CR*. 9. Pus tan fort ponh hieu (en *R*) mi eys dechazer *CR*; (ponh) poigna *A*, puoig *D*, pueg *N*.

II. 10. falh *Rf*. 11. Plus *ADMf*. 12. que falhirs *C*. 13. Mas endreich dieu es p. *A*, Mos en dreiz deu peccaç D; (O c'es) Et es *Mf*, Oçes *N*; endres dieus *C*, e. die *M*. 14. blamez *A*, blasmens *N*; (endreg) con dreit *D*, entre *R*. 17. (recebr') resemble *AD*, reseble *N*, ressembr *f*. 18. (que) qui *MN*.

III. 20. Qe nos (Qeus *D*) par dun t. *AD*; (Que) Qui *N*; (un) o *CR*, *lacking N*; torbador *D*. 21. (es) ese *D*; (e) o *CR*, ese *N*. 22. pils *N*. 23. Sill fai dan nilh sobrecor *M*, Sil ten uil nil c. *f*; Si launis *A*; laus nis *R*. 24. Dautra cors far cos p. *D*; Dautra fars *C*; partiria *f*. 25. (o) a *D*, *lacking f*; (faria) sabria *M*. 26. Qui honra so que (cheu *D*) deuria uil (car *D*) tener *AD*; (que) cheu *N*. 27. Que son tengutz contra dieu e temer *CR*; Qui so *DM*, Qui eso *f*, Qui son *N*; (qu' onrar) corar *D*, contra *N*.

IV. 28. Bem (Ben *N*) fara *ADN*, Ben feira *M*, Ben fara *f*; castics *A*. 29. Si creis per c. *A*, Si creis c. *DN*, Qui cre ses c. *M*, Si crezes c. *f*. 30. Mans *NR*; beus dic *C*, ben dir *M*. 31. no *lacking D*. 33. chaistiar *D*; (que) qei *ADN*, qeus *Mf*, quel *R*; ualdriã *D*. 34. *lacking ADN*; laisme (laismen *f*) qaitan (car tan *f*) me perdria *Mf*. 35. sa *lacking f*; (qui·lh) qui *DMNf*; met son lezer *M*, met alazer *f*. 36. En fill daze bateiar *M*; (bateja) baça *N*; çorn ne ser *N*.

V. *lacking M*. 37. A mi mezeis *A*. 38. Me *C*; en fatz clamor *A*, en fauc clamor *f*. 39. *lacking f*; Qel es un (us *D*) fort crois m. *AD*, Que leschai croi m. *N*, Que les chien creys m. *R*; los uils *C*. 40. *lacking f*; Mas (Men *D*) ueiaire mes assatz *AD*; uenseran *CR*, ueçeran *N*. 41. *lacking f*; Quom *CNR*, Con *D*; fai satal *D*, falsa cal *R*. 42. *lacking f*; Qieu eus no *A*, Queu ues no *DN*; uenzazia *D*. 43. *lacking f*; neus si bem uolia *A*; lauseia *DN*. 44. *lacking f*; e crescal *ADN*. 45. *lacking f*; om *lacking C*; pec honrar *D*, peç honrar *N*.

VI. *lacking Mf*. 46. (A'N) En *DNR*; cortis *CN*, cortal *R*. 47. Socor *R*, Sator *AN*, Sabers *D*; (que) ques *C*; mons trais *N*.

TRANSLATION

I. Like a foolish money-changer, I have changed bad for worse. And so there are two follies. But nevertheless I am sensible enough to see my own foolishness. And if my own good sense does not chastise me for it and if I follow always my folly, no one should pity me, but my misfortune should give pleasure, since I strive after my own dishonor.

II. For, if I erred in the greater matter, I have erred more in the lesser: wherefore the error is doubled, so that it (?) is a sin in respect to God, a subject of reproach in respect to fame, a crime in respect to courtesy, a shame in respect to one's love, and a loss in respect to receiving another's property. Therefore, the man who is striving to be worthy should guard against it.

III. Therefore tell me, Sirs! In what way does she wrong a troubadour who is known and recommended and exalted by the best, if she shame or discredit him? How would she conduct herself in another affair? That is easy to guess, since she honors what she should despise and despises what she should honor and fear.

IV. I shall make a stronger reproach, even though she does not believe the reproacher. But if you do not love praise and do not fear shame, how will you know what honor is? And what boots it to reproach? It would avail me naught, for he who baptizes an ass's son by day or night loses the chrism which he puts on it, and his time likewise.

V. So I blame myself, not another, about these love affairs. The contemptible wretch with sinful bargains will overcome me, so that she may do me such a dishonor. I could not ever avenge myself so well, even if I slew her. May God grant him life and increase his knowledge! And no man could pray for or wish her worse than that.

VI. I make known to Sir Rainier of the Courtly Vale that there is no help I hope for from my darts (cutting words).

NOTES

Seven MSS: *ACDMNRf*. The relationships between the MSS are very difficult to determine exactly. The poem evidently perplexed the copyists as much as it does modern interpreters. The group *AD* is clearly established; cf. vv. 17, 20, 26, 33, 34, 40. *N* often agrees with *AD* (6, 17, 33, 34, 44), sometimes with *D* alone (27, 29, 42, 43, 45, 46), and once with *A* alone (47). The groups *CR* (6, 7–9, 20, 27) and *Mf* (6, 33, 34) are likewise fairly certain. The only possible stemma would be a tripartite one along the lines indicated.

In view of the rather defective text in all the MSS, the reconstruction has of necessity been somewhat eclectic. The choice of readings lies between *CR* on the one hand and *AD* on the other. Except in lines 7–9, where *C*'s reading seems to be grammatically impossible, we have followed *C*, with some evident corrections.

This is the most difficult, and also the most personal, of all of Aimeric's songs. Most of the rest seem to be literary exercises, at least in large measure. The love, or loves, he sings in them are conventional. But a real emotion breathes through this piece. Aimeric had evidently deserted a first love, who treated him badly, for a second, who treated him worse. Is this the same situation as that referred to in songs 7 and 14? For similar sentiments, caused by a like betrayal, cf. the piece VIII of Jausbert de Puycibot (ed. Shepard, pp. 25–28).

1–2. This beginning may have been suggested by the line of Folquet de Marseille (ed. Stronski, VI, 27): *Mas ben deu hom camjar bon per meillor.*

7–9. On the principle of the *lectio difficilior*, one should prefer the reading of *CR*. But we have been unable to find a single example of *plazer* transitive, in the sense "take pleasure in." This seems to exclude the possibility of accepting line 8 as these MSS have it. Moreover, since *M* most commonly goes with *CR*, but opposes them here, there is likelihood that the reading adopted is correct.

13. I am not too sure how one should interpret *O c'es*, whether as *O s'es*, as *O qu'es* (rather unlikely for these MSS), or even as *Oc es* (FMC).

17. Exactly what is meant by this line is hard to determine.

19–23. Only by taking this sentence as a question is it possible to translate the *Que* in line 20.

23. *contracor*. Apparently a rare word in Provençal. Levy (*SW*, I, 344) cites only two examples, with the meaning "entgegen laufen, eilen." In the *PD* however he adds the meaning "déroger," which fits this passage.

35–36. Cnyrim, *Sprichwörter*, no. 497.

40. It is likely that the original had *ueniara* (supported by the *ueiaire* of *A*); but we have not ventured to introduce this conjecture into the text.

44–45. To understand these lines, it seems necessary to assume that the *'l* of 44 refers to *lo vil* of 39, while the *'l* of 45 means the lady who betrayed the poet.

46. *En Rainier de Val Cortes* may be a *senhal*. At all events, the person designated is unknown.

47. The word *tratz* is evidently used figuratively here, meaning "sharp, cutting words."

5

"AL REI QUE TEN EN PES"

The single stanza found in *H*, and numbered by *Bartsch* as the fifth of Aimeric's poems, was later recognized to be only a stanza of poem 49.

6

I. Amics Albertz, tenzos soven
Fan assatz tuit li trobador,
E partisson razon d'amor
E d'als, qan lur platz, eissamen.
Mas ieu faz zo q'anc om non fes,
Tenzon d'aizo qi res non es;
Q'a razon pro·m respondrias,
Mas al nien vueil respondatz;
Et er la tenzos de non-re.

II. N'Aimerics, pueis del dreg nien
Mi voletz far respondedor,
Non voil autre razonador
Mas mi meteus. Mon eiscien,
Be·m par q'a razon respondes
Qi respon zo qe res non es.
Us nienz es d'autre compratz.
Per q'al nien don m'apellatz,
Respondrai com? Calarai me!

III. Albertz, ges callan non enten
Qe·l respondres aja valor;
Ni mutz non respon a segnor,
E muz non diz vertat ni men.
S'ades callatz, con respondres?
Ja parlei, qe·us ai escomes.
Nient a nom; donc, si·l nomatz,
Parlares, mal grat qe n'ajatz,
O no·i respondretz mal ni be.

IV. N'Aimerics, nuil essernimen
No·us aug dir, anz parlatz error.
Folia deu hom a follor
Respondre, e saber a sen.
Eu respon a "non sai qe s'es"
Con cel q'en cisterna s'es mes,
Qe mira sos oils e sa faz,
E s'el sona, sera sonatz
De si meteus, c'als non i ve.

V. Albertz, cel sui eu veramen
Qi son' e mira sa color,
Et aug la voz del sonador,
Pueis ieu vos son primeiramen;
E·l resonz es nienz, so·m pes:
Donc es vos—e no·us enoi ges—
Nienz, s'aissi respondiatz.
E si per tal vos razonatz,
Ben es fols qi de ren vos cre.

VI. N'Aimerics, d'entrecimamen
Sabetz, e fai vos hom lauzor;
Si no·us entendon li pluzor,
Ni vos mezeus, zo es parven.
Et es vos en tal razon mes
Don ieu issirai, mal qe·us pes,
E vos remanretz essaratz;
E sitot mi matracejatz,
Ieu vos respon, mas no·us dic qe.

VII. Albertz, zo q'eu vos dic vers es:
Doncs dic eu qe om ve non-res,
Qar s'un flum d'un pont fort gardatz,
L'ueil vos diran q'ades anatz,
E l'aiga can cor s'i rete.

VIII. N'Aimerics, non es mals ni bes,
Aizo de qe·us es entremes,
Q'atrestam petit issegatz
Co·l molinz q'a roda de latz,
Qe·s mou tot jorn e non vai re.

VARIANTS

I. 1. Amic a^1; albert Oa^1, nalbert *R* (*and likewise in the later stanzas, each MS being consistent*), nalberz *M;* tenso *MR;* seuen Oa^1. 2. (assatz) aras *R;* (tuit li) llautre *M*. 3. E parton se razos *R*. 5. com mays no f. *R;* om *lacking* a^1. 6. daqo *M*, de so *R;* qi ies *O*. 7. (Q'a) Car *R;* pro *M*. 8. (al nien) a me Oa^1, a nien *M*. 9. Eli tensos es *M*.

II. 10. Naimeric ORa^1 (*and so throughout*), Naimeris *M;* (del dreg nien) respondedor *M*. 11. (respondedor) dun dreg nien *M*. 12. Noi *MR;* (voil) qier *M*. 13. Mas sol mon sen tan solamen *M*, Mas mon saber solamen *R*. 14. (Be·m) Ben a^1, Prom *R;* (q'a) car *R;* respozes *M*. 15

Qa so r. qe *M,* Saisous r. que *R;* non es res R. 16. (Us) Cus *R.* 17. E pos a nien ma. *M.* 18. Respondra *a*[1]; (com) cora *Oa*[1]; calayramen *R.*

III. 19. Nalbertet *M;* ges *lacking M;* callar *M.* 20. (Qe·l) Que *R;* Que dei auer nulha v. *M.* 21. (Ni) Qar *M,* Que *R.* 22. (E) Ni *MR;* (diz) di *M.* 23. Doncs si callas *M.* 24. Jaus parlieu *R,* La parlli ieu *M;* (Ja) Iai *Oa*[1]; (escomes) comes *M.* 25. (donc) e *M.* 26. Respondres *M.* 27. E non dires ni mal ni be *M;* (no·i) non *R.*

IV. 29. ans sembla derror *R;* d' *lacking Oa*[1]. 30. E folia *Oa*[1]. 32. (Eu) Prous *R;* (a) e *Oa*[1]. 34. Ques *R;* sos hueilh *M.* 35. E uen autre ques fayssonatz *R;* (E s'el) E si *M.* 36. cautre noy ue *R.*

V. 37. yeu soy sel *R.* 38. Qe mir mos hueilhs e ma c. *M,* Queus sen es mira sa c. *R.* 39. E vos la votz del s. *M,* E vos lo vout del orador *R.* 40. *lacking M;* (ieu) en *a*[1]. 41. Si per aisso vos raçonatz (=44) *M;* El retint *R;* (pes) penz *a*[1]. 42. Doncs est vos nientz e nous pes *M,* Donc e uos no uos e. g. *R;* (vos) uous *a*[1]. 43–45. *Here M substitutes 57–59, which also occur in their proper place:* Qar sil flum de laiga gardatz Vostr hueilh diran no uos nanaz E laigon plus cor si rete. 43. Nienz fatz sim r. *R;* respondratz *O.* 45. Ben es nessis qi de reus cre *R.*

VI. 46. lentrecimamen *R.* 47. e portaus nom l. *M,* per com vō fa l. *R.* 48. (Si) E *MR.* 49. (Ni) Neys *R;* (so es p.) mon escien *MR.* 50. (mes) pres *R;* Et es en uos en tal *a*[1]. 52. essaiatz *a*[1] eisseratz *M,* issaratz *R.* 53. (mi) mieus *R.* 54. Yeus r. mays nous vuelh dir que *R;* Respon uos ieu *M.*

VII. 55. Albert *M* (*as well as Oa*[1]*; see line* 1); so qieu dic vezers es *M;* so cuelh ditz *R.* 56. Per qieu dic *M;* qei coue non res *Oa*[1]. 57. (s'un) sil *M,* si *R;* dun aiga g. *M,* dun aut pon g. *R.* 58. Vostr hueilh d. *M.* 59. E laigon plus cor *M;* (can) on *R;* (s'i) se *R.*

VIII. 62. Cans es un pauc escigatz *R;* petit petit i. *O;* esgardatz *M.* 63. qe roda es latz *R.* 64. (Qe·s) Es *M.*

TRANSLATION

I. Friend Albert, all the troubadours compose *tensos* quite often and debate a question of love or of something else, likewise, when it pleases them. But I am composing what no one ever made,—a *tenso* about nothing. You would answer well to a real question; but I wish you to answer to nothing. So this *tenso* will be about nothing.

II. Sir Aimeric, since you wish to make me an answerer to a mere nothing, I do not wish to have any other debater but myself. In my opinion, I think that he makes a good reply who answers that it is nothing. One nothing balances the other. Since then you invite me to a debate about nothing, how shall I answer? I'll keep silent.

III. Sir Albert, I don't think that a silent answer is worth anything. A dumb man does not answer his lord, nor speak the truth nor lie. If you keep silent all the time, how will you answer? I have spoken to you already, for I challenged you. The subject is—nothing; therefore, if you name it, you'll speak in spite of yourself, or you will not answer the challenge either well or ill.

IV. Sir Aimeric, I don't hear you speak with discernment; on the contrary, you talk erroneously. One should answer foolishness with folly, wisdom with sense. So I answer this "I don't know what" like a man in a cistern who looks at his own eyes and face; and if he utters a word, he will be echoed by himself, for he doesn't see anything else in it.

V. Sir Albert, that is who I am really, a man who speaks and looks at his own face; and I hear the voice of the speaker, for I speak to you first. But the echo is nothing, as I think. So you are—and don't let this irk you—nothing, if you answer thus. And if you argue yourself into that quandary, he is a fool who believes you about anything.

VI. Sir Aimeric, you do know confusing arguments, and people praise you for that, even if most of them do not understand you,—nor do you understand yourself, it seems. And you have got yourself into a quandary that I will get out of, however it irk you; and you will remain stuck in it. Though you knock me down, I answer,—but I do not say a word.

VII. Sir Albert, what I tell you is true. I tell you that one can see nothing; for if you watch a river closely from a bridge, your eyes will tell you that it is you who are moving and that the running water is still.

VIII. Sir Aimeric, this thing that you challenged me to debate is neither good nor bad. You won't get anywhere with it, any more than a mill with a wheel beside it, which turns night and day and doesn't go anywhere.

NOTES

Four MSS: *MORa*[1]. Of these, *O* and *a*[1] seem to be copies of the same original (cf. Bertoni, *Il canzoniere provenzale di Bernart Amoros*, pp. xvi–xxi). *R* and *M* are not so close either to each other or to *Oa*[1], though they have common divergences from *Oa*[1] in vv. 12, 22, 48, 49, in addition to those noted below. We have adopted *a*[1] as base.

Critical editions: W. P. Shepard, in *Modern Philology*, XXIII, 23–28; and Jean Boutière, in *Les poésies du troubadour Albertet*, pp. 84–87 (no. XIX). Both follow *Oa*[1] (Shepard, the orthography of *a*[1], Boutière that of *O*). The present text differs only slightly from Mr. Shepard's earlier text.

This *tenso* with Albert (de Sestaro) was probably suggested by the piece *No sai que s'es* of Raïmbaut d'Aurenga (published by Appel, *Prov. Chrest.*, p. 77). The earliest specimen of a song about nothing is the *Farai un vers de dreit nien* of William of Poitou (no. 4 in Jeanroy's edition, p. 6).

3. This meaning of *partir*, "take part in a debate," is not given by Raynouard or Levy, but it derives easily from such expressions as *partir un joc*, *partir una tenso*. The reading *razos* of *R* would perhaps be preferable (see the note on 19, 1), but *razon* is intelligible.

8. The reading of *Oa*[1] is hypometric, so we have followed *MR*. So does Boutière. One could emend: *vueil que respondatz*.

14. Boutière: *responz es*. He translates this and the following line: "il me paraît évident qu'on peut trouver une réponse pour un sujet raisonnable, mais qui répond à ce qui n'existe pas?" This seems to strain the syntax somewhat, and the rime *es: es* in successive lines is questionable.

18. Here again *MR* have the correct reading, as the measure shows. Boutière: *respondrai c'or calarai me*.

23–24. The rime here and elsewhere indicates that the reduction of -ts (*-tz*) to -s had been accomplished by Aimeric's time. This sound change, though it took place early in many regions, does not appear often in the rimes of the troubadours (see Grandgent, *Old Provençal*, p. 47; also Schultz-Gora, *Provenzalische Studien*, I, 8 and 28). The reduction may or may not be shown in the spelling of the MSS (as it is here).

24. Shepard: *Ja parl ieu;* Boutière: *ja·i parlei*, "j'ai déjà pris la parole"; but the function of *i* is not clear.

30–31. Cnyrim, *Sprichwörter*, no. 559.

32. Again we (like Boutière) have preferred the reading *a* of *MR* to *e* of *Oa*[1], because it seems that all through the *tenso* the poets are thinking of Raïmbaut's *No sai que s'es*.

36. Boutière: *c'autre no·i ve* (with *R*).

39. Boutière: *vos* (for *aug;* with *MR*).

43. Boutière: *respondratz* (though he rejects the form in a note).

44. For *se razonar per*, "acknowledge oneself to be," see Bernart de Ventadorn (ed. Appel), XX, 48. This meaning is not given by Raynouard or Levy. Boutière: "et si vous vous défendez de telle manière."

46. *entrecimamen*. Sole example of this word. Raynouard (II, 396) gives the translation 'entrelacement," and connects the word with *cima*. Levy (*SW*, III, 80) also cites this passage, but refuses to explain the word. The verb *tressimar, entressimar* is however used by Gavaudan (ed. Jeanroy in *Romania*, XXXIV, 497ff.). Mistral (*Trésor dou Félibrige*, II, 1044) cites the New Provençal *tressimaci*, "micmac, chose inextricable, trafic, agencement." The meaning here is evidently "entanglement, confused reasoning." We are inclined to think that the word belongs to the family of Provençal *tressar*, Old French *tresse, tresser*. The development of meaning is somewhat the same as in Italian *intreccio*.

53. *matrasejatz*. Apparently the sole example of the word in Old Provençal. See Raynouard, IV, 168. Not cited by Levy in the *SW*, but given, with a question mark, in the *PD*. The word is evidently derived from *matras*, "levier, javelot." Mistral (*Trésor*, II, 297) cites New Provençal *matrassa*, "frapper avec un matras, maltraîter." Albert uses the word here playfully.

56. Boutière: *doncs dic eu qe·i cove non res*, "et je dis que le néant convient à notre entretien (?)." This is the reading of *Oa*[1], but the meaning and the connection with the rest of the stanza are far from clear. We prefer the reading of *MR*.

57–59. A comparison probably due to the schools. A century later, Cardinal Nicolas de Cusa argued that a boat in rapid motion might seem at rest to a person seated in it. See Hobson, *The Domain of Natural Science* (Cambridge, 1923), p. 183.

62. For the verb *issegar, eissegar*, see *Flamenca*, v. 1044. Paul Meyer translates "exécuter, parfaire," and this meaning suits well here. See also Levy, *SW*, II, 333. Boutière: "vous obtenez des résultats aussi nuls que le moulin."

7

I. Amors, a vos meteussa·m clam de vos,
Car en mi etz intrada solamen
Et en Midonz non intratz eissamen,
Si que l'afans d'amdos comunals fos;
Mas vos laissatz lieis e retenetz mi,
Car mi trobatz senes totz engans fi,
E datz a lieis gaug et a mi dolor.
Los huoills e·l cor vos en trac ad auctor.

II. E fai ben pauc d'esfortz, so sabetz vos,
E grand orguoill e mal esseignamen
Cel que cellui combat que no·is deffen;
Puois es pecatz et avols vengazos.
Mas vos o faitz de mi tot atressi
Cum cel qui pres repren e mort auci.
Aver voletz l'aip del bon servidor
Qe·l sieu deserv, tant vol servir aillor.

III. Mas tot m'es bel, pros dompna, tant am vos,
Et amei vos anz q'ie·us vis, finamen;
E qan vos vi, amei vos per un cen,
E chascun jorn creis l'amors per un dos.
Gen mi sebret a la vista e·m parti
La vostr' amors d'un' altra qe·m trahi;
Mas tout m'avetz mal e donat pejor,
S'Amors ab vos e Merces no·m socor.

IV. Que per vos pert lieis e ges non ai vos,
Cum cel qui vai sos cairels pertraen
E per l'un pert l'autre. Tot aissi·m pren;
E meron mal vostras bellas faissos.
Vostra beltat blasmatz car m'abelli;
Apres blasmatz Amor car m'enardi.
E s'ieu i fatz nescies ni follor,
Non blasmetz mi mas vos eissa et Amor.

V. A! cum m'ant mort vostre beill huoill e vos
Ab un esgart qe·m feiron doussamen,

Q'ieu cujava c'o fesson veramen,
E non era mas geins e tracios!
Paucs fo l'esgartz qe·m vitz et ieu vos vi,
Dompna, mas puois es cregutz enaissi
De pauc en gran e de gran en major,
De sospir en plaing e de plaing en plor.

VI. *Dieus mi sal vos, domn', et a vos sal mi,*
Quar be m'es ops et a vos atressi:
A mi per so qu'enanz vostra lauzor,
Et a vos quar suy vostr' om e·us azor.

VII. Anc la dolsors puois del cor no m'issi
Des q'ie·us baisiei las mans, si·m dolsezi;
Neis ma bocha ditz que n'ac tal dolsor
C'anc non tastet mais tant dolsa sabor.

VIII. Vas Tolosa, al comte palaizi,
Duc e marques, chanssos, ten ton cami,
Car el val tant q'en la soa valor
Auria asatz ad un emperador.

VARIANTS

I. 1. A uos amors *C;* meteissamen *Fa*, meteismamen me *T*, medisam *c*. 2. Quar etz enme *CERf;* entradas. 3. E (Car *R*) non intretz en (*lacking Q*) midonz (ma domna *FaIKUc*) *CEFaGIKMQRUcf*. 4. dambes *N;* dams cominalmen fos *DFaIKTc*. 5. vos *lacking A;* laissetz *Fa;* (lieis) luy *R*. 6. (senes) ses *C;* tot enian *CEFaGNQRUc;* (fi) e fi *C*. 7. ab mi *GQ*. 8. Veus quem eschay car soi fis amador *R;* cor en (uon *IKf*) pues trair (traira *IK*) *CIKf;* (e·l cor) don plor *G*, *lacking Q;* (vos) nos *D;* (en) ne *E*.

II. 9. fai petit desfortz *A*. 10. (E) En *D;* (mal) paud d *R;* eissamen *D*. 11. Hom qi bat cell qui ges non si defen *M;* combat celui *IK;* (combat) abat *DT;* (no·s) nous *GQ*. 12. (Puois) Et *CEMR;* (es) er *D*[c]*;* (avols) davol *C*, aols *IK*, auos *D*, auol *T*, mala *M;* uenasos *c*, penizos *C*, punizos *R*, sospeissos *M*. 13. vos *lacking T;* (o faitz de mi) amors o fas *M;* fag *f;* de mi *lacking E*. 14. Concel cel repren *T;* (repren) rete *CN;* (qui) quel *EFaMNRTf*, qil *U*, quis *D;* (e mort auci) el mort auci *CEFaMNR*, o mort auci *U*, e puois lauci *AT*, e poisa lauci *D*. 15. Auer lo uoletz laip *D;* (del) de *DD*[c]*GQRUcf;* sufridor *E*. 16. Qua dan dels sieus uol seruire alhor *C;* Qui seu *D*, Qal seu *GQ*, Qe seus *c*, Quel sieus *IKMR*, Cals sieus *f*, Qels seus *EFa*, Qassi *U*, Qels (sieus *lacking*) *D*[c]*;* desert *N*.

III. 17. (m'es) me *C;* (pros) ma *R;* (tant) car *CEMR*, cant *T*. 18. (Et amei vos) Et amauaus *EFaIKMcf*, Et amaua *C*, Eus amaua *R;* amai *GQ;* (qu'ie·us) qe uos *Tc*. 19. ui uos *GQf*. 20. Et a totz jors *CEMR;* (creis l'amors) am uos mais *f*. 21. Gen (Sen *E*) mi sobret (semblet *EM*) quan la uistan (uistam *M*) parti *CEM;* sembret *Dc;* com la uistam per si *R*, a la uistam parti *T*. 22. Li *M;* quen *I*. 23. (Mas) Quar *CEMR;* (donat) dat *T*. 24. Sab (Sam *C*) uos amors e merces (merces et amors *CR*) *CEFaIKMR*.

IV. 25. (Que) Quar *CEFaGIKMQRf*, Qa *Uc*, Quieu *N;* ges *lacking E*, si *M*. 26. vai *lacking T;* (sos) los *R*, son *EMN;* cairel *EMN;* perd traien *U*. 27. E pert lun per lautre tot amsi pren *T;* (E) Que *CEFaGIKMNRUcf;* pren *lacking Q*. 28. (E) En *M;* (meron) meromen *T*, mer en *N;* mals *U;* uostra bella faissos *N*. 29. Vostras *FaT;* beltaz *Gcf;* blasm mais *Fa;* (car) que *CEFaMRT;* car anc la ui *f*. 30. (Apres) E pueys *CEMR;* blasm mais *Fa;* (car) que *CEMRT;* menanti *CM*, menati *E*. 31. (E) Car *R;* (s'ieu) sai *Q;* i *lacking DITU;* (ni) e *NU;* folors *T*. 32. No blasma mi mauos essi amor *T;* (vos) ues *D;* (eissa) dona *f;* et *lacking U*.

V. *lacking Fa*. 33. (cum m'ant) coman *CN*, c. ma *Q;* li uostr hueilh enueios *M;* uostr b. h. *U*, uostres bels hueils *ER*. 34. qe feron *U;* (doussamen) simplamen *GQf*. 35. (Q'ieu) Qen G, Ieu *EM*, Qiem *R*, Qe *c;* (c'o fesson) queu f. *C*, qe f. *QUc*, cos f. *T*, que fossa *EM*, queissi fon *N;* leyalmen *CEMR*. 36. (era) eras *T*, em *Q*, *lacking C;* (geins) guerr *CEMR*, engian *T*, engein *Q;* (e) o *Q*, *lacking U*. 37. *lacking G;* quan mi uitz ez ieus ui *CIKNQRf*, qan me uis et eu uos ui *c*, qan uos me uis eus (et eus *M*) ui *EM* (me *in margin in M, to be inserted as indicated*), ce me ueins e uos ui *T*, quan me uist eu uos ui *U*, que me uiz et eus uos ui *D*. 38. *lacking G;* Mas a totz jorns dona creys enaissi *CEMR;* pois ses *DT;* gregutz *N*. 40. E de sospir en planh de planh en plor *EGMQ*, E de sospir en planh e de planh (*for* de planh: torn en *R*, creis en *f*) plor *CRf*.

VI. *lacking ADFaGIKNQUcf;* VII *in T*. 41. me salue dona uos e e uos mi *R;* domna et a uos mi *M;* domn' *lacking T;* e uos sal mi *T*. 43. (so) tal *EMT;* (qu'enanz) cenas *T;* (lauzor) ualor *R*. 44. (a vos) a mi *E;* car soi uostre causidor *T*.

VII. *lacking EFaMRf;* VI *in T*. 45. Anc puois del cor la d. non issi *IK*, Anc la dolor del cor puois no meisi *T;* la *lacking Q*. 46. D'is cois basei *D*, Deis cous basei *T*, Des quos b. *N;* dolzi *Uc*, dolzet si *G*. 47. *lacking U;* (Neis ma) Qeis la *G*, Per meus la *Q;* (ditz que n'ac tal) dins nac tan gran *C*, dis (dinç *c*) tan nac gran *GIKNQc*. 48. (mais tant) de tan *CGIKNQUc;* dolz *U;* sabors *T*.

VIII. *lacking DEFaGMNQRTUc*. 50. chanso *Cf;* (ten) tei *C*, tien *I*, tiei *K*.

TRANSLATION

I. Love, I make my complaint about you to you, for you have entered me alone; and you did not enter into my Lady also, so that the torment of both should be mutual. But you leave her and keep me, for you find me loyal, without deceit; and you give her joy and me sorrow. I can bring my eyes and my heart as witnesses to that.

II. He who fights against a man who does not defend himself makes few efforts and (shows) great pride and ill breeding,—that you know. It is a sin and an evil vengeance. But you act in regard to me exactly like the man who recaptures the captive and slays the dead. What you wish is to have the character of the good servant who disserves his own people, because he wishes so much to serve others.

III. Yet everything is right with me, worthy Lady, for I love you; and I loved you before I saw you, loyally; and when I saw you, I loved you a hundred fold, and my love grows twofold every day. Your love at first sight severed and parted me from another lady who betrayed me. But you have taken from me ill and given me worse, if with you Mercy and Love do not help me.

IV. Through you I lose her and I have not you, like the man who goes shooting away his bolts and loses one for the other. So it is with me. Your fair face deserves blame. Blame your beauty, then, which pleased me so; and then blame Love, who emboldened me so. Thus, if I am doing a stupid or mad thing, do not blame me, but yourself and Love.

V. Ah! how your fair eyes and you have slain me with a look which they gave me so sweetly! I believed that they did it loyally; but it was naught but deceit and treason. Slight was that look when you first saw me and I you, Lady; but ever since it has been growing thus from slight to great and from great to greater, (and I turn) from sighing to pining and from pining to weeping.

VI. May God keep you for me, Lady, and me for you, for that is needful for me and for you too: for me, because I exalt your praise; and for you, because I am your man and I adore you.

VII. Since first I kissed her hands, the sweetness of them has never left my heart, so greatly that sweetened me. My mouth even says that it felt such sweetness from it that never has it tasted so sweet a savor.

VIII. Toward Toulouse, to the Count Palatine, Duke and Marquis, go thy way, Song, for he is so worthy that an emperor would be content if he had his worth.

NOTES

Seventeen MSS: *ACDD^cEFaGIKMNQRTUcf*. Of these, *D^c* contains only the second stanza, *Fa* only the first four stanzas. The first and fifth stanzas are quoted in the *Breviari d'amor*, 29162 and 28925 respectively (Variants: 1. *A vos amors*. 2. *Car es en me*. 3. *non intretz en midons*. 6. *trobatz mi ses tot engan e fi*. 8. *cor ne pues trair az autor*. 35. *que fosso*. 37. *quan me vis et ieus vi*. 38. *Mas a tot jorns dona creis enaissi*. 40. *E de sospir*). Berenguier de Noya quotes lines 9–14 in his *Mirall de trobar* (ed. Anglade, in *Homenaje . . . Menéndez Pidal*, I, 678. Variants: 9. (*fai*) *say*. 12. *Que es; venjance es*. 13. *o* lacking; *tots altres*. 14. *Si cum cell qui el pres rete ol mort l'auci*).

The group *CEMR* is clearly established (lines 12, 17, 20, 21, 23, 30, 35, 36, 38). *T* joins this group in preserving the first envoi, and in several variants (14, 29, 30). *CEMR* may be divided into *CR* (12) and *EM* (35). Other smaller groups are: *ADT* (?, 14), *GQf* (19, 34; *GQ* alone: 16, 18); *Uc* (25) is likely, but less clear than usual; *IK* we take for granted. The position of *N* is doubtful, as is that of *Fa* and *D^c*. And it seems impossible to construct any satisfactory stemma.

Base: *A;* the lines in italics, from *C*.

1–8. Cf. Bernart de Ventadorn (ed. Appel, 28, 9):

> A totz me clam, senhor,
> De midons e d'Amor,
> C'aicist dui traïdor,
> Car me fiav' en lor,
> Me fan viur' a dolor.

9. Here *A*'s reading is isolated and can hardly be maintained against the agreement of all the other MSS.

9–16. Another evident reminiscence of Bernart de Ventadorn (ed. Appel, 10, 9):

> Amors, e cals onors vos es
> Ni cals pros vo·n pot eschazer,
> S'aucizetz celui c'avetz pres,
> Qu'enves vos no s'auza mover?

14. The isolated reading of *AD* is less forceful than that of the other MSS, and is almost certainly wrong.

19–22. Cf. Folquet de Marseille (ed. Stronski, II, 41):

> Trop vos am mais, dona, qu'ieu no sai dire,
> E quar anc jorn aic d'autr' amor desire
> No m'en penet, ans vos am per un cen,
> Car ai proat l'autrui captenemen.

It is evident that Folquet likewise had forsaken another lady for the present object of his vows and verses.

20. For the phrase *per un dos*, cf. Aimeric's poem 21, line 23, and Folquet de Marseille (ed. Stronski), XVIII, 66.

33–34. A frequent conceit with the troubadours. Cf. Bernart de Ventadorn (Appel, 1, 50):

> E·lh vostre belh olh m'an conquis,
> E·l doutz esgartz e lo clars viz.

46. *doussezir*. The only two examples of the word in Raynouard (III, 66) are from Aimeric: his one and 20, line 7; not in Levy, *SW*.

7a

(Aimeric de Peguilhan)

I. Anc al temps d'Artus ni d'ara
No crei qe hom vis
Tan bel colp cum en las cris
Pris Sordels d'un' engrestara;
E se·l colps non fo de mort,
Sel qe·l penchenet n'ac tort;
Mas el a·l cor tan umil e tan franc
Q'el prend en patz toz colps pois no i a sanc.

(Sordello)

II. Anc persona tan avara
No crei qe hom vis
Cum a·l veils arlots meschis,
N'Aimerics ab trista cara.
Sel qe·l ve a pez de mort;
E se tot a son cors tort
E magr' e sec e vel e c op e ranc,
Mil aitans dis . . . q'el no fes.anc.

READINGS EMENDED

I. 2. No crei qe nuls hom vis. 3. crins. 5. colp non di fo. 6. pezenet. 8. (a) e.
II. 10. *like* 2, *above*. 11. veil arloc meschins. 12. naimeric. 15. cloc. 16. aitan.

TRANSLATION

I. (Aimeric de Peguilhan). I do not believe that a man ever saw, in Arthur's time or nowadays, so lovely a hit as Sordello took on his hair from a narrow-necked flask. If the blow was not mortal, that was the fault of the man who combed him; but he has a heart so humble and so noble that he takes in peace all blows when there is no blood drawn.

II. (Sordello). I do not believe that a man ever saw a character so greedy as that old, contemptible beggar, Sir Aimeric with doleful face, has. He who sees him is worse than dead; and although his body is twisted and dried up and old and lame and halt, a thousand times he said . . . than he ever did (?).

NOTES

One MS: *P.*

Critical edition by De Lollis, *Vita e poesie di Sordello di Goito,* p. 149. Printed also in De Bartholomaeis, *Poesie prov. storiche,* II, 78. We have in general followed De Lollis in his few emendations.

This exchange of *coblas* has the same metrical structure and, except for *a*, the same rimes, as number 9, between Aimeric and Guilhem Figueira. Probably, as De Lollis suggests (*op. cit.*, pp. 5–6), all these coblas refer to the same incident, as does likewise another *cobla* by a certain Paves (Pillet-Carstens, 320, 1). The latter has been edited by Bertoni, *I trovatori d'Italia,* p. 301. This *cobla* indicates that the scene of this "flyting" was Florence, which is also confirmed by the form *Jacopis* (Giacopino) in 9. Paves's *cobla* is as follows:

> Anc de Roland ni del pro N'Auliver
> Non fo auzitz us colps tan engoissos
> Cum scels qe fez Capitanis l'autrier
> A Florença, a·N Guillem l'enojos;
> E no fos ges d'espada ni de lanza,
> Anz fo d'un pan dur e sec sus en l'oill,
> Q'estop' e sal et ou, aital mesclanza
> L'i mes hom destenprada ab orgoill.

Unless we assume that the *Guillem* of this *cobla* is Guilhem Figueira, there is no proof that it is directly connected with our 7a or 9.

2. We have followed De Lollis in emending this line (and line 10) to correspond with the similar one in 9.

4. *engrestara.* On this word, a *hapax* in Old Provençal, see Levy, *SW,* III, 1, and Chabaneau in *Revue des langues romanes,* XXVII, 263, note 2.

8. *a.* The MS has *e*, emended by De Lollis, followed by De Bartholomaeis, to *ve*. An easier emendation seems to us to be *a*.

11. It is not easy to understand the construction of this sentence. Is *a* in this line the equivalent of *habet* or of *ad*? If the former, as we assume, then *persona,* v. 9, must have the meaning "nature, character."

16. This line is hypometrical by two syllables. The meaning is so doubtful that no emendation is possible.

8

Anc mais de joy ni de chan,
Ni de solatz mantener,
Non agui, al mieu parer,
Tan bo ni tan ferm talan;
Ni anc mais no mi plac tan
Cum era·m platz d'Amor sa mantenensa,
Per qu'ieu la vuelh mantener et honrar
E contra selhs defendr' e razonar
Qui·n fan clamor alques per non-sabensa.

II. E selh que si van claman
D'Amor an pauc de saber;
Quar, segon razon e ver,
Hieu venserai razonan
Selhs qui s'en van rancuran,
Qu'Amors no fai mal ni desconoissensa,
Per que nulhs hom s'en deia rancurar;
Ni ges Amors no pot apoderar
Neguna re, ses grat d'altra valensa.

III. Ni fin' Amors—so vos man—
Non a, ni non pot aver,
Ab se forsa ni poder
Ni nulh cosselh pauc ni gran,
Si l'huelh e·l cor no li dan;
Mas so qu'als huelhs platz ez al cor agensa
Vol fin' Amors que no·i pot contrastar.
Per so non deu Amor ochaizonar
Tan quan los huelhs e·l cor, a ma parvensa.

IV. Quar li huelh son drogoman
Del cor, e l'huelh van vezer
So qu'al cor platz retener;
E quan ben son acordan
E ferm tuit trei d'un semblan,
Adoncas pren veray' Amors nasquensa
D'aisso que l'huelh fan al cor agradar,
Qu'estiers no pot naysser ni comensar;
Mas per lo grat dels tres nays e comensa.

V. Per lo grat e pel coman
Dels tres, e per lor plazer,
Nays Amors, qu'en bon esper
Vai sos amics cofortan;
Per que tuit li fin aman
Sapchan qu'Amors es fina bevolensa
Que nays del cor e dels huelhs, sens duptar,
Que l'uelh la fan florir e l cor granar—
Amors qu'es frugz de la vera semensa.

VI. Per qu'ieu acli merceyan
Mos huels e·l cor ses tener
Ves Amor, qu'ab ferm voler
Se van trastuit percassan
De mas honors trair enan
E de mos bes ses gienh e ses temensa;
Per qu'ieu los dei grazir e merceyar,
Quar ilh man fait de tal enamorar
Don sui paguatz ses plus ab l'entendensa.

VII. Chansos, vai dir a·N Blacatz em Proensa
Qu'el fai valor valer e pretz prezar,
Qu'om lui lauzan no pot sobrelauzar,
Tant es valens e fina sa valensa.

VARIANTS

I. 1. Anc mais ne de ioy D^a; iois *GQ*. 2. Ni de solatz *lacking* R^2; mantenir *U*. 3. aigui *E*, agiu *P*; (parer) poder *N*. 4. (bo) ben *U*; (ni) in *Q*. 5. (no mi) nom *EQ*, no me D^a, no men *L*. 6. (era·m) era *IKU*, eran *DP*; (d'Amor sa) damorosa *ER*; (sa) si I^2; manteneza *GP*. 7. (qu'ieu) que R^2; (la) lo *G*. 8. Encontra DI^2K^2LPU; defendre a r. *Q*, defendra e r. *D*. 9. (Qui·n) Qui *CEP*, Quen D^aIKNR^2, Que *RU*; clamors *N*, claman *P*; alquels *N*; non chalensa R^2.

II. 10. (E selh que) E qals qals *D*, E qals qe $D^aGII^2KK^2LNPR^2c$, E qual ques *EQR*, E qui que *U*; selhs *C*; sen an $DD^aII^2KK^2LNP$, sen nam *U*, nan *ER*. 11. (an) a $D^aEGIKQRR^2Uc$; pauch *P*. 12. (e ver) e uezer DI^2K^2, auer *N*. 13. (Hieu) Ieu en I^2K^2L, E un *U*, Eu len *c*. 14. *lacking D*; Cel *U*; uaun *E*; ranguran *N*. 15. (no) nom R^2. 16. (s'en) en *c*; (deia) denha R^2, degua *c*; (rancurar) blasmar *N*. 17. (no) nom CR^2, non *IK*. 18. Deguna R^2; (re) res PRR^2, rem *U*; gratz *L*.

III. 19. (Ni) A *IK*; fins *IK*; (so vos) sous *ERU*, cho uos *LP*. 20. (a) ai *Qc*; (ni non pot) ni pot $DEII^2KK^2RR^2$. 21. (forsa) forz ha *P*; (ni) in *G*. 22. nuillz DGI^2K^2LQ; conseillz I^2K^2, conseui *L*. 23. Sils oils *N*; oilz *GQ*; cors $DD^aEI^2K^2c$; nol li RR^2, no lo i L. 24. so *lacking* $DI^2K^2LR^2U$; (qu'als huelhs) qa soill *U*; (ez al) nil *E*. 25. Poil *N*; fins *IK*; (no·i) non *U*, nol *N*, noil c. 26.

Doncx non deu hom amors o. *R*^{2}; (so) qom *D*^{a}*IKUc*, con *N*, cho *L;* (non) nos *L;* dei *P;* occhailonar *N*. 27. (quan) com *ELPR*^{2}, con *N;* e cor e ma *c*.

IV. 28. li oillz *GNQ*, los oilh *U;* drugaman *G*, drugoman *Q*, drucoman *N*. 29. els oils *N*, eli oill *Lc*, elis oilh *U*, eill oillz *P;* (van) uarai *E*. 30. (So) Ezo *U;* (qu'al cor) calor *R*^{2}; (cor) corp *P*, *lacking U*. 31. son ben *C;* concordan *G*. 32. totç *LN;* treis *NU;* (semblan) talan *IK*. 33. Ladoncas *N*, Adonc *c;* (veray') uer *EQR*, uerais *IKU*, ueira *L*, leials *N;* (nasquensa) ualensa *CEGQR*. 34. (D'aisso) Daquo *D*^{a}*GQ*, Da que *IK*, Da so *P*, Dacho *L*, Da po *N;* que oill *D*^{a}*IK*, qe li oill *LP*, qals oils *N*, qas oilhs *U;* a cor *GQ;* a gardar *IKNR*^{2}. 35. (no) noy *R*^{2}; naise *c;* (ni) e *U*. 36. lo *lacking D;* los grat *GQ*, los gratz *L*, la grat *R*^{2}; tres *lacking U*.

V. 37. la grat *R*^{2}, lo gratz *L;* (e) a *E;* pels *c*. 38. Del treis a per l. p. *N;* (lor) lo *R*^{2}, *lacking D*. 39. (Nays) Si ais *N;* (qu'en) qem *U*, qe *c*. 40. (sos) lur *L;* conortan *L*. 42. (es) en *U*. 43. Qen nais *I*^{2}*K*^{2}*U;* dels oils e del cor *NR*^{2}*U;* duptan *U*, doptare *c*, duptanza *Q*. 44. Quels oils *NR*^{2}*U;* (e·l) et *c;* cors *D;* grauar *G*, egranar *E*. 45. (qu'es) qe *L;* (de la) de lor *DGI*^{2}*K*^{2}*LNPQUc*, del cor *D*^{a}*IK;* (semensa) nasquenza *IK*.

VI. 46. (qu'ieu) qieus *R;* (acli) adui *P*. 47. Mes *P*, Los *U;* (e·l) et *c;* cors *Dc;* (ses) se *R*^{2}; (tener) temer *D*^{a}*GII*^{2}*KK*^{2}*LNR*^{2}*c*, temor *U*. 48. Ves Amor *lacking DI*^{2}*K*^{2}; (Ves) Et *D*^{a}*GIKNPQc*, Ad *LR*^{2}*U;* (qu'ab) qua *U*, ab *R*^{2}. 49. Sen *DNPU;* (van) uai *U*, uasi *N;* trestutz *L*, trastoz *N*, tuit iorn *U;* perchanchan *I*, perchan *N*, percazhian *P*. 50. ma honor *DI*^{2}*K*^{2}*PR*^{2}, mais honor *N*. 51. E de bes zeingh e sens temensa *N;* ses neguna faillenza *G;* (gienh) ghabs *U*. 52. Per qeu li uoill grazir *U;* (los) lo *N*, lous *R;* deu *D*^{a}*IKN*. 53. (Quar ilh) Camit *N*, Qe *U;* ma *R*^{2}*U;* (tal) tant *c*. 54. (Don) Dom *D;* (ab) en *E*, al *P;* atendensa *CER*.

VII. *lacking D*^{a}. 55. Chanson *CELNQRR*^{2}*Uc;* (a·N) en *DGII*^{2}*KK*^{2}*LPU*, em *Qc;* blancatz *DK*^{2}*PQU*, blançaz *N;* prodença *N*. 56. (Qu'el) Qe *c;* ualer ualor *IKU;* (e) el *U;* (prezar) preiar *II*^{2}*KK*^{2}*Q*, preçare *c*. 57. (Qu'om) Con *U*, Cũ *I*^{2}*K*^{2}; (lui) lus *N;* (lauzan) lauian *I*^{2}*K*^{2}, lauan *R*^{2}, lauçam *Q;* sobrel lauszar *L*, saber lauzar *D*. 58. (sa) sua *U*.

TRANSLATION

I. Never had I such a good, firm will to uphold mirth and song and good fellowship according to my power, nor did it ever please me as much as now the upholding of Love pleases me. Therefore I wish to uphold and honor him and defend and justify him against those who complain of him, somewhat through ignorance.

II. Those who go about complaining of Love have little wit; wherefore, according to reason and truth, I shall overcome by my argument those who go about reproaching him, for Love does no ill or folly for which one should complain of him; nor can Love ever gain mastery over anything without the help of some other power.

III. I tell you this: loyal Love has not, nor can have by himself, force or power or any authority little or great, unless the eyes and the heart give it to him; but what pleases the eyes and delights the heart, loyal Love wills that no one can withstand it. Therefore, no one should accuse Love, but the eyes and the heart, in my opinion.

IV. The eyes are the interpreters of the heart, and the eyes see what it pleases the heart to keep. When they are in accord and firmly of one mind, then true Love is born from what the eyes make pleasing to the heart. Otherwise it cannot be born or begun; but by the will of all three it is born and begins.

V. By the will and by the command of the three and by their pleasure, Love is born, who goes comforting his faithful friends with good hope. Therefore, let all faithful lovers know that

Love is a loyal affection which springs from the heart and eyes, without fear, for the eyes make it flower and the heart makes it bear fruit,—Love which is the fruit of the true sowing.

VI. Therefore I bow down thankfully without cease my eyes and my heart toward Love, for all of them seek to promote my honors and my welfare without guile or fear. Therefore I ought to give them thanks and gratitude, for they have made me love a lady of such worth that I am content with the expectation alone.

VII. Song, go and tell Sir Blacatz in Provence that he gives worth to worthiness and repute to reputation, for one cannot, praising him, overpraise him,—his worth is so worthy and true.

NOTES

Seventeen MSS: $CDD^aEGII^2KK^2LNPQRR^2Uc$. The reference to *N* is not given by Pillet-Carstens. The poem (anonymous) appears there (f. 106) after the poems of Peire Milon. The second, third and fourth stanzas are quoted in the *Breviari d'amor*, lines 29435, 29377, and 29394 respectively (Variants: 23. *Selh cors e l'uuelhs*. 26. (*non*) *nos; encaizonar*. 29. (*van*) *fan*. 33. (*nasquensa*) *valensa*. 34. *De so*. 35. *Estiers*).

The song is ascribed to Aimeric in $CD^aEGIKQRUc$ and in the *Breviari d'amor*, to Guillem Figueira in $CRegDI^2K^2R^2$, to Giraut de Borneil in *P;* it is anonymous in *LN*. That this song is Aimeric's and not Guillem Figueira's can hardly be disputed. Figueira's only *chanso* (no. 5) contains nothing similar, while the same thought and even the phraseology may be found in other poems of Aimeric. Levy, in his edition of Guillem, does not claim the song for his poet. Critical edition by Levy, *op. cit.*, pp. 58–63.

Levy establishes a complicated stemma for this song. We feel that he brushes certain difficulties aside too lightly. How, for example, can one explain the agreement of *GQ* with *CER* in the striking mistake *ualensa* for *nasquensa* (l. 33), if they belong to totally different families? And the agreement of *P* with *GQ* is much less uniform than his stemma would lead one to suppose (cf. 8, 50). We feel that no satisfactory stemma can be constructed: the relationships are too complicated, the contaminations too numerous. Nevertheless, some of Levy's groups are well established: D^aIK (45), DI^2K^2 (12), *CER* (54). It seems likely, furthermore, that R^2 and *U* (as well as *L*, which was inaccessible to Levy) are closely related to DI^2K^2 (24). Line 48 would point to a group $D^aGIKNPQc$, but this is not too well confirmed elsewhere.

Base: *C*.

This song is one of the best known expositions of the medieval theory of the origin of "courtly" love, and as such has been frequently quoted (see Jeanroy, *Poésie lyrique*, II, 119–120, and Wechssler, *Kulturproblem des Minnesangs*, I, 379–380). That the eyes awaken love in the heart by the sight of beauty is a conceit which goes far back, through the scholastic philosophers to Aristotle and Democritus.

6. For the pleonastic use of the possessive *sa*, see Meyer-Lübke, *Rom. Gram.*, III, 89–90; the same usage is found in 46, lines 41–42.

10. Levy: *quals que s'en an*.

11. Levy: *a pauc*.

23. *no li dan*. When both objects are of the third person, the direct object pronoun is often omitted in Old Provençal, as in Old French. See Meyer-Lübke, *op. cit.*, III, 402, and Schultz-Gora, *Altprovenzalisches Elementarbuch*, p. 124.

28–30. For this conceit, cf. the quotations from the troubadours and Minnesinger (and also Dante) given by Wechssler, *op. cit.*, pp. 282–283.

31. *C*'s reading is here isolated.

32. *trei.* The two eyes and the heart.

33. The reading *ualensa* (*CGEQR*) seems clearly erroneous.

45. Levy: *lor.*

47. *ses tener,* though clearly the preferable reading, seems to be found only in this one passage, quoted by Levy, *SW*, VIII, 151.

54. Levy: *atendensa.* We prefer *entendensa,* which has much better MS support.

9

(Guilhem Figueira)

I. Anc tan bel colp de joncada
No cuit qe hom vis
Com det l'autrer Jacopis
A·N Guillelm Testa-pelada;
Qe, qi qe n'aia desport,
El aia ira e desconort,
E, setot ac de joncada·l cap blanc,
Mantas vez l'a agut negre de sanc.

(Aimeric de Peguilhan)

II. Anc tan bella espazada
No cuit qe hom vis
Com det N'Auzers sus el vis
A·n Guillelm Gauta-segnada,
Q'el vis lo feri tant fort
C'un petit n'a l'un oill tort,
E·l cill qe sol aver negr' er a blanc
E·l cais plus ros d'escerlatra e de sanc.

READINGS EMENDED

I. 1. iocanda. 5. Qe qi naia desport.

TRANSLATION

I. (Guilhem Figueira). I think that no man ever saw so fine a hit with a cheese as Giacopino gave the other day to Sir William Shaven-head. Whoever takes pleasure in it, he may well feel wrath and sorrow. Although he had his head white with the cheese, many times he has had it black with blood.

II. (Aimeric de Peguilhan). I think that no man ever saw so fine a hit with a sword as Sir

Auzer gave, up in his face, to Sir William Branded-cheek, for he wounded him so sorely in the face that he almost has one eye gouged out by it, and the eye-brow once black is now white and the jaw redder than scarlet and blood.

NOTES

One MS: *H*. Aimeric's *cobla* is quoted by Barbieri, *Poesia rimata*, p. 113; there are no significant variants.

Critical edition by Levy, *Guilhem Figueira*, p. 55. Also printed by De Bartholomaeis, *op. cit.*, II, 76.

Evidently connected with 7a, and may refer to the same event, a row in a Florentine tavern. See the notes to 7a, and the Introduction.

We have followed Levy in his two emendations (lines 1 and 5), but retained the orthography of the MS.

1. *joncada*. For this word, see Levy, *SW*, IV, 263, and also his remarks on this passage in his edition of Guilhem (p. 99). It seems to be another *hapax*.

3–4. Who these men were we have no means of knowing.

11. N'Auzers is likewise unknown.

12. Levy takes this Guillelm Gauta-segnada to be Guilhem Figueira, and quotes (pp. 11–12 of his edition) these lines of Sordello (437, 33; p. 149 in De Lollis's edition of Sordello):

Sitot m'assail de serventes Figera
Ab sa lenga falsa e menssongieira,
Sofrir lom taing, tal paor ai nom feira
Ab l'espada ab qel feri N'Auziers . . .

This certainly seems to refer to the same incident, and we may accept Levy's identification.

10

I. Era par ben que Valors se desfai,
E podetz o conoisser e saber,
Quar selh que plus volia mantener
Solatz, Domney, Larguez', ab cor veray,
Mezur' e Sen, Conoissens' e Paria,
Humilitat, Orguelh ses vilania,
E·ls bos mestiers totz ses menhs e ses mai,
Es mortz! Guillems Malespina marques,
Que fo miralhs e mayestre dels bes.

II. De bos mestiers el mon par non li say,
Qu'anc no fon tan larcs, segon mon parer,
Alexandres de manjar ni d'aver,
Qu'elh non dis "non" qui·l quis ni trobet plai;
Ni ges Galvains d'armas plus non valia,
Ni non saup tan Ivans de cortezia,
Ni·s mes Tristans d'amor en tan d'assay.
Hueymais non er castiatz ni repres
Negus, si falh, pus lo miralhs no·y es.

III. On son eras siei dig plazent e guai
E siei fag plus poderos de poder,
Que·ls autres fagz fazian desvaler?
Oi Dieus! cum son escurzit li clar rai
Qu'alumnavan Toscan' e Lombardia,
Per que quascus anava e venia
Ab lo sieu lum ses dupt' e ses esmai;
Qu'aissi saup Pretz guizar, tan fon cortes,
Cum l'estela guidet los reys totz tres.

IV. Per cui venran soudadier de luenh sai,
Ni·l ric joglar que·l venian vezer
Qu'elh sabia honrar e car tener
Plus que princeps de sai mar ni de lai?
E manhta gen ses art, ses joglaria,
Per lo sieu don, on negus no falhia,
Que manh caval ferran e brun e bay
Donava plus soven, ez autr' arnes,
De nulh baron qu'ieu anc vis ni saubes.

V. Belhs senher cars, valens, ieu que farai?
Ni cum puesc sai vius ses vos remaner,
Que·m saubes tan dir e far mon plazer
Qu'autre plazers contra·l vostre·m desplai?
Que tals per vos m'onrav' e m'aculhia
Que m'er estrans cum si vist no m'avia;
Ni ja nulh temps cambi no·n trobarai,
Ni esmenda del dan qu'ai per vos pres,
Nez ieu non cre qu'om far la m'en pogues.

VI. Lo senher qu'es us en personas tres
Vos valh' aissi cum ops ni cocha·us es.

VARIANTS

I. 1. destai *a*^{1}. 2. (podetz) poder *D*. 3. volra *a*^{1}, nolia *D*. 4. (ab) e *E*. 5. (Mezur' e Sen) Largueze sen e *E*. 7. (E·ls) El *a*^{1}; (totz) tant *ABD;* (e) o *IK;* (mai) maia *D*. 8. (Guillems) lonratz *AB;* malaspina *ABDIK*, malespinal *E*. 9. maistre *E*, maystres *R*.

II. 10. (De) Dels *a*^{1}. 11. fo larcs tant *a*^{1}. 12. alixandris *I*, alassandris *K*. 13. (Qu'elh) Que *IK;* (qui·l) qui *D;* qui quel ne trobes plai *R;* (quis) ques *DEIKa*^{1}; (ni) nil *ABa*^{1}, nei *IK*, non *D*. 14. (Galvains) guillem *C*, -lem *E* (*after a mutilation*), .g. *IKR;* Ni ges darmas galuains *AB;* darmar *E*. 15. (Ivans) diuars *C*, ioans *R*. 16. en tant (tans *R*) assai *ABDIKRa*^{1}. 17. (er) es *a*^{1}; castiez ni remes *D*. 18. miralh *CDER*.

III. 19. (On) En *DIK*. 20. Eil sieu *B;* (de) del *ABDIKa*^{1}. 22. Ai *A;* escurit *DIK*, esclarzit *C*. 23. Qenluminauam *a*^{1}. 25. (Ab) A *ABD;* (lum) nom *CEIKR*. 26. *lacking I;* (guizar) gazaignar *D*, guiar *a*^{1}. 27. la stella *D*.

IV. 28. veran *K*, veirai *I*. 31. princes *ABD*, prince *IK;* (sai) sa *IK*. 32. maintas (mainta *a*^{1}) gens *ABa*^{1}; (ses j.) e ses j. *E*. 33. los seus dos *a*^{1}; (no) nos *a*^{1}. 36. anc *lacking IK;* sabes *a*^{1}.

V. 37. (ieu) e *AB*. 38. sai ses uos uius *ABDEIKRa*^{1}; romaner *IK*. 39. Qem sabiatz tant dir e far p. *AB;* Qen *a*^{1}; sabes *D;* far e dir *E*. 40. uostrom *IK;* m *lacking D*. 41. macuilla *E*, macuilliua *IK*. 42. (Que) Qi *a*^{1}. 43. nom trobaria *IK*. 44. (per) de *ABDIKa*^{1}, en *E*. 45. (Nez) Ni *ABERa*^{1}, Ne *DIK;* (la) lo *R*.

VI. *lacking a*^{1}. 46. ques una person en (persona *AB*) tres *ABDIK;* (personas) persona *CR*. 47. (valh') uoill *D;* ni chozauses *D*.

TRANSLATION

I. Now it is very evident that human worth is dead; and you can well recognize and know that, for he who was most desirous of upholding good breeding, lady-service, generosity, with an upright heart, moderation and good sense, knowledge and friendliness, humility, pride without baseness, and all good deeds without decrease or increase, is dead,—William Malaspina, the Marquis, who was the mirror and possessor of all good qualities.

II. I know not his peer in this world for good actions, for, in my opinion, Alexander was not so liberal in banquets and gifts, since he (Malaspina) never said "no" to anyone who besought him, nor picked a quarrel with him. Gawain was not more valiant in arms, nor Yvain so learned in courtesy, nor did Tristan undergo so many trials in love. Now no one, if he go astray, will be reproved, since the mirror of all is here no longer.

III. Where are now his gay and pleasing words, his acts, mightier than might, which made others' deeds seem of little worth? Ah, God! How are those bright rays dimmed which lighted Tuscany and Lombardy! Everyone came and went under the protection of his light, so courteous was he, for he could guide Honor without doubt or fear, just as the star guided the three kings.

IV. For whom will now come here the troopers from far away and the famed minstrels, who came to see him? He honored and held them dear, more than any prince here or overseas. Many folk (came here) too who had no art or minstrelsy, for his gifts, which he denied to no one. He gave many a steed, gray or brown or bay, and other gear also, more often than any baron whom I ever saw or knew.

V. Fair, dear and worthy Lord, what shall I do now? How can I remain alive here without you? You treated me so well in words and deeds that all other favors I scorn, in comparison with yours. Certain men, on your account, were wont to honor and welcome me, who now will be like strangers who have never seen me. I shall never, at any time, find one to take your place or who will make amends for your loss. I do not believe that anyone can do that for me.

VI. The Lord who is one in three persons, may He help you according to your need and want.

NOTES

Nine MSS: *ABCDEIKRa*[1]. The text of *E* has suffered somewhat from the excision of a miniature. Critical edition by De Bartholomaeis, *Poesie prov. storiche*, I, 238. Stemma:

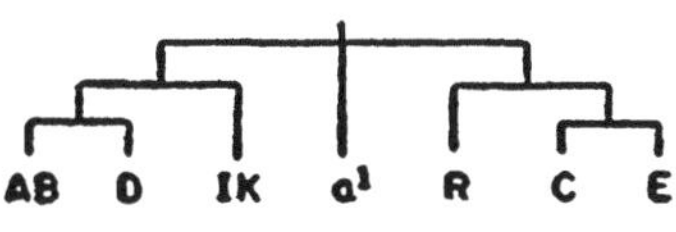

ABDIK: 31, 46
ABD: 7, 25
AB: 8, 37, 46
IK: 7, 13, 31, 36

CER: 20, 44 (-*E*)
CE: 14, 16

The order of poems in *CER* had some weight in the preparation of this stemma; the three must have had a common source:

C:	17	20	23	38	24	45	10	22	11	49	2	26
E:	17	20					10	22	11	49		26
R:	17	20		38			10	22			2	26

The curious similarity of *CEIKR* in 14, 25 does not strain the limits of coincidence excessively, although we might admit some contamination of sources here. In 19, where *DIK* agree against *AB*, the original of the last two simply corrected an obvious mistake. The readings of *C* seem preferable, ordinarily, to those of *AB*, so we have adopted that MS as base. De Bartholomaeis uses *A*, but emends it frequently.

On William Malaspina, for whom this *planh* was written, on his relations with Aimeric, and on the Malaspina family and their relations with the troubadours, see our Introduction and also Jeanroy, *Poésie lyrique des troubadours*, I, 239 ff. William died in 1220, which fixes the date of this poem.

13. The expression *trobar plai* seems not to occur elsewhere, so that the interpretation of the line is doubtful. We have followed De Bartholomaeis, who translates: "egli non disse di no a chi lo richiese, nè creo liti."

14. After some hesitation, we have rejected the *Guillem* of *CE* in favor of the *Galvains* of *ABDa*[1]. It is true that the *.g.* of *IKR* would surely be interpreted as *Guillem;* but if our stemma is correct, the testimony of *a*[1] (from another source, as it apparently is) adds much weight to that of *ABD;* for the coincidence of *CEIKR*, see above. Furthermore, in the following lines Aimeric cites two other heroes of the Arthurian cycle, Yvain and Tristan; and Gawain would seem a more likely companion for them than William (of Orange?). And, since Aimeric is speaking of William Malaspina, would he introduce another William without some further identification?

15. The variants of *CR* can be explained as scribal errors.

25. The reading *lum* of *ABDa*[1] is clearly preferable to the *nom* of the other MSS, considering the context.

37. For the order *ieu que farai*, not uncommon in Provençal and Old French, see Meyer-Lübke, *Rom. Gram.*, III, 808, and especially Tobler, *Vermischte Beiträge*, I, 55–56.

38. *C*'s reading is here isolated, but there seems to be no compelling reason for changing it.

II

I. Ara parra qual seran enveyos
D'aver lo pretz del mon e·l pretz de Dieu,
Que bel poiran guazanhar ambedos
Selh que seran adreitamen romieu
Al sepulcre cobrar. Las! qual dolor
Que Turc aian forsat nostre senhor!
Pensem el cor la dezonor mortal
E de la crotz prendam lo sanh senhal
E passem lai, que·l ferms e·l conoissens
Nos guizara, lo bos pap' Innocens.

II. Doncs, pus quascus n'es preguatz e somos,
Tragua s'enan e senh s'e nom de Dieu,
Qu'en la crotz fo mes entre dos lairos,
Quan ses colpa l'auciron li Juzieu;
Quar, si prezam leialtat ni valor,
Son dezeret tenrem a dezonor;
Mas nos amam e volem so qu'es mal
E soanam so qu'es bon e que val,
Que·l viures sai, qu'es morirs, non es gens,
E·l morirs lai, viures sades, plazens.

III. No deuria esser hom temeros
De suffrir mort el servizi de Dieu,
Qu'elh la suffri el servizi de nos,
Don seran salf essems ab sant Andrieu
Selh que·l segran lai vas Monti-Tabor;
Per que negus non deu aver paor
El viatge d'aquesta mort carnal.
Plus deu temer la mort esperital
On seran plors ez estridors de dens,
Que sanhs Matieus o mostr' e n'es guirens.

IV. A! vengutz es lo temps e la sazos
On deu esser proat qual temon Dieu,
Qu'elh non somo mas los valens e·ls pros,
Quar silh seran totz temps franchamen sieu
Qui seran lai ferm bon combatedor
. . . .

E franc e larc e cortes e leyal;
E remanran li menut e·l venal,
Que dels bos vol Dieus qu'ab bos fagz valens
Se salvon lai; ez es belhs salvamens.

V. E si anc Guillems Malespina fon bos
En est segle, ben o mostra en Dieu,
Qu'ab los prumiers s'es crozatz voluntos
Per socorre·l sant sepulcr' e son fieu;
Don an li rey colp' e l'emperador,
Quar no fan paz ez acort entre lor
Per desliurar lo regisme reyal
E·l lum e·l vas e la crotz atretal,
Qu'an retengut li Turc tan longuamens
Que sol l'auzirs es us grieus pessamens.

VI. Marques de Monferrat, vostr' ansessor
Agron lo pretz de Suri' e l'onor;
E vos, senher, vulhatz l'aver aital.
El nom de Dieu **vos** metetz lo senhal
E passatz lai, que pretz ez honramens
Vos er el mon, et en Dieu salvamens.

VII. Tot so qu'om fai el segl' es dreitz niens,
Si a la fi non l'aonda sos sens.

VARIANTS

I. 1. cals sera *R;* ceraun *E;* (enveyos) voluntos *R.* 3. bels *DER;* (ambedos) ab bels dos *R.* 4. Cill qi *D.* 5. (Las) dieus *R;* (qual) tal *C.* 6. truc *D;* aian *lacking R, space left blank;* forchat *D.* 7. Pensen *D;* (el) al *E,* del *D,* de *R.* 8. prenguam *R;* (sanh) gran *R.* 9. lai . . . conoissens *lacking E.* 10. *lacking E;* guidaro *D;* la papa ignoscens *R;* (bos) bom *C.*

II. *lacking E.* 12. (s'e) sel *R.* 13. Quen cros *R.* 14. (Quan) Qa *D,* Hon *R;* iudei *D.* 15. (Quar) E *R;* presan *D;* (ni) e *R.* 16. tenren *D.* 17. aman *R.* 19. Quel viures chai ques morirs veramens no es gens *D,* Quel vieure sai es a totz defalhenz *R;* (qu'es) que *C.* 20. El moris lai vera vida vivens *D,* Del morir lay serem tos tems iauzens *R;* (sades, plazens) sai desplazens *C.*

III. *lacking E.* 21. Non d. hom esser ia t. *R;* E non *D.* 22. (el) al *R.* 23. soffrit *D.* 24. serem *R;* sals *CR.* 25. Selhs *CR,* Cill *D;* (que·l) que *DR;* (vas) a *R;* montatabor *D.* 28. la mort *lacking D,* lamor *R.* 29. Don pot fogir tristor e perdemens *R;* sera *D.* 30. Que s. M. en mostra en es garens *D.*

IV. 31. *lacking E.* 32. *lacking E;* (On) E *R;* cals *R.* 33. Qu'elh non somo *lacking E;* mas quan los v. *E.* 34. (Quar silh) Caquels *R;* (sieu) seus *R.* 35. Que seran lay fi e bo sofridor *R;*

segran *E*. 36. *lacking CDE*, Ni afortit ni bon combatedor *R*. 38. E remanguan li vencut el logual *R*. 39. (qu'ab bos) cabos *D*, los be *R*. 40. (Se) Ques *R;* saluom *E*.

V. 41. Si francx g. m. es bos *R;* E *lacking D;* guillem *CE*. 43. Cap *R*. 44. (son fieu) car seu *R*. 45. (rey) ren *D*. 47. (reyal) leial *E*. 48. (lum) loc *R*. 49. Que an tengut *R;* retenguz *D*. 50. us *lacking D;* (grieus) grans *R;* (pessamens) espauenz *D*, marrimens *R*.

VI. 51. *lacking R*. 52. *lacking R;* Agan lo pretz sobretoz el onor *D;* (de) en *E*. 54. (El) E *DE*. 56. mons *R*.

VII. *lacking R*. 57. (Tot) Tan *D*. 58. l' *lacking E;* auonda *D*.

TRANSLATION

I. Now it will be evident who will desire to have praise from the world and honor from God, for they can win both loyally, those who will soon be pilgrims in order to regain the Sepulcher. Alas! how grievous it is that the Turks have done violence to our Lord! Let us ponder in our hearts that deadly dishonor. And then let us take the holy sign of the cross and pass over-seas, for the good Pope Innocent, the strong and wise, will guide us.

II. Therefore, since each one is bidden and summoned, let him go forward and take the cross in God's name, God who was suspended on the cross between two thieves when the Jews slew Him for no fault. If we prize loyalty and courage, we shall feel dishonored by His disinheritance. But we love and desire what is evil, and despise what is good and worthy. Life here, which is death, is not noble; and death yonder is a happy and pleasing life.

III. No one should be afraid to suffer death in God's service; for He suffered it to serve us; and, for that reason, all will be saved with Saint Andrew, all who will follow him on yonder toward Mount Tabor. Therefore, no one should have any fear of dying in the flesh in this journey. One should rather fear dying in the spirit, where there will be weeping and gnashing of teeth, as Saint Matthew demonstrates and guarantees.

IV. Ah! the time has come and the season when a test must be made (to see) which men fear God, for he summons only the bold and the good, for those will be freely His who will yonder be steadfast and good fighters . . . and noble and courteous and generous and loyal. The mean and vile will remain here, for God wills that only the good be saved yonder, by good and worthy deeds; and it is a noble road to salvation.

V. If ever William Malaspina was held worthy in this world, he shows it now in God's service, for he took the cross among the first, right willingly, in order to save the Holy Sepulcher and His fief. The kings and emperors are much at fault, since they do not make peace and accord among themselves, in order to deliver the royal kingdom, the light, the sepulcher, and the cross also, which the Turks have held so long that even to hear of it is a grievous thought.

VI. Marquis of Montferrat, your ancestors held the glory and honor of Syria; and may you, Lord, wish to have it too. In God's name, put on the holy sign and pass over yonder, for that will give you fame and honor in this world, and salvation in God.

VII. Everything that one does in this world is just nothing, if at one's latter end one's conscience does not help one.

Four MSS: *CDER* (vv. 9–33 are illegible in *E*). Critical edition, Appel, *Chrestomathie*, p. 110; adopted, with some changes, by De Bartholomaeis, *Poesie storiche*, I, 189 ff.

The four MSS seem to be quite independent of one another. *R* alone has tried to replace verse 36 by means of a not very successful filler. In view of the order of poems in *CE* (see the notes to number 10), we should be inclined to think these MSS derived from a single source; but nothing of what is left in *E* gives very strong confirmation of this belief. We have chosen *C* as base.

For the date of this crusading song, see our Introduction, De Bartholomaeis, *loc. cit.*, and Lewent, *Das altprovenzalische Kreuzlied*, p. 28. The year 1213 seems to be the most likely time.

10. The "good Pope" is Innocent III.

19–20. Appel, *Prov. Chrest.*, p. 110, gives up any attempt to reconstruct these two verses. De Bartholomaeis arrives at a text by combining the readings of *C* and *D*. But, with two slight corrections, *C*'s text gives a satisfactory sense. The adjective *sade* (or *sabe*) is rare in Provençal. Raynouard (V, 128) and Levy (*SW*, VII, 394) each cite two examples, none from a troubadour. The word must however have been known to Aimeric. It was evidently not recognized by the scribe of *C*.

30. The allusion is to Matthew, VIII, 12.

32. *deu esser proat*. An impersonal construction similar to *Ara parra* in line 1.

36. Verse evidently lacking in the original of all four MSS. *R* has simply made two verses out of one. De Bartholomaeis follows *R* without remark or comment.

45–46. As shown by De Bartholomaeis, *op. cit.*, p. 189, this allusion fits the suggested date well. The kings are Philip Augustus of France and John of England. The emperors are Otto of Brunswick and Frederick II of Hohenstaufen, rivals for the imperial crown at that time.

48. It is not quite clear what Aimeric means by *lo lum;* but see Lewent, *loc. cit.* For *vas*, meaning "Holy Sepulcher," see Levy, *SW*, VIII, 591. De Bartholomaeis translates literally: "il lume, il vaso e la croce."

51. For the connection of the Montferrat family with the Holy Land, see especially Schultz-Gora, *Die Briefe des Trobadors Raimbaut de Vaqueiras am Markgraf Bonifaz I von Montferrat.*

12

I. Atressi·m pren quom fai al joguador,
Qu'al comensar jogua mayestrilmen
A petits juecs, pueis s'escalfa perden,
Que·l fai montar tan qu'es en la folor;
Aissi·m mis ieu pauc e pauc en la via,
Que cujava amar ab mayestria
Si qu'en pogues partir quan me volgues,
On sui intraz tan qu' issir non puesc ges.

II. Autra vetz fui en la preizon d'Amor,
Don escapei; mas aora·m repren
Ab un cortes engienh tan sotilmen
Que·m fa plazer mo mal e ma dolor;
Q'un latz me fetz metr' al colh ab que·m lia,
Don per mon grat mai no·m desliaria;
E nulhs autr' om que fos liatz non es,
Qui·l deslies, que ben no li plagues.

III. Anc mais nulh temps no trobei liador
Tan ferm lies ab tan pauc liamen,
Que·l liams fo d'un dous bays solamen,
Don non truep sai qui·m desli, ni alhor.
Enliamatz sui tan que, si·m volia
Desliamar, ges far non o poiria;
Qu'Amors, que lai m'enliamet e·m pres,
M'enliama sai plus fort per un tres.

IV. A ley del fer que va ses tirador
Vas l'aziman que·l tira vas si gen,
Amors, que·m sap tirar ses tiramen,
Mas tirat m'a sevals per la melhor;
Quar si d'autra melhuirar me sabia,
Tant am lo mielhs que be·m melhuiraria;
Mas melhuirar no cre que m'en pogues.
Ve·us per que m'a part las melhors conqes.

V. Na Gentils Cors, formatz plus gen que flor,
Aiatz de me qualacom chauzimen,
Quar muer per vos d'envey' e de talen;

E podetz o proar a ma color,
Quan vos remir, que·s trasva e·s cambia;
Per que fora almorn' e cortezia
Q'Humilitatz merceyan vos prezes
D'aquest cochat, sofrachos de totz bes.

VI. Be·m platz Guillems Malespina·l marques,
Quar conquier pretz e Pretz a lui conques.

VII. Na Beatritz d'Est, lo bes qu'en vos es
Fa melhoirar las autras ab lors bes.

VARIANTS

I. 1. co *R;* (al) ad *c.* 2. comezar *G;* iogab *AB*, iuega *M;* maestrament *ABDGIKMNPSUc*, maistrablemen *L*, mot sotilmen *R.* 3. Al *NPSU;* petit ioc *GIKLMNPQRSUcf;* e pois *U;* se chaufa *Q*, secalfa *K.* 4. Qil *U;* (tan) tro *ABEM;* folia *E.* 5. (Aissi·m) Aissi *GIK;* (e) a *DGLPQSUc.* 6. (Que) Quieu *ABEGLQRSU*, Qem *Mc*, Quen *f;* (ab) per *IKLN*, a *MPQSUc.* 7. Si qiem *AB*, Si quem *LPSc*, Que men *Rf*, Don mi *M;* (quan me) corã *f.* 8. (On) Er *ABGMQU*, Ei *L*, Ar *IKNSc*, Or *P*, E *R*, Es *f;* (intraz) uiratz *E;* (ges) ge *I.*

II. 9. Quatra *L;* (fui) sui *P;* las preyzos *R.* 10. escampei *ABU;* (aora·m) auram *E*, aram *D*, eram *c*, era mi *AN*, eras mi *BMf*, era men *IK*, aeran *G*, aoras me *L;* reten *ABD*, repen *K.* 11. Ab un esgart don mos cors sescompren *IKLN;* engieinh cortes *M;* (tan) trop *f;* subtilmenz *D.* 12. (Que·m) Que *IK*, Qen *c.* 13. Qum *U;* las *MRUf*, laiç *c;* (me fetz) ma fach *R;* (fetz metr') mis *c;* (metr') entr *C;* (al) el *CLM;* (colh) cor *ABMR;* (ab) a *U;* quen *IK.* 14. Dom *D;* (per) a *L;* (mai) ia *IKN;* (no·m) nos *R*, non *Uf.* 15. E mais nul hom el mon l. non es *IKN;* En nul *U;* fos si liatz *L;* (que) qen *GMQR*, qim *U.* 16. (Qui·l) Quel *L*, Ques *R;* desligues *L*, desles *D.*

III. 17. nulz temps *GMPQSUc*, nuis temps *D.* 18. Qe tan ferm *PS;* (ab) a *PSc.* 19. Que le liams *M;* (d'un dous bays) cortz dun bras *GIKNPQSUc*, dun bras tan *R*, dun embras *f;* dous *lacking EM.* 20. (Don) E *IKNR*, Donc *U;* (qui·m) qil *RU*, qin *P*, quem *N;* deslie ni aisi ni alhor *R.* 21. (sui) foi *E;* qẽ sim *Q.* 22. podia *GQ.* 23. Car fin amors qel sieu liam ma pres *M*, Lamors quieu lai mellia en ten pres *f*, Quamors quem (quel *DE*) liamen em (ha *E*) pres *CDE;* qem ma enliamet e pres *U;* qil lai *Q*, ques lai *N;* mo (mon *c*) liamet *Sc*, mo liament *P.* 24. Meliama *PSc*, Melliam *Q*, Mem liama *U*, E menliama *f;* (sai plus) ades *U*, chai plus *Q;* (tres) cent *D.*

IV. 25. (del) de *ADRf;* des fers *PS;* (va) ual *D*, uas *Q.* 26. ladiman *DGQ;* laiman *IKMUf;* (tira) tra *G*, tirael *N;* (vas) uai *EN*, uau *GIKMQSUf*, uan *P*, uao *c;* (si gen) seguen *Ec*, siguen *GIKNRUf*, segen *M.* 27. (que·m) quen *IN*, que *R;* timen *DN* (*later corrected to* tiramen *in N*). 28. Ma si tiratz siuals *R;* tira ma *PSc;* (melhor) gensor *E.* 29. (Quar) Que *GIKNPQRSUcf;* (si) sieu *IKN;* (sabia) podia f, saubia *DGQU*, sabria *PSc.* 30. E am tant *PS;* (be·m) ben *BIKPQSUcf.* 31. Mau *U;* meillur *E;* (que) queu *IKNR;* (m'en) me *Q*, mi *PSUc;* poguges *G.* 32. Per qem par la meillur qun es *c;* per la melhor *IKNPRSU;* pert *Q;* la melhors *f.*

V. 33. (Na) A *ABDFaGIKNPRSUcf;* plus gen formatz *FaIKN;* format *C;* onrat genser de flor *R;* (que) de *ABDEIKMNPRSU*, *lacking c;* flors *C.* 34. (Aiatz) Prengaus *N;* (qualacom) alcun *G*, cal que *R*, qal alcun *Q*, qalqun *c*, calocom *IK;* iausimen *G*. 35. (Quar) Quieu *ABDFaGIKNPRSUcf*, Qe *Q*; (per) de *M;* (d'envey') denuenia *G*. 36. E de poder *D;* (o) lo *PSc;* (a) per *R*. 37. Que souenet entrasu (entrasuz *N*) en (e *N*) cambia *IKN;* (Quan) Cam *P;* (que·s) que *DPSUc*, quem *FaR*, quen *f;* (trasva) trebailla *ABD*, muda *MU*, trauail *c*, trasu *PS;* (e·s) e *FaGPQSUc*, em *Rf;* chabia *G*. 38. E fora grant a. e c. *GQf*, E per que fora a. e c. *Fa*, Que fora a. e granz c. *PSc*, E feyratz y a. e. c. *R*, Per que fora grans c. *E*, Per que fora hueimais grantz c. *M;* (fora) for *D;* amorn *D*, almosina *Uc*. 39. Cumilitatz e merces uos p. *AB;* Sumilitatz *IKN;* preges *PS*. 40. (cochat) chaitiu *AM*, forfait *IKN*, coichos *PSUc*, coitat *E*.

VI. *lacking Rf*. 41. (Be·m platz) Dieus sal *IKN*, Ben p. *GPSc;* guillem *C*, guillis *N;* malespina m. *ADGIKMNPQSc*. 42. (Quar) Que *IKN;* (lui) lieys *C*, li *Sc*, el *IKN*.

VII. *lacking ABDf*. 43. Na *lacking P;* (d'Est lo) daquest *EM*, de lo *C*, lo gran *R;* (bes) ben *CEGMQRU*. 44. (Fa) Fai *GQU*, Fan *CN*, Faitz *EM*, E a *c;* m. a las autras lor bes *GQ;* (lors·bes) los bes *PSUc*, a pales *R*.

TRANSLATION

I. What has happened to me is what happens to the gambler, who at the start plays masterfully for small stakes, then grows hot as he loses, so that he increases his stake till he is in a mad state. So I have entered little by little in the road (of love), for I thought that I could love masterfully so that I could get out of it when I wished; but now I am so far in that I cannot get out at all.

II. Once before, I was in Love's power, but I escaped. Now he seizes me again so subtly that he makes me take pleasure in my woe and my pain. He had a noose put around my neck to bind me, from which I would never unbind myself by my own will. Yet there is no man in bonds who would not be gladdened if some one should unbind him.

III. Never before did I find a captor who bound so firmly with so small a noose, for the noose was made of one sweet kiss only; and I shall find no one, here or elsewhere, to unbind me. I am bound so tightly that, even if I wished, I could not free myself; for Love, who once bound and seized me *there*, binds me *here* with a three-fold bond.

IV. Like the iron which, without anyone to draw it, goes toward the magnet which pulls it to itself, Love, who can pull me without a pull, has at least pulled me most by the best (of ladies). For if I knew that I could better myself, I so love the best that I should do so; but I do not think that I can better myself. You see now how Love has overcome me above the (power of the) best (to charm me).

V. Lady Fair Body, more fairly formed than a flower, have some pity on me, for I die of desire and of longing for you. You can test that by my color, which fades and changes when I look at you. Therefore, it would be a charity and a courtesy if Humility should lay hold on you, showing mercy to wretched me, deprived of all good things.

VI. The Marquis William Malaspina pleases me well, for he conquers fame, even as Fame has conquered him.

VII. Lady Beatrice of Este, the good qualities which are in you make better other ladies with their good qualities.

Nineteen MSS: *ABCDEFaGIKLMNPQRSUcf*. Of these, *Fa* contains only lines 33–40, *L* only lines 1–18. Stanzas one and three are quoted in the *Breviari d'amor*, lines 33947 and 28993 respectively (Variants: 3. *petit joc*. 6. *Quieu*. 7. *quem pogues*. 8. *E soi*. 19. (*dous bays solamen*) *embrassamen*. 23. *me lia em ten pres*. 24. *plus fort que per*). De Bartholomaeis (*Poesie storiche*, I, 232) prints lines 1–12 and 41–42, from *A*. Critical edition, Shepard, in *Studies for William A. Read*, Louisiana State University Press (Baton Rouge), 1940, p. 174. The present edition is substantially a reprinting of this; a few minor changes are noted below.

The variant readings are so numerous and so diverse that it is necessary to abandon any hope of establishing a stemma. Some MSS which generally agree in all particulars show in this piece a few curious differences. Such are, for example, *A* and *B* (lines 25, 40), *C* and *E* (lines 4, 8, 28, 38), *G* and *Q* (10, 24). One can, however, distinguish certain groups which generally go together, as, for example, *IKN* (6, 11, 14, 15, 20, 29, 33, 40), *PSUc* (31, 40, 44). The group *GQ*, though less clearly defined (22, 44), evidently exists. But no constant large families can be determined.

Base: *C*.

1–4. This comparison of the lover to the gambler was used by several troubadours before Aimeric, notably by Folquet de Marseille; cf. Stronski's edition, XI, 1–5:

> Sitot me soi a tart aperceubutz,
> Aissi cum cel qu'a tot perdut e jura
> Que mais non joc, a gran bonaventura
> M'o dei tener car me sui conogutz
> Del gran engan qu'Amors vas mi fazia.

9. Aimeric alludes in several other songs to an earlier love from which he had escaped; cf. 7 and 14.

13–24. Allusions to the *latz* of Love are frequent. Here Aimeric probably had in mind the comparisons used by Giraut de Bornelh (Kolsen's edition):

> Qu'eu·m sui d'un latz
> Pel col lassatz
> A vos donatz. (8, 65)

> E si·m tenetz pres el liam. (32, 49)

> Ges leus non ateis lo liams
> En que cudei c'ams nos prezes. (33, 34)

13. *C*'s reading is here isolated and does not give a satisfactory sense.

23. The reading of *C* is metrically incorrect.

25. This comparison of the attractive force of love to that of a magnet is rather common among the troubadours. Cf. Aimeric's poem 24, lines 1–2, and this from Bernart de Ventadorn (ed. Appel, 26, 40):

> E si·m sui de Midons lonhans,
> Vas se·m tira com azimans
> La bela cui Deus defenda.

Likewise, Folquet de Marseille (ed. Stronski, XVII, 16):

> Q'eissamens cum l'azimans
> Tira·l fer e·l fai levar,
> Fazi' el mains cors dreissar.

But the passage which most resembles the present one is found in the single poem of Bernart Tortitz (Appel, *Provenzalische Inedita*, p. 42):

> Aissi quo·l ferr la peira d'aziman
> Tira vas se fin' Amors solamen.

But it is impossible to determine the date of Bernart's life, so it may be that he is imitating Aimeric, rather than the reverse.

33. Reading *Na Gentils Cors*, we must take this expression as the *senhal* by which Aimeric designates his lady; if we read *A* for *Na* (with the majority of the MSS), we could interpret the phrase as meaning little more than "Ah, fair lady."

34. The same line is found in a poem of Pons de Capduoil (ed. Napolski, XII, 30). As the two poets were contemporaries, it is impossible to determine which was imitating the other—if indeed there was an imitation; the line is not too unusual for two poets to invent it independently of each other.

35. *C*'s reading *Quar* is isolated, but there is no compelling reason for changing it.

43. *C*'s *de* is isolated, and does not fit with the same MS's *Fan* (44); we take it therefore to be a slip, and adopt the reading *d'Est* of the majority of the MSS. The *daquest* of *EM* is a curious misunderstanding of *Est* as a demonstrative. But, whatever the reading, the lady in question is certainly Beatrice of Este, whose name is coupled with that of William Malaspina in a number of *tornadas*. See the discussion in the Introduction.

44. The *Fan* of *CN* could be justified (as *Fa·n*), but seems a little strained; we have therefore preferred the reading of the majority of the MSS. Shepard's earlier edition: *Faitz*.

13

I. (Figera)

Bertram d'Aurel, se moria
N'Aimerics anz de Martror,
Digatz a cui laissaria
Son aver e sa ricor
C'a conques en Lombardia
Suffertan freit e langor?
Ço·m dison gl' albergador.
Pero ben fez la Metgia,
E dis del rei gran lauzor,
Sol q'el so tegn' ad honor.

II. (Aimeric de Peguilhan)

Bertram d'Aurel, s'aucizia
N'Auzers Figera·l deptor,
Digatz a cui laissaria
Lo seu fals cor traidor,
Plen d'enjan e de bauzia
E d'enoi e de folor,
D'anta e de desonor?
Ni putans qi menaria?
Ni arlot ni bevedor
Qe farian de seignor?

III. (Bertram d'Aurel)

N'Aimeric, laissar poria
A·n Çoanet lo menor
L'enjan e la tricharia,
Car el viu d'aital labor,
E l'enoi e la folia
A N'Auzer lo fegnedor,
Et a·N Bude·l desonor,
Et a·N Lambert la putia,
E·l beure a·N Conplit-Flor,
E·ls arloz a N'Amador.

IV. (Lambert)

Seigner, scel qi la putia
M'en laissa, s'en fai honor,
Qu'eu m'o teing a manentia
Qi m'en fai prez ni largor,
C'anc a nuill jorn de ma via
No voill far autre labor,
Qe fotres m'ac tal sabor
Qu'eu ne laissei la clerzia
E teng mon vet per prior
E lo con per refreitor.

READINGS EMENDED

8. mezia. 11. Bertram daurel s. . . . 12. d ptor. 16. denoiz. 25. lenoiz. 38. queu ni laissei la clerezi a.

TRANSLATION

I. (Figera) Bertram d'Aurel, if Sir Aimeric should die before All Saints' Day, say: To whom would he leave his possessions and his riches which he gained in Lombardy, by suffering cold and pain? The inn-keepers tell me that. But he composed the Song of the Physician and spoke great praise of the King, provided that he deem *that* an honor.

II. (Aimeric de Peguilhan) Bertram d'Aurel, if Sir Auzer should kill Figera his debtor, say: To whom would he leave his false and treacherous heart, full of deceit and guile, of vexation and folly, of shame and dishonor? Who would lead harlots? What would tramps and topers do for a lord?

III. (Bertram d'Aurel) Sir Aimeric, he could leave deceit and trickery to Sir Johnny the Lesser, for he lives by such a trade, and vexation and folly to Sir Auzer the hypocrite, dishonor to Sir Bude, lechery to Sir Lambert, drinking to Sir Perfect-Flower, and the tramps to Sir Lover.

IV. (Lambert) Sirs, he who leaves lechery to me does himself honor, for I think *that* a kind of riches which brings me fame and abundance, so that never do I wish to do any other work any day of my life. Copulation pleases me so well that I forsook a clerical life for it, and now I regard my penis as prior and the vagina as refectory.

NOTES

One MS: *H.*

Critical edition by Levy, *Guilhem Figueira,* p. 56, also by De Bartholomaeis, *Poesie storiche,* I, 250–252.

De Bartholomaeis puts this "diverbio guillaresco" in the year 1220, soon after Aimeric had composed his *Metgia* in honor of the King-Emperor Frederick II. The interlocutors, according to him, were four jongleurs, assembled at some point on the Via Emilia to await the passing of the Emperor. All that seems to us doubtful. De Lollis (*Vita e poesie di Sordello di Goito,* p. 4) connects these *coblas* with the similar jovial exchanges of insults in 7a and 9. Bertoni (*Rambertino Buvalelli,* p. 67) denies this, with good reason. Nor is it probable that *Lambert* is Rambertino; in this opinion we follow Bertoni. *Figera* may well be Guilhem Figueira, and *Aimeric* is our poet. The date and the other identifications must be considered doubtful. All we know is that these *coblas* were composed after the *Metgia.*

2. For *Martror* with the meaning "All Saints' Day," see Levy, *SW,* V, 133. The word is preserved in modern Provençal.

6. The word *langor,* curiously enough, is not to be found in either the *PD* or the *SW* of Levy. It is cited by Raynouard, *Lex. rom.,* IV, 16–17.

8. The *Metgia* is the well-known poem, no. 26, in praise of Frederick II.

11–12. We have preferred Levy's reconstruction of these lines (*Guilhem Figueira,* p. 56, also pp. 11–12) to that of De Bartholomaeis: *se moria N'Auzers Figeral doptor.*

20. We also accept Levy's interpretation of this verse (*op. cit.,* p. 100).

35. *via* here is for *vida,* for the rime's sake. The form is found in several troubadours. See Levy, *op. cit.,* p. 100, also his *SW,* VIII, 756.

38. Levy reconstructs this verse (with thanks to Tobler): *Qu'eu'n laissei la clerezia;* De Bartholomaeis: *Qu'eun i laissei la clerzia.*

39. The word *vet,* an evident cognate of Old French *vit,* is not to be found in Raynouard's *Lex. rom.,* nor in Levy's *PD* or *SW.* Why?

14

I. Car fui de dura acoindanssa
Vas vos al comenssamen,
Taing qe·n prendatz vengamen
Ab brau respost o ab lanssa.
Q'anz q'ie·us ames, m'ametz vos ses engan,
E tornei vos, bona dompna, en soan
Per tal que m'a trazit ses desfianssa.

II. S'ie·us fui a la comenssansa
Fals, ara·us am finamen.
E sai qe·m diretz soven
Que fraitura d'autra amanssa
Mi fai venir vas vos humilian,
E q'ieu vos vau minten e galian,
Ni ges no·us am en faitz, mas en semblanssa.

III. De gran forfaich gran venganssa,
So ditz Dreitz per iutgamen;
E Merces ditz eissamen:
De gran tort gran perdonansa.
Ambedui son e mains luocs d'un semblan,
Et e mains luocs se van contrarian;
Car Dreitz auci, e Merces a pietanssa.

IV. Doncs si dreich ni vostr' onranssa
Gardatz, ni·l mieu faillimen,
Ja no m'aurez chausimen;
C'alz mals da Dreitz malananssa.
Qe·l faillimens q'ieu fi vas vos tant gran
E l'onramens c'avetz sobre mi tan
Creisson m'amor e mermon m'esperanssa.

V. Puois conoissetz ses doptanssa
Q'ieu failli nesciamen,
No·us sia lo mals en men,
Mas del ben aiatz membranssa.
Si pro no·m faitz, sivals no·m fassatz dan;
E del benfaich sia en vostre talan,
Q'ie·us atendrai senes desesperanssa.

VI. Reis d'Aragon, qui·l vostre gai semblan 36
Vei, ben pot dir: De bon pair bon enfan.
Car bon pretz cuoill cel qui semena honranssa.

VARIANTS

I. 1. Can f. *T*, Sar f. *R*, Sieu f. *U*, Tant sui *c;* dura cordansa *P*. 2. al comencamen *T*, alla comensansa *R* (la *expunctuated*). 3. Tan *QU*, Tant *c;* (qe·n) com *Q*, *lacking P;* prenda *E;* ueçamen *Q*, ueiança *N*. 4. (Ab) A *GQUc;* (brau) mal *ADEIKNP;* (o ab) o a *Q*, et ab *Uc*, o *G*, cab *IK* (c *changed to* o *in later hand in K*); longansa *Uc*. 5. Anz *Uc;* qeu a. *Uc;* m'ametz *lacking N*. 6. Et ieu torneus *CJRT*, Et ieus tornei *M*, Et eu torn uos *GQ*, Et eu misius *Uc*, E torner uas *P;* (bona) bela *Q;* domna nen soan *T;* (soan) loan *G*. 7. tal *lacking G;* qa ma trais *Q*, ce trai ma *T;* deifiaça *N*.

II. 8. Sieu *EMNUc*, Sieu uos *T*, Si cus *P*, Dieus *C;* (fui) sui *D;* al comensamen *A*. 9. (ara·us) ara uos *MT*, arans *P*, aruos *Uc*. 10. (qe·m) que *CRUc;* dizetz *R*, dretç *T*. 11. francura *QT*, franchura *P*. 12. uas uos uenir *R*, uar uos u. *Uc;* (venir) tornar *NT*, *lacking C;* vos *lacking D;* humilmen *E*, humeliar *N*. 13. *added in margin, in later hand, in N;* Quar ancse uau *CT*, Et ancseus uauc *R*, E qancsios uai *GMQ;* mentenc *IK*. 14. (Ni) Non *GQR*, E *CJMTUc;* (ges) qieu *M;* en fach nous (no uos *T*) am *CT;* (no·us am) non uas *U*, no uan *c*, lacking *GQR;* (en semblanssa) per. s. *C*, en bela s. *R*, enulla s. *Q*.

III. 15. uenians *T*. 16. (ditz) de *P*, di *J;* (per) de *D*[c]*GQ*, iuzamenz *D*, uizamen *D*[c]. 17. merce *CRT;* di *JP*. 18. granz t. *GQ;* granz p. *G*. 19. (Ambedui) Car amdui *D*[c]*GQ*, Que amdui *CRT*, Qes andui *M*, Amdui *DEJP*, Qambdui *Uc;* son *lacking Q;* manh luec *CDEJMNPRTUc*, maiç loc *Q;* d'un semblan *lacking D*. 20. Et . . . luocs *lacking D;* Et *lacking T;* (e) a *N;* manh luec *CDEJNPUc*, maint locs *GQT;* uan se *JP;* contraria *J*, contralian *c*. 21. Que *CMT*, Qa *U*.

IV. 22. (si dreich ni) sendreg la *R;* (ni) en *AD* e *E*. 23. (nil) nil nil *D*, nul *P*, lo *R*. 24. non a. *CGIKMRTUc*, nam a. *D;* aurei *c*. 25. Qual mal *CIKMNRT*, Qel mal *Uc;* (da Dreitz) daretz *CD*[c]*RT*, dona d. *EJP*, dartz *N;* da *lacking Uc*. 26. falhimen *CDEGIJKNPQRUc;* (q'ieu) quie *P*, qeus *c*. 27. onramen *CEIJKNPRTUc;* sobra *EJ*. 28. mamors *T;* merma *C*, mormon *D*, mern *T;* masperanssa *DGQU*.

V. 29. (Puois) Vos *R;* (doptanssa) conoisses *D*. 30. Qe f. *c;* failh *P*. 31. *lacking NP;* Nous siol mal souinen *M*, Nom sian li mal nozen *R;* (No·us) Non *Q*, Non uus *U;* (sia) si *T;* lo mal *CTUc;* (en men) amen *U*. 32. dels bes *CMR*, del bene *c*. 33. Si non faitç mal seuals nom tegatç dan *T;* noi . . . noi *Uc;* (pro) be *CMUc;* (fassatz) tengatz *CJMc*, aia *U*. 34. ben far *CMTUc;* (en) al *RUc*, el *JP;* (talan) coman *CIKMNRTU*, man *c*. 35. Quieu *CMUc;* sens *T;* desperanza *GT*.

VI. *lacking MTUc*. 36. (gai) bel *A*. 37. Ben ue *N;* Vei *lacking R;* pot ben *EJP;* dire *R;* paire *IKR*, par *GQ;* pair bon enfan *lacking P*. 38. *lacking P;* (Car) Que *C;* (cel) ce *Q;* semana h. *G*, sesma h. *Q*.

C has this additional envoi:

La comtessa de Cumenge prezan
Pot hom lauzar, quar es ses tot enguan:
Bona ves Dieus, e ves Pretz ses eguansa.

TRANSLATION

I. Since I was distant toward you at the beginning, it is fitting that you take vengeance for it with a harsh answer or with a lance. For before I loved you, you loved me without guile, and I scorned you, good Lady, for one who has betrayed me without a challenge.

II. If I was false to you at the beginning, now I love you faithfully. And I know that you will often tell me that the lack of another love makes me come humbly to you, and that I am lying to you and deceiving you, and that I do not love you in deed, but in semblance.

III. For a great crime, great vengeance: so says Justice by way of judgment; and Mercy says, in the same way: For a great wrong, great forgiveness. Both are, in many places, of the same opinion, and in many places they contradict each other; for Justice kills, and Mercy has pity.

IV. So if you consider Justice or your honor or my fault, you will never be indulgent to me; for to the evil, Justice gives misfortune. The fault which I committed against you (which was so great) and the great excess of honor that you have over me, increase my love and diminish my hope.

V. Since you know for certain that I sinned from ignorance, do not bear the evil in mind, but remember the good. If you do me no favors, at least do me no harm; and let the (question of) reward be as you wish; for I shall wait for you without despair.

VI. King of Aragon, whoever sees your joyous countenance may well say: From a good father comes a good child. For he who sows honor reaps good worth.

NOTES

Seventeen MSS: *ACDD^cEGIJKMNPQRTUc*. Of these, *D^c* contains only the third and fourth stanzas.

In view of the evident contamination of sources, it is impossible to construct a satisfactory stemma. No groups (other than *IK*) remain constant throughout the poem. But the following deserve mention: *Uc* (5, 6, 12, etc.), *GQ* (6, 37), *JP* (20, 34, etc.; but cf. 4, 6, 33). Certain lines (14, 31, 33, 34, 35) point to a group *CMTUc;* according to 9 and 21, one could subdivide this *C-MT-Uc*. *E* agrees fairly often with *JP* (25, 37). *D^c* appears to be related to *GQ* (15, 19), while *R*, though fairly independent, has much in common with various members of the group *CMTUc* (10, 13, 25, 32, etc.). From the order of poems in the MSS, I am inclined to admit likewise the groups *AD* and *IKN*, though these groups are not always confirmed by the variants. But these are only tangled threads, which do not arrange themselves readily into a pattern.

Base: *A*.

The situation underlying this poem (Aimeric leaves a lady who has betrayed him, and begins to love another) is similar to that in song 7, written during the same period, and may possibly be the same situation as that described in 4, which cannot be dated.

4. *brau respost*. We have rejected *A*'s *mal* in favor of *brau* (found in nine MSS), because the phrase *brau respos* occurs in a poem of Folquet de Marseille (Stronski, XII, 6), from which Aimeric borrows an image in another poem (21, line 14) written in the same period as the present song.

6. *tornar en soan*. Levy, *PD*, lists only *metre en soan, tener a soan;* but in the *SW* (VII, 675) he gives examples with *tornar*. All three expressions seem to mean the same thing.

19–28. Cf. no. 27, lines 24–28, and the reference there to Folquet de Marseille (Stronski, VII, 35).

37. Cnyrim, *Sprichwörter*, no. 166; cf. 42, line 37.

38. Cnyrim, *Sprichwörter*, no. 153.

39–41. See the variants for an extra envoi, appearing only in *C*. Nothing about the envoi marks it as spurious, but I hesitate to accept it on the testimony of this one MS. Aimeric undoubtedly knew the lady in question. See our Introduction.

15

I. Cel qui s'irais ni guerreia ab Amor
Jes que savis non fai al mieu semblan,
Car de guerra vei tart pro e tost dan,
E guerra fai tornar mal en pejor.
En guerra trob, per q'ieu no la volria,
Viltat de mal e de ben carestia;
Mas fina Amors, sitot mi fai languir,
A tant de joi qe·m pot leu esjauzir.

II. Qe·ill plazer son plus qe·il enoi d'Amor,
E·il ben qe·il mal, e·il sojorn qe·il afan,
E·il gaug qe·il dol, e·il leu fais qe·il pesan;
E·il pro qe·il dan son plus, e·il ris qe·il plor.
Non dic aissi del tot que mal no·n sia;
E·l mals c'om n'a val mais que si·n garia,
Car qui ama de cor non vol garir
Del mal d'Amor, tant es dolz per sofrir.

III. Ancaras trob mais de ben en Amor,
Qe·l vil fai car e·l nesci gen parlan,
E l'escars larc, e leial lo truan,
E·l fol savi, e·l pec conoissedor;
E l'orgoillos domesga et homelia;
E fai de dos cors un, tant ferm los lia.
Per c'om non deu ad Amor contradir,
Pois tant gen sap esmendar e fenir.

IV. S'ieu l'ai servit, pro n'ai canje d'Amor,
Ab que ja puois non agues mas aitan;
Q'en mains luocs m'a faich tant aut e tant gran
Don ja ses lieis non pogra aver honor,
E maintas vetz m'engart de vilania
Que ses Amor gardar no m'en sabria,
E mains bons motz mi fai pensar e dir
Que ses Amor no·i sabria venir.

V. Bona dompna, de vos teing e d'Amor
Sen e saber, cor e cors, motz e chan.
E s'ieu ren dic que sia benestan,

Devetz n'aver lo grat e la lauzor
Vos et Amors, qe·m datz la maestria.
E si ja plus de ben no m'en venia,
Pro n'ai cambi segon lo mieu servir;
E si fos plus, ben saubra·l plus grazir.

VI. Chanssos, vai t'en de ma part e d'Amor
Al bon, al bel, al valen, al prezan
A cui servon Latin et Alaman
E·l sopleion cum bon emperador,
Sobre·ls majors a tant de majoria,
Largueza e pretz, honor e cortesia,
Sen e saber, conoissensa e chausir—
Ric de ricor per ric pretz conquerir.

VARIANTS

I. 1. que *AIJKNOPScf;* (ni) ne *I*, in *Q;* (ab) amb *f;* amors *PQ*. 2. (Jes) E *O;* saui *U;* (al) ab D^c. 3. Qar hom a tart (a hom tart *D*, hom atrai *PS*) pro de (en *MPS*) guerre (guerra *PS*) tost dan *D*D^c*GIKMNOPQSUc;* Qe *U;* (vei) uen *Cf;* (pro) bens *f*. 4. En quera D^c, Qe g. *O*, E gueram *N;* fas *Q;* mal tornar *C;* (mal en pejor) de mal p. *O*. 6. del mal *Q;* (ben) ioi *D*. 7. (Mas) Mai *J*, E *C*D^c*GIKMNOPQSUcf;* fins amor *U;* se tut *U*, se tu *c*. 8. (A) Ai *PSUc*, De *Q;* del ioi *IKQ;* (qe·m) quen *IKOQ*, qe *PS;* (leu) ben *B*, tost *GIKOQ*, tot D^c, tuest *N;* (esjauzir) far iauzir *U*, esbaudir *f*, çausir *c*.

II. 9. Cels plaisirs *D*, Quels plazers *f*, Queil placers *Q*, Li plaiser *O;* (plus) mais *PS;* li nueih *f*, li noi *O;* (d'Amor) denan *O*. 10. (E·il ben qe·il mal) El ioi qel dol *M*, Els bes quels mals *f;* bes *D*. 11. (E·il gaug qe·il dol) El ben qel mal *M;* (gaug) ioi *GIKOPQSU;* (e·il leu) eleo *O*, leu *P;* fas *DOU*, fag *PS; for* 11 *and* 12, *c has:* El ris qel plor e leu fais qel pesan. 12. (pro) prous *D*, plos *U;* dans *D;* (plus) mais *PS*, plu *O;* som pus el pron quel dan *f;* (plor) pros *Q*. 13. Pero non dic del tot *f;* (dic aissi) dieu ges *PS*, dic aiso *O;* de tot *IK;* quel *DOQ;* mals *JMf;* noi *DGIKNOQcf*, no *C*. 14. Qieu nam tro mais los mals qen s. g. *M*, El mal plas plus que sin gueria *N;* Mas lo mal *c*, Qel mal *PQU*, El mal *D*, Qe mal *S;* com nai *O;* (val mais) plus plaz *GQ*, plaz plus *OPSUc;* (que) qen *Q;* (si·n) sim *I*, sen *DUc*, qim *S*, qan *P*, q (*with a cross-bar on the stem*) *O*. 15. Car (E *IKN*) selh quama *CGIKMNOPQSUc;* (vol) pot *GQ;* languir (*later corrected to guerir*) *J*. 16. Dells mals *Mf;* (es) les *IKN*, son *Mf;* (dolz) durs *D;* (per) a *OUc*.

III. 17. Enqer sai plus (eu *OU*, *lacking N*) dautres (dautre *GQUc*) bes (ben *OUc*) en (ni *O*) amor *GIKNOQUc;* (Ancaras trob) Enquera truep *C*, Encara sai *M*, Enqer sai eu *PS*. 18. (car) pro *GIKNOQUc*, pros *C;* neissis *OQc;* (gen) ben *GOPQSU*. 19. escas *CJM*, escarcs *Q*, escartz *PS*, esclars *A;* larcs *DOU;* leials *OUc;* les truan *O*. 20. E fol *O;* sauis *QUc*, sain *M;* (pec) per *Q*, faitz *IK*. 21. (domesga) domest *DIKNc*, domestg *CMPS*, domesta *O*, demest *U*, domesqu *J*, domesca *GQ*, domesia *f;* (et) es *DS*, *lacking M;* humilian *M*. 22. E de dos cors fai un *Cf;* E *lacking O;* cor *OQUc;* (ferm) gen *C;* lo lia *PS*, les lia *Uc*. 23. Pero (Doncs *O*) non deu (de *Oc*) hom *OUc;* (non) nos *J;* (ad) uas *PS*. 24. (Pois) Car *f;* (gen) ben *O;* amendar *U*, comensar *C*, e emendar *P;* (e finir) al finir *f*, es fermir *U*.

IV. 25. Sieus ai *f*, E eu lai *O;* (pro n'ai) ben ai *GOU*, ben nai *IKNc*, eu ai *Q;* cambi *CGIJK*-

MNOQf, canbis *PS*. 26. (Ab que ja) Ia qe *Uc;* (puois) plus *CGIJKMNOPQSUc*, pus *f;* (non agues) nom (non *PQSUc*) fassa (fezes *OQ*, faç *c*) *CIKNOPQSUc*, non portes *G;* mai *f;* daitan *PSU*. 27. Que *ABCNQ;* maint loc *IKNPSUc*, mainh locs *CGQ*, manz loc *O;* (m'a) man *P;* tan gran e tan aut *D*, tant alt e gran *c*, aut e tan gran *O*. 28. Qe noi saupra auenir ses amor *f*, Qe ses amor noi p. a. h. *S;* On *GMQUc*, Qe *OPS;* (ja) ges *Uc;* ses lui *GOQUc;* noi *P;* (pogra) saubra *O*. 29. Manta ues *N*, moutas uetz *C;* me gart *DGJOQU*, mi gart *ACMc*, me trai *PS*. 30. *lacking O;* Ques *I*, Qar *Uc;* me *N;* (sabria) poiria *IKMNPSf*. 31. *lacking O;* maint *GIKNQUc;* bon *NPSUc*, bes *Q;* mot *NPSU;* ma faig *IKf*. 32. Qar *Uc;* non sabria un dir *ABD*, noi poiri auenir *MUc*, nom porria uenir *O*, noi pogreu deuenir *PS*, noi saubra auenir *f*.

V. 33. Bella *IKN;* (d'Amor) amor *U*. 34. Sen e saber e cor moz e chan *P;* Saber e sen *f;* Sein *D;* sabers *c;* cors e cor *CDGMOQ;* mot *c;* (chan) talan *Uc*. 35. (s'ieu) sanc *M;* (ren dic) fai ren *Ucf*, ren fatz *CDO*, faz ren *PS*, ren fis *M;* qi *M*, qem *DGOf*, qen *QU*, queus *IJKN*. 36. Deues *Mc*, De uen *O;* (n'aver) auer *GOQUc;* (lauzor) ualor *Q*. 37. qe mi datz *O*, qem donaz *PS;* maistria *IJKMOPS*. 38. *lacking C;* (si) cant *f;* (plus) puois *D;* bes *Af;* uenria *f*. 39. Pron nai *Uf;* (cambi) cange *U*, de cange *c*, daitan *PS;* (segon) selonc *M;* (servir) albir *U*, arbir *c*, nalbir *C*. 40. E sil fos plus *IK*, E sil plus fos *N*, E si plus fos *CDO*, E sim fes plus *A*, Sil plus hi fos *JMf*, Se plus nagues *PS*, Mas se (sel *Uc*) plus fos *GQUc;* ben o saupra grazir *M;* (saubra·l) sapia *U*, saubra *O*, sabria *Pc*, sabra *N;* (plus g.) miels g. *f*.

VI. *lacking Of*. 41. Chansoneta *J*, Chazon *D;* dama part *GU*, de part mi *JM;* (d'Amor) clamor *Q*. 42. Al pro al ric *CD*, Al pro al larc *PS*, Al bon al ric *M;* eal b. eal u. eal p. *U;* (valen) cortes *J;* prezen *B*, presa *D*. 43. (servon) sopleion *J;* (Latin) tyes *C*, tieis *M*. 44. (E·l) E *CGMQUc;* (sopleion) sopliom *PS*, sopreian *c*, sopream *U*, sieruon *J;* (cum) qan *D*, torn *Q;* emberador *Q*. 45. (Sobre·ls) Sobres *PS*, Contrals *Uc*, Contral *GQ;* maior *MQ*, meillors *PS;* (a tant de) a una *CDM*, aura *QUc*, aura ia *G;* (majoria) senhoria *JN*. 46. *lacking D;* Honor e pretz largueze (ualor e *M*) c. *CIJKMN*, Conoissenza largeze c. *GQUc*, Valor e sen largeze c. *PS*. 47. Larcs es de cor damar (donrar *DM*) e de seruir *CDM*, Mesure sen saber (parlar *Uc*) entendre dir *GQUc;* (conoissensa e chausir) conoisser e grazir *PS*, e conoisense c. *N;* iauzir *J*. 48. Valens de fag e de pretz enantir *CM*, Valen de fauz rics de pretz enantir *D*, Proez e (e *lacking Q*) cor ric de prez enriqir *GQ*, E toz bons (bon *U*) aibs de prez enriquir *Uc*, Naz de ricor fai fin prez enriqir *PS;* (ricor) ric cor *A;* bon pretz *A;* (conquerir) enrequir *JN*.

TRANSLATION

I. The one who is vexed with Love or wages war upon him is far, in my opinion, from acting like a wise man. For from war I see advantage (coming) late and harm early, and war turns bad into worse. In war I find things on account of which I should not wish it: abundance of evil and dearth of good. But faithful Love, although he makes me pine away, has so much of joy that he can easily make me rejoice.

II. For Love's pleasures are more than his annoyances, and the good things than the bad, and the diversions than the toils, and the joys than the pains, and the light burdens than the heavy; and the advantages are more than the harms, and the smiles than the tears. In speaking thus, I do not mean that that there is no evil (which comes) from it; but the sickness that one has from it is better than if one got well of it. For he who loves from the heart does not wish to be cured of the disease of love, it is so sweet to endure.

III. I also find more good in Love because he makes the wretched friendly, and the silly man a clever talker, and the stingy generous, and the rogue trustworthy, and the madman wise, and the simpleton learned; and the proud he tames and humbles; and of two hearts he makes one, so strongly does he bind them. Therefore one should not oppose Love, since he knows how to correct and to finish so nicely.

IV. If I have served him, I have an ample reward from Love, though he do no more than this. For he has made me so high and so great in many places from which without him I could never have had honor. And many times I keep myself from vileness, against which, without Love, I could not guard myself. And many fine words he makes me think and say, to which, without Love, I could not attain.

V. Good Lady, from you I hold, and from Love, sense and knowledge, heart and body, words and song. And if I say anything that is fitting, you and Love should have the thanks and the praise for it, you who give me the mastery. I have good reward from him according to my service; and if there should be more, I should certainly know how to be grateful for the more.

VI. Song, go, in my name and in Love's, to the good, the fair, the valiant, the worthy man whom Latins and Germans serve and to whom they bow as to a good emperor. He has so much superiority over the highest, generosity and worth, honor and courtesy, sense and knowledge, judgment and discernment, (he who is) rich in riches to conquer rich worth.

NOTES

Nineteen MSS: *ABCDD^cGIJKMNOPQSUcf* and *Ve.Ag*. Only the first stanza appears in *D*^c. Stanzas one, two, three, and five are quoted in the *Breviari d'amor*, lines 28786, 29317, 31977, and 33276 respectively (variants: 1. *que*. 3. (*de*) *per; ve*. 4. *mal tornar*. 7. *E*. 13. *no*. 15. *cel quama*. 17. *bes*. 18. (*vil*) *mal*. 19. *escas*. 20. *domesc e lhumilia*. 21. *de dos cors fai un tan gen*. 24. *comensar*. 34. *cors e cor*. 38. *bes*. 40. *Sil plus i fos; saubrial*).

We have not been able to use *Ve.Ag*. We have chosen *B* as our base.

The order ot stanzas is as given here, except for the following MSS:

M: 1-2-3-5-4-6
Of: 1-2-3-5-4
U: 1-3-2-4-5-6
PS: 1-5-2-3-4-6

CJ, O, and *j* have envois not found in other MSS; these are quoted at the end of the Notes.

De Bartholomaeis prints stanzas one and six in his *Poesie storiche* (II, 168); not a critical edition.

The variants are exceedingly numerous, and the relationships of the MSS more confused than usual. It is impossible to construct a satisfactory stemma. Certain groups, however, stand out: *ABD* (32, etc.; but cf. our remarks concerning 45–48, below), *IKN* (33, 40), *GQ*, *Uc*, *PS*. *GQ* and *Uc* often go together (40, 45, 46, 47), and *O* has much in common with *GQ* (8). *J* goes now with *ABD* (3, 7, 15, 17, 18), now with *IKN* (35, 46). The agreement of *CDM* in 45–48 is remarkable. Here, as frequently elsewhere in this poem, we must admit a contamination of sources. In general, these last four lines caused trouble. In addition to the version of *CDM*, there are the independent versions of *GQ*, *Uc*, and *PS*.

The poem is full of commonplaces, which could be matched in many another troubadour poem. These lines from Peire Rogier (ed. Appel, V, p. 51, lines 15–21) contain much of the same vocabulary, as well as the same ideas:

Si·l ioys d'amor no fos tan fis,
Ia non agra durat aitan,
Mas no y a d'ira tan ni quan,
Que·l dans n'es pros e·l mals n'es bes

E soiorns, qui plus mal en tray;
Demandatz cum! qu'ie·us o diray:
Quar apres n'aten hom merce.

3. *C*'s *ven* makes a little smoother sense, but the compiler of *C* had the habit of modifying texts to make them easier, and we do not feel obliged to follow him here.

6. *viltat* in the sense of "abundance" is noted by both Raynouard (V, 544) and Levy (*SW*, VIII, 778); Levy quotes these lines from Aimeric.

13. *mal no·n*. The reading *mals no·i*, which would seem preferable by our standards, actually occurs only in *f; no·i* alone is much better attested, but I think we are not obliged to reject *B*'s *non*, which is also well supported. As for *mals*, it does not occur in a single one of the older MSS: only in *JMf;* to accept their authority against that of *ABIK* and the rest seems excessively arbitrary. I suspect that our zeal for syntactical "correctness" has falsified more than one Provençal and Old French text.

16. *per*. Cf. these lines of Peirol (366, 27), quoted by Raynouard (IV, 502): *La flam' escon-duda Es greu* per *amortir* "difficile *à* éteindre."

25. Raynouard and Levy distinguish between *cambi* and *camge;* but, judging by the variant readings here and in 39, it seems that to the copyists at any rate the two were only forms of the same word, and that *cambi* was the commoner of the two.

29. *engard*. Apparently a rare word. It is not in Raynouard. Levy (*SW*, II, 500) quotes one example from the *Cour d'amour*, and another from Aimeric (38, line 12). But he questions this second example, for the reading of the better MSS is *esgardar*. The reading *gard* (*ACDGJ-MOQUc*) would perhaps be better here; but I have not ventured to change a reading of *B* supported by *IKN*.

30, 32. This illogical use of *que*, although not particularly difficult to understand, is not explained or illustrated by Raynouard or Levy.

48. I follow De Bartholomaeis in inserting "he who is" in the translation. The logical connection is loose, and, in view of the large number of variant readings, the text is probably faulty. For the pun on *Frederic*, see poem 26, lines 41–42.

CJ have this envoi, which I quote in the text of *C* (the variants of *J* are only orthographic, except *nom uoilh* for *no me uolrai* in the third line):

Bona domna, la genser etz que sia;
Vas uos azor e soplej nueg e dia.
Iamais de uos no me uolrai partir,
Qu'en tot lo mon nõ pogra miels chauzir.

O has these envois (compare the first two lines with the envoi to poem 2):

Na Zoana d'Est, dir no sabria
Tant de lauzor com a uos couenria,
Car uos sabez lo bens melz far qõ dir,
Tals bens cõ deo sobr' altres bẽs ĝçir.

Na Biatrix, del oilz del cor uos mir.

Bergert (*Damen*, p. 96) tentatively accepts this as part of the poem, and identifies "Na Biatrix" as Beatrice of Mangona, because Beatrice of Este was a nun when this poem was written (evidently after 22 November 1220, when Frederick was crowned emperor). But I agree with Zingarelli (*Intorno a due trovatori*, pp. 30–32) that the unsupported testimony of *O* is too weak a foundation for much of a structure. It seems more likely that these lines were added later. As Zingarelli says: "Non è il primo caso di strofe spurie aggiunte ad una poesia di trovatore celebre."

And, finally, *f* has still another envoi, written in a different hand, in different ink, around the name of the author of the following poem (Uc de la Bacalaria):

Bona dõna, q̃m tenetz en baillia,
Si tot nom ual la uostra senhoria,
De uos amar nom tuelh nim uuelh giquir,
Car sai q̃ mielhs nõ poiria chauzir.

16

I. Chantar vuilh.—Per qe?—Ja·m pladz.
—Ja te·n eras tu laichatz?
—O eu.—Fols es tu. Qin' es
De cui chantas?—Fola res,
De la gensor q'el mon sia.
—Oc, ben leu; mas si tu·l cres,
Altre no·t creiria ges.
  —Per deu, si faria

II. Toz hom qe vis sas beutatz.
—Es tan pros com lo·m lauçaz?
—La melher q'anc dieus feçes.
—Doncs fas tu ben qe cortes.
—Et eu, fol, no t'o diçia?
—Si be.—Doncz, de qe·m mescres
Sai?—Si es. Platz mi.—E sos bes
  Non entremetria,

III. S'aisi no fos la vertatz.
—Era, vos, qar me digatz!
—E qe?—Ama·us tan ni qan?
—Vai tu, mensongier truan;
Ela per qe m'ameria?
En tant qant soleilhs resplan,
N'a tan pro ni tan preçan.
  Fol, co·s tanheria

IV. A mi sos genz cors hondratz?
—Ben es doncs nesis e fatz.
—Cum?—Car as mes tot afan,
A guisa de fol aman,
La on ga res no·t valdria.
—Cre me tu qe merseian,
Aman, sirven, e preian
  Conqer hom amia

V. Tost o tard, don . . .—Er aujatz,
Qe ben es hom enguanatz.
—Non es ges. Saps qe m'a sors?

—Eu no.—Us conortz: q'Amors
Restaura tot en un dia
Qant qe a mesfait alhors;
Per qe·m sofri sas dolors
En paç tota via

VI. E·ls afans qe m'a . . .—Tardatz.
—Las, eu mur!—Cum?—Soi nafratz.
—Qui·t nafret?—Del mon la flors.
—Qe flors es?—De las melhors.
—Per qe fetz?—Qar se volia.
—Be·l cre; don atens socors?
—De leis, qe sa granz valors
M'es suaus medgia.

VII. Garir ses leis no poiria
Per re de mas greus dolors,
Q'asi·m nafret gent s'amors,
Non sai con m'estia.

VIII. Na Beatrix, cui jois guia,
D'Est, q'es flors de las gensors
E mellier de las meillors,
Meillura tot dia.

READINGS EMENDED

1. qem. 5. fia. 7. nol te creiria. 9. sa. 29. *This verse is placed after* 32. 36. conort. 43. flor. 44. la. 46. aten. 47. gran. 48. medgria. 51. naifret. 54. la.

TRANSLATION

I. I wish to sing.—Why?—It pleases me.—Have you ever ceased to do so?—Yes.—You are crazy. What kind of woman is it of whom you sing?—You crazy thing, of the noblest woman in the world.—Yes, very likely; but if you believe that, another would hardly believe you.—By God, so would believe

II. Every man who saw her beauty.—Is she as worthy as you praise her to me?—The best that God ever made.—In that case, you act like a courteous gentleman.—Did I not tell you so, you fool?—Yes, indeed.—Then why do you doubt me now?—So it is; I agree.—I shouldn't undertake (to sing) her good qualities

III. If the truth were not thus.—Now, pray, tell me.—What?—Does she love you at all?—Away, you lying knave! Why should she love me? In all the lands that the sun shines on, there is no one so worthy or so honored. Fool, how could

IV. Her noble, honored person be suitable for me?—Then you are an ignorant fool.—How?—Because you have, like a foolish man, gone to so much trouble in a cause from which you will receive no profit.—Believe me, by suing, loving, serving, and begging, a man wins a lady

V. Sooner or later, from whom . . .—Now hear! For a man is easily deceived.—Not at all. Do you know what has come to me?—No.—A comforting thought: that Love makes up in one day for all the wrongs he has done elsewhere; wherefore I suffer his woes always in peace,

VI. And the torments that he has . . .—You pause.—Alas, I am dying!—How?—I am wounded.—Who wounded you?—The flower of the world.—A flower, you say?—Of the best.—Why did she do it?—Because she wished to.—I believe it; from whom do you expect aid?—From her, for her great worth is a sweet medicine to me.

VII. Without her, nothing could cure me of my grievous woes, for the love of her wounded me so gently that I do not know how I am.

VIII. Lady Beatrice of Este, whom Joy guides, who is the flower of the noblest and the best of the best, grows better every day.

NOTES

One MS: *c*.

Critical edition by Appel, in *Revue des langues romanes* XXXIV, 7. We have followed Appel in his few emendations, and for the most part in his punctuation. The hardest problem is to decide which words are to be given to the poet and which to his imaginary interlocutor; it is here that we have ventured in one or two cases (e.g., line 15) to differ with Appel. Lines 1–12 and the tornada are printed by De Bartholomaeis, *Poesie storiche*, I, 230.

This poem, whose dialogue form suggests Peire Rogier, adds nothing to the stature of Aimeric as a poet. It is easy to see why it occurs in only one MS.

3. Appel has an interesting note on the origin and development of the word *qin'* (*loc. cit.*).

7. Appel does not introduce the emendation *no·t creiria* into the text, but suggests it in a note.

15. Appel translates "Je sais", and punctuates *Doncz, de qe·m mescres?—Sai, si es, platz mi e sos bes.*

17. Berenguier de Noya, in his *Mirall de trobar* (c. 1400), quotes this and the following lines thus (see Anglade in *Homenaje ofrecido a Menéndez Pidal*, Madrid, 1925, I, 678):

S'axi no fos la vertatz
Eras vos car me digatz
A que Amors tant ne quant
Vays tu mesonger tavanço (*sic*)
La per quam amaria.

On the basis of this, we depart from Appel's reading *Sai, si no fos.*

27. Appel suggests the correction *ton afan.*

30–32. Cnyrim, *Sprichwörter*, no. 45.

41. Appel asks "Lisez *cargatz* au lieu de *tardatz*?" He does not break up the line.

17

I. De so dont hom a longuamen
Ben dig entre·ls conoissedors,
S'en ditz pueys mal vilanamen,
Es a tot lo meynhs dezonors;
Qu'aisselh que si mezeis desmen
Del ben qu'a dig, no m'es parven,
Des qu'es trobatz ben dizen fals,
Que·l dej' om creire dizen mals.

II. Se disses al comensamen
Los mals ans que·l besdigz fos sors,
Dissera plus cubertamen,
E semblera ver als pluzors.
Mas pero ben aven soven
Qu'aisso qu'om cre blasmar, defen.
Doncs non es, d'ome qu'es aitals,
Lo besdigz bos ni·l maldigz mals.

III. C'us qu'en dis ben premeiramen
Que de bas aut pojet amors,
E·n dis apres mal sotilmen
Per far semblar sos mals pejors
E per plus enguanar la gen,
Ab proverbis dauratz de sen
Et ab parauletas venals
Vol far creire del ben qu'es mals.

IV. Non es bes, qui fa d'avinen
Segon lo mon so qu'es valors,
E qui·s garda de falhimen
On pus pot, e creys sas lauzors?
Si es; mas no·n pot far nien
Si non a l'amayestramen
D'Amor, qu'es mayestre lials
Qu'ensenh' a triar bes de mals.

V. Qu'el cor nays, on Amors s'empren,
Essems Ardimens e Paors;

Qu'en saviez' a l'ardimen,
E·l volpilhag' en las folhors.
E pueys es arditz eissamen
De larguez' e d'ensenhamen,
E volpilhs d'escassez' e d'als
Que fos vilania ni mals.

VI. Per so·m par que qui ditz mal, men,
Del majestre qui dona·l sen
Cum sia hom valens e cabals
Ni cum se pot gardar de mals.

VII. Quar val plus e conoys e sen
Na Johana d'Est, et enten,
Vuelh segon lo dreg jutge quals
Deu hom dir d'Amor, bes o mals.

VARIANTS

I. 1–7 *lacking E*. 1. Daiso *D^aD^cIJKOPR;* hom hom *C*. 2. Bel *D^a;* dic *O*. 3. Sin *D^cJPR*, Si en *O*. 4. Les *D^c;* totz *IK*. 6. Dels bes *O*. 7. Des que *D^aD^c;* (ben) ren *C*. 8. deiam *P*, deion *O;* (dizen) diz *D^a*.

II. 9. Sel *R*. 10. Los bes ans quels (que *IK*) mals ditz fos sors *D^aIK;* Lo mals *P;* quel ben dig *EJOP*, quels bels ditz *R*. 12. sembla *EJP;* uers *C;* (als) a *D^aEIJKOP*. 14. (qu'om) nom *P;* blasma *O*. 16. Lo ben digz *EO;* bos *lacking IK;* (bos nil) ben lo *O;* mals dit *IK*.

III. 17. (Cus) Us *C*, Sus *IK*, Duns *O*, Cun *P;* (qu'en) que *R;* (ben) liei *P*, *lacking D^aIK*. 18. (Que) Don *O;* poges *I*, paget *O*. 19. (E·n) Ne *O;* sitilmen *IK*. 20. sos mals semblar *O*. 21. (enguanar) decebre *O*. 22. peruerbis *D^aIKO*, uerbis *E;* dautratz *D^a*, daurag *O*. 23. paraulas *IKP*, parauletus *O*. 24. Volc *O;* de ben *E*, del bes *O;* qu'es *lacking P*.

IV. *lacking O*. 25. be *R;* (qui) que *D^aIK;* (fa) sap *J*. 28. sa lauzors *CR*, sas lamors *P*. 29. *lacking E;* mals no *R*. 30. *lacking E;* laministramen *JP*. 31. *lacking E;* Damors *C;* (qu'es) que *R;* mastre *P*. 32. *lacking E;* ben dels mals *R*, bes da mals *D^a*.

V. *lacking E*. 33. (Qu'el) Del *O;* cors *J;* amor *CD^aR*, amans *P*. 35. (Qu'en) Cant *R;* sameza a l. *O*. 36. (E·l) E *CJPR;* (en) e *D^aIK;* la folors *IKP*. 37. (pueys es) pocis *O*. 38. languesza e d. *P*. 39. olpils *D^aKR* (*initial* u *added in R above line*), uolpiz *O*. 40. Qe sos ni lama ni mals *O;* uilanie *D^a*.

VI. *lacking E*. 41. Cer *D^a* (*small* p *in margin*); (so·m) son *IK;* que *lacking JP;* (qui) qun *O;* mal man *O*, malamen *IK*, mal uilanamen *JP*. 42. qui *lacking I;* dona lo sen *O*. 43. homs *C*.

VII. *lacking E*. 45. (e sen) ẽsen *R*. 48. damors *JR;* ben *O*.

TRANSLATION

I. If one boorishly speaks ill of that concerning which one has long spoken well among those who know, it is at the very least a dishonor; for he who belies himself about the good that he has said, it does not seem to me, since he is revealed as a false sayer of good, that one ought to believe him when he says evil things.

II. If he had said the evil things at the beginning, before speaking well had come forth, he would have spoken more covertly, and it would have seemed true to most people. But it often happens that one defends what one means to blame. Therefore, the good words of a man of this sort are not good, nor his evil words evil.

III. For he who speaks well of Love at first, before it has risen from low to high, and afterwards subtly speaks ill of it in order to make his pains seem worse and to deceive people more, —with proverbs gilded with sense and with venal little words he wishes to make one believe that good is evil.

IV. Is it not a good thing, if a man does fittingly that which is meritorious according to the world, and if he guards himself from error as much as he can, and increases his good repute? Yes, it is; but one cannot do anything of this without the instruction of Love, who is an honest instructor who teaches how to distinguish good things from bad.

V. For in the heart where Love is kindled, there are born at the same time boldness and fear; for he (Love; or the heart?) has boldness in (doing) wisdom and cowardice in (doing) follies. And then he is bold likewise with generosity and good breeding (he bestows these qualities freely), and cowardly in niggardliness and anything else that might be baseness or evil.

VI. For this reason, it seems to me that he lies who speaks ill of the teacher who gives the knowledge how one may be noble and excellent, and how one can guard oneself from evils.

VII. Because Lady Johana of Este is most worthy and knows and perceives and understands, I wish her to decide justly which one should say of Love, good things or bad.

NOTES

Ten MSS: *CD^aD^cEIJKOPR*. Only the first stanza appears in *D^c*. Lines 5–8 are quoted in the *Breviari d'amor* (variants: 5. *aicels*. 7. *Pueis; dizens*. 8. *deion*). The poem is anonymous in *O*. De Bartholomaeis (*Poesie storiche*, II, 127) prints stanzas I and VII, after *O*.

The only clear groups of MSS are *D^aIK* (10, 17), *JP* (30, 41), and probably *CR* (12, 28). Lines 22 and 36 hint at a division *D^aIKO—CJPR*, but this is not certain (cf. *IKP* in 23 and 36: *la folors*). So little is left in *E*, after the excision of two miniatures, that its affiliation cannot be established; but cf. *EJP* in 12. The relationships are not definite enough to allow us to construct a stemma. Base text: *C*.

For the theme, compare poem 40, and see the references there to Folquet de Marseille. The two poems, 17 and 40, were probably composed about the same time.

11. *cubertamen*. That is, the lie would not then have been so obvious.

12. *als pluzors*. Levy (*SW*, VI, 400) quotes Crescini's comment: "Di solito l'uso di *plusor* è ristretto al nom. pl.," and adds: "Ich kann auch keinen Beleg von *los pluzors* beibringen." We have one here, assuming that the reading of *CR*, which we have adopted, is correct; and it seems on the whole preferable to that of the other MSS.

15–16. Cf. 40, lines 5–10.

45. Raynouard and Levy give no examples of the absolute use of *sentir;* it seems to mean "to be gifted in perception."

18

I. D'avinen sap enganar e trahir
Qui d'avinen sap trahir trahidor;
E sel que faill d'avinen vas Amor
Sap d'avinen ses faillimen faillir,
C'al mieu semblan ses faillimen faillis
Cel que cellui qui vol trahir trahis;
Mas ieu non sai autrui trahir mas me,
E ma dompna trahis e me e se.

II. C'a mi mezeus mi cuja far aucir,
Aissi cum fai l'austarda per temor:
Qand ve venir o l'aigla o l'austor,
A terra·is fer per plus viatz morir;
Per que pieitz ha de mort cel que languis.
Mas per razon no vuoill esser aucis
Qe·ill renda mal per mal ni ben per be,
Puois ab sofrir no·i posc trobar merce.

III. Assajarai si ja·m poirai gauzir
De lieis ab mal dir ni ab desonor,
Puois no m'en gau ab precs ni ab lauzor
Qu'eu en diga, sufren ni ab servir.
C'assatz troba soven, so m'es avis,
Encausadors cel que fuich ni·s gandis;
Doncs, s'ai fugit e non encausiei re,
Encausserai so c'ai fugit ancse.

IV. Aissi co·l sers poigna en si delir,
Que·is venz e·is fraing e·is combat per vigor,
O ai ieu faich lonc temps per ma follor;
Per que no·m vuoil ges desenfolletir,
Enanz on plus follei, plus m'abellis:
Doncs per qe·m clam s'ieu eis m'enfolletis
Ab escien? Mas ges fols no·is recre
De follejar tro la foudatz si ve.

V. Trop parlars notz, qe·m n'er a desmentir,
Dompna, e torn l'amar gen en dolsor;
Per que qui sap servir a son seignor,

Ops l'auria qe·il saubes deservir:
Car fols mi par cel que totz temps servis
A son seignor qand li o desgrazis;
E non per so que vas vos mi malme,
Enanz ai pres del menassar refre.

VARIANTS

I. 2. saub *K*. 3. cils *T;* qui *D*[c]*EM*. 4. Belhamen sap ses f. f. *C*. 5. *lacking D*[c] (?); Camon semblan *EM*. 6. (que) qi *D*[c]*M;* (qui) quel *CDD*[c]*K*, qil *MT*, q *EI*. 7. (sai) aus *CEIKM;* mi *T*. 8. E ma dona sap trair mi e se *D*[c]*IKT;* (e me e se) autrui e se *A*, e se e me *E*.

II. 9. A mi *IK;* (mi cuja) cuiaua *C*, me cuiaua *EIK;* ausire *T*. 10. (Aissi) Si *T;* lastarda *IK*. 11. Cauei uenir *T;* (o l'aigla) laigla *T*, laiguilla *IK*, daut laigla *C*, la agla *D;* lastor *T*. 12. En terras f. *C*, En terra f. *EM;* (morir) aucir *A*, au morir *D*. 13. Pero *CEIKM*. 14. *lacking IK;* (per razon) per aquo *CE*, per aisso *M*. 15. Quel *CDIK*, Qieilh *M*, Cil *T;* reda *T*. 16. a sofrir *IKT*, ab suffriz *D;* (no·i) no *IKT*, non *CDEM;* puoc *T*.

III. (V *in EM*). 17. Tot assaiarai sim poirai i. *E*, Veirai si ia en poiria i. *M*, Assaiarai sim poiria i. *C;* (ja·m) gia *T;* porai *D*, poerai *IK*, poria *T*. 18. a mal dir ni am d. *T*. 19. Puois non giau am p. *T;* prec *E*, pretz *CM;* am l. *T*. 20. siruen ni ab suffrir *C*, souen ni ab sufrir *EM*, soffron et a seruir *IK*. 21. Quassatz troba som es auis (uis *E*) *CE*, Qar pro troba cassatz ço mes uis *M*, Cassatz troba (trobom *DT*) souen encusador (encachador *D*, ecasador *T*, encaisaris *IK*) *ADIKT*. 22. Aicel que fuich (fuiz *D*) trop souen nis (ni *DT*) gandis *ADIKT;* Encausador *E*, Dencaussadors *M;* ni g. *E*. 23. *lacking EM;* Donc sieu ai fag quanc non encaussei re *C;* Doncs ai fugis *D*, Doncs sai fugir *A*, Doncs ai fugir *T*, Doncs ai fugit *IK;* noi encauei re *IK*. 24. *lacking EMT;* Eucauserai *IK*, Encaussarai *C*.

IV. (III *in EM*). 25. Caisi *E;* ser *E*, serps *D*[c]*;* ponha si eys delir *CE*, poinhaen sieis delir *M*. 26. Que suzes f. *C*, Ques ue es f. *E;* e (os *K*) conbat *IK;* (vigor) fortor *C*. 27. Mai eo fait lomcs temps *T;* loncs t. *IK;* tẽp *D*. 28. Per que no uuelh ges del sen follezir *C;* Per quieu *EM;* (no·m) non *D*[c]*M*, nõ *IK;* (ges) ia *M;* desfoletir *T*, deenfolletir *IK*, dessenfolezir *D*[c]. 29. o plus *IK*, om plus *T;* (follei, plus) mi fai mal *IK*, folleg plus *C*. 30. Dans *D*[c]*;* (per) de *DD*[c]*EIKMT;* me folletis *C*, menfollezis *D*[c]. 31. Amb e. *T*, Az e. *D*[c]*EM;* mas ges folls no se recre (ges *expunctuated*) *M;* fol *C*. 32. foudat *ADT*, foudalz *M*, faudatz *IK;* (se ve) len ue *C*, laue *E*, llaue *M*.

V. (IV *in EM*, *lacking IK*). 33. (Trop) Prop *C;* parlar *CDEMT;* noiz *D;* que men a d. *C*, quar mer a d. *E*, qar uen a d. *M*. 34. Don ops agra a lamar gran doussor *M; Et* dõpna *et T;* (e) en *DE;* (gen) guan *C;* (en) e *T*, *lacking E*. 35. Qar cell qi sap gen seruir a seinhor *M;* saup *E;* amb son s. *T*. 36. (l'auria) li auria *T*, auria *CD;* (qe·il) que *C;* saupes *M*, sabes *T*. 37. fol *DET;* tut teps *T*. 38. (qand) ca *T*, pos *M;* (li o) el lo *A*. 39. (que) quieu *CE*. 40. Enas a pres *T;* (del menassar) ab la boca *E*, per uos seruir *M;* (refre) lo fre *CEM*.

TRANSLATION

I. He knows how to deceive and betray fittingly, who knows how fittingly to betray a traitor; and he who sins fittingly against Love knows how to sin fittingly without sin, for in my opinion he sins without sin who betrays one who wishes to betray (him); but I know how to betray no other than myself, and my Lady betrays herself and me.

II. For she almost makes me kill myself, just as the bustard does through fear: when it sees the eagle or the goshawk coming, it casts itself to the ground in order to die more quickly; because he who languishes has worse than death. But I do not wish to be killed for the purpose of returning to her evil for evil or good for good, since with suffering I cannot find mercy in her.

III. I shall try whether I can have my pleasure of her through slander or dishonor, since I have no pleasure of her through entreaties or through praise that, suffering or serving, I speak of her. For he who flees and runs away finds pursuers very often, I believe; so, if I have fled and not pursued anything, I shall pursue what I have always fled.

IV. Just as the stag labors to destroy himself, who overcomes and breaks himself and fights vigorously, so I have done for a long time, through my folly; because I do not wish at all to become sane again, rather, when I am most insane, I am most pleased. Then why do I complain if I myself knowingly drive myself mad? But a madman does not give up being insane until the madness goes away.

V. Too much talking does harm, Lady, for I shall have to deny what I have said, and the bitter turns pleasantly into sweetness; wherefore he who knows how to serve his lord, ought to know how to do him disservice: for he seems foolish to me who serves his lord all the time, when the lord is not grateful to him for it. And (I say this?) not because I am conducting myself badly toward you; rather, I have put a check on my threatening.

NOTES

Nine MSS: *ACDD^{c}EIKMT*. *D^c* contains only stanzas one and four; other omissions are noted in the Variants. Berenguier de Noya quotes the first four lines; see Anglade, in *Homenaje . . . Menéndez Pidal*, I, 679 (only significant variant: 3. *vay s'amor*). The poem is anonymous in *IK*, and ascribed to Uc de Pena in *CReg*. Stemma:

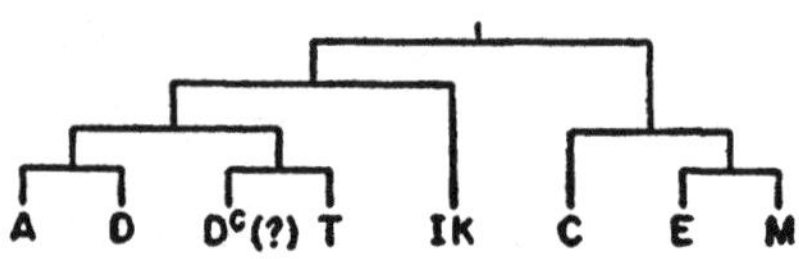

ADD^{c}IKT: 21–22 (-*D^c*, which does not contain the stanza)
ADD^{c}T: 7 (*aus* would seem to be the original reading)
AD: 12 (where *D* started to copy the *aucir* that appears in *A*, then made the obvious correction to *morir*)
CEM: 32, 40 (*lo fre*, unless this is the original reading)
EM: the order of stanzas (I, II, IV, V, III), 5, 20, the omission of 23–24, 28, 32
For further confirmation of the division *ADD^{c}IKT* and *CEM*, see lines 14, 25. The position of *D^c* is doubtful, but a comparison of lines 7 and 8 suggests some relationship with *T*.

The common original seems to have been fairly corrupt: in lines 8 and 11, one syllable was apparently lacking, and most copyists used their ingenuity to fill out the meter; this explains the surprising groups indicated by the variants in these lines, for coincidence in these simple corrections is to be expected. Our text is based on that of *A*.

The text is not very satisfactory. It is hard, however, to be sure whether the incoherence of the poem is due to a faulty text or to the author's struggles with the childish paradoxes that he is developing, and the verbal gymnastics with which he chose to develop them. It would be charitable to think that this is one of his early poems.

21–24. Cf. Folquet de Marseille (ed. Stronski), I, 17, taken from Ovid's *Quod sequitur fugio, quod fugit ipse sequor* (*Amores*, II, 19, 36; see Stronski, p. 78*):

So que m'encaussa vau fugen
E so que·m fugh ieu vau seguen.

25. *delir*. The word, which Raynouard defines and illustrates (III, 23), was omitted by mistake from Levy's *PD*.

26. *Que·is venz*. The meaning seems to be "who overcomes, exhausts himself." This reflexive use is not illustrated in Raynouard or Levy.

40. *refre*. The word is not given by Raynouard or Levy. The correct reading may be *lo fre* (*CEM*), though it is hard to see why *ADT* would change this to a non-existent word. We may easily assume a noun *refre*, connected with the word-family *refrenar*, *refrenador*, *refrenamen*.

19

I. De Berguedan, d'estas doas razos
Al vostre sen chausetz en la meillor,
Q'ieu mantenrai tant ben la sordejor
Q'ie·us cuich vensser, qui dreich m'en vol jutgar:
Si volriatz mais desamatz amar,
O desamar e que fossetz amatz.
Chausetz viatz cella que mais vos platz.

II. N'Aimerics, doncs auria sen de tos
Si eu lo mieills non chausia d'amor.
Totz temps vuoill mais qe·m teignan per seignor
E que desam e c'om mi teigna car;
C'anc en amor non vengui per musar,
Ni anc non fui d'aqels desfasendatz;
Qe·l gazaing vuoill de dompnas e de datz.

III. De Berguedan, nuils hom desamoros
Al mieu semblan non a gaug ni honor;
C'aissi cum sens val mais sobre follor,
Val mais qui serv e·n fai mieills ad honrar
C'aicel qe vol penre e non donar.
Per q'ieu vuoill mais esser paubres honratz
C'avols manens e desenamoratz.

IV. N'Aimerics, tot enaissi o faitz vos
Cum fetz Rainautz qand ac del fruich sabor:
Que s'en laisset non per autre temor
Mas car non poc sus el cereis montar,
E blasme·l fruich car aver ni manjar
Non poc; e vos etz ab lui acordatz,
C'aisso que non podetz aver blasmatz.

V. De Berguedan, car vos etz malgignos,
Cuidatz qez eu sia d'aital color?
Non sui, q'en loc de gauch pren la dolor;
Mas bos respieitz m'aiud' a sofertar,
Per qu'eu vuoill mais ses consegre enchaussar
Que conseguir so don non fos pagatz,
Car mil d'autres val us bens desiratz.

VI. N'Aimerics, mainz de gaillartz e de pros
N'ai vistz faillir tot per aital error.
Qe·l cors d'En Ot del caval milsoudor
En fo vencutz car no·l laisset brochar;
Que si de prim l'agues faich enanssar,
Cel qe·l venqet fora per el sobratz:
Per c'om deu far, quan pot, sas volontatz.

VII. De Berguedan, cella q'ieu teing plus car
Vuoill mil aitans mais amar desamatz
C'ab autra far totas mas volontatz.

VIII. Bar N'Aimerics, ja no·us cuidetz gabar!
Que s'amassetz aissi cum vos vanatz,
No·us foratz tant de Tolosa loignatz.

VARIANTS

I. 1. En berguedan *R* (*and so throughout*), De breguedan *DIK* (*and so throughout*), Den bergada *M*, De bergueda *Q*. 2. A vostre sen *CIKR*. 3. mantenria *IK*, matendrai *Q*, manterai a^{1}; (tant ben) tan gen *MQ*, *lacking IK;* (la) lo *R*. 4. Qeu cuit uezer *D*, Qeus uencerai *M;* qi dreit lam vol iugar *Q*, qi lam vol drech iurar *M;* (m'en) mi a^{1}. 5. amar desamaz *D*. 6. e *lacking* a^{1}. 7. (Chausetz viatz) Aras chauzetz *R;* (viatz) dambas *M;* (mais) plus *MQ*.

II. 8. Naimeric *ADR*a^{1}, Saimeric *Q;* don *IK;* aurieu *CDIKM*a^{1}; (de tos) dotos *C*. 9. Sel mielz nõ c. d. *IK;* (lo) del *CD;* iauzia *D*. 10. Tostẽps sapchatz uuelh mais esser senhor *CR*, Toç tems sapchaç q̃ uoil esser segnor *Q*, Totz temps mi plai qom mapelle seinhor *M;* (qe·m teignan) qem teigno a^{1}, quen tengom *IK*, com teĩgna *D*. 11. (que) qieu *M;* (teigna) tenhaen *C*, tenguon *IK*, tegnem a^{1}. 12. Qieu non sui ges ab amor per musar *M* (*last four words added in margin*), Qeu no ueng ges en amor p. m. *Q;* (C'anc) Car *A;* (en) eu en a^{1}; (vengui) ueigau a^{1}. 13. Ni nõ sui ges *AQ* (*added in margin in M*), Ni anc no suy *R;* desfazedaz *D*, des fat sendaç *Q*. 14. Que g. *C*, Que gazanhar *R;* de domne de datz *R*.

III. 15. De bergeda *M*, O bergueda *Q* (*see above, line* 1); nuls hons desamo moros *Q*. 16. A mon s. *CDIK*, A mo s. *R*a^{1}; (gaug) ben *MQ;* hononor *M*. 17. sen *MQR*. 18. e fai mais *CMR*, e fai meillz *IKQ*a^{1}, es fai meillz *D;* ontar a^{1}. 19. *lacking C;* Car sel *D*, Qe cell *MQ;* e *lacking R*. 20. Per qieu am mais paubre esser honratz *M*, Per que amais paubres esser omtaz *Q;* (qu'ieu) quẽ *I;* paubretz a^{1}. 21. Qe rics ses iois (sex ioi *Q*) e d. *MQ;* (e) ni *D*.

IV. 22. Naimeric *ACQR*a^{1}; (enaissi) aysi *R*. 23. ranauz *IK*, rainarz *MQ*, rainart *CR;* (qand) e quãt *Q;* del frug ac s. a^{1}; fru *Q*. 24. Non sen laisset ges (laisegges *Q*) per a. t. *MQ;* (autre) autra *CMQR*a^{1}. 25. car *lacking Q;* seriers *C*, cerçer *D*, cerser *IK*, cirier *M*, serier *R*, cerier a^{1}, ciresier *Q*. 26. Blasmet lo f. *R*, E blasmal f. a^{1}; (car) quant *CIKMQR*a^{1}. 27. (etz) netz *C*, nest *IK*, nes a^{1}, est *M*, es *QR*, ses *D;* (ab lui) nab lui *Q*, ni lui luy *R*. 28. Qar so *M*, Qan ço *Q*, Que so *R;* (podetz) pedeç *Q*.

V. 29. De bergueda *Q*, De bregedan *M*, De bergadan a^{1} (*see above, line* 1); (etz) el *Q;* gignons *K*, guiscos *M*. 30. Cuidaz uos dunc qeu sia d. c. *Q;* (qez eu) quieu *R*. 31. pren la adolor

Q. 32. bon *CR;* ma uida *CDR;* confortar *MQ*. 33. encassar *IK*. 35. (Car) Qe *MQ;* mils *D;* (val) uas *a*[1]*;* un bes *R*.

VI. 36. Naimeric *ACQRa*[1]*;* (mainz) mais *C;* mãs g. e pros *R*. 37. uist *DIKMQR*, uitz *a*[1]. 38. (Qe·l cors d'En Ot) Quel cors denoc *C*, Qel cors donet *MR*, Qel cors donot *Q*, Qel coredors *AD;* cors d'En Ot del *lacking a*[1]. 39. (En) Ne *Q*, E *R;* (no·l) non *M*, uol *I;* (brochar) enanzar *a*[1]. 40. *lacking a*[1]*;* Que sil laises de primas enansar *R*, E sil laisseç de prim ben enanzar *Q*, E sil laisses ab . . . (?) ben auansar *M* (*partly illegible*)*;* (l'agues faich) lo laisses *CIK*. 41. Sol quel uenques fora pres e s. *R;* per lui *Q*. 42. (c'om) cum *Q*.

VII. 43. De bergeda *MQ*, De bergadan *a*[1]*;* quieu plus tenc car *C*. 44. mays mil aitans *R;* mils *a*[1]*;* aitan *D;* desemaç *Q*. 45. mas *lacking I*.

VIII. *lacking M*. 46. Bar naimeric *ACR*, Bars naimerics *IK*, Ua naimeric *Q*, An aimeric *a*[1]*;* cabar *IK*. 47. Qe saguesseç conques zo que cercaç *Q;* tant cum (cant *R*) aissius u. *CIKR*, tan cous u. *a*[1]*;* (vanatz) comtaz *D*. 48. (No·us) Non *D*, Nos *Q*.

TRANSLATION

I. De Berguedan, of these two alternatives choose the one which in your opinion is the better, for I shall maintain the worse one so well that I think I shall overcome you, if one is willing to grant me justice: Whether you would rather love unloved, or not love, and be loved. Choose quickly the one which pleases you more.

II. Sir Aimeric, I should have the sense of a child if I did not choose the better (part) of love. I would always rather be considered the lord, and not love, but be held dear; for I never came to love to waste my time, nor was I ever one of those who are content to be spectators; I want to win with ladies and at dice.

III. De Berguedan, no man who does not love has, to my mind, either joy or honor; for just as sense is better than folly, so he who serves and who acts more honorably is better than he who wishes to take and not to give. Wherefore I would rather be poor and honorable than rich but vile and out of love.

IV. Sir Aimeric, you act just as Reynard did when he had a taste for the fruit: he gave it up not for any other fear, but because he could not climb up into the cherry tree, and he said the fruit was bad because he could not get it or eat it; and you agree with him, since you blame what you cannot get.

V. De Berguedan, since you are a disloyal man, do you think that I am of the same breed? I am not; for instead of joy I take pain; but good expectation helps me to endure, because I would rather pursue without attaining than to attain that with which I would not be pleased; for one wished-for good is worth a thousand others.

VI. Sir Aimeric, I have seen many excellent and good men go astray through that very mistake. For Sir Otto of the priceless horse was conquered thereby, because he did not let him run; if he had let the horse go ahead at first, the one who conquered him would have been overcome by him: therefore, one ought to fulfill one's desires, when it is possible.

VII. De Berguedan, I would a thousand times rather love unloved her whom I hold most dear, than fulfill all my desires with another.

VIII. Valiant Sir Aimeric, don't try to brag! For if you loved as much as you boast (that you do), you would not have come so far away from Toulouse.

Ten MSS: *ACDIKMQRa¹d*. Since *d* is copied from *K*, we have neglected it. The relationships of the MSS are complicated and confusing. The most satisfactory stemma that can be devised is probably this:

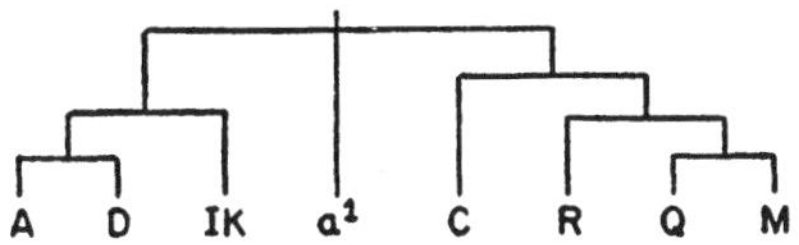

ADIK: 24
IK: 3, 46, etc.
AD: 38, 40, 47
CMQR: 10, 23
MQR: 17, 27, 38, 40
MQ: 3, 4, 7, 16, 24, 32, 35

*a*¹ has no constant agreement with any other MS.

But it is very hard to explain the many groupings that are in contradiction to this stemma: *IKQa*¹, 18; *CDIKMa*¹, 8; *CD*, 9; *AMQ*, 16; etc. Can coincidence account for them all? One thing that makes certainty of MS filiations impossible is the fact that, while there are an unusually large number of variants, most of those involving more than two MSS are not obviously wrong; the method of "common error" for establishing families of MSS therefore becomes arbitrary and unreliable. For an unsuccessful attempt to apply other methods to this poem, see W. P. Shepard, "Recent Theories of Textual Criticism," in *Modern Philology*, XXVIII, 136. We have based our text on that of *A*.

1. *razos*. For the meaning "alternative (in a *partimen*)," see Levy, *SW*, VII, 62, where this passage and one other are quoted.

13. *desfasendatz*. The only example of the word in Raynouard (III, 276) and Levy (*SW*, II, 140); both quote this passage. Raynouard translates "imbécile, ignorant." Levy thinks this meaning unlikely, in view of the word's origin, and says: "Es ist eigentlich 'unbeschäftigt, müssig,' hier wol 'der sich mit müssigen Zuschauen begnügt,' synonym *muzador*." Jeanroy (*Anthologie des troubadours*, p. 81): "soupirants inactifs."

17–21. Cf. Folquet de Marseille (Stronski's edition), XIII, 38:

> Quar miels gazanh' e plus gen
> Qui dona qu'aicel qui pren,

and VII, 9:

> Per que n'a mais us paubres s'es joyos
> Q'us rix ses joi qu'es tot l'an cossiros.

22–27. The reference is apparently not to the *Roman de Renard*, but to the well-known fable; however, since the *Roman de Renard* was so popular, the name Renard could be given to any fox. Allusions to the same fable, without the name Renard, but with cherries instead of grapes, occur in the *tenso* of Bernart (de Ventadorn?) and Peirol (Appel, *Bernart von Ventadorn*, p. 277, lines 38–41):

> E la volps al sirieir dis o:
> Can l'ac de totas parts cerchat,
> Las sirieias vi lonh de se,
> E dis que no valion re,

and in the poem *Amis et Amiles* (ed. Hofmann, 1882, line 571).

23. *sabor*. Levy (*SW*, VII, 407) quotes this passage to illustrate the use of *aver sabor de* to mean "desire, crave;" see also Stronski, *Folquet de Marseille*, p. 264.

24. *autre temor*. Although I have found no other example of the word as masculine, I hesi-

tate to reject the reading of four good MSS (*ADIK*). Latin *timor* was masculine, and Aimeric makes the similar word *color* unquestionably masculine in 32, 30; likewise *error* in 39, 26.

26. *blasme·l.* See the note on 36, 7.

28. Cnyrim, *Sprichwörter*, no. 703.

29. *malgignos.* Raynouard (III, 456) and Levy (*PD*) give only the meaning "maladroit," the former with a quotation from Bernart de Venzac: *Prims sens fai home malginhos*, "Mince sens fait homme maladroit." That meaning hardly fits here, unless Aimeric means simply that Guilhem's argument is not clever. Jeanroy (*op. cit.*, p. 82) translates: "parce que vous êtes un déloyal," which seems much more to the point.

38. This line caused the copyists as much trouble as it has given to critics and translators (see, for example, Jeanroy, *op. cit.*, p. 82, note). Evidently "En Ot" was no better known then than he is now, for the scribes altered the phrase *cors d'En Ot* in several ways, *AD* even reaching the word *coredors*, which at least makes some sense in the context; a^1 simply omitted the phrase; only *IK* have what seems to be the correct reading (I am not absolutely certain that it is). The use of *cors* in such combinations as *mos cors* "I" (see Aimeric's poem 22, line 32), *vostre cors* "you," etc., is familiar; I do not recall another case of its use with *de* and a noun, as here, although there is no logical objection to such an extension. It may be that Guilhem is referring, not to a literary text, but to some actual event that both he and Aimeric had witnessed, there in Catalonia.

46. *Bar.* Neither Raynouard nor Levy lists an adjectival use of *bar* or *baro* with a proper name, as here, or with any noun; and I have found no other cases of such a use. But the reading is well supported, and the meaning seems clear.

48. Guilhem may be referring here to Aimeric's difficulties with his first love, in Toulouse, as related in the *Vida*.

20

I. De fin' amor comenson mas chansos
Plus que no fan de nulh' autra sciensa,
Qu'ieu non saubra nien s'amors no fos;
Ez anc tan car no compriei conoissensa,
Qu'ab belh semblan aissi cum fai traïre
Me vai doblan quascun jorn mo martire,
Qu'en la boca·m fes al prim doussezir
So que m'a fag pueys al cor amarzir.

II. Si de Merce acuzar fos razos,
Digna fora de ma desbevolensa,
Qu'Amors vens mi e Chauzimen amdos,
Ez us non a d'els poder que lieys vensa.
Per so·m cuja de tot en tot aucire,
Quar sap e ve que Merces n'es a dire.
Pero no·m vol ges solamen aucir,
Abans mi fai languen piegz de morir.

III. Piegz a de mort selh que viu cossiros,
E non a joy, mas dolor e temensa,
Pueys ve la ren que·l pogra far joyos
On no troba socors ni mantenensa.
E doncs hieu, las! qui sui d'est mal suffrire,
De mil dolors, fos d'un sol joy jauzire!
E ja no fos mas per mi escarnir,
Si·m degra far ab belh semblan languir.

IV. Mas non a tort, qu'ieu am lieys a rescos
Ins e mon cor e no·l n'aus far parvensa.
D'aitan sol fas a guiza d'orgulhos
Quar ges de lieys aus aver sovinensa;
Mas ieu non puesc ad Amor contradire:
So que·l platz am, e so que·l platz adire;
Pero cum folhs mi vuelh enfolhetir,
Quar encaus so qu'ieu no vuelh cosseguir.

V. Que·l sieus cars pretz es lo mielher dels bos,
Pueys la beutatz es eguals la valensa.
Cum plus remir ni vey d'autras faissos,

Ades m'es vis que sa beutatz agensa;
Per qu'ieu no·lh aus preyan mon cor devire;
Savals denan li fremisc e·lh sospire:
Quar sa beutatz fai ma boca mudir,
Mas sospiran la·n cug far avertir.

VI. Dels huelhs no vey lieys cui de cor remire,
Per qu'ensems plor mesclamens e sospire;
E si·s laisses a Merce covertir,
Dreit for' hueymais que·m fes vas si venir.

VII. Reys d'Aragon, tant aguizatz que dire
Als ben dizens q'us no sap on se vire,
Qu'a l'un bon fag faitz l'autre cosseguir,
Per qu'om tem dir lo ben pel mielhs gequir.

VARIANTS

I. 1–7 (*to* al prim) *lacking E, because of the excision of an illumination.* 1. comenza ma chansos *DSc.* 2. (Plus) Mais *AIK;* fai *DSc;* nuli *D;* autren s. *IKN.* 3. (Qu'ieu) Car *NRf;* sabria *RSc;* niem fors *D.* 5. fai atraire *C,* fals traire *DSc.* 6. (Me) Or *D;* chaschus ior *N;* (mo) lo *D,* li *Sc.* 7. Que *CR,* Ca *A,* Quem *D;* bocam am fes *D;* al primer dolcir *Sc,* al prim dolse *D.* 8. So qeram fai inz al cor a. *A;* al cors *f,* el cor *IKNRSc,* el cors *D;* amarguir *R,* amartir *c.*

II. 9. acauzir *E;* fon *f.* 10. fora *lacking c.* 11. (mi) lieys *ENRScf,* li *D;* iauziment *c.* 12. Et eu sai ben qua poder *D,* Et usau na del poder *S,* Eus aima del poder *c,* E uers non a de poder *f;* (d'els) en *A,* de *EIKNR* (*added later, above the line, in R*); (lieys) lui *c.* 13. Per so me uol *DSc;* del tot *Scf.* 14. (ve) ues *f.* 15. Per so *AIK,* E pois *D;* non *NSc,* nõ *DR;* (ges solamen) del tot uiatz *C;* aucire *c.* 16. (Abans) Enans *AIK;* (languen) aman *AEIKNRf.*

III. 17. Pretz *I;* (viu) uio *D,* uieu *R.* 18. iois *DSc.* 19. Qan ue *ADIK;* (ve) ues *f;* (que·l) qem *c.* 20. (On) E *D,* Ar *Sc;* (socors) sosteing *Sc.* 21. las *lacking f;* (d'est) del *DScf.* 22. (fos) fors *DS;* sol *lacking E;* (joy) ben *A.* 23. (ja) ça *D;* (no) noill *AIK;* (mi) un *Sc.* 24. (Si·m) Son *Sc,* Gim *f;* (ab) al *c,* a *D.*

IV. 26. Et en mon cor *DSc;* (e no·l n'aus) e noill aus *IK,* e non aus *Dc,* non aus *S;* fare p. *S;* pauença *N.* 27. Daitan fatz ieu *ADIKf;* (sol) eis *ENR,* en *Sc.* 28. (ges) sol *AEIKNRf,* soi *DSc;* souença *c.* 29. al amor *DSc.* 30. e so ques uol aire *E,* et so qell desplaz aire *S,* so qell desplaz aire *c, lacking D.* 31. *lacking f;* enfolezir *RSc,* esfoletir *D.* 32. (Quar) Qe *Sc,* Qeu *D;* encautz *A;* (qu'ieu) que *AR;* (vuelh) aus *ADIKNSc,* puesc *f.*

V. 33. Quels *IK,* Que *Sc;* son *Sc;* rics prez *Sc,* ris prec *D;* (lo) so *D, lacking E;* meillor(s) *NRSc;* del *DNSc.* 34. (es eguals) que ual a *f,* es egual *CEIKS;* (la valensa) a uolenza *Sc.* 35. (Cum) Quant *DSc;* ne uez *D,* ni ueg *Sc.* 36. (sa) la *C.* 37. (no·lh) non *E,* uoil *c;* (aus) posc *DSc;* mon cor preyan *DSc,* pregar ni cor *f.* 38. (Savals) Senals *D,* Mas qan *A,* Mas que *IK;* fremics *f;* (e·lh) et *DSc.* 39. *lacking DSc.* 40. *lacking DSc;* la cug *ER.*

VI. *lacking A.* 41. *lacking DSc;* (lieys cui de cor remire) ley mas del cor la remire *ERf* (la r *lacking E because of a cut*), leis mas del cor la mire *N,* mais del cor la remire *IK.* 42. *lacking DSc.* 43. (a) ab *Sc.* 44. (fes) fas *C,* fezes *Ef;* (vas) uer *D.*

VII. *lacking DScf*. 45. (aguizatz) agratz *E*, demostratz *AIK*, aguiratz *R;* (que) de *C*. 46. (ben) bons *IK*. 47. ben faich *A*. 48. (tem) ten *IK;* per *ER*.

TRANSLATION

I. My songs begin with the theme of faithful love, more than they do about any other knowledge, for I would know nothing if Love did not exist. Yet I never bought knowledge so dearly, for with fair pretenses, like a traitor, he doubles every day my misery. At the beginning he made that taste sweet in the mouth which afterwards turned bitter in the heart.

II. If it were right to accuse Mercy, it were worthy of my displeasure, for Love overcomes me and Mercy too; and neither one of us has the power to conquer him. Therefore he thinks to slay me utterly, for he knows and sees that Mercy is lacking. However, he does not wish to slay me quickly and wholly; rather he treats me worse than death, for I pine away.

III. He who lives in desire is worse than dead. He has no joy, only pain and fear, for he sees the creature who could make him glad, but finds in her neither help nor support. So I, alas, who suffer this ill,—would that I might rejoice in one joy, instead of a thousand sorrows! Even if it were but to mock me, she should at least make me pine away with a fair pretense.

IV. But she is not wrong, for I love her in secret, deep in my heart; nor do I dare to make a show of it. In this alone do I act like a proud man, in that I dare to remember her at all. But I cannot withstand Love. I love what he wills, and I hate what he wills. Therefore, like a madman, I wish to lose my mind, for I pursue what I do not wish to attain.

V. Her precious repute is the best of the good, for in her beauty and worth are equal. The more I look at other ladies' faces, the more it is my conviction that her beauty adorns all. Therefore I do not dare to lay bare my heart in prayers to her; at least I tremble and sigh before her. Her beauty makes my mouth mute; but I think to tell her of it by my sighs.

VI. I do not see with my eyes her whose image is in my heart. Therefore I weep and sigh together, in mingled wise. If she should let herself be converted to mercy, then it would be right for her to summon me to her side.

VII. King of Aragon, you provide the fine speakers with so much to speak about that no one of them knows where to turn. You make one noble deed follow another, so that one fears to praise you, lest he omit something better.

NOTES

Eleven MSS: *ACDEIKNRScf*. The most satisfactory stemma that can be established is probably this:

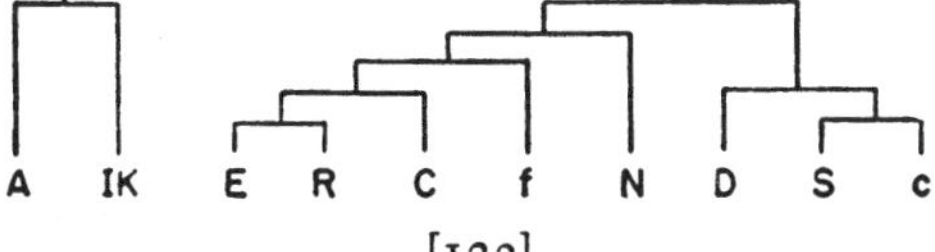

The main division rests largely on line 11, where *ACIK* have what would seem to be the correct reading; whatever division we make, we must admit that *C* at least had access to a MS of the other family, so the presence of the correct reading in *C* here is not an insuperable obstacle. For the smaller groups:

AIK: 2, 15, 16, 23, etc.
DSc: 1, 5, 13, 26, etc.
Sc: 7, 20, 23, etc.
ERf: 41 (here *C* has corrected a metrically wrong reading), 32
ER: 40, 48

The exact arrangement of *CENRf* is not certain, but there seems to be little doubt that both *N* and *f* belong with this group (3, 11); we place *N* as it is here because of line 32; in line 27, we may have to admit that *f* had access to a MS of the other group. As for *D*, its position with *Sc* appears certain, despite an occasional agreement with *AIK* (19, 27), due either to chance or to contamination of sources.

We have chosen *C* for our base.

A conventional love song, with little originality. But the commonplaces are so frequent that it is generally impossible to determine where Aimeric has taken the thought.

7. *doussezir.* See the note on poem 7, line 46.

10. *desbevolensa.* This is the only example of the word in Raynouard (V, 564); not in Levy, *SW*.

11. The *li* or *lieys* of the majority of the MSS seems to make nonsense.

12. *d'els.* This reading of *C* has no other MS support, and may possibly be wrong. According to our interpretation, one would expect *de·ns* (cf. Appel, *Chrestomathie*, p. xiv; no examples); but that reading does not occur in any of the MSS. Was the third person possible in such a case? The text of *DScf* is so different that no comparison is possible. If we read *de* (with *EIKNR*) or *en* (with *A*), we should probably take *us* not as "one," but as "usage, habitude" (Levy, *PD*): even becoming used to my loving her would not make her yield.

21. Cf. Folquet de Marseille (ed. Stronski), VIII, 13:

> E, s'entre tans mals n'ai un be,
> Ja no·us er dans ni desonors.

25–26. Cf. Folquet de Marseille, VII, 49:

> Qu'ins e mon cor l'amarai a rescos.

31. *mi vuelh enfoletir.* Only *enfolezir* is listed and exemplified as a reflexive verb by Raynouard (III, 352) and Levy (*SW*, II, 494; *PD*, 147), and Levy distinguishes in meaning between the two verbs. Three MSS (*RSc*) offer the reading *enfolezir;* but we do not feel obliged to change the reading of the majority of the MSS. Two verbs so similar in form and meaning were bound to be confused in time, even if they were once distinct, which seems open to question.

36. *agensa.* Although giving the meaning "plaire," neither Raynouard (III, 463) nor Levy (*SW*, I, 33) illustrates that use without an object, as here.

37. *devire.* The word seems clearly to mean "reveal." This meaning is not given in the dictionaries. Levy, *PD:* "diviser, partager; séparer; disperser; reconnaître." Cf., however, Folquet de Marseille (Stronski, IX, 25): *No vos ausi tot mon maltraich devire*, "Je n'ose pas vous retracer tout mon malheur."

In *Sc*, there is this extra envoi; text of *c:*

> Oi mais pois lo dous temps gais ue
> E la douça donna plaizenz
> En cui es preç iois e iouenz.

(*S:* lodoros temps gais ue.)

21

I. Destretz, cochatz, dezamatz, amoros,
Aissi cum selh qu'aman plor' e feuneia,
Vos vauc ancse merceyan en perdos;
Ez on plus vos mercey, mi desmerceya
Lo vostr' erguels qu'a Merce tol poder
De merceyar, pros dona de bon aire,
E quar vos sui merceyan fis amaire,
Segon Merce me degratz ben voler;
E si Merces merceyan no·m defen,
Endreg d'Amor pretz pauc merceyamen.

II. Pero ben sai que·m notz plus deves vos—
So qu'a mi par que plus valer mi deya—
Vostre rics pretz e l'avinens faissos
E·l guays solatz qu'ab mezura pareya
E·l sens que·us fa conoisser e vezer
Lo mal e·l be, e·us es fis cosselhaire
Del mal gequir e del ben dir e faire;
Per que no·n faitz forfaitz ni non-dever
Mays qu'enves mi cui faitz planher soven:
Ve·us lo mieu dan e·l vostre falhimen.

III. E quar ab sen etz plus guay' e plus pros
Ez aquelha que mielhs parl' e cunhdeya,
Devetz gardar vostre pretz per un dos.
Cum plus cai d'aut, pretz plus franh e pesseya;
Mas pretz mesclatz ab sen no pot chazer.
Doncs, de que·m fatz parliers ni chastiaire?
Qu'ab sol jauzen que·m fezes pauc ni guaire,
Ren no·us pogr'om blasmar ni vil tener.
Ez ieu quier vos, en luec de jauzimen,
Lo belh semblan, qu'autre pro no·i aten.

IV. Grans for' a mi ez a vos paucs lo dos,
Tan mi destrenh vostr' amors e·m guerreya;
E fa·m soven irat e tart joyos
E·m defen so que chauzimens m'autreya.
Mas savals mielhs m'en deuriatz valer
Al meynhs d'aitan quar vos sui merceyaire,

Si be no·m faitz, que no·m fessetz mal traire,
E del benfait fos al vostre plazer,
Qu'ie·us servirai preian tan lonjamen
Que·m faretz ben, o morrai vos serven.

V. En Castelha, al valen rey N'Amfos,
Quar es lo mielhs qu'om auja el mon ni veya,
Ans qu'alhor ans, vai de part mi, chansos,
Qu'elh melhura quan autre reys sordeya.
De guazanhar pretz et de retener
Nulhs reys non lh'es pars ni nulhs emperaire,
Per qu'es totz sols, qu'om no·l pot trobar fraire;
Qu'eu·m meravilh cum pot en lui caber
Lo pretz qu'elh tolh e raub' ez embl' e pren
E compr' ades, e no·n dona ni·n ven.

VI. La reyna de Tolosa eissamen
Val sobr' autras si cum aurs sobr' argen.

VARIANTS

I. 1. Destre *I;* desamant *U;* amors *N.* 2. cama *R,* qe man *U,* qa maint *AB;* feunia *ABCR.* 3. (vauc) uan *D;* anse *K,* ab sen *R.* 4. (mi) uos *R.* 5. uostrorgoillos *IK;* (qu'a) qab *U,* a *f.* 7. Ep pos uos soi D; fin *C.* 8. degaz *U,* de degras *f;* ualer *AB.* 9. merce *C;* (no·m) non *DUc.* 10. damos *f;* pauc pretz *R;* mercean *U.*

II. 11. quen nos *DIKc,* qe noz *U;* (deves vos) doc uas uos *C,* denan uos *R,* domna ab uos *IK.* 12. So qe mi *Uc,* So camin *IKN;* (plus) mais *IKNUc.* 13. ric *CIKNRc,* fins *M;* e las plazens f. *R.* 14. guai *CMRUcf;* solat *f.* 15. (sens) fei *R;* qe fai *U,* qeu fais *c.* 16. *lacking D;* Lo ben el mal *AB;* queus es *ABN,* uos es *RU,* uos el *cf;* fin *C.* 17. De mal *RUc.* 18. nom *CKN,* mon *I;* foriatz *N;* mon deuer *I,* nom deuer *K.* 19. (qu'enves mi) qant uas mi *ABIKNR,* enues mi *Mf;* (cui) qui *C,* quem *IKR,* quẽ *N.* 20. Ves *Uc;* dan uostre lo f. *U,* dan e uostre f. *c;* falimenz *N.*

III. 21. sens *Uc;* gais *U.* 23. per per uns dos *c.* 24. (Cum) On *IKMNf,* Don *R;* pus aut cay *R,* plus daut chai *IKMNUc;* plus frainh pretz *f.* 25. mesclat *CIKNUc,* gardat *R;* quab sen *C,* ab sem *N,* per sen *R.* 26. (de) e *IKN;* quen *I,* quẽ *C;* fai *M,* fauc *f.* 27. Cab quem fessetz iauzen petit ni g. *R;* Qual sol *C;* gauzem *BUc,* cauzent *IK;* qen *M;* fet ses *N;* pau *C;* (ni) o *MNf.* 28. (Ren no·us) Res nous *CM,* Ren nos *IKN,* Ren non uos *U,* Ren nos uos *c,* Nous o *AB,* No uous *R,* Don nous *f.* 29. Et ieu preiraus *ABN,* Et eu penraus *IK,* Et ieu prenc uos *R,* Et eu presera uos *U,* Et eu pregrera uos *c;* chauzimen *R.* 30. *lacking D;* (qu'autre pro) cautre faich *ABIKNUc,* quen alre *R;* (no·i) non *ABRc.*

IV. 31. ab uos *U.* 32. (e·m) et *Uc.* 33. Em fai *ABIKMNR,* E fa *Uc;* souen dirat (irat *B*) estar ioyos *AB.* 34. En *c,* Qan *B;* iausimen *Uc;* m' *lacking C.* 35. Mas uos siuals men (mi *IKN*) d. u. *ABIKNUc,* Mar er siuals me d. u. *R,* Pero siuals miels d. u. *f;* deuria *CN;* uoler *DM.* 36. de tan *D;* sui fis amaire *AB.* 37. (Si) Pois *IKN;* non fas *M;* que ñ f. *D;* fassat *f,* fet ses *N.*

38. ben faitz *IKN;* (fos) fas *R*, uos *IK;* (al) el *M*, en *Uc*, a *D;* (plazer) uoler *f*, lezer *IKN*. 39. Qeu *U*, Qen *c*, Que eus *N*. 40. (faretz) fezetz *IK;* morra *C;* serueu *D*.

V. 41. En castel al *Uc*. 42. Ques lo meiller *AB;* com augera ni *IKN*, qom aoga eram (era ni *c*) *Uc*. 43. ans *lacking Uc;* de (da *U*) ma part *NRUc*, da part mi *M*. 44. autre rey *CMR*, autra ren *Uc*. 45. (et) ni *IKNRUc;* de *lacking Uc*. 46. Noill (Non *IKN*) es nulhs reis pars *ABIKNUc*, Non li es pars n. r. ni *R;* Nulh rey *C;* non illes pars *M;* (ni nulhs) ni *Uc*, *lacking I*. 47. (sols) sels *R;* (no·l) noi *Uc;* (fraire) faire *D*, paire *Uc*. 48. Qem *Uc*. 49. (qu'elh) qi *c*, que *R;* tol rauba embla *R*, tot embla e raube pren *f;* embra *Uc*. 50. En (E *R*) con pranc (planc *I*) se *IKNR;* (E) El *f*, En *B;* (e) ni *ABD;* ni uen *MUc*, nien *f*.

VI. *lacking DMRUcf* (*space left blank in M*). 51. La reyna de bon ensenhamen *C*, La reina de bolen eissamen *N*.

TRANSLATION

I. Distressed, afflicted, unloved, loving, like the lover who weeps and is sad, I crave your mercy always, but in vain; and when I seek it most, your pride, which takes from Mercy the power of granting mercy, refuses it most to me, worthy and well-born Lady. Since I am your faithful lover, beseeching mercy, according to Mercy you should wish me well. And if Mercy, seeking mercy, does not defend me, I prize Mercy little where love is concerned.

II. But I know well what harms me most in your eyes,—what it seems to me should help me most,—your noble fame, your graceful manner, your gift of gay social intercourse, equal to your moderation, and the wisdom which makes you recognize and see evil and good and which is your faithful counselor about forsaking evil and saying and doing good. Therefore you do no wrong nor unrighteousness, except toward me whom you make often lament. Behold my hurt and your wrong!

III. Because with wisdom you are the gayest and worthiest and she who speaks best and is most attractive, you should doubly guard your fame. The farther it falls, the more is fame broken and shattered; but fame mixed with wisdom cannot fall. Therefore, why do I make myself a talker or a censor? For a single favor that you might grant me, small or insignificant, no one could blame you or belittle you. In place of a favor, all I seek of you is a kind look; no other advantage do I expect from you.

IV. Such a gift were great for me and small for you, since love of you so masters me and wars on me and makes me often sad and tardily glad and forbids me to take what Pity grants to me. At least you should help me, because I am he who craves your pity, thus much, that if you cannot treat me well, you will not make me suffer. Let the kind deed be according to your pleasure, for I shall serve you with prayers so long that you will finally do me a kindness —or I shall die in your service.

V. Into Castile, to the valiant King Alfonso, the best whom one can hear or see in the world, before you go elsewhere, go, in my name, Song, for he grows better where another king grows worse. No king nor emperor is his peer in winning fame or keeping it. Therefore he is all alone: one cannot find his brother in fame. I wonder how he can keep within himself the fame which he seizes and steals and robs and takes and buys always, and does not give away or sell.

VI. The Queen of Toulouse likewise is prized more than others, as gold is more prized than silver.

NOTES

Twelve MSS: *ABCDIKMNRUcf*. The most satisfactory stemma that can be established is probably this:

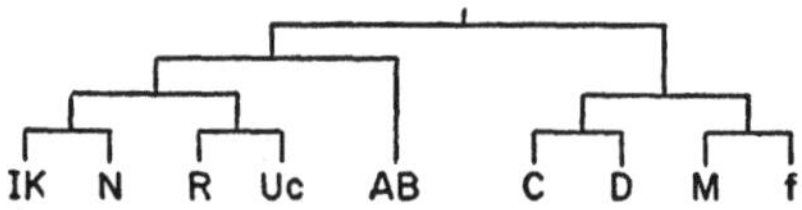

ABIKNRUc: 29, 30, 46 (-*R*)
CDMf: 19, 30 (lacking in *D*), 35, 46
IKNRUc: 45
IKN: 12, 28, 37, 38, 42
RUc: 17, 43 (+*N*)
Uc: 20, 38, 44
AB: 8, 16, 28
CD: 19
Mf: 19
Actually, the groups *RUc*, *CD*, and *Mf* are not very certain; but the other groups and the main divisions seem well defined.

We have chosen *C* for a base.

1. *Destreitz, cochatz.* Cf. Peire Vidal (ed. Anglade, XL, 49): *E destreitz e coitos.*

3–10. For the repetition of ***merce***, and the phrase ***merces merceyan*** (line 9), cf. Ponz de Capduoill (ed. Napolski, XIX, 37):

> Chauzimens es, quan pot merce trobar
> Selh qu'ab merce quier merce merceyan, etc.

23. *per un dos*. See the note on poem 7, line 20.

24. Compare Folquet de Marseille's lines (ed. Stronski, XII, 10):

> Pero, qan faill cel qu'es pros ni prezatz,
> Tant cant val mais tant n'es plus encolpatz.

26. The nominatives *parliers* and *chastiaire* are apparently used in this not uncommon construction because *de que·m fatz* is equivalent to "why do I become?" Cf. Folquet de Marseille, XVIII, 43: *Qui·s fan plus* frevol *de glassa.*

51. *C*'s reading is evidently an attempt to patch up an illegible or incomprehensible line. It will be noted that no other MS of the group to which *C* belongs contains the ***tornada***. The same "Queen of Toulouse" appears in poem 46; as we have explained in the Introduction, she is Eleanor, daughter of Alfonso II of Aragon, and wife of Raymond VI of Toulouse.

22

I. De tot en tot es er de mi partitz
Aquelh eys joys que m'era remazutz.
Sabetz per que suy aissi esperdutz?
Per la bona comtessa Beatritz,
Per la gensor e per la plus valen,
Qu'es mort'! Oi, Dieus! quan estranh partimen,
Tan fer, tan dur, don ai tal dol ab me
Qu'ab pauc lo cor no·m part quan m'en sove.

II. On es aras sos belhs cors gen noiritz,
Que fo pels bos amaz e car tengutz?
E·i venia hom cum si fezes vertutz,
Que ses son dan saup far guays los marritz.
E quan quascun avia fag jauzen,
Tornava·ls pueys en maior marrimen
Al comïat, qu'om no·n avia be,
Des qu'en partis, que no·i tornes dese.

III. Que·l sieus solatz era guays e chauzitz,
E l'aculhirs de "Ben siatz vengutz";
E sos parlars fis ez aperceubutz,
E·l respondres plazens ez abelhitz,
E sos esguars dous, um pauc en rizen,
E sos onrars plus onratz d'onramen.
De totz bos ayps avia mais ab se
Qu'autra del mon, e de beutat, so cre.

IV. Per cui er hom mais honratz e servitz?
Ni per cui er bos trobars entendutz?
Ni per cui er hom tan gent ereubutz?
Ni per cui er belhs motz ris ni grazitz?
Ni per cui er belhs chans fagz d'avinen?
Ni per cui er domneys en son enten?
Diguatz per cui ni cumsi ni per que!
Hieu non o sai, ni mos cors non ho ve.

V. Domna, Jovens es ab vos sebelhitz,
E Gaugz entiers sosterratz e perdutz.
Ja·s tenia sol per vostras salutz

Totz hom ses plus per rics e per guaritz.
Dol pot haver qui vi vostre cors gen,
E qui no·l vi, dol—mas non tan cozen.
Autra vista no·i poc metre pueys be,
Tant ac lo cor, qui·us vi, del vezer ple.

VI. Na Beatritz, Dieus, qu'es ples de merce,
Vos acompanh ab sa mair' ez ab se.

VARIANTS

I. 2. Aquel eis eis i. D^a; romazutz D^a*IK*. 3. (suy) sun D^a; enaysi *R*. 5. (valen) plazen D^a*IK*. 6. (Oi) o *IK*, uei *E;* (quan) tan *R*. 7. (ab) en *E*. 8. Ca pauc D^a*IKR*, Quan pauc *E;* (part) faill D^a*IK;* (m'en) mi *R*.

II. *lacking E*. 10. Qe fon bels bons *IK; in R* bels *has been expunctuated and* pels *substituted*. 12. sap *IK*. 13. cascus *R*. 16. (qu'en) qem D^a*IK;* (que) si D^a*IK*, qui *R*.

III. *lacking E*. 18. aculhir *C*. 20. respondre *C*D^a*IKR*. 21. ses esgart D^a; rien *R*. 22. (E) O *C*.

IV. *lacking E* (Order of verses: 25, 28, 27, 26, 28, 29, 30, 31, 32 D^a; 25, 28, 26, 29, 30, 31 *I;* 25, 28, 27, 26, 29, 30, 31 *K;* 25, 27, 26, 28, 31, 32 *R*). 25. (e) ni D^a*IKR*. 27. *lacking I;* hom may tan gen *R;* (ereubutz) reseubutz D^a*KR*. 29. *lacking R;* Ni per cui er hom mais (mais hom D^a) en pensamen D^a*IK*. 30. *lacking R;* De far tals faitz que fosson dauinen D^a*IK*. 32. *lacking IK;* (ho ve) o coue D^a.

V. 35. (Ja·s) Qes D^a*IK;* cenia D^a; pel *IK;* uostra D^a*R*. 36. Tot *C;* plus *lacking I*. 38. (no·l) nous *E;* consen *I*. 39. Dautra D^a*IK;* (be) re D^a*IKR*. 40. (ac) anc D^a, nac *IK;* (del) de *ER*.

VI. 42. a sa maire ab se D^a.

TRANSLATION

I. That same joy which was left me now is taken from me entirely. Do you know why I am so afflicted? For the good Countess Beatrice, the noblest and most worthy of all, who is dead. Ah God! what a cruel loss, painful and hard to bear! It causes me such woe that my heart well nigh breaks when I think of it.

II. Where is now her fair, well nurtured body, which was loved and held dear by all good folk? Men came to see her as if she could work miracles, for without harm to herself she could make the afflicted happy. And when she had made each one joyful, they became afterwards still more downcast at parting, for no one, after he had left her, was happy if he did not go back to her at once.

III. Her conversation was gay and polite, her greeting was "Be you welcome", her speech witty and intelligent, her answers pleasing and agreeable, her glances sweet, smiling a little, and her way of doing honor more honorable than Honor. She had more good qualities and more beauty than any other lady in the world, I believe.

IV. By whom will one now be honored and served? By whom will good verse-making be heard? By whom will one be made so nobly happy? By whom will fine words be greeted with a smile and rewarded? For whom will fair songs be made in a pleasing way? For whom will lady-service be in one's intention? Tell me for whom or how or for what. I do not know, nor do I see how it can be.

V. Lady, Youth is buried with you, and all Joy is interred and lost. Once, every man thought himself noble and healthy by your greeting alone. He who has seen your fair body may well feel sorrow; and also he who never saw it, but not such poignant grief. He could never put the sight of any other lady in your place, because, once he had seen you, his heart was always full of that vision.

VI. Lady Beatrice, may God, who is full of mercy, place you beside his Mother and Himself.

NOTES

Six MSS: *C*D^{a}*EIKR* (stanzas II–IV have been cut out of *E*).
Stemma:

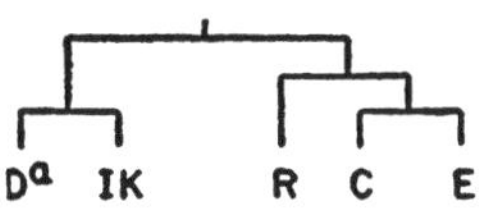

D^{a}*IK:* 16, 25–28 (order), 29, 30
IK: 10, 35
CER: no obviously faulty readings in common, but cf. 5, 8 (*part, faill*), 35, 39, where it would be possible to take either the version of *CER* or that of D^{a}*IK* as the true reading. As for the grouping *CE*, it is supported by line 39 (re, be); but so much is lacking in *E* that its position is doubtful. The common order of poems (10, 22, 11, 49) in *CE*, however, makes a common source likely. We have chosen *C* as our base.

A ***planh*** for a Countess Beatrice, whom one would be tempted to identify with Beatrice of Este. We have discussed the difficulties raised by this identification in our Introduction, and they are considerable. Other possibilities are likewise discussed in the Introduction; but they must remain only possibilities, since our knowledge is not extensive enough to permit us either to prove or to disprove them.

20. ***abelhitz***. An active use of the past participle, not illustrated in Raynouard (II, 207); the word is not in Levy, *SW*.

25–32. This stanza caused the copyists much trouble. No two MSS (not even *IK*) have the same lines in the same order. It may be that our text follows *C* too closely, and that lines 29–30 as we present them are an invention of the scribe of *C*. They are quite different in D^{a}*IK*, which agree among themselves. But D^{a}*IK* are derived from a single source, and these lines may equally well have been inserted there to fill an existing lacuna. Since they do not occur at all in *R*, it seems likely that the original was faulty, and that various attempts were made to correct it. The order of verses is also questionable, and neither logic nor syntax is of any assistance. We follow *C* throughout the stanza, even where it stands alone, because it is the only MS which has eight lines arranged according to the proper rime-scheme, and any deviation from it would have to be arbitrary and subjective. Furthermore, if *C* is wrong in reading *ereubutz* for *reseubutz* in line 27, its wrong reading is a mistake in the right direction, away from banality.

28. *ris.* This transitive use is not clearly illustrated in the dictionaries.

30. *en son enten.* If *C*'s reading is correct, the *son* refers very loosely indeed to the *hom* of line 27.

32. *mos cors*, i.e., "I." Cf. poem 19, line 38, note.

23

I. Domna, per vos estauc en greu turmen.
Senher, que folhs faitz, qu'ieu grat no·us en sen.
Domna, per Dieu, aiatz en chauzimen!
Senher, vostres precs hi anatz perden.
Bona dona, ja·us am ieu finamen.
Senher, et ie·us vuelh pietz qu'a l'autra gen.
Domna, per so n'ai ieu lo cor dolen.
Senher, et ieu alegre e jauzen.

II. Domna, ja muer per vos sens nulh cofort.
Senher, ben trop n'auretz faich lonc acort.
Domna, ja es ma vida piegz de mort.
Senher, so·m platz, sol que no·us n'aya tort.
Domna, de vos non ai mas desconort.
Senher, e doncs cujatz qu'ie·us am per fort?
Domna, ab un semblan m'agratz estort.
Senher, respieit no·n aiatz ni conort.

III. Domna, vauc doncs alhors clamar merce.
Senher, anatz de sai; qui vos rete?
Domna, no puesc, que vostr' amors me te.
Senes cosselh, senher, o fa de me.
Domna, trop mal mi respondetz ancse.
Senher, quar piegz vos vuelh qu'az autra re.
E doncs, dona, no·m faretz ja nulh be?
Senher, aissi er cum disez, so cre.

IV. Amors, gitat m'avetz a "no m'en cal."
Amics, per Dieu, no·us en puesc far ren al.
Amors, e vos ja meretz de tot mal.
Amics, per so vo·n trairai san e sal.
Amors, per que·m fetz chauzir don' aital?
Amix, ieu vos mostrei so que mais val.
Amors, no puesc sofrir l'afan coral.
Amix, per so queiram autre logual.

V. Amors, en tot quan faichs vos vei falhir.
Amix, a gran tort me voletz laidir.

Amors, e doncs per que·ns voletz partir?
Amix, quar greu m'es quan vos vey morir.
Amors, ja no cujetz qu'alhor me vir.
Amix, per so pessatz del ben soffrir.
Amors, sembla·us si ja·n poirai jauzir?
Amix, oc vos, sufren et ab servir.

VARIANTS

I. 2. Seingner folls es que null grat nous en sen *M;* fols i fatz *LN;* en *lacking LN.* 3. (en) er *M.* 4. (hi) en *L;* ananz *IK.* 5. iauz am *R.* 6. eu uoill *IKf,* ieu uos uuelh *R;* qaz autra gen *Mf;* autre *N.* 7. ieu *lacking D;* (lo) mon *M.* 8. alegres e i. *L,* alegre i. *N.*

II. 9. (ja muer per vos) eu m. p. u. *IK,* per uos morrai *M;* (nulh) tot *MR;* conort *L.* 10. (ben) bon *D;* naues *f.* 11. *lacking N;* (es) mes *M;* mortz *R.* 12. *lacking N;* sol quieus (quieu *Mf*) non (noi *Mf*) aia tort *DIKMf;* qieu *L;* (n'aya) haia *L;* tortz *R.* 14. E doncs seinher *M;* (e doncs) adonc *L;* per *lacking LN.* 15. ab un bel semblan *DL;* magr estort *L.* 16. S. de me non auretz mais c. *N;* S. ia respieg *f;* (no·n) noi *LM.*

III. 17. (vauc) ual *D;* (doncs) men *M.* 18. (de sai) desait *M,* dazai *N,* daz haia *L,* dazen *R,* dols aia *f,* e doncs *C;* quieus rete *f,* qe os reren *L.* 19. (que) qar *L.* 20. Senher senes c. *M;* fas *IKM,* fatz *Lf.* 22. (vos) os *L.* 23. Adonc *L;* (no·m) non *MN.* 24. com uos d. *MNf.*

IV. *lacking L.* 26. non puesc faire *M,* non puesc far *f;* (ren al) en cal *D.* 27. *lacking Df;* (meretz) mires *IKN.* 28. *lacking D;* (per so vo·n) per sous en *IKMNRf;* trairei *C,* tranrieu *N.* 29. Amors e per que *I;* fezes *IK;* dona tal *IK.* 30. (ieu vos) ieus *N.* 32. qiran *D,* quiram *I,* qerres *M,* queretz *f;* (logual) iornal *D.*

V. *lacking L.* 34. (laidir) maldir *DM.* 35. E doncs amors *M;* (que·ns) queus *f,* quen *I,* qem *KM.* 36. (quan) qar *DMNRf;* grieus *M;* (morir) pertir *D.* 37. (no) nos *M;* alor *C.* 38. per so *lacking f;* de ben *IMf.* 39. (sembla·us) sabrai *M;* poira *M.* 40. uos oc *M,* o uos *D.*

TRANSLATION

I. Lady, I am in grievous torment because of you.—Sir, you act like a fool, for I feel no gratitude to you for that.—Lady, for God's sake, have pity on me!—Sir, you are wasting your time in prayers.—Good Lady, I love you truly.—Sir, I hate you worse than anyone else.—Lady, that afflicts my heart.—Sir, my heart is gay and joyful.

II. Lady, I am dying for you without hope.—Sir, you have clung to that desire too long. —Lady, my life is worse than death.—Sir, I am glad of that, provided that I do not wrong you.—Lady, I get nothing but affliction from you.—Sir, do you think that I will love you by force?—Lady, one glance would have saved me.—Sir, have no hope or expectation of that.

III. Lady, I go therefore to ask pity of another.—Sir, go; who is keeping you?—Lady, I cannot; your love holds me here.—Sir, it does that without asking my advice.—Lady, you always answer me too badly.—Sir, that is because I hate you more than anything.—So then, Lady, you will never be kind to me?—Sir, it will be just as you say, I believe.

IV. Love, you have cast me out into "I don't care".—Friend, for God's sake, I cannot do otherwise.—Love, you deserve then altogether evil.—Friend, I shall get you out of this sound and well.—Love, why did you make me choose such a lady?—Friend, I showed you the worthiest.—Love, I cannot endure the woe of my heart.—Friend, let us seek therefore another abiding-place.

V. Love, in everything you do I see you err.—Friend, you wish to insult me very wrongfully.—Love, why then do you wish to part us?—Friend, because it afflicts me to see you die. —Love, do not think that I shall ever turn to another woman.—Friend, bethink you then! You must be patient.—Love, does it seem to you that I shall ever be happy?—Friend, yes, by dint of suffering and service.

NOTES

Nine MSS: *CDIKLMNRf*. The first three stanzas are quoted in the *Breviari d'amor*, line 30696 (variants: 1. (*greu*) *gran*. 7. *cors*. 9. *per uos morrai*. 10. (*n'auretz*) *auetz*. 12. *sol quieu non aia tort*. 15. *Don am un bel semblan*. 18. *mal aia quieus rete*. 20. *faitz*. 22. *qua nulha re*. 23. (*ja nulh*) *altre*. 24. *Enaici er cum o dizetz*). Critical edition (not using all MSS) in Bartsch-Koschwitz, *Chrestomathie*, col. 175–177. With two exceptions (noted below) our edition differs from this one only in orthography.

The only even moderately constant groups are *IK*, which one can take for granted, and *Mf* (6, 13, 24, 26, 38). A couple of variants would point to a group *LN* (2, 14), but this is hardly decisive evidence. Further, one cannot go. It seems likely, from the number of lines missing from various MSS, that the original text was corrupt or illegible in spots. A stemma is out of the question.

Base: *C*.

A fictitious *tenso* between the poet and his Lady (I–III) and between the lover and Love (IV–V).

2. For the locution *far que* plus a nominative, common enough in Old French and Old Provençal, see the references in Appel's *Chrestomathie*, glossary (*far*).

10. *acort*. The dictionaries give no examples of just this use of the word, although there can be little doubt of the meaning here.

12. Bartsch-Koschwitz: *sol qu'eu·s non aia tort*.

14. *per fort*. Raynouard (II, 429, under *cuidar*) quotes this passage, and translates "très fort." Levy (*SW*, III, 571) corrects this to "gezwungenerweise," which seems preferable.

18. *de sai*. The original text evidently puzzled the copyists here. We adopt the reading which has the best MS support, but with a feeling amounting almost to certainty that it is incorrect. For one thing, it is very weak. For another, this simple phrase would not have caused the slightest difficulty, and the MSS would have been unanimous in preserving it. Surely what Aimeric wrote was a word or phrase corresponding to the Old French *dehet ait* "cursed be he." But, as far as we can discover, this does not occur elsewhere in Provençal (though

the *Breviari*'s reading *mal aia* supports our conjecture), and we have not ventured to introduce into the text a form made out of whole cloth. (Bartsch-Koschwitz also read *de sai.*)

22. *quar.* For a similar elliptical use of *quar*, see line 36; "(I do so) because."

28. Bartsch-Koschwitz: *per so·us en trairai.*

38. *del ben soffrir.* The infinitive used as a noun, with the article, is common enough in Old Provençal; see poem 37, line 7, *del far.*

39. We have found no other use of *semblar* construed thus, with *si.*

40. *oc vos.* The use of a personal pronoun with the word for "yes" is fairly frequent in Provençal, as in Old French. Cf. Folquet de Marseille (ed. Stronski), I, 41; III, 51, etc.

24

I. Yssamen cum l'aÿmans
Tira·l fer e·l trai vas se,
Tir' Amors mon cor ancse,
Qu'es forser e mais tirans;
E mos fortz cors atressi,
Quar es forssatz, forssa mi;
Per qu'ieu, a forsa de vos,
Domna·us am totas sazos.

II. Pero maltraitz ni afans
No·m dezenansa ni·m te
De vos servir mielhs de be,
Quals que·m sia pros o dans.
Mas fag m'avetz Ansessi
Mon cor que per vos m'auci,
Que·m sol esser fis e bos,
Mas ar m'es fagz enginhos.

III. Qu'ieu solia esser clamans
De mos huelhs mas d'autra re;
Mas era·m clam, per ma fe,
De mo fals cor mil aitans,
Qu'er non ai cor, so·us afi,
Qu'al prim que·m vis ez hie·us vi,
S'emblet de mi a rescos,
Don hieu remanh ses cor blos.

IV. Ves vos fis, ves me truans,
Es mos cors, e sai per que:
Quar neguna no·s capte
Tan gen, ni es tan parlans,
Ni acuelh tan be ni ri.
E sabetz quals ni cossi?
Qu'al partir l'avols e·l pros
N'es ses vostre dan joyos.

V. Tant es cuenhd' e benestans,
Guaya, la genser qu'om ve,

E·l pretz, aissi co·s cove,
Es, segon la beutat, grans;
Per qu'Amors pres e chauzi,
Quar es plus fin' al plus fi,
Qu'ie·us fos fis ez amoros,
Ez hieu soi plus fis qu'anc fos.

VI. Quar sui plus fis dels amans
E no·m biays ni·m recre,
Non per mi, mas per merce,
Vos fos, pros domna, prezans
Que·m fetzsetz ric de mesqui.
Sol d'aitan pus no·m cambi,
Suffretz qu'ie·us am em perdos,
Ez er grans lo guazardos.

VII. Totz lo mons s'acord' ab mi,
Ves on qu'ieu an enaissi,
Que·l rics reys valens N'Amfos
Es de totas bontatz bos.

VIII. De la contess' atressi
De Sobeiratz so·us afi:
Que sos pretz e sa faissos
Es l'us belhs e l'autre bos.

VARIANTS

I. 2. ***added in margin in** N;* (e·l) e D^c; ua se *D*. 3. (ancse) a se *AE*, ia se *DJ*, ues se *IK*, ab se *R*. 4. (forser) plus fortz *C*, forsor D^c, forseis *J*, for sors *R;* (mais) plus *ADD*^{c}*EIJKNR*. 5. (fortz) folz *AEJ;* cor D^c*R*. 6. es *lacking I;* (forssa) forsan *R*. 7. Per quieu (que ieu *R*) forsaz de uos *NR*. 8. tota sazos *N*.

II. 9. mals traitz *AD*. 12. Cal *I;* quen D^c*EIJ;* sial pros ol dans *EJ*. 13. (fag) frach *R;* m' *lacking DD*^{c}*E;* amsesi *IK*, enaissi *R*. 14. Que mos cors per uos mausi *D;* Mos cors *R*. 15. Quen *I*, Que *R;* soli esser *EJ*. 16. era *EJ;* (m'es fagz enginhos) mes fals (fols *D*) e ginhos *ADEJ*, mes fals engignos *IK*, me fatz e. *N*, me fals e gignos D^c, mes contrarios *R*.

III. 18. (mas) plus *AEIJK;* (d'autra) que de *R*. 20. mon cor fals *D*. 21. Quar *E*. 22. quen *I;* (ez hie·us vi) et eu uos ui *DEJN*, et uos mi *R*. 24. (Don) Et *ADIKR;* remas *ADEIJKR*.

IV. 25. Pos iois fis uai mi truanz *N* (*corrected much later to* Ves uos fis), Pus que fis ioys mes t. *R;* (Ves) Bes *IK*. 26. E mon cor *R;* (sai) sabetz *EJ*. 28. Tant ben nis (ni *R*) tant gen p. *AR*, Tan ben ni est bon e p. *N*. 29. (be) gen *JR*. 30. (ni) e *R*. 31. lauol *C*, laols *IKN*.

V. 33. benestan *R*. 34. Que la gensser es com ue *ADEJ;* gensor *IKNR*. 35. cous coue *AE*. 36. (Es) Que *CIKNR;* la (las *R*) beutatz *DNR*. 37. (pres e) pretz li *R*, aissi *AD*, *lacking EJ*.

38. (es) etz *CIJKN;* (fin' al) fi ual *R.* 39. Queus sui francs et a. *D,* Et ieu plus fis a uos *EJ,* Queu soi fis et a. *R.* 40. Et plus leials quanc mais fos *DEJ,* E fols lo plus fis canc fos *R,* E sols plus fis canc fos *N;* (soi) sol *C.*

VI. 41. Car sol *A;* (fis dels) fizels *DEJ,* leials *A.* 42. (ni·m recre) nin cre *D,* en re *EJ.* 43. Nom *N.* 44. pro *C.* 45. Quen *I.* 46. non *D.* 48. (er) es *A;* guizardos *EJ,* guizerdos *A,* giardos *D.*

VII. 49. sab cord *D.* 50. Vezon *R;* (an) am *R.* 51. Quel ualen ric rey nanfos *R.*

VIII. *lacking DJR.* 53. antressi *N.* 54. (De) Se *A;* (so·us) uos *A.* 55. sas faissos *ACEIK.*

TRANSLATION

I. Just as the lodestone draws and drags the iron toward it, so Love draws my heart always, Love who is stronger and more powerful; and my strong heart likewise, because it is forced, forces me. Therefore I, by force of you, Lady, love you always.

II. Therefore neither pain nor suffering can dishearten me, nor hold me back from serving you better than well, whether it bring me profit or loss. But you have made of my heart an Assassin, who kills me for your sake; for it was wont to be faithful and true to me, but it has now become a deceiver.

III. I was once wont to accuse my eyes more than anything else; but now, by my faith, I accuse my false heart a thousand times as much. Now, I assure you, I have no heart; for the first time you saw me and I you, it fled from me in secret, so that I remain deprived of a heart.

IV. My heart is faithful to you, but false to me; and I know why: because no lady bears herself so nobly, nor is so apt of speech, nor welcomes nor laughs so well. And do you know whom or how? Because, at parting, the good and the bad are alike joyous about you, without any hurt to you.

V. She is so graceful, so perfect, so gay, the noblest that one can see; and her reputation, as is fitting, is, according to her beauty, great (her reputation is as great as her beauty). Therefore Love, since he is most loyal to the most faithful, took and chose me to be faithful and loving to you; and I am more faithful now than I ever was.

VI. Since I am the most faithful of lovers and never go astray or draw back, it would be laudable, honored Lady, for you to make me happy instead of wretched, not for my sake, but for Mercy's. Solely because I never change, suffer me to love you without reward, and great will be my guerdon.

VII. Everyone agrees with me, wherever I go, that the brave and valiant king, Lord Alfonso, is endowed with all good gifts.

VIII. In regard to the Countess of Sobiratz, I assure you likewise that her fame and her face are the one fair and the other great.

NOTES

Ten MSS: *ACDD^cEIJKNR.* Of these, *D^c* contains only the first two stanzas. The first stanza is quoted in the *Breviari d'amor,* line 29010 (Variants: 3. (*ancse*) *vas se.* 4. *plus fort e plus.* 5. *cors fols*).

The following stemma indicates the relationships fairly well, although there are minor deviations from it:

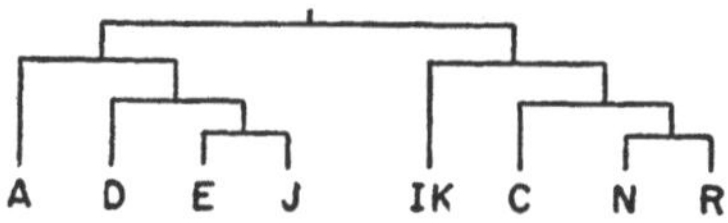

ADEJ: 16, 34
DEJ: 41, 42
EJ: 15, 16, 26, 37, 39

CIKNR: 36
IK: 3, 16, etc.
CNR: 3, 16
NR: 7, 25

Base: *C.*

1–2. See the note on poem 12, lines 25–27.

4. *forser.* This original reading was evidently rejuvenated to *plus fortz* by the copyist of *C.*

11. *mielhs de be.* I am inclined to follow Stronski (edition of Folquet de Marseille, glossary: *miels*) in taking this as a simple adverbial phrase rather than as a *senhal,* here as well as in Folquet's poem XX. It is quite possible that Aimeric is imitating Folquet in this use, as he does often enough elsewhere. For a further discussion, see Stronski's edition, p. 32*.

13. This metaphor of the Assassins recurs in a slightly different form in poem 42, lines 28ff. See F. M. Chambers, "The Troubadours and the Assassins," in *Modern Language Notes,* April, 1949, p. 245.

28. One should undoubtedly take *tan parlans* with *be* in the next line, though the ambiguous phrasing is not very flattering.

30. The sense of the line is clear, although the exact reference of *quals* is not; I take it to mean "what sort of persons (she welcomes)," but this may be straining the words a bit.

32. That is, your reputation does not suffer.

36. The *Que* of *CIKNR* gives no satisfactory sense. But even reading *Es,* with the other MSS, one still has some difficulty with the line. I take it to mean that the lady's reputation is as great as her beauty, or perhaps that her reputation in the matter of beauty is great. But I must confess that either interpretation strains the meaning of *segon.*

44. It seems necessary to take *prezans* with *Vos fos,* rather than as a modifier of *domna,* if one is to arrive at an acceptable meaning for the line.

25

I. En Amor trob alques en qe·m refraing,
C'al meins d'Amor mals o bes no·m sofraing,
Ni eu per mal no·m loing d'Amor ni·m fraing;
On plus m'auci plus vas Amor m'afraing.
Mas non conosc c'Amors vas mi s'afraigna,
Ni eu non ai d'Amor poder qe·m fraigna.
Res no·m sofraing, sol c'Amors no·m sofraigna,
Car ses Amor non sai en qe·m refraigna.

II. D'Amor no·m puosc partir, c'Amors mi pren,
E qan m'en cuich emblar plus mi repren
Ab un esgart don mos cors s'escompren,
Qe·m fai venir de lieis en cui m'enpren.
Mas a son dan no·us cuidetz que m'enprenda,
Ni per autra mos fins cors s'escomprenda,
Don hom per fals amador mi reprenda,
Q'en lieis es tot, si·l platz, qe·m lais o·m prenda.

III. C'aissi sui faitz del tot al sieu coman
Que nuilla ren non desdic q'ella·m man.
Pero d'un ben la prec que no·m desman
C'al comenssar mi promes del deman;
Don fai pechat oimais que no·m demanda
E grans merces sivals car no·m desmanda;
Mas ieu tenc ben per desman si no·m manda,
Pero assatz qui non desditz comanda.

IV. En lieis son tuich li bon aip c'om retrai,
Estiers que greu promet e leu estrai,
Per q'ieu non puosc sofrir lo mal q'ieu trai
Si cal que ben Amors no m'en atrai.
Mas pero ben o mal cal q'ieu n'atraia
Sofrirai tot, que ja per mal qu'eu traia
No m'estrairai d'amar, qui qe·is n'estraia,
Ni ja nuill temps non vuoill q'om m'o retraia.

V. Dompna, en vos ai mon cor tant fin e ferm
Que ges non ai poder que l'en desferm.
Abanz vos jur sobre sainz e·us afferm

Cum plus m'en cuich partir, plus mi referm;
E si Merces qe·ls partimens referma
Per chausimen en vos plus no s'aferma,
Totz mos affars s'i destrui e·is desferma,
C'autra del mon no vuoill que m'estia ferma.

VI. L'adreitz Conratz Malespina referma
Don e dompnei, si que chascus aferma
Que de bon pretz no·is laissa ni·s desferma,
Per c'om en lui deu tener prova ferma.

VII. Na Biatritz d'Est, tant etz fina e ferma
Qe·l vostre sens no·is camja ni·s desferma,
Don vostre laus si meillura e s'aferma;
E puois mos chans e mos digz o referma.

VARIANTS

I. (*In C the first four verses are mutilated by the excision of a miniature.*) 1. amors *JR* (*and so, frequently, in the rest of the poem*); algues *c*, ales *Sg;* en quen *K*, a qem *U*. 2. Cal mens al mal damor bes non sofrain *f;* mal al be *GQ*, ben o mal *R*, mal o ben *SUc*, mals o ben *N;* non *DMQSU;* (sofraing) refraing *IK*. 3. Ni en *Q*, Ieu *R;* damor nom (nim *S*) loing *CMRS;* damar *Q;* (ni'm) ni *M*, min *U;* flaing *c*. 4. *lacking Sg;* On plus maues *D*, On mai ma uei *f;* (On) Com *IJKMNSUc;* (*the second* plus) e *A*, *lacking Dc;* (vas) uer *M;* amar *Q* (*and so frequently*); me flaing *c*. 5. *lacking Q;* (Mas) E *JRSg;* no *lacking Sg;* sofraigna *c*, saffraing *Fa*. 6. (eu) ges *M;* damor non ai poder *CFaGIJKMNQRSUcfSg*, non ai poder damor *D;* (que·m) que *R;* flagna *c*. 7. Re *Q*, Ren *NSUcf;* (*first* no·m) non *FaU;* no sostaingna *D*. 8. (Car) Mas *M*, Ni *FaSg;* reflagna *c*.

II. 9. non *NSU;* pusc jens partir *Sg*. 10. (E) Qe *S;* (m'en) me *QUc;* (cuich) puesc *R;* (emblar) partir *CFaMNRU*, luynar *Sg;* mi *lacking Sg*. 11. *lacking G;* si (sen *R*) compren *MRUSg*. 12. *lacking G;* Quen *IN;* (venir) plaizer *U;* (de lieis) celei *QU*, sela *Rf;* (en) de *RU;* me pren *AU*, mespren *Q*. 13. (a son) aizo *U*, al seu *S;* dan *lacking Uc;* (no·us) non *CDGIJKMNQSUcf*, nos *RSg;* (cuidetz) cug ges *CGQRfSg;* (que) quieu *JMNRSUcSg;* (m'emprenda) lam prenda *C*, mesprenda *GQf*, mi prenda *Sc*, reprenda *U*. 14. *lacking Sg* (*with this line added after* 15: Anc clam merce midons con que menprenda); mon fin cor *DN*, mos fis cor *Fa;* (per) por *S*, ues *R;* si comprenda *M*. 15. Don ia nulhs fals amadors *C*. 16. *lacking f;* quem laissa *A*, qen lais *IKM*, qe lais *R*, qe illais *U;* o prenda *MSc*, comprenda *R*.

III. (IV *in CMR*). 17. Aissi *CGJMQSUcf*, Car ieu *R;* a sieu *N*, a son *IKS*. 18. (non) noylh *CUc;* de dic *Q;* qelan mant *S*, qeu li man *U*, qil o man *c*, quella man *f*. 19. (Pero d'un ben) Pero lo ben *S*, Mais duna res *R;* (que) quil *Sc;* (no·m) non *DQSc*, nol *U*. 20. desman *D*. 21. (Don) Un *Sg;* (fai) sol *Sc;* no mi manda *M;* (no'm) non *DIKNQSUc*. 22. *lacking f;* greu m. *G*, gran merce *MNR;* (sivals) daitan *R;* (car) que *CJMc*, *lacking G;* (no·m) non *DQSUc;* demanda *R*. 23. (ieu) eus *c;* ben *lacking R;* deman *N;* (si) sil *Uc*, qi *MR;* (no·m) no *Rc;* desmanda *c*. 24. (qui) que *Dc;* nom *U*.

IV. (III *in CMR*). 25. Quen *Sg;* totz los bos aibs *R*. 26. (que) car *Sg;* (e) ẽ *G*. 27. nom *R;* qui en t. *IK*, quen t. *GQSg*. 28. cals qe bes *RSg*, cal ben *IK;* (Amor no m'en atrai) o merces nom atrai *N;* (Amors) merces *CGMQRSUcfSg;* non matrai *c*, non mi atrai *S;* atraia *Q*, uetrai *f*. 29. *lacking Q;* (Mas pero) Emperol *RSg*, Ma perol *c*, Perol *U;* ben ol mal *cSg*, bes o mals *R*, mal o ben *DGJ*, mal ol ben *U;* cal qieu en traia *AIK*, qual que matraya *CNSc*, cal qem natraia *DJM*, cals qieu traia *R*, qal qe me traia *U*, cal qez ieu traia *f*. 30. *lacking f;* (tot) leu *MS*, eu *Sg;* mals *R;* qien traia *DIJKMQ*, qem traia *Uc*, qem atraia *S*. 31. Nom nestrarai *M*, Nom nestrai *R*, Non estarai *Sc*, Non esterai *U;* damor *IK*, damors *J*, lacking *U;* qi qen astraia *S*, qi qen estraia *GQ*, qi qe me nestraia *c*, qi qis n. *Uf*. 32. Qe ia *Uc*, Mi ia *Q;* (temps) teing *D*, iorn *M;* (q'om m'o) qom o *Mf*, qẽ *G*, com me *Nc*.

V. 33. Domna ieu uos ai *A*, Domna uos ai *c*, Damar leys ai *Sg;* lo cors *Q;* tan *lacking U;* e *lacking f;* e tan ferm *R*. 34. Qeu *DIKN;* non nai *U*, non a *R;* (ges) res *RSg;* (que) qeu *CFaIKMNf*, quel *RSg;* (l'en) lem *NS*, lom *Uc*, ne *Sg*, me *R;* deferm *U*. 35. Enans *CFaGMQRfSg;* sobrels s. *Sg;* e aferm *M*. 36. On plus *C*, Que can *RSg;* (m'en) me *IKMNUc;* (partir) luynar *Sg;* (mi) men *FaNQ*. 37. *lacking N;* (E) Mai *f*, Mas *GQSg;* (si) sil *U*, sel *c;* (qe·ls) qel *QU*, al *R*, qe *S*, qil *c;* pertemença *c*. 38. Per iauçimen e uos plus nus saferma *N*, Per xausimen pus uas mi non la ferma *Sg;* (Per) E *M*. 39. *lacking Gc;* Tot mon afar *CMN;* (s'i) se *DMNQR;* destrai *N*, desclau *f;* (e·s) e *NQSU*, ses *R;* (desferma) ferma *R*. 40. *lacking f;* Qautre *c;* (del mon) mais uos *CDFaGIJKMNQRSc*, mais *U*, mas il *Sg;* (m'estia) mesteu *A*, mestei *FaJ*, mestec *DIK*, mestic *G*, hestic *Q*, mesti *N*, mistea *U*, mestes *MS*, mesteia *c*, sia *R*, m sia *Sg;* ferm *c*.

After V, *U adds this cobla:* Lai on uos es me uao rendre per pres Bona donna caisi mai enapres Ab fin amor qem fai estar ab pres De ben amar qe non sia repres Ma dieus mi lais tan uiure tro qeu prenda Vostre bel cors dedins çambra o reprenda Qe semblan mer donna cab dieu mi prenda Ab qe merces en uostre cors saprenda.

VI. *lacking GMNQRUcfSg;* VII *in CS*. 41. (Conratz) conrat *S*, coralz *K*, coral *I*, cora *D*, guillem *CJ*. 43. non laissi ni d. *S*. 44. *lacking A* (*text given is that of I*); Per qe en lui es ades ualor ferma *S*.

VII. *lacking Nf;* VI *in CS*. 45. d'Est *lacking CMRUScSg;* (fina e) de beutat *CR*, de bontat *SUc*, de bon pretz *MSg*. 46. Qe *GMQSUc;* (sens) prez *MS;* (no·s) non *SUc*, de bon pretz *MSg*. 46. Qe *GMQSUc;* (sens) prez *MS;* (no·s) non *SUc;* (ni·s) ni *Sc;* deferma *I*. 47. *lacking GMSg;* (Don) De *Uc;* (laus) sen *Q;* (si) anç *Uc*, *lacking R;* meillor anz saferma *S*. 48. Anz puei ades e mos chantz o referma *M;* (E puois) Que *Sg;* mos diz e mos chanz *GQ*, mos ditz e mos cors *R*, mos diz en ren no *S;* (o referma) se desferma *S*, co referma *R*, eus (uus *U*) referma *Uc*, mo referma *C*.

TRANSLATION

I. I find in Love somewhat of solace, for at least I lack not ill or good from Love; nor do I, for ill, depart or take myself away from Love. The more he maltreats me, the more I humble myself before him. But I do not see that Love humbles himself before me, and yet I have not the power to depart from him. I lack nought, if I lack not Love, for without Love I know not in what to seek solace.

II. I may not part from Love, since Love seizes me; and when I think to steal away from him, he seizes me again more firmly, by means of a look which fires my heart and which he sends upon me from her who snares me. But think not that I am snared to her hurt, nor that my faithful heart will ever be kindled by another woman, for which one might blame me as a false lover. In her, if she will, is all power to take me or to leave me.

III. I am so mindful of her commands that I gainsay nought which she commands me to do. However, I beg her in her turn not to gainsay a favor which she promised me about a question I put to her at the beginning. Hence she commits a sin in that she does not question me, and at the same time she is very merciful in that she does not gainsay me. I hold it nevertheless to be a gainsaying if she does not send for me. Yet it is evident that whoever does not gainsay commands.

IV. In her are all the good qualities that are told of men, save that she is slow to promise and swift to retract. Therefore I cannot endure the woe I suffer, unless Love bring me some good with it. But whatever of good or ill I may bring upon myself, I shall endure all, for never for ill that I endure shall I cease loving, whosoever may cease; nor do I wish that anyone should ever accuse me of that.

V. Lady, my heart is so faithful and true to you that I have no power in me of taking it away from you. Nay, I swear by the saints and I affirm that the more I think to part from you, the more I remain. Yet if Pity who heals all dissensions abide not in you by your grace, all my cause is ruined and overthrown, since I will not that any other lady in the world, save you, be constant to me.

VI. The upright Conrad Malaspina abounds in largess and lady-service, so that every one asserts that he does not cease nor desist from seeking good fame. One should find in him therefore a true witness.

VII. Lady Beatrice of Este, you are so faithful and constant that your mind wavers not nor is shaken, wherefore your glory grows and abides. My song and my words affirm that forever.

NOTES

Seventeen MSS: *ACDFaGIJKMNQRSSgUcf*. Of these, *Fa* contains only stanzas one, two, and five. Jaufre de Foixa quotes lines 25–27 (ed. Paul Meyer, in *Romania*, IX, 68. Variants: 25. *(lieis) luy; on.* 26. *Estres; (greu) tart.* 27. *E eu; los mals*). Critical edition by W. P. Shepard, in *Speculum*, II, 297. De Bartholomaeis prints stanzas one, six, and seven in *Poesie storiche*, I, 226 (not a critical edition).

Our variants for *Sg* are taken from Massó y Torrents's diplomatic edition in the *Anuari*, 1907, of the Institut d'Estudis Catalans, p. 429. This MS and *N* were not available to Mr. Shepard when he made his earlier edition. The only important deviation from that edition is that we have followed the orthography of the base MS (*A*) instead of making it conform to the standards of *C*. Minor changes will be noted below.

The variant readings are very numerous, and indicate considerable contamination of sources. In the main, *ADIK*, often joined by *J*, stand apart from the rest of the MSS (cf. particularly line 28, and stanza VI). Other fairly constant groups are *GQ* (2, 31, etc.), often joined by *f* (13, 37); and *SUc* (45, 46), with *Sc* often standing apart (13, 31, etc.). The order of stanzas confirms these groupings, at least in a general way:

1-2-3-4-5-6-7 *ADIJK*
1-2-3-4-5-7 *GNQUcSg* (*U* has an extra stanza after 5)
1-2-3-4-5 *f*
1-2-3-4-5-7-6 *S*
1-2-4-3-5-7-6 *C*
1-2-4-3-5-7 *MR*

The order of stanzas three and four suggests another group, *CMR*, which is supported by a fairly consistent agreement in the variants. But there are so many individual deviations from all these groups, and so little consistency in the relations of one group with another, that it is impossible to construct a satisfactory stemma.

Base: *A*.

A song in derivative rimes, like number 47. For discussions of this verbal juggling, see Mr. Shepard's earlier edition (*Speculum*, II, 296–297) and Jeanroy, *Poésie lyrique*, II, 90. As Shepard says, "the poetical value of such *tours de force* is of course slight."

17. Shepard: *Aissi* (with the majority of the MSS, but *A*'s *Caissi* also has good support).

17–24. Shepard: "The sequence of thought in this strophe is confused and paradoxical. It may be paraphrased as follows: Whatever she commands, I do. When I first wooed her, she promised to ask me a favor. She has not done so. That's too bad; but not as bad as retracting the promise would be. Not asking is retracting; but yet not retracting is asking." I am not too sure that I follow this, especially about the Lady's promising to ask the poet a favor; that may be what Aimeric had in mind, but the expression is far from clear.

26. Shepard: *retrai* (for *estrai*). This is evidently a slip; the word was repeated by mistake from the line above.

34. Shepard: *qu'ieu* (for *que*).

40. *m'estia*. For a similar treatment of *-ia* as one syllable, see 48, line 27. Elsewhere, Aimeric counts this ending as two syllables (10, 30: *sabia;* 11, 21: *deuria*).

41. Shepard: *Guilhems*. It is true that Aimeric had a particular fondness for William Malaspina, and addressed many songs to him, frequently in company with Beatrice of Este; one would therefore expect to find William here. That, I think, is exactly what the copyists of *CJ* (the only two MSS which give the name of William) felt when they saw *Conratz* in the text they were copying. An error of this sort would be very easy, while the reverse would be hard to explain. Shepard argues, furthermore, that the agreement of *CJ*, which agree in so little elsewhere, is significant. The same argument could be adduced for the agreement of *S* with *ADIK* in reading *Conratz* (or something like it), since *S* more commonly goes with *C*. De Bartholomaeis, who follows *A*, reads *Conratz*.

26

I. En aquelh temps que·l reys mori, N'Amfos,
E sos belhs filhs qu'era plazens e bos,
E·l reys Peire de cui fon Araguos,
E·N Dieguos qu'era savis e pros,
E·l marques d'Est e·l valens Salados,
Ladonc cugei que fos mortz pretz e dos,
Si qu'ieu fui pres de laissar mas chansos;
Mas ar los vey restauratz ambedos.

II. Pretz es estortz, qu'era guastz e malmes,
E Dons gueritz del mal qu'avia pres,
Q'un bon metge nos a Dieus sai trames
Deves Salern, savi e ben apres,
Que conoys totz los mals e totz los bes
E mezina quascun segon que s'es;
Et anc loguier no·n demandet ni ques,
Anz los logua, tant es francs e cortes.

III. Anc hom no vi metge de son joven
Tan belh, tam bo, tan larc, tan conoissen,
Tan coratgos, tan ferm, tan conqueren,
Tam be parlan ni tam ben entenden,
Que·l be sap tot e tot lo mal enten,
Per que sap mielhs mezinar e plus gen,
E fa de Dieu cap e comensamen,
Que l'ensenh' a guardar de falhimen.

IV. Aquest metges sap de meggia tan,
Et a l'engienh e·l sen e·l saber gran,
Qu'elh sap ensemps guazanhar mezinan
Dieu e secgle. Guardatz valor d'enfan!
Que·l sieu perden venc, metent e donan,
Sai conquerir l'emperi alaman.
Hueymais cre ben, quom que·y anes duptan,
Lo fag qu'om di d'Alixandr' en comtan.

V. Aquest metges savis, de qu'ieu vos dic,
Fon filhs del bon emperador Enric,

Et a lo nom del metge Frederic,
E·l cor e·l sen e·l saber e·l fag ric,
Don seran ben mezinat siey amic
E·l trobaran cosselh e bon abric.
De lonc sermon deu hom far breu prezic,
Que ben cobram lo gran segon l'espic.

VI. Be pot aver lo nom de Frederic,
Que·l dig son bon e·l fag son aut e ric.

VII. Al bon metge maiestre Frederic
Di, meggia, que de meggar no·s tric.

VARIANTS

I. 1. tẽp *D;* rey *CIN;* nafos *D.* 2. E *lacking D;* fills plazens cortes e bos *AB;* (plazens) ualens *N;* (bos) pros *C.* 4. diego *ACENRa*^{1}, dego *IK;* quera ualenz e bos *N.* 6. Adoncs *ABDa*^{1}*;* cuieu *a*^{1}. 7. (qu'ieu) que *D.*

II. 9. gatz *E,* guast *N.* 10. E doncs geriz *D,* E don guerisc *R,* Et eu garitz *a*^{1}*;* don *CE.* 11. nos a sai dieus trames *E;* (sai) soi *D,* sa *R.* 12. sauis *D.* 13. (Que) Qel *a*^{1}. 14. segon *lacking B.* 15. (ni ques) nin qes *BDIKN,* ni pres *A.* 16. Qel loga lor *a*^{1}*;* (los) lor *IK;* tant francs es *B.*

III. 18. Tant larc tant bel tant bon tant c. *A,* Tant larc tant bon tant bel tant c. *B.* 20. bel parlan *R.* 21. Qel *repeated D* (Qel Qel); be *lacking R.* 24. garda *N.*

IV. 25. metge *CIKNR;* (meggia tan) metgi aitan *ENR,* metiai tan *D,* mitzi aitan *IK.* 26. e saber *a*^{1}. 27. meizinar gazaignan *A.* 28. Dieus *R;* (e) el *ABDIKNa*^{1}. 29. uenz *a*^{1}. 30. Saup conqerer *a*^{1}. 31. (quom) cor *Aa*^{1}*;* (que·y) qe *a*^{1}, qui *D;* (anes) amics *I.* 32. Los faitz *AB,* Lafait *D;* dalixandre comtan *ABEa*^{1}, daleysandre daleysandre comtan *R,* dalisandrin comdan *IKN,* dalisandre condan *D.*

V. *lacking N.* 33. metge saui *CDEIKR,* saui metges *a*^{1}. 34. (Enric) nenric *C.* 35. lo non *D.* 36. *lacking D;* el saber elafic *AB.* 38. Eu trobarai *a*^{1}, E trobaran *IR,* Ei trobara *D;* (e) el *I.* 39. (deu hom) deuem *ER.* 40. (cobram) cobran *D,* troban *a*^{1}*;* gra *E.*

VI. *lacking N.*

VII. *lacking N.* 44. Dil *a*^{1}; mezina *I;* del *a*^{1}*;* meiar *D,* maniar *E,* mengar *IK;* (tric) teic *D.*

TRANSLATION

I. At that time when the King, Lord Alfonso, died, and his son, who was gracious and good, and King Peter of Aragon, and Lord Diego, who was wise and worthy, and the Marquis of Este, and the brave Salado, then I thought that Worth and Largess were dead, so that I well nigh gave up my singing; but now I see both of them restored.

II. Worth, which was wasted and spoiled, is saved, and Largess is cured of the illness which had seized it, for God has sent to us here, from Salerno, a good physician, wise and well taught, who knows all the ills and all the good things, and who doctors everyone as suits him best. He has never asked nor sought a fee; but he fees others, so liberal and courteous is he.

III. Never did one see a physician as young as he, so fair, so good, so generous, so knowing, so brave, so firm, so victorious, speaking and listening so well, since he knows entirely what is good and understands entirely what is evil. Therefore he can doctor better and more nobly. He makes God his leader and chief, who teaches him how to keep from sin.

IV. This physician knows so much of medicine and has such great wit and sense and knowledge that he can win both God and the world by his doctoring. Look! how wise a youth! Losing his own money, spending and giving, he came here to conquer the German empire. Now I believe indeed, though I once doubted them, the deeds men tell about Alexander.

V. This wise physician, of whom I am telling you, was the son of the good Emperor Henry. The name of the physician is Frederick, of noble heart and mind and wisdom and action. So all his friends will be well doctored and will find in him counsel and protection. One should make a short preaching out of a long sermon: for we gather the grain according to the ear.

VI. Well may his name be Frederick, for his words are good, his deeds lofty and rich.

VII. To the good physician, Master Frederick, say, O Medicine, to make no delay in doctoring.

NOTES

Ten MSS: *ABCDEIKNRa*[1]. Critical text (not using all MSS) in Bartsch-Koschwitz, *Chrestomathie*, col. 179. De Bartholomaeis reprints Crescini's text from the *Manuale* (p. 289) in *Poesie storiche*, I, 246. These texts are based primarily on *A*.

The versions are remarkably uniform, and striking divergences are largely individual. For this reason, it is impossible to construct a valid stemma. The following groups are recognizable: *AB* (2, 36), *ER* (39), *IKN* (32). From line 6 we obtain a group *ABDa*[1], which is moderately constant elsewhere. *C* apparently belongs with *ER* (15, 28). But the evidence is not sufficient to indicate any larger groups.

Base: *C*.

1–5. For a discussion of the patrons mentioned here, see our Introduction. They are, in order: Alfonso VIII of Castile, his son the Infante Ferdinand, Peter II of Aragon, Diego López de Haro, and Azzo VI of Este. Salados is unknown; we have discussed in the Introduction De Bartholomaeis's theory that Aimeric uses this name to designate William Malaspina. De Bartholomaeis (*loc. cit.* and *Memorie della Reale Accademia di Bologna*, serie 1, vol. VI, pp. 69 and 101) dates the poem in the fall of 1220, between Frederick's arrival in Italy and his coronation. This date seems likely enough, and it is true that William Malaspina was dead at that time, and that he was one of Aimeric's favorite patrons; but Aimeric calls him by his proper name everywhere else, and none of the other patrons here are designated by *senhals*. We are therefore not convinced that *Salados* is William.

2. Bartsch-Koschwitz: *plazens, cortes e bos* (for *qu'era*, etc.); in earlier editions, Bartsch reads as we do.

6. B-K: *Adoncs;* in earlier editions, Bartsch reads *Ladoncs*.

15. B-K: *nin pres;* in earlier editions, *ni'n ques*.

18. B-K: *Tan larc, tal bel, tan bon, tan conoissen;* in earlier editions, Bartsch follows our order.

24. *ensenh' a guardar*. Other editions read *ensenha gardar*. But Levy (*SW*, III, 35) says he can find no sure example of *ensenhar* without a preposition before an infinitive, and quotes one clear example with *a*. We follow him in this.

28. B-K: *Dieu el segle.*

31. B-K: *cor que·i;* in earlier editions, Bartsch reads *cum quei.*

32. B-K: *Los faitz . . . d'Alixandre comtan;* in earlier editions, Bartsch: *Lo fag.*

36. B-K: *e l'afic;* likewise De Bartholomaeis, who translates "e la premura"; but Bartsch, in earlier editions, reads *el fag ric.*

39. B-K: *devem far*. De Bartholomaeis translates "*Dopo* lungo sermone," etc., which may be stretching the meaning of *de* a little, though it helps the sense. By *prezic*, Aimeric apparently means a sort of exhortation, a final appeal, at the end of a sermon. But I must confess that I do not know precisely what Aimeric had in mind when he wrote this and the following line. The two lines are quoted by Cnyrim, *Sprichwörter*, no. 600.

41–42. For a similar play on the name *Frederic*, see Guillem Figueira (ed. Levy), 7, lines 63–64:

> Belhs amics Taurel, vos e ma dona Dia
> Devetz ben amar selh c'a nom *de ric fre*.

See also Jausbert de Poicibot (ed. Shepard), XI, 55–60:

> E del sieu pretz es autors
> Lo sieus noms rics benestans,
> Qu'el a *fre de ric* per ver;
> Per refrenar vils faitz e retener
> Qu'us non toc a son pretz cabal,
> *Fre de ric* e man port' aital.

27

I. En greu pantais m'a tengut longamen
Qu'anc no·m laisset ni no·m retenc Amors,
Et a·m sajat de totas sas dolors,
Si que del tot m'a fag obedien;
E quar mi sap esforciu e sufren,
A·m si cargat de l'amoros afan
Que·l melhor cen no·n sufririon tan.

II. Qu'amar mi fai mal mon grat finamen
Lieys qu'ilh m'a fag cauzir part las gensors;
Et agra·m ops que·m fes chauzir alhors,
Qu'assatz val mai guazanhar en argen
Que perdr' en aur, segon mon essien;
Mas ieu o fatz a ley de fin aman,
Qu'ieu fug mon pro e vauc seguen mon dan.

III. E s'ieu cum fols sec mon dan folamen,
A tot lo mengz m'er la foudatz honors,
Qu'ieu ai ja vist faire mangtas folhors
Que tornavon a saber et a sen,
Et ai vist far mangz fagz saviamen
Que tornavon a folhia trop gran,
Per qu'ieu cug far sen quan vauc folhejan.

IV. E vos, dona, qu'avetz valor valen,
Aissi cum etz mieller de las melhors,
Valha·m Merces et oblit vos ricors
E no·i gardetz Razo, mas Chauzimen;
Que so que l'us pueja, l'autre dissen:
So que Merces creis, Razos vai merman.
Si·us platz, aucir mi podetz razonan.

V. Pauc vos calra del mieu enansamen,
S'aissi gardatz vostras valens valors,
Lo dous esgart e las frescas colors,
Qu'enquera·m so el cor vostr' uelh rizen,
Li cortes dig amoros e plazen.
E quar ieu plus soven no·us vau denan,
A pauc miey huelh estra mon grat no·i van.

VI. Reys d'Arago e flors d'essenhamen,
Fuelha de gaug, frugz de bos fagz donan,
Vos etz de pretz mayestre ses enjan.

VII. Coms Cumenges, grat e merces vos ren,
Quar ses donar m'avetz donat aitan
Qu'endreg d'onor val un don aut e gran.

VARIANTS

I. 2. Cac *f*, Qar *Uc;* non . . . non *DGP;* (ni no·m) e nom *c*, e non *U*, ni mõ *G;* amor *O* (*and rimes in* -or *throughout*). 3. (Et) Anz *MRR*^{2}*;* ma s. *R*^{2}, massaiet *M*, massaie *R*, ai saiada *O*, am sazit *f;* a·m *lacking I;* (de totas) ab t. *ADIKMNPRR*^{2}*S*, a t. *GQf*, de tota *a*^{1}, del tot *Uc;* sa dolor *a*^{1}. 4. Si quels *O;* de tot *C;* obedienz *a*^{1}*f*. 5. (sap) saup *IKN*, sa *S;* (esforciu) afortit *Ca*^{1}, forcer si *O;* e sufrens *a*^{1}*f*, o sufren *G*. 6. An si *S*, Aisi *O;* cargaiz *O*, gardat *R*, gargat *f*. 7. Quels (Quel *N*) melhors *CNRR*^{2}*f*, Qei m. *Uc;* (cen) tent *O;* soffriron *O*, soffrion *P;* (tan) aitan *Oa*^{1}.

II. *lacking N*. 8. (Qu'amar) Amar *ADD*^{c}*FaMOPRR*^{2}*SUa*^{1}*c*, E amar *Q;* me fan *R*^{2}*;* (mal) man *U*, ses *GQR*^{2}*f*, ster *P*, ster ster *S*, *lacking a*^{1}*;* folamen *RR*^{2}. 9. Leis las gensors de totas las melhors *R*, Lei li huelh cꝑ man fag chauzir en la iensor *R*^{2} (Lei *expunctuated*); (qu'ilh) cui *ADUc*, qui *GOQSa*^{1}*f*, que *D*^{c}*FaIKMP;* iauzir *Uc;* (part) per *GOPQSUa*^{1}*c*, de *M*, en *IKf*, mest *ADFa;* la meillor *Oa*^{1}, las melhors *CM*, la gensors *DSUc*. 10. E foram (fora *A*) mieills *ADR*, E ualgram mais *M*, E agran obs *Oc*, E foram obs *D*^{c}*FaGQf;* saghes (agues *R*, caghes *R*^{2}*U*) chauzit aillors *MRR*^{2}*U*. 11. (en) ab *R*, ni *Q*. 12. Ca *Q;* perdir en *P;* (en) ab *R;* per lo mieu e. *ADFa*. 13. Et eu fatz o *AD*, Et eu o fatz *Fa*, Mais eu lai fag *O;* o *lacking RUa*^{1}*c;* fiz *a*^{1}*;* (a ley) allies *f*. 14. (Qu'ieu) Que *AGIKQRR*^{2}*Ucf*, Qui *DM;* son pro *M;* (seguen) segur *O*, seguir *a*^{1}, sercan *RR*^{2}*;* son dan *M*.

III. 15. E ieu *R*. 16. (m'er) mes *ADFaGMOPQSa*^{1}*f*. 17. (Qu'ieu) Que *I*, Qar eu *Uc;* (ai ja vist faire) ai uistas faire *FaNPS*, ai (nai *f*) uistas far *GIKQRR*^{2}*f*, aia uist faire *D;* ja *lacking Ua*^{1}*c;* far foldatz maintas sazos *A;* (faire) far *Uc*. 18. *lacking Q;* Qe torna ben *O;* (saber) honor *A*. 19. *lacking Q;* Et ai uistas mantas folias faire sauiamen *R;* uistz *A;* maint faig *IKNa*^{1}, maint faitz *OSc*. 20. Qi torna ben *O*, E tornauon *S*. 21. Per quom *O;* (cug) auch *Q;* (quan) tan *D*.

IV. 22. (E) Mas *M*, Ma *GQ;* caues ualor e sen *MR*. 23. Tan can uos es *R;* miellers *C;* etz bona (meiller *FaPRS*) part (pars *PRS*) las meillors *ADFaIKNPRR*^{2}*SUc;* las meillor *O*. 24. Prendaus *ADR*, Menbreus *FaGIKNPQR*^{2}*Sf*, Valaus *a*^{1}, Val ac *O;* (oblit) obri *O;* (vos) uostre *c*, uoi *U*. 25. (no·i) no *COa*^{1}*;* (Razo) merce *N;* iausimen *U*. 26. Qar (Que *AGQ*) lus poia so que *AFaGIKNPQSUc*, Que car lus p. so que *f*, Que lus puogna ço que *D*, Que se lun p. so que *R*^{2}*;* Caiso que *R*. 27. So que razos creis merces uai merman *C*, So que razos creys merces razos u. m. *R*^{2} (*first* razos *expunctuated*), Que raison creis merces uauc amerman *O;* (So) E so *Uc*. 28. (Si·us platz) Sieus p. *R*, Seus p. *S*, Pero *R*^{2}, E sa uos p. *Uc;* auciderm p. *c*.

V. 29. Vauc *O;* carra *PSUc;* (del) de *c;* enantimen *MR*. 30. (S'aissi gardatz) Si uos membra *IK*, Se uos membratz *O*, Se uos souen *PS*, Sius remembra *ADD*^{c}*GNQRR*^{2}*Ucf;* uostra *AIKNOPRR*^{2}*Ua*^{1}*cf;* ualen *NRUa*^{1}*c;* ualor *OR*, lauzors *GQ*. 31. (Lo) Los *M*, El *ADOR*, Nil *D*^{c}*GIKNPQR*^{2}*Sa*^{1}*f*, Nel *U*, Del *c*, Ni *f;* (dous esgart) d. esgartz *ACM*, gent parlar *Uc;* (e) ni *D*^{c}*GIKNPQR*^{2}*Sf*, ab *Oa*^{1}*;* la fresca colors *ACIKNORR*^{2}*SUcf*. 32. *this and* 33 *are interverted in*

O; Que mon cor son uostres u. r. *R,* Cades me son uostr uelh el cor r. R^2; (Qu'enquera·m so) Can cor mistan *O,* Quem (Quen *K*) queiram son *IK;* (el) al *AD^cGIKNOPSUa^1cf,* als *Q;* (rizen) plazen *c.* 33. Eill doutz esgart *ADRR^2Uc;* (Li) El *D^cGIKMNOPS,* Els *Qf;* e lamoros paruen *M;* (plazen) riden *c.* 34. E car ades non uos estau d. *AD,* E car nous uenc ieu plus s. d. *f;* (quar) qan *GQUc;* ieu *lacking G;* (vau) uenc *D^cIKNOR^2*. 35. Fan men estar fals lauzengiers truan *R^2;* (A) Per *ADP,* Ab *f;* (estra) estier *IKMNOUa^1c,* estrau *D,* estiers *D^cGQ,* otra *R;* (grat) grã *f.*

VI. *lacking DMORUa^1cf.* 36. Rei de ragon *GQ;* (e flors) flors etz *CR^2*, e caps *A.* 37. e fatz los frutz donan *R^2*. 38. mastre e ses enjan *Q.*

VII. *lacking DGMOQRR^2Ua^1c.* 39. gratz *A;* (grat e) cin cent *PS;* merce *S.* 40. Car senes dar *A,* Qe ses donar *PS.* 41. Qe las honors ualon don riche (riche et *S*) gran *PS;* (d'onor) damor *AIKf;* un don autre gran *CK.*

TRANSLATION

I. Love has kept me in grievous torment for a long time without either letting me go or keeping me, and has tested me with all his sorrows, so that he has made me truly his subject. Because he knew me to be steadfast and long-suffering, he has burdened me so with the pains of love that the hundred best (lovers) would not endure so much.

II. In spite of myself, he makes me love faithfully her whom he made me choose from among the best. It would have been profitable to me if he had made me choose another, for, as it seems to me, it is far better to make a profit in silver than to take a loss in gold. But I am acting like a faithful lover, for I flee my own profit and pursue my loss.

III. Even if I, like a fool, pursue my loss foolishly, at least that folly will be an honor to me, for I have seen many follies done that turned out to be wisdom and sense, and I have seen many things done wisely that turned out to be great follies. Therefore, when I act foolishly, I think that I am, in reality, acting sensibly.

IV. And you, Lady, who have famous fame and are best of the best, may Mercy aid me with you and may it forget your high rank; and may you heed not Reason, but Mercy. What one exalts, the other abases; what Mercy increases, Reason diminishes. So, if it please you, you may kill me by your reasoning.

V. My advantage will matter little to you, if thus you consider your great fame, your sweet glance, your fresh colors, for your laughing eyes and your courteous, loving and agreeable words are still deep in my heart. Because I cannot go more often into your presence, my eyes go there almost in spite of myself.

VI. King of Aragon, flower of good manners, leaf of joy, fruit of good and generous deeds, you are the master of all fame, without any doubt.

VII. Count of Comminges, I give you thanks and gratitude, for, without giving, you have given me so much as to equal a great and permanent gift, as far as honor is concerned.

NOTES

Twenty-one MSS: *ACDD^cFaGIKMNPQRR^2SUa^1cfg*. Of these, *D^c* contains only stanzas two and five; *Fa* only stanzas two, three, and four; we have not consulted *g*. *R* gives the poem to Aimeric de Belenoi, R^2 to Peire Vidal; but the attribution is not doubtful. Stanza three is quoted in the *Breviari d'amor*, line 28645 (Variants: 17. *ja* lacking. 19. *manh fait*. 20. *tornava*).

It is impossible to construct a satisfactory stemma. Such small groups as one finds among the MSS are not constant throughout the poem, and no consistent larger groups can be discovered. The largest measure of agreement is found in the following cases: *AD*, often joined by *R* (10, 11, 24, 31) or *Fa* (9, 12, 13, 34); *GQf* (3, 8, 11, and most of the important variants); *PS* (8, 30, 41); *Uc* (3, 31); Ca^1 (5, 30), with which *O* in particular seems to have something in common (3, 4, 9).

Base: *C*.

5. *esforciu*. We adopt the reading of all the MSS except Ca^1.

9. *C*'s reading *las melhors*, though supported by MOa^1, is pretty clearly wrong. The word *melhors* appears in the rime in line 23, where the sense demands it more than here; and Aimeric is careful not to repeat his rime-words in the body of a poem. Almost the only exceptions are intentional refrain-rimes.

11–12. Cnyrim, *Sprichwörter*, no. 689.

24–28. Cf. song 14, lines 19–28, and Folquet de Marseille (ed. Stronski) VII, 34: *conosc e sai Que Merces vol so que Razos dechai.*

26. Cnyrim, *op. cit.*, no. 406.

27. Cnyrim, *op. cit.*, no. 214.

40. Evidently the Count of Comminges had given Aimeric not gifts but praise.

28

I. Gaucelms Faiditz, de dos amics leials
Al vostre sen me digatz zo qe n'es:
Qan a l'un d'els ven de sa domna bes
Et a l'autre danz e destrics e mals,
Si qe negus non a poder qe·s vir,
Qals se deu plus esforzar de servir
Sidonz? Pero endreit d'Amor jutjatz,
E pois celui qe·us volretz razonatz.

II. N'Aimerics, ges non es plaitz comunals,
Q'aicel cui ve d'Amor en totas res
Danz e destrics deia esser tan cortes
Endreit sidonz de servizis corals
Com cel cui son complit tuit sei dezir.
Non es razos, ni hom non o deu dir,
Qe s'esfortz tan hom desaventuratz
Com fiz amics q'es leialment amatz.

III. Gaucelms Faiditz, entendeires venals
Degra penre si com vos avetz pres,
Qu'aitals amics non serv sa domna ges,
Si non conois qe·l servirs sia sals.
Non es esfortz ni fai tan a grazir
Qui d'un gran be sap l'altre far issir;
Mas qi del mal pot be far, zo sapchatz,
Ab gen servir, deu esser dobles gratz.

IV. N'Aimerics, gen razonatz zo q'es fals,
E·l razonars non es mas nescies.
Com auzatz dir qe·l drutz cui val Merces
Non deia esser de servir plus cabals
Qe·l desamatz qe·s deuria aucir?
Foll' er domna si·us fai de si jauzir,
Si senz benfag vales e·us esforsatz;
E si·us fai be, qe ja re no·n vaillatz!

V. Gaucelms Faiditz, car vos es totz aitals,
Cuidatz que eu aia de vos apres?

E donc no·s deu esforzar demanes
Lo paubres, tan c'al manen si' egals?
Pero mais vol lo malaptes garir
C'us autre sanz al malaveig fugir,
E deuria·s cel q'es pauc enansatz
Esforzar plus qe cel q'es plus prezatz.

VI. N'Aimerics, trop es afars desegals,
Qe vos digatz qe drutz on pres s'es mes
Non deia miels gardar zo q'a conqes
Ab proeza et ab fachs naturals
Qe cel qe re non a mais lo cossir.
Non a qe gart, anz se fai escarnir;
E sos servirs es perda e foudatz,
Pois a sidonz res qe·il fassa no·il platz.

VII. Gaucelms, lo coms de Fois qe·s fai grazir
Nos sabra be jutjar e devezir,
Q'estiers per vos, si doncs no m'esforzatz,
Non pueis esser per dreit apoderatz.

VIII. N'Aimerics, be sabra lo miels chauzir
Lo valenz coms, e·l ver jutjar e dir,
Qar cel sap miels lo dreit d'Amor assatz
Qe n'es soven alegres et iratz.

VARIANTS

I. 1. Gaucelm faidiz *GMr*, Gaucelm faidit *CNa*^{1}, Gauselins faidiz *𝔔*; Faiditz *lacking* *D*^{a}; (leials) corals *CD*^{a}*GIKM𝔔r*. 2. (Al) A *D*^{a}; (me) men *IK𝔔*. 3. d'els *lacking G𝔔;* de sa domna ue bes *CG𝔔*. 5. Si que poder non a negus *C;* que uir *Ca*^{1}. 6. Qual *CD*^{a}*GM𝔔;* dieu *D*^{a}; (plus) meillz *M;* offorçar *G*. 7. Sidonz *lacking CG𝔔;* per so *IK;* (en) segon lo *C*. 8. E celui pois *G𝔔*, E pueys ayssel *C*, E pueis cella *r;* que uos u. *D*^{a}, qe uoleç *G𝔔*, que uos tretz *r*.

II. 9. Ges naimericx *C;* Naimeric *GN𝔔a*^{1}*r*. 10. Qe cels (cels *lacking 𝔔*) qil ue damors *G𝔔;* Que cel *CM*. 11. *a*^{1} *runs this and* 12 *into one verse:* Danz e destrics deia esser amics corals; tan deya star *c. C;* deg *D*^{a}*IKr*. 12. (Endreit) En ues *CGN𝔔r;* (sidonz) damor *M;* coral *C*, leials *M*. 13. Con se *D*^{a}, En cel *𝔔;* (dezir) uoler *r*. 14. (ni) e *G𝔔;* non o deu hom dir *CG𝔔;* no lo *M*. 15. Que tan sesfortz *CG𝔔;* Qeu *D*^{a}; desauenturos *G𝔔*. 16. (q'es) quecs *IK*, queys *C*.

III. 17. Gaucelm faiditz *GMN*, Gaucelm faidit *a*^{1}*r*, Gauselin faiditz *𝔔;* entendedors *C*, entendedor *G*, entendor *𝔔;* enals *M*. 18. Degran *C;* (penre) chauzir *CG𝔔*. 19. Que tal amic *C*, Que tals amics *G𝔔;* non *lacking 𝔔;* sers *r*. 20. Silh non *C*, Si noil *G𝔔;* seruir *CG𝔔*, seruizi *r;* sial sals *IK*, sia als *M*. 21. (Non es esfortz) Non es ges fortz *C*, Ni sesforz tan *G𝔔*, Non esfors *IK;* (ni) nil *r*. 22. Qui dun be sap far un autre uenir *C;* (d'un gran be sap l'altre) dun be (bes

G) sap autre be D^aD^cGIKQr, dun be sap autre *N*. 23. (del) de CD^aM; sap far be D^cGQ, sap be far *Cr*, pot far be D^aIKM. 24. A ben seruir *Q*; doble D^aIKr, doblel *M*; grāz *G*.

IV. 25. Naimeric *N*; Gen razonatz naimericx *C*. 26. El razonatz *r*, El razonar *GQ*; mais con esciens *Q*, mas mas n. *I*, mals n. a^1. 27. (Com) Son a^1; ausest M; (qe·l drutz) cal d. D^aIK, que dreitz *C*; qe·l *lacking Q*. 28. (deia) degra *N*; (de servir) ues sidons *CGQr*; (cabals) ses sals *r*. 30. Fols *GQ*; (er) es *CGNQr*; si·us fai de si *added later in* a^1; sil fai *GQ*. 31. (Si) Pus *CGQr*; bes faiz *GQ*; (valetz e·us) ualenz eus *I*, u. nus *r*, ualer uos *C*; (e·us esforsatz) e uos forçaz *GQ*. 32. E faretz mal que ia be no uullatz *C*, E si faiz mal ben que ia no uaillaz *GQ*; (be) en *N*, *lacking* a^1; (no·n) no a^1; uoilhatz *r*.

V. *lacking CGQ*. 33. Gaucelms ben sai que (car D^a) uos etz t. a. D^aIK; Gaucelms ben sai que car es t. a. *Mr*; Gaucelm faidit a^1. 34. quieu *r*; naia D^aMr. 35. (no·s) no a^1. 36. Los *IK*, Le *Mr*. 37. E uol trop mais *r*; Per so *IK*; plus D^aIK; (lo malaptes) loing mal an pres *N*. 38. autres D^cMr; al malautes D^a, a malauei *M*, a malaueis *N*; al malaveig fugir *lacking r*. 39. *lacking r*; Et deuria D^a, Es deuria *IK*; (enansatz) malmenatz a^1. 40. *lacking r*; plus quel ques pauc enansatz *N*; (plus) mais *M*; qes enausatz a^1, qes pro p. D^c.

VI. *lacking CGQr*. 41. Naimeric Na^1; (afars) le fatz *M*; non egals a^1. 42. (m'es) me a^1. 43. conquis *N*. 44. proezas D^aIKM. 45. Qaicel D^aIK; (qe re) qaten *M*. 46. (gart) grat *IK*; (anz) az a^1. 48. ren que fassa non platz D^aIK.

VII. *lacking CGQr*. 49. Gaucelm a^1, Gaucel *N*; (Fois) fau *N*. 50. Nos o sabra iuiar *M*. 51. (vos) nos a^1, ren *M*; no men forsatz D^aIKM. 52. (Non) Nous a^1; (puesc) poc *N*; (per) por *N*; (dreit) uos *M*.

VIII. *lacking CGQr*. 53. Naimeric Na^1. 54. Le ualenz coms mas una reus uuelh dir *M*; iuiamen dir D^a, iuramen dir *IK*. 55. Qes hõ auist qera paupres presatz *M*; Caisel D^aIKN; los dretz D^a, lo dreitz *IK*. 56. E pueissas fon manenz des abaissatz *M*; (Qe) Qui *N*.

TRANSLATION

I. Gaucelm Faidit, tell me your opinion about two loyal lovers. When to one of them good fortune comes from his lady, and to the other woe and distress and ill, so that neither of them has the power to turn aside (from her), which one should strive the more to serve his lady? Judge this question in accordance with Love's law, and then defend your choice.

II. Sir Aimeric, it is by no means a common arrangement for a man who gets from Love woe and distress in all things to be as diligent in sincere services towards his lady as the man whose desires are all fulfilled. It is not right, and one should not say, that the unhappy lover should strive as hard as the faithful lover who is loyally loved.

III. Gaucelm Faidit, the venal wooer would make such a choice as you have, for such a lover serves his lady only when he knows that his services are well paid. It is no effort, nor is it praiseworthy, for a man to make one good fortune produce another; but you should know that, if he make good come from ill by faithful service, his reward should be double.

IV. Sir Aimeric, you argue cleverly for what is false, and your argument is mere foolishness. How dare you say that the lover whom Mercy favors should not be more perfect in his service than the unloved wretch who would do best to kill himself? The lady will be a fool who permits you to take your pleasure of her, since you find profit in striving without reward; and should she do you a favor, may it not profit you!

V. Gaucelm, because you are like that, do you think that I have learned (my way of life) from you? And should a poor man then not strive straightway to be equal to the rich? Nay, the sick man wishes more to be cured than another, in health, to avoid a sickness; and he who has prospered little in love should strive harder than one who is more honored.

VI. Sir Aimeric, this business is too one-sided, in that you say that the lover who gets his reward should not strive harder to keep what he has won by dint of prowess and praiseworthy deeds than the man who has got nothing but vain desire. The latter has nothing to keep, and is mocked for his pains; and his lady-service is vanity and folly, since nothing he can do will please his lady.

VII. Gaucelm, the Count of Foix, that worthy man, will know how to judge and decide this debate; and, unless you use force, I cannot otherwise be rightfully overcome by you.

VIII. Sir Aimeric, the worthy Count will certainly be able to make a just decision, for that man knows more of the law of Love who is often glad and sorry because of him.

NOTES

Eleven MSS: *C$D^a$$D^c$GIKMNQ$a^1$r*. Of these, D^c contains only a few lines (21–24, 37–40), and *CGQr* only the first four or five stanzas (as indicated in the Variants). The following stemma represents fairly accurately the relations of the MSS:

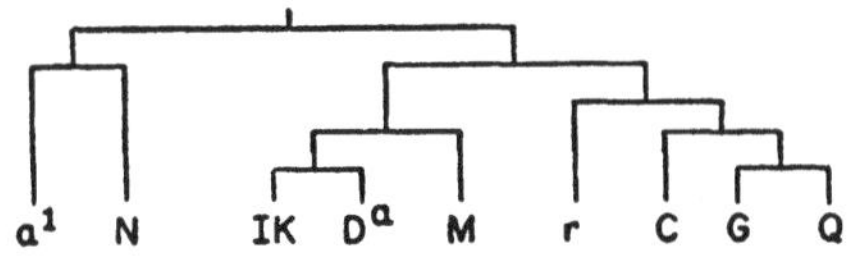

The main division rests on lines 1, 22, 23, 33; in line 1 especially, there can be little doubt that *Na^1*, though standing against all the other MSS, have the correct reading (cf. *corals* used again in line 12).

D^aIKM: 23, 51

D^aIK: 27, 37, 45, 48

CGQr: 28, 31

CGQ: 3, 7, 14, 15, 17, etc.

GQ: 8, 10, 15, 20, etc.

The agreement of *N* with *CGQr* in 12 and 30 must, I think, be attributed to coincidence, as the MSS otherwise have little in common. It would seem that *r* took the lines of stanza five which it contains from a MS related to *M* (these lines are not in *CGQ*). The position of D^c is doubtful.

None of the MSS offers a flawless text. On the whole, that of a^1 seems most satisfactory, and we have used it as our base; but where a^1 stands alone against a better reading in the other MSS, we have followed the majority. The text of lines 11–12 (insofar as it is defective in a^1) comes from *D^aIK*.

A *partimen* with Gaucelm Faidit on the subject: Which of two lovers should strive harder to serve his lady, one who receives her favors, or one who does not?

20. *sals*. I can find no other example of this use of the word. The closest listed in Levy (*SW*, VII, 447) is *aver salv* "gut angewandt haben"; cf. *Flamenca* (Meyer's second edition, v. 1571):

> Be i ac salva sa noiridura
> E son estuzi e sa cura.

22. The text of a^1, which receives at least partial support from *N*, seems clearly preferable to that of the other MSS on grounds of euphony.

33. The text of *Na^1* provides a much better introduction to line 34 than does that of the other MSS.

48. *a sidonz . . . no·il platz*. Pleonastic use of the object pronoun, still common enough in several of the Romance languages.

29

I. Hom ditz que gaugz non es senes amor;
Mas hieu no·i truep mas enueg e pezansa,
Qu'anc no·n aic joy que no·m costes un plor,
Ez enaissi dobla ma malanansa.
. . . .
Qu'al prim q'eu vi ma domna ez ylh me
M'agra be ops qu'adoncs no vis ieu re.

II. Anc mai mey huelh no·m foron traïdor;
Mas eras m'an trayt ses desfiansa.
Quar m'an trahit, assatz an trahit lor,
Qu'ilh en ploran quasqun jorn ses duptansa.
En pren lo cors ez ieu lo jorn venjansa:
Lo cors del sieu sospir que va ab se,
Ez ieu del dan e del mal que m'en ve.

III. A lor ops an chauzit en la gensor
Mey huelh e pres, segon la lor esmansa;
Mas a mos ops cauziron la pejor,
Pus descobrir non l'aus ma fin' amansa,
Qu'atressi puesc la reyna de Fransa
Amar. Aisso no·m pot vedar, so cre,
Pus non l'enquier ni l'aus clamar merce.

IV. E non guardetz Paratge ni Ricor,
Dona, vas mi, mas vostra benestansa,
Quar ben podetz de bon faire melhor,
Ez er lo pros mieus e vostra l'onransa;
Quar no fai trop qui·lhs enansatz enansa,
Mas qui·lhs humils enansa e soste,
Dieu ez amics e bon pretz en rete.

VARIANTS

I. *lacking O.* 1. sens amors *T.* 3. Anc *R,* Qe anc *c;* (no·n) noi *c;* aic un gioi *T;* (no·m) non *c;* un plurs *T.* 5. *lacking in all five MSS.* 7. Be magra obs *R;* non vis en re *c,* noi vis re *T.*

II. 8. *lacking O;* (mey) nos *T;* (no·m) non *Tc*. 9. *lacking O*. 10. *lacking O;* (an) ay *R;* an traids lor *c*. 11. *lacking O*. 12. Et cum lo cor enprent lo giorn v. *T;* lo cor *Oc;* (ez ieu) en eus *C*, en eis *R*. 13. Lo cors *lacking T*, Lo cor *CORc;* dels seus sospirs *c;* sospir *lacking O;* qen ac (qe nan *Tc*) ancse *OTc*. 14. ieu *lacking T;* del mal e del dan *OTc*.

III. 15. (A) Per *O;* causida la meglior *T*. 16. (e pres) espres *O;* (la lor) lo cor *T*. 17. a mon ops *O*. 18. ma malananansa *Tc*. 19. Quatressim *CORc*. 20. (no·m) non *c*. 21. ni li aus *T*.

IV. 22. Non esgardatz *T*, Non esgardez *c*, Do nes garetz *O;* parages *O*. 24. (ben) bem *R;* faire de bon m. *O*. 25. pro *CRTc;* e vostra ner (er *T*) lonransa *OT*. 27. (qui·lhs) quis *c*, quil *O*. 28. Dieus *CT;* Deu et amics bon pres en reve *O*.

TRANSLATION

I. People say that joy cannot be without love; but I find nothing in it but care and trouble, for I never had a joy from it that did not cost me a tear. Thus it doubles my woe . . . . The first time that I saw my Lady and she me, it would have been profitable to me if, at that time, I had seen nothing at all.

II. Never before were my eyes traitors to me, but now they have betrayed me without warning. Since they betrayed me, they have betrayed themselves too, quite enough, for they weep over it every day, without any doubt. My heart and I take vengeance on them daily for it, my heart for its sigh which goes with it, and I for the hurt and harm which come to me from them.

III. My eyes have, for their profit, chosen and taken the noblest, according to their opinion. But, for me, they chose the worst, for I do not dare to reveal to her my faithful love, so that I might just as well be in love with the Queen of France. She cannot forbid me this, I think, since I do not seek her love nor do I dare to beseech mercy from her.

IV. Lady, heed not Rank nor Riches in your treatment of me, but your honor, for you can change it from good to better; and the profit will be mine, the glory yours. He who exalts the exalted does not do very much; but he who exalts and upholds the humble gains thereby the favor of God and friends and fair renown.

NOTES

Five MSS: *CORTc*. Attributed to Arnaut de Maroill in *Tc;* anonymous and incomplete in *O* (vv. 12–28), appearing as part of poem 50. Stemma:

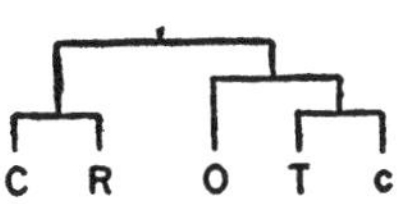

CR: 12
OTc: 13 (*qen ac ancse*), 14, 25 (*-c*)
Tc: 18 and attribution to Arnaut de Maroill
In line 25, *c* has corrected an obvious metrical error, and so returned to the correct reading.

For the general theme, and especially for the first few lines, compare Aimeric's poem 39.

1. Cnyrim, *Sprichwörter*, no. 1.

8–11. Cf. Folquet de Marseille (ed. Stronski), I, 1–6:

Ben an mort mi e lor
Mei huel galiador,
Per que·s tanh qu'ab els plor,
Pos ylh so an merit,
Qu'en tal don' an chausit
Dont han fach fallimen.

Cf. also Aimeric's poem 43, lines 22–24.

12. *lo jorn.* The nearest approach to this usage that I can find is in cases like Bernart de Ventadorn (ed. Appel), 31, 27:

Cen vetz mor lo jorn de dolor.

13. I am not sure what Aimeric means by *va ab se.*

28. *rete.* Cf. *retener lo camp* "Herr des Schlachtfeldes bleiben" (Levy, *SW*, VII, 288). Raynouard (V, 341) gives the meanings "attraper, rattraper."

30

I. Ja no cujey que·m pogues oblidar
Lo dan qu'ai pres d'amix e de senhors;
Mas lo gran dan oblid' om pels majors,
Qu'aisso es dans que no·s pot esmendar;
Que·l melher coms del mon e·lh mielhs apres—
Lays m'o, que tugh sabetz be del marques
D'Est, quals era; no·l vos qual lauzar ges—
Mortz es; mas hieu no cre que negun temps
Morisson tan de bos costums essemps.

II. Qu'elh fon savis, conoyssens, e saup far
A mezura, tan qu'era sa valors
El plus alt gra pojad' e sos pretz sors,
E sostener que no·s pogues baissar
La saup ab sen, pueys fo larcs e cortes,
Humils als bos ez als mals d'orguelh ples,
E vas domnas adregz en totas res,
E vertadiers a son poder totz temps,
Que·l cor e·l sen e·l fait hi mes essemps.

III. Autre dol ai que m'es greus a durar,
Del guai comte verones, qu'era flors
De gran beutat e de totz bes colors.
Qui·ls sieus bos aips vos volia comtar,
No·ls poiria totz retrayr' en u mes;
Ne non es hom qui tener se pogues,
Se·ls auzia, que del cor no·l plainsses.
Per so quar mais no falhiran totz temps
Aquist duy dol que son vengut essemps.

IV. Senher marques, vos faziatz donar
A tals cui dars no fora ja sabors,
Pueys faziatz als menuz donadors
Creysser lor dos quant auzian parlar
Del vostre fait cum era sobremes.
Qui fara mais los belhs dos ni·ls grans bes?
Ni de qual cort venra tan rics arnes
Cum fazia de la vostra totz temps?
Quar negus tant cum vos no·n dav' ensemps.

V. Senher marques, que faran li joglar,
A cui fezetz tans dos, tantas honors?
Mas un cosselh non sai als trobadors:
Laisso·s morir ez ano·us lai sercar,
Quar sai no vei guaire qui de lor pes,
Quar vos no·y etz ni·l valens coms no·y es.
Pauc nos laisset Dieus vas que trop n'a pres.
Si! Laysset tant que durara totz temps,
Plangz e sospirs e dolors tot essemps.

VI. Aquelh vers Dieus que fo ez er totz temps
Los met' amdos em paradis ensemps!

VARIANTS

I. 1. Anc *C*, Ça *D*, Qa *I;* nom *R*. 2. danz *D;* damic *IK*. 3. lo granz dans *DIK;* oblidon *DIK;* pel maior *C*, per lo maior *E*, per maior *R*, pel maiors *DIK*. 5. melhor *CDR;* cors *DR*. 7. (D'Est) Del *IK;* (no·l) no *DIK;* vos *lacking E;* (qual) cals *I;* (ges) gens *D*. 8. Mortz es *lacking CR;* Pos mortz es *E*. 9. Moris om *D;* tans *CIKR;* bon costum *DIK;* (costums essemps) castiamens *E*.

II. 10. savis e conoissens *DE;* sap *DIK*. 12. pozad *D*, poiat *ER*, poiatz *C*, poiar *IK;* sos pretz *lacking E*. 14. (La) Lo *IKR;* sap *I;* (cortes) contes *D*. 16. E bos darmas adreichs en totas tens *D*. 17. tot temps *IK;* tepms (*sic*) *D*. 18. Quel cor el sen i met el fait e. *DIK;* el faitz *CR*, els faitz *E*.

III. 19. greus ad uzar *R*. 20. ver ont es *C*. 22. Quil seu *D*, Qil seus *IK*. 23. retrar *IK*. 24. (qui) que *DER;* (se) sen *E*. 25. de cor *DIK;* (no·l) non *DEIK;* plaisses *CER*, plangues *D*. 26. (quar) que *IK;* faillia *IK;* null temps *DIK*.

IV. 29. (cui) qui *C;* dar *CDR*, donars *IK;* ja d. no fora sabors *DIK*. 30. (als) al *D*. 31. lurs *R*. 32. Del vostre (vostres *K*) faitz *IK;* eran *IK*. 33. (belhs) grans *E*. 34. tanz *IK*. 36. (dav') donava *E*, dad *D*.

V. 37. faraun *E*. 38. fedes *D*. 40. Laisses *I;* (ano·us) anons *K*, anos *DI*, anol *ER;* (lai) lais *DIK*. 41. (Quar) Que *IK;* (qui) que *K*. 42. (ni·l) nel *D*. 43. Pauc los lauset deus *D*. 44. Sil *R;* (que) quel *D;* durera *DIK*.

VI. 46. ver *CDR*.

TRANSLATION

I. Never did I think that I could forget the losses I have had of friends and lords; but one forgets a great loss for those which are still greater; and this is a loss which cannot be made good, for the best and wisest count in the world—I leave off, for all of you know what manner of man the Marquis of Este was: no need to praise him—is dead. I do not believe that ever so many good customs died together.

II. He was wise, intelligent, and knew how to act with moderation, so that his fame had mounted to the highest places and his glory risen up. He knew how to uphold it with wisdom, so that it could not sink, for he was generous and courteous, humble toward the good, full of pride toward the evil, and toward the ladies upright in all things, and truthful always as much as he could be, for he put into these things heart and mind and action all together.

III. Another sorrow I have, grievous to endure, for the gay Count of Verona, who was the flower of beauty and paragon of all good qualities. If anyone wished to tell you his good qualities, he could not mention them all in a month; nor is there any man who, if he heard them, would not mourn him heartily. Therefore, these two sorrows, which came together, will never cease.

IV. Lord Marquis, by your liberality you made certain men give gifts to whom giving would not (otherwise) have been agreeable, since you caused the small givers to increase their gifts when they heard tell of your actions, how liberally you gave. Who will now make the fair gifts or the great alms? From what court will come now the rich costumes, as they did always from yours? No one gave as many of them together as you.

V. Lord Marquis, what will the minstrels do now, to whom you gave so many gifts, so many honors? I know but one good counsel for the troubadours to follow: let them die and go look for you beyond the grave, for here on earth I see no one who thinks of them, since you and the worthy Count are here no longer. God left us little and took too much away. Yea! He left us what will endure forever, moaning and sighing and sorrow all together!

VI. May that true God, who was and will be forever, put them both together in Paradise!

NOTES

Six MSS: *CDEIKR*, which fall into the customary groups *DIK* and *CER*, thus:

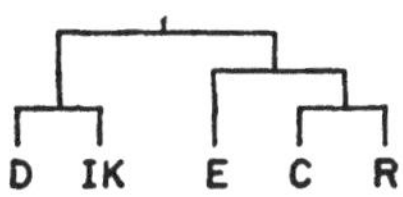

DIK: 3, 7, 9, 40

IK: 2, 7, 12, 17, etc.

CER: 25, 40 (-*C*)

CR: 5, 8

In 40, we may assume that *C* has corrected a mistake preserved in *ER*. Various occasional agreements can be attributed to coincidence: *DE* 10, *CDR* 5, *DR* 5 (*cors;* see the note on this line).

The poem has been edited critically: De Bartholomaeis, *Poesie storiche*, I, 182–186. This text is apparently based on *D*, with extensive borrowings from *IK*. We have chosen *C* as our base.

A *planh* on the death of Azzo VI of Este and Bonifazio di San Bonifazio. Date: November, 1212. See our Introduction, and the comments and quotations from sources in De Bartholomaeis, *loc. cit*. Aimeric's poem 48 is another *planh* for the same two men.

5. *coms*. It may be, since Aimeric calls Azzo *marques* in line 6, that we should read *cors* "person" here (with *DR*); whichever way the confusion went, it is easy to see how an *m* (shaped something like a 3) and an *r* could be confused in the script of these copyists.

6. *Lays m'o*. Although I have found no exact parallels to this construction, the meaning seems clear. De Bartholomaeis: "ometto ciò."

8. De Bartholomaeis: *qu'e negun temps*. This reading is perhaps preferable (the sense is the same, in any case); but it is noteworthy that none of the MSS have *qu'en*, which we should expect as a variant of *qu'e*.

18. De Bartholomaeis: *els faitz*, which is equally good; but cf. *vostre fait*, in the same sense, in line 32.

21. *colors*. Levy (*SW*, I, 283) suggests the translation "splendeur; das was Farbe, Glanz verleiht." De Bartholomaeis, reading as we do, nevertheless translates "di ogni bel colore." The word is surely almost a synonym of *flors* in line 20: that which is excellent of its kind. The reading *bels* for *bes*, implied by De Bartholomaeis's translation, is not warranted by any of the MSS.

44. De Bartholomaeis puts a comma at the end of line 43, and reads: *Si laisset, tant que*, etc., which he translates: "se lasciò, ciò che durerà sempre, pianti," etc.

31

"LANQUAN CHANTON LI AUZEL EN PRIMIER"

This poem, attributed to Aimeric by four MSS, and to Guillem Rainol d'At by another, is almost certainly not the work of Aimeric. See the section of the Introduction dealing with attributions, and, for a critical text and elaboration of the reasons for denying it to Aimeric, our article in *Romance Philology*, II, 83. For purposes of greater accessibility, we reproduce in an appendix the text of the poem, but not the variant readings.

32

I. Li fol e·il put e·il filol
Creison trop e no m'es bel;
E·il croi joglaret novel,
Enojos e mal parlan,
Corron un pauc trop enan;
E son ja li mordedor,
Per un de nos dui de lor,
E non es qui los n'esqerna.

II. Greu m'es car hom lor o col
E non lor en fai revel.
Non o dic contra·N Sordel,
Q'el non es d'aital semblan
Ni no·is vai ges percassan,
Si co·il cavallier doctor;
Mas qan faillon prestador,
Non pot far cinc ni sieis terna.

III. Lo marques part Pinarol,
Que ten Salus e Revel,
Non vuoill ges que desclavel
De sa cort ni an loignan
Persaval, que sap d'enfan
Esser maestre e tutor,
Ni un autre tirador,
Qu'eu no vuoil dir, de Luserna.

IV. Aitals los a cum los vol,
Lo marques, Encantarel,
Nicholet e Trufarel,
Que venon ab lui e van,
E non del tot pel lor dan.
Be·is son trobat d'un color:
Aitals vassals tal seignor!
Dieus lor done *vita eterna.*

V. Ar veiretz venir l'estol
Vas Malespina e·l tropel,

Don an la carn e la pel;
Et ades on pieitz lor fan,
E meins de merce lor an.
Trop son li combatedor
E pauc li defendedor:
Mort son si Dieus no·ls governa.

VI. Estampidas e romor
Sai que faran entre lor,
Menassan en la taverna.

VARIANTS

I. 2. non es belh *CIK*. 4. Enveyos *CR*. 7. des nos *D;* (dui) dos *A*, *lacking D;* des lor *DIK*, deus lor *C*. 8. (los) lor *D;* quils n. *C*.

II. 9. (m'es) es *CR*, er *IK;* lor acol *DIK*. 11. contral sordel *DIK*. 12. daitan s. *IK*. 15. faillol p. *IK*. 16. .v. nils sincs *IK*, cinc ni cincs *C*, .v. ni .vi. *R*, .v. sul cincs *D*.

III. 17. (part) par *D*. 19. No vuelh que ab si mapel *C*. 20. En sa cort don vau lunhan *C*. 21. Per soval *D*. 22. Esser maestrador *DIK*, Esser maystre tuor *R*. 23. (tirador) tuador *C*.

IV. 26. (Encantarel) den cantarel *DR*, den cautarel *C*, de cantarel *AIK*. 27. (e) el *CDIKR*. 29. (pel lor) per lor *CDIK*, per los *R*. 30. (Be·is) Ben *CDIK*, Bes *R*. 31. A tals vassals *CR*. 32. (done) do *CDIKR*.

V. 34. malaspinal t. *C*. 36. (fan) an *I*. 40. Mortz *CIKR;* si *lacking I*.

VI. 41. E. errimor *IK;* rimor *R*. 42. (que) quen *CIKR*.

TRANSLATION

I. The fools, the wicked, and their offspring grow too numerous; and that is not to my liking. The contemptible new minstrels, tiresome and slanderous, are getting too forward. Already the backbiters are ahead—two of them for one of us; and there is nobody who scorns them for it.

II. It grieves me when one takes that from them and does not oppose them. I do not say that against Sir Sordello, for he is not like them nor does he persecute us like the learned knights. When money-lenders are lacking, he cannot make a five or a six into a double three (?).

III. The Marquis from near Pinerolo, who holds Saluzzo and Revello, I do not wish him to lock out of his court nor keep at a distance Percival, who knows how to be the teacher and guardian of the boy, nor another leech from Luserna, whom I do not care to name.

IV. He has them just as he wants them, the Marquis: Encantarel, Nicholet and Trufarel, who go and come with him, not at all to their loss. They are all of the same color; like vassals, like lord. May God give them *vita eterna*!

V. Now you will see the band and the troop coming towards Malaspina, of which they have the flesh and the hide. Always when they treat them worse, the less mercy they have for them. The fighters are too many, the defenders are few. Dead they are, if God does not lead them.

VI. I know that they will stamp and roar about it among themselves, uttering threats in the tavern.

NOTES

Six MSS: *ACDIKR*. Critical editions: Witthoeft, *Sirventes joglaresc*, p. 69; De Bartholomaeis, in *Studj romanzi*, VII, 297, and again, substantially the same text, in *Poesie storiche*, I, 241.

The MSS differ materially in only one or two lines, and it is almost impossible to construct a really satisfactory stemma. *IK* of course go together (12, 15), and the group *DIK* seems well established (11, 22). Depending on which version we accept as correct, lines 7, 16, 30 indicate either *CDIK* or *AR* as groups containing common mistakes. But these groupings conflict with others: *CR* (4, 31), *CIK* (2), *CIKR* (40), *IKR* (41). We may discount some of these latter as mere coincidences; and we may assume that *D* had access to a MS related to *A*. With these reservations (and they amount to a very big "if"), we propose the following stemma as perhaps the best that can be devised:

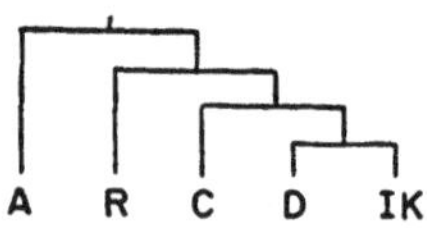

Our text is based on *A*.

This *sirventes* is a recognizable imitation of a *sirventes* of Bertran de Born (80, 28; Stimming, no. 15), from which Aimeric has taken not only his meter and his rimes, but also several whole phrases. He has also assumed some of Bertran's fine frenzy and not a little of his difficulty; for the poem is full of obscure allusions. It has been the subject of numerous commentaries and studies, to which we shall have occasion to refer in the notes. Opinions have differed widely over details, but there seems to be general agreement that the Marquis is Manfred III of Saluzzo, who succeeded his grandfather, at the age of ten, in 1215, and ruled until 1244. The references to his guardians date the poem in Manfred's minority. The young man was declared of age in 1220, according to De Bartholomaeis (above references); and this scholar would date the poem in that year, shortly after the death of William Malaspina, believing that Aimeric would not, during William's lifetime, have said that Malaspina was in danger of being overrun by the persons whom he is attacking in the poem. This is a good guess, but I do not know that we are obliged to accept the date as definitely proved; as De Bartholomaeis himself admits, young Manfred did not exercise his full powers until some years later.

1. According to Jeanroy (*Romania*, XLI, 141, a review of De Bartholomaeis's article in *Studj romanzi*), *put* and *filol* together mean approximately "débauché" (cf. the meanings of the corresponding feminines).

2. *m'es bel.* Bertran de Born, the poem mentioned above (Stimming, no. 15), line 50: *de cui m'es bel.*

8. *n'esqerna.* Bertran de Born, *ibid.*, line 67: *qui que·m n'esquerna.*

9. Witthoeft and De Bartholomaeis: *lor acol.* Jeanroy (*loc. cit.*) prefers our reading: "leur permet cela."

15. Jeanroy: *faillol* (with *IK*).

16. A puzzling line, which has exercised the ingenuity of editors and critics. The reference is plainly to various throws of dice: Sordello could not win at dice without stakes advanced by money-lenders. But, in view of the divergent MS readings, the text is not certain, and the exact interpretation is still less so. We agree with Levy (*SW*, VIII, 181) that none of the emendations and translations that have been offered for *ni sieis* are entirely satisfactory (*ni s'ieis* "nè, se esce"; *nis s'ieis* "pas même s'il amène"; *nil eis* "e essi nemmeno"; *ni neis* "ni même"). According to Semrau, *Würfel und Würfelspiel*, p. 70, *terna* was a better throw than *cinc;* this eliminates the suggestion *ni neis;* the others are simply not very convincing. Shall we understand: "without money advanced by lenders, Sordello cannot make a five or a six into a *terna* (a double three)"? That is, he cannot turn moderate luck into good luck without their help. Bertran de Born (line 70) has: *Be puosc far cinc et ilh terna*, which does not help us much. Perhaps the original here had: *.v., .vi. ni terna*, or, better, *.u., .ui. ni terna*, which would make sense of a sort, and in which the *ui* and *ni* could easily be confused. On the whole, this seems to us the most likely possibility; but we have not ventured to introduce the emendation into the text. Neither it nor the other suggestions can explain the readings of the other MSS, which, incidentally, have been given rather carelessly by previous editors.

21. *Persaval.* Both Schultz-Gora (*Zeitschrift für r. Ph.*, VII, 205) and De Bartholomaeis reject the identification with Perseval Doria, which had been suggested by Cavedoni. De Bartholomaeis (*Studj rom.* VII, 325) suggests Bonifazio di Piossasco, called in various documents by the nickname *Percevallus;* he was associated in the regency for Manfred with the latter's grandmother.

23. *tirador.* De Bartholomaeis, *tuador*, synonymous with *tutor* in line 22. Jeanroy prefers to keep the reading of the majority of the MSS, and refers to Mistral's Modern Provençal *tiradou* "sangsue, personne avide, qui soutire de l'argent par finesse." Levy (*SW*, VIII, 233) thinks this at least possible.

24. *de Luserna.* Schultz-Gora (*loc. cit.*) and Witthoeft identify the *tirador de Luserna* as Peire Guilhem de Luserna, following Cavedoni (*Trovatori provenzali alla corte de' Marchesi d'Este*, p. 43). De Bartholomaeis (*Studj. rom.*, VII, 320) doubts this, since according to his reading of the preceding line this person would have to be one of the young marquis's guardians. He suggests Willelmus Billiator de Luserna, who was at the court of Saluzzo at the time. Even with our reading in line 23, this identification is perhaps preferable, since we have no indication that Peire Guilhem was ever at Saluzzo.

26. We take *lo marques* as the subject of the verb in line 25, the three names that follow as objects of the same verb. We read *Encantarel*, with Bertoni (*Annales du Midi*, XXIV, 217), though *En Cantarel* would not be impossible; one could even take the honorific *En* as ironic. A greater difficulty is that all the MSS have a *de* before this name. Witthoeft takes the line to mean "the Marquis of Encantarello," which would have to be ironic, since there was no such marquis. We may assume that all the copyists interpreted the line in this same way, or that their common original did so, which is not impossible; this would explain the *de*. A further difficulty, however, is that three of the MSS (*AIK*) have *de cantarel*, not *den cantarel;* this is against an *Encantarel.* Jeanroy accepts *Encantarel;* De Bartholomaeis and Schultz-Gora (*Prov. Stud.*, II, 125) prefer *En Cantarel.* This person is perhaps the same as the *En Cantarel* (or *Enc.*) of a poem of Amoros dau Luc (22, 1; ed. by Schultz-Gora, *loc. cit.*), who is otherwise unidentified. *Cantarel* could be a nickname; Levy (*SW*, I, 200); "gerne, häufig singend."

27. *Nicholet* is unknown. There seems to be no reason to identify him, as Schultz-Gora did (*Zs. für r. Ph.*, VII, 214) as Nicolet de Turin, though of course this may be right. *Trufarel* is probably a nickname. Raynouard translates "railleur, moqueur, farceur"; cf. Mistral's Modern Provençal *trufarèu* "qui aime à se moquer, railleur"; De Bartholomaeis, "truffaldino"; Jeanroy, "coquin." Levy does not decide among these meanings in the *SW*, but in the

PD he gives "railleur?". All the MSS but *A* have the definite article with the name; but it may equally well have been used without, so we retain the reading of *A*.

30. *Be·is*. Jeanroy prefers *Ben;* but the reflexive occurs in both *A* and *R*. Notice that *color* here is masculine.

31. Cnyrim, *Sprichwörter*, no. 174a.

32. We follow Levy (*SW*, VIII, 513, under *trufarel*) in keeping *A*'s reading *done*. Bertran de Born (line 16) scans *vid' eterna*, and Aimeric would probably follow his example.

35. This line is not clear. De Bartholomaeis reads *donan*, "giving," but we agree with Jeanroy that *don an* "of which they have" is more likely, since these jongleurs were evidently more inclined to take than to give.

35–37. Jeanroy: "Plus on (les 'défenseurs' du v. 39) les maltraite (les assaillants), moins ils (ceux-ci) épargnent leurs ennemis." But the lines are very confusing.

39. De Bartholomaeis puts a question mark at the end of this line; our punctuation seems to us somewhat better.

40. Bertran de Born (line 56): *cui bos pretz governa*.

33

I. Lonjamen m'a trebalhat e malmes
Sens nulh repaus Amors en son poder,
Si que del tot m'a vencut e conques;
Mas era·m te guay ez en bon esper,
Qu'a mos huelhs a mostrada la gensor
Ez e mon cor enclauza la melhor,
Per que del tot m'an guazanhat mei huelh
E tenc en car mon cor pus que no suelh.

II. Mezur' e sen, qu'es razitz de totz bes,
Joven, beutat, conoissens' e saber
Pauzet en lieys Dieus quan la nos trames,
E volc que fos (per so quar sap valer)
Sa valensa plus valens de valor
E s'onransa plus honrada d'onor.
No cre, per qu'ieu de lieys no·m lunh ni·m tuelh,
Qu'altr' ab tans bes se viesta ni·s despuelh.

III. Que·l belh semblan plazen e·l mot cortes,
E·l dous esguart biaissat e·l plazer,
Qu'ab mezura fai e di quan luecs es,
La fan a toz blandir e quar tener;
Qu'om no la ve que no·n digua lauzor,
Qu'a mi mezeis fan doblar ma dolor,
Quan lur aug dir cum parla ni acuelh,
E platz m'en mais lo mals on plus m'en duelh.

IV. Anc no cugei mais avenir pogues
A nulh home, ni ges no sembla ver
Que sa dolors l'abelis ni·l plagues;
Mas a mi platz on plus me fai doler,
Que lo mieus mals es de fin amador,
Per qu'es un pauc atempratz en doussor.
Pero soven de lagremas en muelh
Mon vis quar no·n l'aus dir lo ben qu'ieu·l vuelh.

V. A mi eys dic lo pus belh prec qu'ieu pes,
E fas cum si la pregav' a parer,
Pueys ab cor fait, quant ai mon cosselh pres,

Venc denant lieys que·l cug dir mo voler;
E quan la vey, no sai s'es per amor
O per temer o per sa gran ricor,
Torn ses parlar mutz, e non per orguelh
Qu'ilh me mostre, ans m'es d'umil escuelh.

VI. Na Beatritz d'Est, anc plus belha flor,
Ni de vostre temps non trobiei melhor.
Tant etz bona, cum plus lauzar vos vuelh,
Ades hi trop pus de be que no suelh.

VII. Senher Guilhem Malespina, l'onor
Avetz de totz los bos aips e d'Amor,
Don vos es pres mielhs c'a·N Gui de Nantuelh,
Car etz valens e d'amoros escuelh.

VARIANTS

I. 1. Luiamen *O*, Loniamens *R;* man t. e mal ires *P*. 3. (m'a) man *P*. 4. (era·m) el em *P;* guay e de bon *C*, iauzen en bon *N*. 5. (Qu'a) Car a *N;* (a) ma *AN*, man *DIKP;* mostrat *NP*. 6. cors *P;* est clausa *N;* (la) li *I*. 7. (Per) Si *O;* gadainat ma m. *P;* (m'an) ma *f*. 8. El temps car mos cors plus qe non soill *P*, E tenc mon cor plus car qe ieu non s. *M;* E tenc nan car *N*, En tenc en car *IKRf;* cors *AOf;* (pus) mai *f;* (que) queu *IKMN*.

II. 9. sens *Mf;* qes de totz bes razitz *A;* raiz *DFaIKOR*. 10. Iouentz beutatz *N*, Iouens e beutatz *f;* conoissanz e *O*. 11. Poisch en len dex *P;* (quan la) qa lan *Fa*. 12. pero *N;* (quar) qe *P;* saup *R*. 13. Sa u. ualens e de ualor *C*, Sa u. ualenz plus de ualor *M*, Sa u. es plus ualent de u. *O;* (Sa) Si *I*. 14. (honrada) honranda *FaN;* (d'onor) damor *O*. 15. Per que de leis non cre miloin nim t. *N;* Ni cre *M*, Nom cre *f;* qeu de loing de ley em t. *P*. 16. Quen tot lo mon tan bella si d. *M*, Ni qualtre si uestre ni d. *P*, Ni cautra tan bes uesta nis d. *N;* (ni·s) ni *D*.

III. 17. Qel b. s. mot gay e c. *P;* (Que·l) Del *O;* (belh) gai *IKR*, gais *Nf;* plazentz *Nf;* (e·l) e *R*, els *f;* (mot) ditz *f*. 18. Eil dous e. de sos huoills eil p. *A*, El douz e. del sei oill plazer *D*, El dous e. quil sap far el p. *N;* esguartz *CN;* biaissatz *C*, bias faiz *P*, baissat *O*. 19. (ab) a *M;* di e fai *DIKMNOPR*, ditz e faitz *f;* can lo luocs es *D*. 20. (La) Lo *C*, Le P*;* fay *P;* a tot *O*. 21. Com non ueuey com non diga l. *P;* (que) com *R*. 22. (fan) fa *O*, fai *NP;* (ma) la *CR;* (dolor) folhor *C*. 23. Qan ilor *P*. 24. platz mi *AMOR*, plaz me me *D;* lo mal *CIK*, los mals *Nf;* (mais) plus *IKNPR;* (plus) mai *f;* mi duelh *ADMO*.

IV. 25. cuiz *P;* cauenir *IKNRf*. 26. hom *P;* (no) nom *AIKP*. 28. Mas am plus com mais em ma dolor *P;* Mas sa plaz *D*. 29. *lacking P;* (Que) Car *IKNRf;* (es) en *O*. 30. *lacking P;* Per quieu sui pauc a. *CM*, Per que un pauc nes a. *N;* (en) ab *Rf*. 31. Per so *P;* larmas *N;* (en) em *P*, mi *M*. 32. Lo uis *CM;* non aus *P*, nol laus *N;* qel u. *NOf*, qil u. *P*.

V. 33. A mi mezeis *NPf*, A mi es *IK;* (prec) plech *P;* (qu'ieu) qe *P*, qem *KR*. 34. (la) leis *IKR*, len *NP*, lils *f;* preger a parer *M*, prech ao parer *P*. 35. Pois a co fag *N*, Pueys ab co fait *P;* nai *AIKRf;* mon cosselh pres *lacking K;* pres *lacking I*. 36. Venc *through* dir *lacking K;* (que·l) el *C*. 37. (no) si *N;* (s'es) sis *C*. 38. O per temer o per temer ricor *P;* O per son pretz *O*. 39. mutz *lacking M;* e non ges per o. *M*, e non genz per egroil *N*. 40. Que me mostre *C*, Quellam mostre *IKNRf*, *lacking P;* (escuelh) acuelh *C*.

VI. (VII *in IKR*) *lacking f*. 41. Valenz beatrix anc *P;* (anc) an *C;* belha *lacking M*. 42. *line added in margin in N;* De (Del *A*) uostre tems no t. ni (*lacking D*) meillor *ADNOP*, De u. t. non ui hom ni melhor *IKR*. 43. (cum) on *N;* (plus) mais *P;* (vos) la *M* (*added above the line*). 44. hi *lacking KP;* (plus) mais *NO;* queu *ADIKN*.

VII. (VI *in IKRf*) *lacking CDMNOP*. 45. Seignen guillem *A*. 46. totz bos aips *f*. 47. gui de lantuoill *IK*.

TRANSLATION

I. Love, in his might, has tormented and mistreated me for a long time without respite, so that he has overcome and conquered me; but now I am joyful and of good hope, for he has shown to my eyes the noblest and in my heart enclosed the best. Therefore my eyes have won me entirely and I hold my heart dearer than I was wont to do.

II. God, when he sent her to us, put in her moderation and sense, which is the root of all good qualities, youth, beauty, knowledge and wisdom; and He willed (because she knows how to be worthy) that her worthiness be more worthy than Worth, and her honor more honored than Honor. I do not believe that any other woman with so many good qualities clothes or unclothes herself; and therefore I do not depart nor take myself from her.

III. Her fair and pleasing looks, her courteous words, her sweet sidelong glances and the pleasing things that she does and says, in moderation and in the right place, make her to be courted and held dear by all, so that no one sees her without uttering her praise. But to me this doubles my woe, when I hear them tell how she speaks and welcomes them; and yet the woe by which I am most grieved pleases me also the most.

IV. I never thought that this could happen to any man, nor does it seem true, that his sorrows could delight and please him. But I take delight in what grieves me most, for my woe is that of a faithful lover, wherefore it is a little tempered by sweet thoughts. For that reason I often wet my face with tears, since I do not dare to tell how much I love her.

V. I say to myself the fairest prayer that I can think of; and I act as if I were begging her to appear, since with a firm heart, when I have made up my mind, I come before her and think to tell her my desire. But when I see her, I know not whether it is through love or fear or her high rank, I turn back silent, without speaking, not by reason of any arrogant bearing toward me, for she is humble in her conduct.

VI. Lady Beatrice of Este, never in your time did I find a fairer flower nor a better. You are so good that when I wish to praise you most, I find in you always more good qualities than I was wont to do.

VII. Lord William Malaspina, you have the honor of all good qualities and of Love; wherefore more good has come to you than to Sir Guy of Nanteuil, for you are worthy and of a loving bearing.

NOTES

Thirteen MSS: *ACDFaIKMNOPRbf*. Of these, *Fa* contains only the second stanza, *b* (which we have not consulted) only the second envoi. Stanzas two and five are quoted in the

Breviari d'amor, lines 29899 and 33770, respectively (Variants: 9. *Mesura sens.* 10. *conoissensa saber.* 14. *E sobr autras.* 33. *Quan mielhs dic lo plus.* 34. (*parer*) *plazer.* 40. (*d'umil*) *de bel*). Barbieri quotes the envoi to Beatrice of Este (stanza six) in apparently the same form as in *b;* see Pillet-Carstens, no. 33 (ed. Tiraboschi, p. 112. Variants: 41. *anc non vi plus bel flor*). The poem is attributed to Blacasset in *P*, and is anonymous in *O*.

De Bartholomaeis (*Poesie storiche*, I, 227) prints stanzas one, six, and seven (after *A*).

It is impossible to construct a satisfactory stemma. Certain small groups seem well established: *AD* (18), *CM* (30, 42), *IKR* (34, 42, order of the envois); but the relations of the other MSS are less obvious. In 17, 25, 29 (-*P*), 40 (-*C*), *IKNRf* seem to form a separate family from *ACDMOP*. But 34, 35 would indicate a group *NP*, to which *f* is added in 33; and this contradicts the division just mentioned. The position of *O* is even less clear.

Base: *C* (for the second envoi, lacking in *C*, the text of *IKR* is adapted to the orthography of *C*).

13–14. Such plays on words appear in a number of poems of Aimeric; cf., for example, poem 18, *passim*.

16. *se viesta ni·s despuelh.* Cf. line 33 of poem 53, wrongly attributed to Aimeric (printed in the Appendix):

D'esser clamans mi desviest e·m despuelh.

Was this line the reason for the attribution to our poet?

24. A commonplace of the troubadours, recurring with monotonous frequency in poem after poem.

25. Another example of parataxis, which is about as common in Old Provençal as in Old French.

33ff. The poet is tongue-tied in his Lady's presence. Aimeric often expresses this thought, as do countless other troubadours. See Wechssler, *Kulturproblem*, I, 260.

34

I. Mangtas vetz sui enqueritz
En cort cossi vers no fatz;
Per qu'ieu vuelh si' apellatz—
E sia lur lo chauzitz—
Chansos o vers aquest chans.
E respon als demandans
Qu'om non troba ni sap devezio
Mas sol lo nom entre vers e chanso.

II. Qu'ieu ai motz mascles auzitz
En chansonetas assatz,
E motz femenis pausatz
En verses bos e grazitz;
E cortz sonetz e cochans
Ai auzitz en verses mans,
Ez auzida chansonet' ab lonc so,
E·ls motz d'amdos d'un gran e·l chant d'un to.

III. E s'ieu en so desmentitz
Qu'aisso no sia vertatz,
Non er hom per me blasmatz,
Si per dreg m'o contraditz;
Ans n'er sos sabers plus grans
Entre·ls bos e·l mieus mermans,
Si d'aisso·m pot venser segon razo,
Qu'ieu non ai ges tot lo sen Salamo.

IV. Quar es de son loc partitz
Domneys que ja fo prezatz,
Mi sui alques desviatz
De joy, tan n'estau marritz,
Qu'entr' amairitz ez amans
S'es mes us pales enjans,
Qu'enjanan l'us l'autre cre far son pro,
E no·i guardo temps ni per que ni quo.

V. Qu'ieu vi, ans que fos faiditz,
Si fos per amor donatz
Us cordos, qu'a dreg solatz
N'issi' acortz e covitz;
Per que·m par que dur dos tans
Us mes no fazia us· ans,
Quan renhava Domneys ses tracio.
Greu es qui ve cum es e sap cum fo.

VI. E non es tan relenquitz,
Si tot mi sui desamatz,
Qu'ieu no sia enamoratz
De tal qu'es sima e razitz
De Pretz, tan qu'a me es dans,
Pus la valors e·l semblans
Son assemblat en tan bella faisso
Qu'om no·i pot neys pessar meluirazo.

VII. Hai! belhs cors cars, gen noiritz,
Adregz e gen faissonatz,
So qu'ie·us vuelh dir devinatz,
Qu'ieu no suy ges tan arditz
Qu'ie·us prec que m'ametz; abans
Vos clam merce merceyans.
Sufretz qu'ie·us am e no·us quier autre do;
E ges d'aquest no·m devetz dir de no.

VIII. Vas Malespina ten, chans,
Al pro Guillem qu'es prezans,
Qu'elh aprenda de te los motz e·l so,
Qual que·s vuelha, per vers o per chanso.

IX. Na Beatritz d'Est, l'enans
De vos mi platz, que·s fai grans.
En vos lauzar s'en son pres tug li bo,
Per que de vos dauri mo vers-chanso.

VARIANTS

I. 1. sui *lacking c;* enquezitz *IK*. 2. cortz *AJQc*. 3. E vuelh que si a. *R;* (qu'ieu) qen D^a, quien *K;* (vuelh) voilla D^a, meil *Q*. 4. lurs *C*D^a*IJK;* chauzir *R*. 5. Chanso *CR*. 6. als de mos dans *R*, als demanz D^a. 7. (non) noi *QUc*. 8. (sol) cant *AJ*, so *I;* lo *lacking Uc*.

II. 9. Esi eu moz mesclaz auziz *U*. 10. (En) E *CJ;* chanzonetta *U*. 11. (pauzatz) passatz *J*, trobatz *Q*. 12. (En) E *CJ;* versetz *AD^a IJK*, vertes *Q;* bos e gen digz *C*. 13. (cortz) croitz *IK*, tortç *Q;* sonet *U;* (cochans) trotans *AJRU*, cointatz *D^a*, coitanz *IK*, toçanç *Q*, choçanz *c*. 14. Ai ieu auzitz *C;* verset m. *U*, verteç maiç *Q*, vers prezans *R*, v. inans *c*. 15. Et ai auzit *A*, E chansos ai auzidas *R;* chanso nec ab *D^a IK*. 16. Els mos abdos dun lonc *R;* (E·ls) E *U;* (gran) grau *c;* el chan el son *Q*, el caszim to *J*.

III. 17. El sieu *D^a*. 18. Caissi non *AD^a IJKQUc*. 19. No uerom *Q*. 20. (m'o) non *Q*, nom *R*. 21. (n'er) er *C*, nes *Uc;* plus *lacking R;* (grans) gratiç *Q*, grazitz *R*. 22. Entrel bons *U;* (bos) pros *Q;* mermatz *R*. 23. (Si) Qi *R;* daiçon *c*. 24. Com non ai ges *Q*.

IV. 25. (loc) loing *U;* (partitz) issitz *AD^a IJK*. 26. que fon ja *R;* preiatç *Q*. 27. Ne soi *R*. 28. Damar *AD^a IJK;* tant estauch *Q*, tan mestau *C*, tan mestai *U*. 29. Car ieu conosc que en mans *R;* Quentre (Qentrels *U*, Qentrel *c*) maritz *CUc;* (ez) els *Uc*. 30. Se mes *c*. 31. Quenganan cre lus lautre *AD^a IJKQR*. 32. non *J;* garda *QRc*, gard *U*.

V. 33. Ieu vi *R;* qel fos *Uc;* faizitz *R*. 34. Sius fos *AD^a IJKQc*, Seu fos *U*, Que si fos *R;* amors *CR;* (donatz) datz *R*. 35. Us coidos qas dreiz s. *U;* cordes *I;* cadieg solatz *Q*, que bel solatz *R*. 36. Nissira cortz *C*, Nissira e corç *c*, Nissi cortz *U;* (cortz e) e ricx *R*. 37. (que·m) qim *Q*, que *R*. 38. Us mes no sol far us ans *R*. 39. (Quan) Que *I;* ses trahizo *A*, ses ochaiszo *J*. 40. Et es be vius qui vi ni sap quo fo *C*, Et es me greu qieu vi e say com fo *R*.

VI. *lacking Q*. 41. (E) Mas *AJ;* Non estau r. *R*. 44. tal qe cima e raitz *Uc;* simeratz *I*, simeraitz *K*. 45. tan qan mi *U;* (tan) per *R*. 46. (Pus) Can *R*. 47. assemblatz *C*. 48. (neys) plus *AJ*, ges *R*; meillur raison *Uc*.

VII. 49. Ab bel cor cars *U;* belh *C;* (cars) gay *R*. 50. E gent adregz e be fagz *C;* Adreg ben afaissonatz (afoissonatz *I*) *IK;* (gen) ben *QRUc*, bechz *D^a*. 51. *lacking J;* So quieu vuelh *C*, So que vuelh *R;* dir *lacking R*. 52. Que ges no soi *R;* (suy) sai *Q*. 53. Vos prec me ametz abans *C;* Qieu prec *A;* (abans) enans *AJ*. 54. (clam) qer *Q*. 55. (e) que *Q;* e non vus quier *U*. 56. *lacking c;* (E ges) E ia *AD^a IJKR*, Ni ia *Q;* daiso *U;* (no·m) non *U*.

VIII. *lacking JQ*. 57. (ten) vai *C;* chanso *R*. 58. prezatz *CUc*. 59. Quelh en prenda de totz los motz el so *C;* (te) tu *R*. 60. Cals *IK;* (que·s) ges *U*.

IX. *lacking QRUc*. 61. (d'Est, l'enans) dels enans *C*. 62. que son grans *C*. 63. (En) Ca *AD^a IJK;* (s'en) si *AD^a IJK;* (pres) mes *J*. 64. Per qieu ab vos *AD^a IJK;* (dauri) dautra *D^a*.

TRANSLATION

I. Many times I have been asked at court how it is that I do not compose "vers"; and therefore I wish that this song be called either "chanso" or "vers". Let the choice of names be theirs. And I reply to the questioners that one does not find or know any difference, except in name, between "vers" and "chanso".

II. I have heard plenty of masculine words in "chansonetas" and feminine words put into good and pleasing "vers", and I have heard short and swift tunes in many "vers", and heard "chansonetas" with long, slow tunes; and also the words of both of one length and the music of one key.

III. If I am given the lie and told that this is not the truth, no one will be blamed by me for that, if some one contradicts me rightly. On the contrary, his knowledge will be the greater for it among good people, and mine will be less, if in that respect he can conquer me reasonably; for I have not all the wisdom of Solomon.

IV. Because Lady-service, which once was honored, has forsaken its lofty place, I have turned away from Joy, so saddened am I by the fact that open deceit has come to pass between lovers, so that when one deceives the other, he thinks to profit by it himself; and they do not consider either the season or the cause or the manner.

V. Before I was exiled, I saw that, if a ribbon was given for love, accord and invitations came out of it with real pleasure. Therefore, it seems to me that now a month lasts twice as long as a year did when Lady-service reigned without treason. Grievous it is to anyone who sees how it is now and knows how it was.

VI. But it is not so forsaken, although I have fallen out of love, that I might not fall in love with her who is the top and the root of Honor, so much so that it hurts me, since worth and good looks are gathered in so fair a face that no one could ever think of bettering it.

VII. Ah, fair and dear one, nobly bred, upright and nobly fashioned, guess what I wish to tell you, for I am by no means so bold as to beg you to love me. On the contrary, I cry you mercy, supplicating you. Suffer me to love you and I ask no other boon of you. You should not say me nay to that.

VIII. Toward Malaspina go, Song, to the worthy and honored William, that he may learn from you the words and the tune for whatever he wishes, "vers" or "chanso".

IX. Lady Beatrice of Este, your lofty fame, which is growing great, pleases me. All good people are set on praising you. Therefore I gild with your name my "vers-chanso".

NOTES

Ten MSS: *ACD*^{a}*IJKQRUc*. Stanza III is quoted by Jaufre de Foixa (ed. Paul Meyer, in *Romania,* IX, 54. Variants: 18. *veritatz.* 20. (*per dreg*) *prover.* 21. (*n'er*) *vey.* 22. *els mieus.* 23. *Sim pot venser d'ayso.* 24. *Que no say ges*). Lines 1–12 and the two envois are printed by De Bartholomaeis, *Poesie storiche*, I, 228–229, after Crescini. Our text is based on *C*.

This stemma, though not entirely satisfactory, indicates the chief relationships of the MSS:

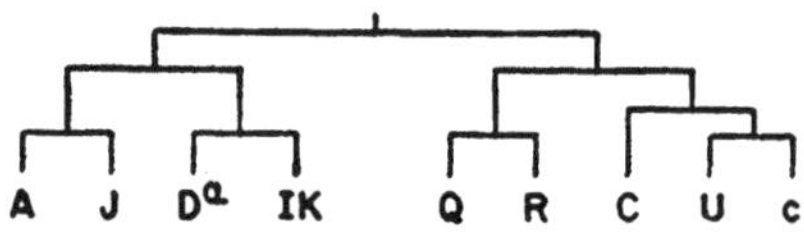

AD^a*IJK:* 12, 25, 28
AJ: 8, 41, 48, 52
D^a*IK:* 15
IK: 13, 50

CQRUc: 12, 25, 28
CUc: 29, 31, 36(?), 56 (*-c*), 58
Uc: 33, 44
QR: 21

The group *CQRUc* is less well established than the group *AD*^{a}*IJK;* the position of *QR* in particular is not too clear, and their relation to each other is much less close than this stemma would imply. The two main divisions are based not on common mistakes, but on widely divergent readings, none of which are necessarily incorrect.

This poem has been widely quoted and often printed, since it is one of the few Provençal discussions of the difference between *vers* and *chansos*. For a lengthy commentary, see Jeanroy, *Poésie lyrique*, II, 64ff. Jeanroy agrees basically with Aimeric, that the names *vers* and *chanso* were used to designate poems of the same metrical form. He adds, however, that *vers* is the older word, gradually supplanted in the sense of "love song" by *chanso*, while *vers* was applied, among the later poets, to poems on moral, religious, or historical subjects; furthermore, this later *vers* was sometimes longer than the standard *chanso*.

By the end of the third stanza, Aimeric has finished his remarks on *vers* and *chanso*, and proceeds, with a lack of transition surprising even in Provençal poetry, to deplore the evil state into which love had fallen. This part of the poem reminds one of Marot's *rondeau* beginning *Au bon vieulx temps un train d'amour regnoit.*

9. *mascles.* This, and *femenis* in line 11, refer of course to masculine and feminine *rimes.* The implication is that, according to the theories, masculine rimes were commoner in *vers,* feminine in *chansos.*

12. *verses,* here and in line 14, is in form a diminutive, equivalent to the *versetz* of *A*D^a*IJK.* The plural of *vers* is *vers.* Cf. *Pois li espont des saumes David tres vers* (*Girart de Rossillon,* in Appel, *Prov. Chrest.,* p. 7, line 399). But there is no real diminutive force here.

13. *sonetz,* like *verses* above, is a diminutive in form, but exactly synonymous with the *so* of line 15. These lines imply that theory demanded a quick movement in the tune of *chansos,* a slow movement in *vers.* According, however, to the *Leys d'amors,* while *Vers deu haver lonc so e pauzat,* it was also true that *Chansos deu haver so pauzat, ayssi quo vers* (Appel, *Prov. Chrest.,* pp. 197, 198).

16. *to.* Does the word here mean musical "mode"?

29. The *amairitz* of the other MSS seems definitely preferable to the *maritz* of *CUc.*

33. *ans que fos faiditz.* Translated "before I was exiled," this could imply that Aimeric still felt a stranger on Italian soil. One could even read into the phrase the idea that he had been obliged to go to Italy against his will, probably by the Albigensian crusade. But nothing else in his poems gives that impression, and his reference to the "bos Pap' Innocens" in poem 11 (date, 1213) shows no resentment against one of the prime movers of the crusade. Of course, the phrase might mean nothing more than "before I came abroad." Or is Aimeric thinking of his forced departure from Toulouse as a result of his first, unlucky love affair? (See the *Vida*).

36. Instead of *N'issi' acortz,* one could read *N'issia cortz,* taking *cort* to mean "courtship"; but we prefer *acort,* "agreement, understanding."

63–64. The readings *En, s'en,* and *de* of *C* are isolated; but, since the stanza is lacking in *QRUc,* they are opposed only by the readings of the other group of MSS, and may therefore represent an equally correct MS tradition. We retain them.

35

I. N'Aimeric, qe·us par d'aqest *novel* marqes?
Guillelm Raimon, be me par aizo qe n'es.
N'Aimeric, meill volgra vos en pareges.
Guillelm Raimon, et eu ben, s'esser poges.
N'Aimeric, lo bon paire volgra sembles o·l fraire.
Guillelm Raimon, et eu be, mas fils es de sa maire.

II. N'Aimeric, mellorar pot, car jovens es.
Guillelm, Deus pod far vertutz et autres bes.
N'Aimeric, en lui agr' ops qe las fezes.
Guillelm, a mi plagra be s'a Deu plages.
N'Aimeric, anz de gaire sabra meill dir e faire.
Guillelm, vist l'ai lonjamen adesmar senes traire.

READINGS EMENDED

I. 1. novel *lacking*. 2. Guillem. 3. par ages.
II. 8. Guillelms.

TRANSLATION

I. Sir Aimeric, what think you of this new Marquis?—Guillem Raimon, I think of him as he is.—Sir Aimeric, I should wish that he appeared better to you.—Guillem Raimon, I also, if it were possible.—Sir Aimeric, I should wish that he were like his good father or his brother.—Guillem Raimon, I also; but he is his mother's son.

II. Sir Aimeric, he may improve, for he is young.—Guillem, God can work miracles and other blessings.—Sir Aimeric, it would be necessary that He work them in him.—Guillem, that would please me well, if it pleased God.—Sir Aimeric, before long he will know how to speak and to act better.—Guillem, I have seen him aim for a long time without shooting.

NOTES

One MS: *H*. Critical edition by Appel in *Prov. Chrest.*, p. 127; twice printed by De Bartholomaeis: in *Studj romanzi*, VII, 335, and in his *Poesie provenzali storiche*, I, 212–213.

A *tenso* with Guilhem Raimon. Aimeric uses the same dialogue form (one-line speeches) in poem 23. The meter is almost identical with that of number 36 (the stanzas being one line shorter), and the rimes of the last two lines are the same. The *marques* is probably Azzo VII of Este, who succeeded to the marquisate in 1215. See our Introduction, and also Bertoni, *Trovatori d'Italia*, p. 17, and the above references to De Bartholomaeis.

1. *novel*. Two syllables are lacking in the MS. None of the other editors have ventured to fill out the measure; we take this suggestion from Jeanroy, *Poésie lyrique*, I, 244, who cites the poem in translation.

3. *pareges*. De Bartholomaeis, in both his texts, which are substantially the same, keeps the *par ages* of the MS, and translates: "vorrei piuttosto che egli vi avesse per amico." This is perhaps ingenious, but it does not impress us as favorably as Appel's emendation *pareges* (imperf. subj. of *parer*).

5. De Bartholomaeis makes two lines of this and 11. We prefer to admit an internal rime (which Aimeric uses elsewhere) and keep the symmetry of the dialogue; it seems likely, furthermore, that this line, containing the same number of syllables as the following, was meant for one line rather than two.

6. We do not know what grievance Aimeric had against the widow of Azzo VI.

11. *anz de gaire*. Levy (*SW*, IV, 16): "binnen kurzem." Levy quotes only this example of *anz de gaire*, but cites, with the same meaning, *en abans de gaire* and *enant que sia gaire*.

36

I. N'Aimeric, qe·us par del pro Bertram d'Aurel?
C'a Breissa joget l'autrer d'un joc novel
E dis doas vez eschah ab un coltel
A·N Guillelm del Dui-Fraire, qe volc l'eschah desfaire;
Mas Bertramz levet del joc can Guillelms cuidet traire.

II. Figera, Bertramz fetz be, car ses apel
Laise·l joc sobre·l maiestre d'En Sordel;
Qe can trop monton revit, non es ges bel;
E·l seus contrajogaire fora tost revidaire.
Doncs fetz qe savis Bertramz, car ses dan s'en saup raire.

III. N'Aimeric, bos jogaire fon Bertramz l'envidaire;
Mas trop tost laisset l'envit qe Guillelms li volc faire.

IV. Figer', anc per lo fraire no fon del joc laissaire
Bertramz, enans per desdeing qe tan pugnav' a traire.

READINGS EMENDED

I. 4. vol.
III. 11. N' *lacking*.
IV. 13. no *lacking*. 14. (enans) mas; (pugnava) pugnua.

TRANSLATION

I. Sir Aimeric, what do you think of the worthy Bertram d'Aurel, who at Brescia played a new game the other day? He said "Check" twice, with a knife, to Sir Guillem of the Two-Brothers, who wished to get out ot check. But Bertram got up from the game when Guillem was about to make a move.

II. Figuera, Bertram did well, since, without a call, he left the game to Sir Sordello's teacher, for it is not a fair thing when the overbids go too high. His opponent would then have quickly been an overbidder. Bertram acted wisely, for he got out of it without loss.

III. Sir Aimeric, Bertram the bidder was a good player; but he left too quickly the bid that Guillem wished to make to him.

IV. Figuera, Bertram left the game not because of the brother, but through scorn when he (Guillem) insisted so on making a move.

NOTES

One MS: *H*. Critical edition in Levy, *Guilhem Figueira*, pp. 57–58. Also printed by De Bartholomaeis, *op. cit.*, II, 74.

The form of this poem is the same as that of number 35, with the omission of one line. And one of the two rimes is the same, and the two poems begin in the same way. Evidently, one was imitated from the other. If we are right in dating number 35 c. 1215, then it must be the earlier, and considerably earlier at that; for Sordello is mentioned in the present poem, and that would place it hardly before 1225. Guilhem Figueira is, then, paying Aimeric the compliment of addressing him in a slightly changed version of one of Aimeric's own meters.

Similarities of a different kind link this poem with 7a, 9, and 13. We have seen that there is a connection between 7a and 9, and the present poem touches both of them in a way. Sordello, the opponent in 7a, is mentioned here; and Guilhem Figueira takes part in both 9 and the present poem. Also, the *Guillelm del Dui-Fraire* of this poem suggests *Guillelm Testa-pelada* and *Guillelm Gauta-segnada* of number 9. And, finally, the subjects are very similar. Number 13 is probably less close; but it is interesting that the debating partners of the present poem exchange *coblas* in 13 with Bertram d'Aurel, who is a leading character in the little incident related here. All four poems may have been written within a short space of time, but the date is uncertain (c. 1225?).

4. *Guillelm del Dui-Fraire*. The person designated, and the point of the nickname, are unknown. Levy suggests Guilhem de la Tor, who exchanged a *tenso* with Sordello (236, 12; cf. line 7, where Guillelm is called Sordello's teacher). The emendation *volc* is accepted by Levy and De Bartholomaeis.

4–5. Levy divides both lines, leaving the first half of five (our numbering) without a rime. De Bartholomaeis divides 4, and leaves 5 in one line. We prefer to print them like the corresponding lines in number 35; see our note there.

5. *levet*. This verb was used intransitively as well as reflexively to mean "get up". Appel cites two examples in the glossary of his *Chrestomathie*. As for *traire*, Levy takes it to mean "draw" (his sword); De Bartholomaeis translates (here and in line 14) "fare la sua mossa". This latter meaning is apparently not given in the dictionaries of Raynouard and Levy; but it seems necessary in the context to carry on the metaphor of a game. To be sure, there is also a pun on the meaning "draw". (In Modern Provençal, *traire uno carto* is used to mean "jeter une carte", according to Mistral, *Trésor*, II, 1022.)

6. *apel*. The word is not in Levy, *SW;* and neither his *PD* nor Raynouard gives any special meaning applicable to games. De Bartholomaeis translates "senza appello (al giuoco)". Does it mean about the same as a call in poker?

7. *Laise·l*. Levy, *SW*, VII, 321, suggests that the MS *laisel* could stand for *laiset lo;* we accept the suggestion. Cf. the similar form *blasme·l* for *blasmet lo* in poem 19, line 26. De Bartholomaeis interprets *laisel* in the same way. He translates "lasciò di giocare col maestro", etc. This is the general meaning, all right; but it leaves the force of *sobre* a little vague. The dictionaries are not very helpful, but the word seems to indicate little more than an indirect object: "to, to the lot of, in possession of". Cf. *Sobre vos cuit, dun monges, que·n tort* (var. *chaira*) *li sorz* (*Girart de Rossillon*, in Appel, *Chrestomathie*, p. 4, l. 216).

8. *revit.* Levy, in his edition and in the *SW* (VII, 321) translates this as "Überbieten" and *revidaire* (l. 9) as "der (im Spiel) überbietet." De Bartholomaeis (who reads *mont' on*) translates this and the following line: "Perchè non è bella cosa che si torni a invitare (*al giuoco*) quando si sale troppo (*con la posta*); (*allora*) l'avversario tornerebbe subito a invitare di nuovo (*rialzando la posta*)." These lines are the only examples of *revit* and *revidador* in Levy, *SW;* but they are evidently modeled on *envit* and *envidador* (lines 11, 12), which are better exemplified. Cf. Fr. Semrau, *Würfel und Würfelspiel*, pp. 83–89. *Envit* exists in French in the form *envi* ("argent qu'on met au jeu pour enchérir sur son compagnon", Littré); Godefroy (*Dict. de l'anc. langue fr.*, III, 315) gives no examples earlier than Rabelais.

10. *raire.* Levy (ed.) emends to *traire.* We are not convinced that this is necessary. De Bartholomaeis keeps *raire*, and translates "se la seppe cavare". Levy (*SW*, VII, 9) gives *se raire* in the meaning "sich davon machen, verschwinden", with an example from *Aigar et Maurin* (ed. Brossmer, l. 1266).

14. *pugnav' a traire.* Levy reads *punhav' en traire*, De Bartholomaeis *pugnu'a traire* (the MS reading). It is hard to see what form of the verb *pugnu'* could be. Some emendation seems necessary, and ours is a little easier than Levy's. Both prepositions (and also *de*) are found after *ponhar:* see Levy, *SW*, VI, 450.

37

I. N'Elyas, conseill vos deman
De lieis c'am mais c'autrui ni me,
Qe·m ditz qe·m colgara ab se
Una nuoich, ab qe·il jur e·il man
Que non la fortz part son talan,
Mas q'eu estei baisan tenen.
Del far digatz m'al vostre sen:
S'es mieils c'aissi sofra et endur,
O part son voler me perjur.

II. N'Aimeric, e·us vauc conseillan
Que, s'ab si·us colga, faitz l'o be,
Car, qui sa dompna en son bratz te,
Fols es s'aillor la vai cercan;
. . . .
Car, s'ieu era ab midonz jazen
E n'avia faich sagramen,
Faria l'o, so·us assegur,
Qui que m'en tengues per perjur.

III. N'Elias, a lei de truan
Me conseillatz er et ancse.
Mal a·i qui del conseill vos cre,
E sai ben qe·il fals vos creiran,
Cill que non amon tan ni qan;
Car Dieu e sa dompna eissamen
Pert qui aisso qe·il jura men;
Per q'al tenen baisan m'atur
Ab cor que del far non perjur.

IV. N'Aimeric, vilania gran
Disetz, e rasonatz desse;
Car, s'ab lieis jatz q'am mais que me,
Ja als no l'irai demandan;
Mas bellamen rizen jogan
L'o farai, puois plorarai m'en
Tro qe·m perdon lo faillimen.
Puois irai pelegrins part Sur
Queren Dieu perdon del perjur.

READINGS EMENDED

II. 14. *lacking A.*
IV. 28. *Nameric.*

TRANSLATION

I. Sir Elias, I ask your advice about the lady whom I love more than anyone else or myself. She told me that I might lie with her one night, provided that I swear to her and promise not to force her against her will and to be content with kissing and hugging. Tell me your opinion about the deed: whether it is better to suffer and endure, or to perjure myself against her will.

II. Sir Aimeric, if she lets you lie with her, my advice to you is to do the deed to her; for he who holds his lady in his arms is mad, if he seeks her elsewhere. . . . If I were in bed with my lady and had taken an oath to her, I should do the deed, I assure you, whoever might deem me a perjurer on that account.

III. Sir Elias, you advise me, now and always, like a rascal. It goes ill with him who believes your advice; and I know well that the false lovers only will believe you, they who do not love truly at all. He who breaks his promised word loses God and his lady likewise. That is why I keep to hugging and kissing, with a firm heart not to perjure myself about the deed.

IV. Sir Aimeric, you utter and defend a great indignity. If I lie with her whom I love better than myself, I shall ask no more of her; but gently, laughing and sporting, I'll do the deed to her and weep about it afterwards till she pardon my fault. Then I'll go as a pilgrim beyond Tyre, seeking of God pardon for the perjury.

NOTES

One MS: *A*. Critical edition: Carstens, in *Die Tenzonen aus dem Kreise der . . . d'Uisel*, pp. 82–83. We follow this text, which is almost exactly that of *A*, with very few changes (punctuation, etc.), as does Audiau, in *Les Poésies des quatre troubadours d'Ussel.*

A *partimen* with Elias d'Ussel on a subject which is almost identical with that proposed by Domna H. to Rofin (249a, 1): My Lady agrees to let me lie with her, provided I limit myself to discreet embraces; shall I keep my promise, or violate it?

7. Carstens quotes Levy, *PD: "far(lo)* 'exprime l'acte de la copulation'." See also Levy, *SW*, III, 380, where several passages of the poem are quoted.

11. *l'o*, here and in 17 and 33; reading suggested by Levy, *SW*, III, 380. Rejected by Carstens (*lo*), but accepted by Audiau.

21. Audiau emends the MS *ai* to *a*.

27. *ab cor que*. Carstens (in a note): "in der Absicht, dass; um zu." Levy, *SW*, I, 358, gives only *a cor de*, "um zu."

32. *rizen jogan*. For the juxtaposition of two present participles here and in lines 6 and 26, above, see the note on poem 3, line 21.

38

I. Nulhs hom non es tan fizels vas senhor
Qu'ieu non sia plus fizels vas Amor;
No solamen en chanso ni en rima,
Mas en totz faitz tenc condregz sos rix fieus
A mon poder e·ls enans plus que·ls mieus,
Que·l sieus enans es mos majer jornals.
Aissi·lh sui fis denan los plus leyals.

II. A mon poder li enans sa honor,
Ez a midons son pretz e sa valor,
Qu'al sieu servir sui dels pes tro qu'al sima.
Aissi sui totz domengeiramen sieus,
Que ges non sui, domna, d'autrui ni mieus;
E pus en ren non sui voutitz ni fals,
Enguarda·us hi, que no·us aus preyar d'als.

III. No·us aus preyar ni·m puesc virar alhor,
Aissi cum selh que s'espert per paor,
Que non fier colp ni·s gandis a l'escrima.
Pero si tenc d'Amor los aspres trieus,—
Vostre l'ancaps e totz lo mescaps mieus,—
Qu'Amors m'auci, mas vos m'etz tan corals,
Per qu'aitals mortz m'es vida naturals.

IV. Mesclamen viu e muer ses valedor
E no sai re loqual d'ams ai pejor.
Be·m n'agra pres si moris a la prima!
Savals, domna, lo termes fora brieus
E no·n fora totz temps lo maltraitz mieus;
Mas no sai bes per qu'ieu camjes mos mals,
Si tot no s'es lo partimens eguals.

V. No sai nulh gaug per qu'ieu des ma dolor.
Guardatz s'ai be camjat sen per folhor.
Quom plus Amors per vos me briz' e·m lima,
Ladonc am mais, mas l'afans m'es tan grieus
Qu'en prop non er mos cors vostre ni mieus,
Qu'Amors e vos m'es tan descominals
Per qu'ai temor l'afans sia mortals.

VI. Chansos, cum selh que es correns e lieus, 36
Ten vas lo rei qu'es tos senher e mieus,
En Aragon, qu'en lui es pretz cabals
E fons de joy e de bos aips loguals.

VARIANTS

I. 2. (plus) mais *A*. 4. Mas en mon chan *D;* (condregz) dreitz *E*. 6. Quels sieus enans *IK*, Que sos seruirs *D;* mos *lacking I;* maiers *CIKNR*. 7. Aisso son *D*.

II. 8. (honor) ualor *EN*, laussor *D*. 9. (valor) honor *EN*. 10. (Qu'al) Al *D;* del pe *DR;* tro quel *N*, tro al *R*, tro la *A*, tro a la *DK*, trol al *E*. 11. totz *lacking D;* domengieiramens *ANR*, don mengieramenz *IK*, domẽ iameniers *D*. 12. Que *N;* ges dona no soi *DE;* sui *lacking I;* (d'autrui) autrui *D*. 13. E pus non sui en ren *A*, E pus nous sui de re *DE;* viratz *A*, vairatz *D*. 14. Esgardatz o *AIK*, Esgardaus doncs *NR* (doncs *inserted in a later hand in N*), Enguardas hi *E*, Gardaz uos hi *D;* queu *N;* non aus penssar dals *D*.

III. 15. Preiar nous aus *DE;* (puesc) uoill *A*. 17. Qe na fier cal ni galdis ni escrima *D;* ni gandis *CIKN;* (a) tras *A*. 18. E per so teng dona los a. t. *D*. 19. Vostres *ACIKR;* (l'ancaps) lo pros *A;* (lo) los *C*. 20. (mas) e *A*.

IV. 22. Mesclamens *CR;* mor e uiu *D*. 23. E re non sai *D;* la cal *A;* dans *EN*, dan *IK;* (ai) es *E*. 24. Ben *D;* (n'agra) fora *ADIK;* sin *E*. 26. E non fora dompna lo mals totz mieus *AIK;* nom *C;* toz tep *D;* mals traz *N*. 27. *lacking D;* (bes) ges *IK*. 28. *lacking D;* non es *C*.

V. *lacking E*. 29. *lacking D;* ioi *A*. 30. *lacking D;* fallor *I*. 31. *lacking D;* me brusem lima *IK*, mabrassa emlia *A*. 32. *lacking D;* Adoncs *AFaIK;* (am) lam *AIK*. 33. *lacking D;* (prop) breu *AFaIK;* uostres mon cor *R;* uostres *C*. 34. (m'es) metz *A*, me *I*. 35. (temor) paor *DFa;* sia lafans mortals *A*.

VI. *lacking D*. 36. Chanson *CR;* (correns) cozens *I*. 37. ton *C;* senhor *C*, senhers *N*, seing *K*.

TRANSLATION

I. No man is so faithful to his lord that I am not more faithful to Love. Not only in song and rime, but in all ways I keep his noble fief in good estate, according to my powers, and better it more than my own, since its betterment is my greatest daily task. Thus I am more faithful to Love than the most loyal.

II. According to my power, I better his honorable estate, and also the fame and good report of my Lady, since I am her servant from foot to head. So I am all hers, like a vassal, so that I belong not at all, noble Lady, to another or to myself. Because in nothing I am inconstant or false, it protects you in this (your fame and your good report), since I dare not beg anything else of you.

III. I dare not beseech you, nor can I turn to another woman, just like the man who is troubled by fear so that he does not strike a blow nor protect himself by fencing. Therefore I keep thus the harsh conditions of Love's truce—yours the gain and mine all the loss. Love slays me; but you are so dear to me that such a death is real life to me.

IV. In a mixed way I live and die, without anyone to help; and I know not which of the two I hold the worse. It would have been well for me if I had died at first. At least, the time of my suffering would have been short and all the woes would not have been always mine. Still, I know well that I would not change my misfortunes, even though the division of them is not equal.

V. I know no joy for which I would exchange my woe. Notice how I have traded wisdom for folly! The more Love bruises and tortures me for your sake, then I love the more; but the suffering is so grievous that in a short time my heart will be neither yours nor mine, for Love and you are so harsh towards me that I fear lest the suffering be mortal.

VI. Song, like a swift and light runner, go straight toward the King who is your lord and mine, in Aragon, for in him is to be found true fame, a fount of joy and a home of all good traits.

NOTES

Nine MSS: *ACDEFaIKNR*. Of these, *Fa* contains only the fifth stanza. Probably the most satisfactory stemma that can be established is this:

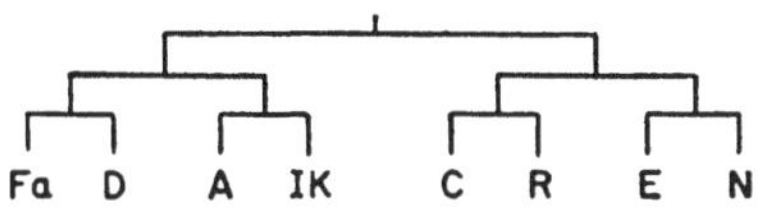

The division into two main groups is based on lines 24, 32, 33; neither reading is necessarily wrong, but it is clear that there were two rather different versions of the poem, which are preserved in these two families. The smaller groups are based on these lines:

AIK: 14, 26, 32 — *EN:* 8, 9
DFa: 35 — *CR:* 22, 36

Unfortunately, other variants do not accommodate themselves so well to this classification. According to lines 12, 15, we should have a group *DE*, to which *A* is added in 13; and, likewise in line 13 (*viratz, vairatz*), *AD* stand against all the other MSS. Can chance or contamination of sources account for these discrepancies? Possibly so. In any case, the relationships are not entirely sure. Base, *C*.

10. Cf. the very similar line of Arnaut Daniel (29, 13; line 14. Canello, p. 105; Lavaud, p. 48): *Qu'al sieu servir suy del pe tro qu'al coma.* Aimeric is evidently copying this expression; he even imitates Arnaut in contracting *a la* to *al*.

14. *Enguarda·us hi.* Neither the reading nor the interpretation is certain. Should we read, with *AIK*, *Esgardatz o*? Levy (*SW*, II, 500), quotes the text as we have it, but cannot decide on a meaning.

18. It would be possible to take *trieus* as "chemins, traces" (Levy, *PD*), rather than as "truce" (cf. 49, line 53, *los trieus de Pretz*); but in view of the metaphor of fencing, we have decided against this.

23. *loqual d'ams*, i.e., to live or to die.

29. Compare Aimeric's line *No sai nulh "oc" per qu'ieu des vostre "no"* (50, line 25).

31. *lima*, lit., "files." This figurative use of the word is not given in the dictionaries. Cf. poem 47, line 2.

34. *descominals.* Cf. *Vas mi a cor descominal* (Gaucelm Faidit, 167, 38; quoted by Raynouard, IV, 290).

39

I. Nulhs hom no sap que s'es gaugz ni dolors,
S'en son poder non l'a tengut Amors;
Mas ieu sai be la dolor e·l turmen
E re no sai quals es la benanansa,
Mas que·m trahi ab sa douss' esperansa.
Pero viatz fug pres qui no·l reten;
Mas lo tenens no·l vol del tot gequir,
Per so que mais lo puesca far languir.

II. Mas mi no ten maltragz, dans ni temors,
Ans sui plus fis on plus crema l'ardors
Vas lieis cui sui sieus mielhs que sel c'om ven;
Mas sos sabers en pren dura venjansa.
Amors, car faitz tan gran desmezuransa?
Mas qui pueja mais que non deu dissen.
Ara conosc que·m vol far penedir
So qu'ilh meteys m'a fait tant abelhir.

III. De lauzengiers ni de mals parladors
No·m clam de re, ans m'es lurs brutz honors,
Per que·l menor de lurs digz non desmen.
Pero dans m'es, mas lo dans m'es honransa,
E sai qu'er bes si·lh belha n'a membransa,
Qu'estiers no·n sap nulhs per mi mon talen;
Qu'adoncs m'espert ieu on plus m'o cossir,
Ez ilh dizo·l so qu'ieu no l'auzi dir.

IV. Ab lieys suy mutz e ben parlans alhors
Ab las autras, e ges aitals errors
No deu esser comtatz per falhimen,
Bona domna, qu'e ma simpla semblansa
Podetz saber mon fin cor ses duptansa;
E vos, si·us platz, prendetz n'esguardamen,
Qu'en luec de fag deu hom voler grazir
A selh quez a voluntat de servir.

V. Si cum val mais davan yvern pascors,
Ez atressi cum sobre amar doussors,
Sobre totas a belh captenemen,
Don mayntas n'an gilozi' e pezansa;
Ez ieu meteys en muer de sobramansa,
Qu'a me sui fals, tant am vos finamen;
E no devetz de tot en tot delir
So qu'ab vos a a viur' ez a murir.

VARIANTS

I. 1. dolor *O, and so for all rimes in* -ors *throughout the poem.* 2. Sin *C.* 4. res *CR;* (la) sa *ORc.* 5. *lacking c;* a sa bona speransa *O;* sa *lacking R.* 6. Pero mult mais senvia cel cosen *Oc*, Pero viatz senveia qui so sen *R.* 7. Que nom (nol *Rc*) rete nim (nil *Rc*) vol del tot gequir *ORc.* 8–14 *are mutilated in C by the excision of a miniature; only these words remain:* . . . mais lo pu . . . Mas mi n . . . ni temors . . . crema lardo . . . mielhs ser . . . ven Mas si . . . veniansa . . . gran desme . . . ia mais que non deu dissen. 8. (lo) me *O*, le *c.*

II. 9. dan ni dolor *O.* 10. om plus erein alaudor *O*, on plus creis ma ardors *R.* 11. Var (Vas *c*) lei cui son tot (totz *c*) seus onom (hon non *c*) defen *Oc.* 12. E pero il prenge dura v. *O*, E per so ilh ne pren ne dura v. *c.* 13. Amor *Oc;* gran *lacking c.* 14. Car qui *Oc;* (mais) pus *R.* 16. Daiso que il ma fait *O*, De so qe il ma fait *c.*

III. 17. lauzengier *O;* mal parledor *O.* 18. en re *R*, en res *Oc;* brug honor *O*, bes honors *R.* 19. menors *Oc;* (digz) duz *c.* 21. E lai car bes si bella na m. *O*, E lais qar bes si bela ana *c;* (bes) bels *R.* 22. no sap de (per *R*) mi nulh mon (mos *O*) talen *ORc.* 23. Adoncs mespert on eu plus mo cosir *O.* Quadoncs mesperc on yeu pus mo cossir *R*, Qadonc mespren qant eu be mo consir *c.* 24. Et elz dizon aizo *O*, E cels dison so *c;* (ilh) els *R;* que ieu *C;* non li aus dir *c*, no laus dir *O*, plus dezir *C.*

IV. 25. (lieys) vos *Oc;* (ben) genz *O*, gent *c.* 27. Nom *O;* comtat *CR*, cointatz *O.* 30. (si·us) siu *C*, sieus *R;* prenetz nes garamen *O;* prendetz *lacking c;* nenguarament *c.* 31. fag lo li de on gradir *Oc*, fag loi deu hom ben grazit *R.* 32. Aicel qia *O*, E sel qia *c.*

V. 33. (davan) denan *R*, denanz *O;* (yvern) ni en *c*, yverns *CR;* pascor *R.* 34. Et enaissi *R;* com sobre mal douçor *c*, con lanbre ma douzor *O*, com sobra mars dossors *R.* 35. Es sus totas de belh c. *R*, Es sobre (sobres *O*) total de b. c. *Oc.* 36. Don motas *R*, Qe mantas *c*, Ne mantas *O.* 38. tan vos am *ORc.* 39. E nom devetz *OR;* del tot *R.* 40. vos a v. *R;* a viure oamorir *O.*

TRANSLATION

I. No man knows what joy or sorrow is if Love has not had him in his power; but I know well the grief and torment, and not at all do I know what the happiness is, save that he betrayed me with his sweet hope. However, a prisoner, if no one holds him, flees quickly; but the holder does not wish to let him go entirely, in order that he may make him pine still more.

II. But neither sufferings, misfortunes nor fears can keep me back. On the contrary, the more faithful I am, the more my passion for her burns, for her to whom I belong wholly, like a slave. His (Love's) wisdom, however, takes a harsh vengeance for it. Love, why are you so overbearing in your actions? He who climbs higher than he should must descend; and now I know that he wishes to make me repent of what he himself made so pleasing to me.

III. I do not complain at all of the slanderers and evil speakers; rather, their talk is an honor to me. So I do not contradict the least of their sayings. It hurts me, to be sure; but that hurt is also an honor to me; and I know that it will turn out to be a blessing, if my Fair One remembers it, since, except her, no one knows by me my desire. The more I lose myself in thought, the more distracted I am; but they (the slanderers) tell her what I do not dare to tell her.

IV. In her presence I am dumb. Elsewhere, with other ladies, I speak well and fittingly. Such embarrassment should not be counted as a fault, good Lady, for by my mere look you can unfailingly know my faithful heart. If you please, take that into consideration, for one should be grateful to him who has the will to serve lovingly, if not the actual power to do so.

V. Just as Easter is preferable to Winter and sweetness to bitterness, so her beauty is exalted above that of other ladies; and many of them feel jealousy and annoyance for that. I myself am dying through excess of love, so that I am false to myself, I love you so truly. You should not destroy entirely him who has to live and to die with you.

NOTES

Four MSS: *CORc*. Of these, *Oc* form a recognizable group (vv. 6, 11, 21, 25, 35). Certain lines (4, 33) indicate that *CR* go together, which would be very usual; but so many variants (4: *la*, 7, 18: *de re*, 22, 31, 35, 38) oppose *C*, with an apparently good reading, to *ORc*, that a stemma of this sort seems more likely:

We have chosen *C* for our base MS.

This poem resembles number 29 in its theme and its opening lines. They may have been composed at about the same time.

8–14. Since the text of *C* is mutilated here, we have followed that of *R* (modifying the spelling somewhat to harmonize with that of the rest of the poem); but in line 10 we have kept the words that remain in *C*.

11. A rather curious construction, but perfectly intelligible.

14. Cnyrim, *Sprichwörter*, no. 398. Cf. Folquet de Marseille (ed. Stronski), I, 7:

E qui n'aut pueia bas deissen.

Aimeric has a reminiscence of the lines immediately preceding this one in poem 29, line 11.

27. *comtatz*. As this refers to *errors* in line 26, we must take this word as masculine, contrary to general usage. Cf. 19, line 24, and 32, line 30, where Aimeric makes other words in *-or* masculine.

40. *So*. *Cel* would seem more likely, but it occurs in none of the MSS.

40

I. Per razo natural,
Segon ma conoissensa,
Deu dir de malvolensa
Be, qui ditz mal d'Amor;
Per que par folhs qui cre
Sel que de mal ditz be,
E quan ditz issamen
De be mal, fai non-sen
Qui son blasme tem ni sa lauzor blan,
Quar no·l ten pro sos laus ni·l blasmes dan.

II. Pauc notz d'ome ni val
Sos digz, a ma parvensa,
Pus non a de falhensa
Vergonha ni paor.
No val ni notz ab me,
Ni entre·ls savis re,
Qu'en lui meteys enten
Lo dan d'aiselh qui men;
E maldigz fals es laus, al mieu semblan,
E bendigz fals blasmes, quar mou d'enjan.

III. E selh que ditz aital
Qu'elh avia crezensa
Que selh que mal comensa
Fenis be, digz error
E parlet contra se.
Doncx enaissi·s cove
De bon comensamen
Aver mal fenimen?
En lui par ver, qu'al comensar cantan
Dis ben d'Amor, et al fenir mal gran.

IV. Quar apres ben dis mal,
Fetz gran desconoissensa;
Mas falsa maldizensa
Mou de fals dizedor.
Donx no falh, ans ave,
Quar ditz so que·lh perte,
Que·l fals falh ver dizen
E·l leyals falh menten,
Qu'atressi falh fals leyaltat menan
Quom lo leyals quan se vai desvian.

V. Una domna leyal
Sai ieu qu'es de Plazensa,
Mas estai en Valensa
Per mielhs gardar Sanhflor
E Mirabel que te,
E Cortezo, per que
Gazanha Benaven
E Belhjoc franchamen,
E ten Guarda e Verona mandan,
E·s bateget lo jorn de sant Johan.

VI. Qui que·s crotle ni estia entrenan,
Malespina esta ferms en l'estan.

VARIANTS

I. 4. (Be) Dir *R;* damor mal *c.* 5. *lacking E;* Per ques fols (fol *GQ*) sel (ce *Q*) qui (qel *G*) cre (recre *IK*) *GIKMNQRUc;* (que) qem *ABD;* par *lacking D.* 6. *lacking E;* (Sel) Lui *GIKQRUc;* (de) del *BDR.* 7. *lacking M;* (quan) car *R.* 8. *lacking M;* (De) Del *ABDEGIKNQRUc.* 9. (tem) ten *U;* (blan) blam *Q.* 10. non naten pro *U*, no aten per *c;* (no·l) no *EGMNR;* (ten) tre *CDE;* (sos) son *C;* (ni·l) ni *DIKQUc.*

II. (III *in ABD*). 11. (d'ome) de mi *RU.* 12. (Sos) Ses *D.* 13. (Pus) Qan *ABDDᶜFaGIKQRc*, Qar *U;* (de falhensa) conoissensa *M*, de faillimen temensa *E*, de ualenza *G.* 14. *lacking E;* Ni non noz ni socor *M*, Temenza ni paor *N.* 15. No ual naiz a me *D;* Nol ual nil notz *C*, Non (Ni *Q*, Nom *E*) notz ni ual *DᶜEFaGIKMNQUc;* (ab) a *DDᶜFaIKMR.* 16. Ni als sauis en re *R;* entrel *IKU;* re *lacking E.* 17. (Qu'en) Qe *U;* (lui) lur *E;* senten *CDᶜR*, menten *E.* 18. (dan) mal *C;* (d'aiselh) daquel *EMN*, de cel *DᶜFa.* 19. (E) Que *ABD*, El *DᶜFaQ*, Car *R;* fals . . . semblan *lacking E;* (es laus) e plans *N;* mieus *IK*, men *GQ.* 20. E bendigz *lacking E*, (E) El *ABDᶜ;* bendig *C*, bes diz *DIK;* blasme *C*, auols *M;* (quar) qan *GQc;* (mou) mo *G;* deman *GQ.*

III. (II *in ABD*, IV *in R*). 21. (E selh) Aquel *EGIKMNQRUc.* 23. *lacking c;* (Que selh), Caicel *AIK;* (mal) be *ABCD.* 24. Fenis be *lacking c;* Feneys *C;* (be) mal *ABCD;* (digz) en *E*, mes *GIKNQRUc.* 25. parlar *c;* contra se *lacking D;* (se) fe *C.* 26. (Donx) Dan *R;* atressis *IK* autressi *EGMNQUc.* 27. (De) Que *C.* 28. (Aver) Aia *C*, Qaia *M*, Far *Uc*, *lacking E;* (mal) auol *R.* 29. De lui dis uer *M*, Quen luy par be *R*, Ellui parlar uer *U;* (par) parer *Q;* (ver) auer *N.* 30. (et al fenir) e dal f. *U*, et a la fi *EMN.*

IV. (III *in R*). 31. (Quar) Qui *AB;* (apres) aprop *AD;* ben *lacking Q.* 32. Fai *AB*, Fe *DUc.* 33. *lacking E;* (Mas) Que *R;* maluolenza *Fa.* 34. fal *U;* fals mal dizedors *R;* dizedors *GIK.* 35. Donc falh enans coue *C*, E no faill ans aue (saue *M*) *EMN*, Ges no faill ans saue *R*, Ges non fail quan sauen *T;* anc *IK*, an *c;* (ave) saue *DᶜFaIKU*, la ue *Q*, lauc *c.* 36. Qe de so que couẽ *T;* Quan *BDDᶜEFaGIKNQc*, Qui *RU;* (que·lh perte) quieill p. *Dᶜ*, q. pete *c*, qel coue (*added above the line*) *N.* 37. Mas (Que *E*, Qel *FaMNR*) leials faill menten *DᶜEFaGIKMNQRUc.* 38. El (E *IK*) fals faill uer dizen *DᶜEFaGIKMNQRUc;* (E·l) E *D.* 39. Catressi fals faill en uan lealtat menan *T;* Catressil *BIKUc*, Atressil *N*, Atressi *E;* falh . . . menan *lacking AB;* fals faill *DDᶜEFaGIKNQUc;* (leyaltat menan) leiall tot m. *D*, leutat m. *M*, leiatatmen *Q.*

40. *lacking AB;* Cõceil leials deuiam *T;* Co falh lials *R*, Com fa leials *U;* (quan) qe *U;* (se) e *D*, sen *QU;* (desvian) definan *EG*.

V. 42. (de Plazensa) desplagenza *U*. 43. (Mas) Mai *C*, Et *ABDMR;* (en) a *ENR*. 44. Per gardar mieilz *D;* (Sanhflor) sa flor *D*, sas flors *G*, honor *E*. 45. (E) En *DM*, *lacking Q;* mirabels *R*. 46. (E) O *B;* corteson *ABD*, cortezon *ER*. 47. Gazaiga (-a *added above the line*) *D;* beniuen *M*. 48. beliuc *U*, beluic *c*, beliueç *N;* (franchamen) eysamen *R*. 49. E ten en garda et en uirona man *R;* (e Verona) eiiarona (?) *D*. 50. (E·s) Ois *A*, E *EGN;* baptezes *G*, bategeç *N;* (lo jorn) el nom *R*.

VI. 51. crolle *DGIKMNQ*, corle *AB*, croil *U*, crod le *c;* ni qi qes nan *U;* nil *R;* estec *IK*, estei *EGMNQ*, esteuc *A*, esteu *BD*, estai *c*. 52. (Malespina) Lo bon marques *U;* ferm *DIK*, en ferm *c;* (en l'estan) entrenan *A*, entretan *B*, en estan *EIKMN*, eniestan *Q*, alestan *U*.

TRANSLATION

I. In my opinion, by a natural reason, he who speaks ill of Love must speak well of malevolence. Therefore, he who believes him who speaks well of evil seems foolish; and when he likewise speaks ill of good, whoever fears his blame or seeks his praise acts foolishly, for his praise does not profit one, nor his blame harm.

II. In my opinion, the words of a man hurt or help little when he has not fear or shame of sin; nor does he hurt or help with me or among the wise, since on himself he draws the sin of the liar. An ill word that is false is praise, to my thinking; and a good word that is false is blame, for it arises out of deceit.

III. He who said that he believed that the man who begins badly ends well spoke in error and talked against himself. Is it therefore likewise fitting that a good beginning should have a bad ending? In him, this seems true, for in the beginning he spoke well of Love in his songs, but at the end very badly.

IV. Since after good he spoke evil, he did a great folly; but a false slander comes from a false speaker. Therefore he does not err, but says what is fitting, since he says what it pertains to him to say. The false man errs when he speaks the truth, and the true man when he lies; for the false man errs when he shows loyalty, just as much as the loyal man when he goes astray.

V. I know a loyal lady, of Piacenza (Pleasing); but she abides in Valensa (Worthy), in order to guard better San Flor (Holy Flower) and Mirabel (Fair Glance), which she holds, and Cortezo (Courtesy); therefore she wins for herself Benaven (Benevolence) and Belhjoc (Good Manners) freely, and she holds in fee Garda (Prudence) and Verona (Sincerity). She was baptized on Saint John's Day (she is helpful to others).

VI. However much others bestir themselves or oppose him, Malaspina stands firm and upright.

NOTES

Seventeen MSS: *ABCDD^cEFaGIKMNQRTUc*. Of these, *D^c* and *Fa* both contain only stanzas two and four, *T* only lines 35–40. Stanza one and lines 35–40 are quoted in the *Breviari d'amor*, lines 28393 and 28034, respectively (Variants: 4. *Ves qui*. 5. (*que*) *quem*. 35. *Ges no falh quan s'ave*. 36. *Qui ditz so quelz cove*. 38. *E leials*. 40. (*se*) *la*).

De Bartholomaeis (*Poesie storiche*, I, 233) prints stanzas one, five, and six, after Mahn's transcript of *C*. Critical edition of stanza five in Zingarelli, *Due trovatori*, p. 35. Edition of the lines from *T* in Appel, *Provenzalische Inedita aus Pariser Handschriften*, p. 325.

The order of stanzas is the same in all MSS, with the following exceptions:

ABD: 1 3 2 4 5 6
R: 1 2 4 3 5 6

From their agreement in this divergent order, *ABD* evidently form a group; the variants confirm this (5, 19). *C* often joins this group (5, 21, 23, 26, 37, 38). *EMN* are another group (18, 30, 35), in which *EN* sometimes stand together against *M* (35, 39). The pairs *IK* and *GQ* are fairly constant, *Uc* a little less so (28). A larger group *GIKQRUc* is likely (6); *EMN* often agree with this group (24, 26), but this may be due to mistakes in *ABCD*. It is not possible to be more specific about the relations of *GIKQRUc*. *D*[c] and *Fa* seem to agree with this latter group, and *T* to stand somewhat closer to *ABCD*. The only stemma that can be constructed consists of these two fragments:

Base: *C*.

For the subject, compare poems 17 and 52. All three songs were probably composed within the space of a year or so, in the neighborhood of 1220, since in 52 Frederick is called "Emperor." The present poem, written while William Malaspina was still alive, may well be the first of the series. There can be little doubt that Stronski, the editor of Folquet de Marseille, is correct in referring the third stanza to his poet (see his edition, p. 60*, and our note on lines 23–24). We have seen Aimeric allude time and time again to the poems of Folquet, whose works he must have known better than those of any other troubadour. And it is true, as Aimeric says (lines 29–30), that Folquet spoke well of Love at the beginning of his career, but condemned it later, when his religious vocation was becoming stronger.

5–10. Compare poem 17, especially lines 15–16:

Doncs non es, d'ome qu'es aitals,
Lo besdigz bos ni·l maldigz mals.

23–24. We accept the readings of the majority of the MSS (23: *mal*, 24: *be*), because in these lines Aimeric surely has in mind the following passage from Folquet de Marseille (ed. Stronski, XIII, 28–31):

Mas ieu avia plivensa
Tant quant amiei follamen
En aisso qu'om vai dizen:
Be fenis qui mal comensa.

As Stronski points out, certain MSS of Folquet's poem have *crezensa* (Aimeric's reading) for *plivensa*.

41–50. We follow Zingarelli (*Due trovatori*, p. 35) in his interpretation of the proper names in these lines. He is probably right, furthermore, in rejecting Cavedoni's theory that the lady "baptized on St. John's day" is Johanna, wife of Azzo VII of Este. As Zingarelli points out (p. 38), this marriage took place in 1221, after the death of William Malaspina (lines 51–52); and it is unlikely that Aimeric would have been interested in Johanna before her marriage to Azzo. It is true, however, that poem 17, on the same subject, is definitely dedicated to Johanna. I do not know that we can be too absolute in rejecting her here. If the reference is not to her, then the lady in question is probably Beatrice of Este, whose name appears so often linked with that of William Malaspina. Incidentally, although it is natural to assume that Aimeric means William Malaspina here, it is not impossible that he is speaking of Conrad or even some other member of the family.

41

I. Per solatz d'autrui chant soven;
Mas pero cora que chantes,
Ni per bon respieich m'alegres,
Ara vei que chant per nien.
E sui a mon dan chantaire,
Si cum l'auzels de bon aire,
Que sap q'es pres e per so no·is recre
C'ades non chant: atretal es de me.

II. En Amor ai lo cor e·l sen
Fermat, e meillur m'en ades,—
Si pogues trobar qui m'ames
Tant ben cum ieu am finamen!
Mas ieu am lieis ses cor vaire
Don sui desamatz amaire.
Et on ieu plus l'am de cor e de fe,
Adoncs creis plus l'amors qe·m lassa e·m te.

III. No m'es vis c'anc plus follamen
Nuills hom per Amor folleies,
Q'ieu am mais que s'autra·m baises
De lieis ses plus l'entendemen;
C'onors m'es; mas que pot faire
Ses emperi emperaire?
Qe·m val honors ni pretz don mals mi ve?
Si fai! qe·l mals que platz es pars del be.

IV. Per so·m so·il mal q'ieu n'ai plazen,
C'anc non vi dompna, loing ni pres,
Mieills disses ni mieills respondes,
Ni tant amesuradamen;
Per que chascus n'es lauzaire,
Puois es del mon la bellaire;
C'anc Natura no mes en lieis, so cre,
Ni plus ni meins, mas aco qe·i cove.

V. Dompna, per merce solamen
Soffrissetz c'un pauc merceies
Merces, e c'un pauc afranques
Merceian vostre dur talen
Vas mi, qe·us sui merceiaire
Totz temps e merce clamaire;
E merceians sui e serai jasse
Vostr' om, clamans: "Merce, merce, merce!"

VI. Lo pros Guillems Malespina soste
Don e dompnei e cortesia e me.

VII. Bels Peragon, cum hom plus sovens ve
Na Biatritz d'Est, plus li vol de be.

VARIANTS

I. 2. Mas ancar qeu per me chantes *c;* Mas *lacking C;* pero *lacking R;* (cora) qom *G;* (que) quieu *CGMPQRc*, qem *B*, qen *DN*. 4. Sai qeu chan *c;* Ar uei *N;* (que) qieu *BGQ*. 5. damh *M*. 6. lauzelh *CR*. 7. Qui sap *added in margin (apparently in the same hand) M;* (q'es) qe *c;* pero non recre *P*. 8. atertal *R*, e atal *M;* (es de me) mesdeue *CP*.

II. 9. Qen *GIKQR;* (lo) el *M*. 10. (meillur m'en) melhuiram *CP*. 11. Sol *M*, Seu *c;* podes *c;* (qui) qe *c*. 12. (Tant ben) Aissi *GIKQR;* ben *lacking M;* finanamen *K*. 13. cors *I*. 14. Donc *c*. 15. ieu *lacking IK;* l'am . . . fe *lacking G;* (l'am) am *IKQ*. 16. Adoncs creis plus *lacking G;* (Adoncs) Doncs *C*, Ades *Rc;* crois *D;* (plus) mais *MR;* (qe·m lassa e·m te) que mal sam te *M*, que me lass em te *C*, quem lacente *DN*, qim lazem te *GQ*, quem laissente (laissemte *K*) *IK*.

III. 17. (No) So *C;* (plus) tan *R*. 18. (per) en *IK;* falhigues *R*. 19. quez autram *IK*, que sautraen *M;* bayes *C*. 20. ses *lacking c;* latendemen *M*. 21. (m'es) es *R;* (que) cos *C*, qet *GQ*, qui *IKRc*, qem *D*[c]. 22. (emperi) esperi *I*, emper *c*. 23. Que ual *IK;* lonor nil pretz *GQ;* si mals men ue *AB*. 24. (que platz) quem fai *CR*, qui p. *DN*, cui p. *P;* par *IK*, pers *P;* (del) de *CDG-IKMNQ*.

IV. 25. Per com fol mal qeu (qen *Q*) naic p. *GQ;* Per so mi son li mal *c;* (so·m) son *M;* (so·il) sonill *N;* (n'ai) na *D*, trac *R*. 26. (loing) lonc *GQ*. 27. Qi tan ben ni tan gent parles *c;* (disses) dieuisses *P*. 28. amesunadamen *C*, ameseradamen *N*. 29. Si que *GIKQc*, Que *R;* (n'es) mes *C*, nos *D*. 30. (Puois) Car *M;* (la) li *M;* belazers *R*. 31. (no) nos *R*. 32. (plus) mais *MR;* (aco) aiso *IK;* (qe·i) qel *c*.

V. 34. Sufretz *MP;* (c'un pauc) queu (quen *IK*) uos *GIKQ*, sel q̃us *R;* (merceies) uos essaies *M*. 35. E merces qun pauc *C*, E cun pauc merce *R*, M. e unc pauc *M*. 36. (dur) dire *Q*. 37. (qe·us sui) qui os es *D*, qi sui *GQ*, qe son *IK*, qeu son *c*, qeu sui *M;* merceyan *R*. 38. Vas uos tot iorn e de merce clamaire *R;* Toz iorn *GQ*, Totz iorns *IK*. 39. Merceyans sui domne serai iasse *C;* Merceiares sui *M;* merceian *FaGIKPQc*. 40. Vostroms totz temps mans ionçhas clam merce *M;* claman merce merce *P*, clamans tro merce may merce *R;* claman *FaGIKQc*, clam *N*.

VI. *lacking P*. 41. Guillem *CGMQc*, .G. *R;* (soste) solbe *G*. 42. (Don) Joi *M;* domnei cortesia et me *c*.

VII. *lacking IKPR (inserted in K in a later hand—Bembo's?—at the top of the page)*. 43. (Bels) Neb *N;* peraguo *C;* (cum) on *CM*, qan *GQc*. 44. (Na) La *ABCD* (*and also the lines added in K*); (d'Est) e *M;* (plus) mais *c;* (li) lo *Q*.

TRANSLATION

I. I often sing for other people's pleasure; but at whatever moment I sang or took pleasure on account of a fair hope, now I sing for naught and am a singer to my own hurt. Just like the gentle bird which knows that it is caught and for that does not cease singing, so it is with me.

II. I have my heart and my mind intent upon Love, and it makes me ever better—if only I could find someone to love me as well as I love faithfully. I love without a fickle heart her whose unloved lover I am; and when I love her most heartily and faithfully, then that love which holds and binds me increases the most.

III. I do not think that ever any man for Love's sake acted more foolishly, for I love more the thought of her, without anything else, than another woman's kiss, since it (the thought of her) is an honor to me. But what can an emperor do without an empire? What avails me honor or fame which brings me ill? Yes, it does (avail me). For the ill which pleases is the equal of the blessing.

IV. Therefore, the ills which come to me from her are blessings to me, for I have never seen a lady, far or near, who spoke and answered so well and so reasonably. For that reason everyone praises her, since she is the fairest in the world, for Nature did not put in her either too much or too little, but just what becomes her.

V. Lady, suffer Mercy to be a little merciful, for Mercy's sake only, and to soften a little, showing mercy, your hard heart in my favor, who am a beggar and claimant of Mercy. Beseeching mercy, I am and always shall be your man, calling: "Mercy, mercy, mercy!"

VI. The worthy William Malaspina upholds generosity and lady-service and courtesy and me.

VII. Fair Paragon, the more frequently one sees Lady Beatrice of Este, the more one wishes her well.

NOTES

Sixteen MSS: *ABCDD^cFaGIKMNPQRbc*. Of these *D^c* contains only stanza three, *Fa* only stanza five; *b* (which we have not consulted) contains an envoi, apparently that quoted by Barbieri. Stanza four is quoted in the *Breviari d'amor*, line 30627 (Variants: 27. *Car non*. 31. (*qe·i*) *quelh*). Berenguier de Noya quoted stanza five in his *Mirall de trobar* (ed. Anglade, in *Homenaje . . . Menéndez Pidal*, I, p. 678. Variants: 33. (*per merce*) *merce merce*. 35. (*afranques*) *lo franx es*. 36. *calen*. 37. *que suy mercenayre*. 39. (*jasse*) *per rase*). And the envoi to William Malaspina was quoted by Barbieri (ed. Tiraboschi, p. 112. Variant: *donnei cortezia*).

Zingarelli (*Due trovatori*, p. 50) prints the poem, after several MSS, but without variants. De Bartholomaeis (*Poesie storiche*, I, 231) prints lines 1–12 and the two envois, after *A*.

In addition to the usual pairs (*AB*, *IK*, *GQ*), two groups seem fairly certain: *GIKQR* (9, 12) and *ABCD* (44, if *La* is really a mistake, as it seems to be). The relations of the other MSS are doubtful. A stemma is therefore out of the question.

Base: *A*.

16. *l'amors qe·m lassa e·m te.* Aimeric remembers the expression of Bernart de Ventadorn (ed. Appel, 17, lines 1–2):

> En cossirer et en esmai
> Sui d'un amor que·m lass' e·m te.

24. *Si fai.* Raynouard (III, 262) quotes another example of this construction (French *si fait*), from Arnaut Plagues.

43. It is not known to whom Aimeric refers as *Bels Peragon*—apparently a man, perhaps another poet.

42

I. Puois descobrir ni retraire
Non aus mon fin pessamen
A lieis de cui sui amaire,
Mout feira gran chausimen
S'ab sos huoills o en parlan
Mi fezes calque semblansa,
Per q'ieu m'enardis preian.
Que s'ella saubes mos mals,
Ja no·il quisera ren als.

II. Ben es fors de grand erranssa
Amics c'ama finamen,
Qand ausa sa malanansa
Dir a lieis en cui s'enten;
Car s'il conogues sivals,
Midonz, l'afan qe·m fai traire,
Plus fora leus mos jornals.
E car non conois mon dan,
Eu muor desamatz aman.

III. Bella dompna de bon aire,
Mieills c'aicel c'om compra e ven
Sui vostr' om senes estraire,
Que no·m vuoill al mieu viven;
Car mos cors si mes denan
Endreich lo fer de sa lanssa.
Amors, per q'ieu tan ni qan
Non puosc esser fraitz ni fals,
Merce·us prec qe·i sia sals.

IV. Car mieills m'avetz, ses doptanssa,
Qe·l Vieills l'Asasina gen,
Que vant, neis s'eron part Franssa,
Tant li son obedien,
Aucir sos gerriers mortals.
So non es greu pauc ni gaire:
Tant vos sui ieu plus leials
Q'ieu m'auci per vos aman.
Donc ben fatz plus qu'il no fan.

V. Al bon rei, fill de bon paire,
Q'es bels e bos eissamen,
Car sap ben dir e mieils faire,
T'en vai, chansos, per prezen,
En Aragon, q'el resplan
Sobr' autres reis e s'enanssa;
Per que sera derenan,
Si cum sol esser, cabals
Mos chans, et eu atretals.

VI. Seign' En Gaston, vostr' onranssa
Onra Gascoigna d'aitan;
C'aissi cum carn salva sals,
La salvatz dels peiors mals.

VARIANTS

I. 2. Nous *C*. 3. (de cui sui) cui sui fis *C*D^a*IKMNRT*. 4. fera D^a*IKMNT*, fara *R*. 5. (S'ab) Quab *CMT;* (sos) sotz *M*. 6. semblan *AEMT*. 7. que eu *IK*, que *R*. 8. (Que s'ella) Las sol quil (que *C*) *C*D^a*MNRT*. 9. cesera *T*.

II. 10. (Ben) Mot *R*. 12. Canc D^a; (ausa) aura *R;* malanza D^a, malanasa *T*. 13. (en) de *T;* (cui) qui *R*, que *E;* (s'enten) saten *CM*. 14. (s'il) si *R*. 15. quen *I*. 16. (leus) letz *R*. 17. (mon dan) lafan *R*. 18. dazamatz *M*, non amatz R.

III. 20. (c'om) ce *T*. 21. (vostr' om) uostres *CRT*. 22. Et serai a mon uiuen *R;* Quieu *E;* (no·m) non *EKNT*, nõ *AI*. 23. mon cor *C;* se met *M*, sames D^a*N*, ses mes *CER*. 24. Endrorg fer *T;* (fer de sa lanssa) fer lan *M;* (sa) la *CR*. 25. *lacking MT;* Don nulh colp non uau duptan *C*. 26. Per quieu en cans ni en als *C*, Per cieu tan ni can en als *T*, Sauos per qieu tan ni can *M;* (Non) Nos D^a*N;* (fraitz) franx *E*. 27. Nous (Nos *M*, Non *T*) puesc esser fragz (frant *T*) ni fals (= 26) *CMT;* (prec) clam D^a*IKN;* (qe·i) que *IK*, qem *R*.

IV. 28. (m'avetz) maue D^a. 29. Quel uielh ansessi la gen *C;* lansesina *EIKRT*, lansesisa *N*, lamsesina D^a. 30. (Que) Quil *A;* (van) can *R;* seran *RT*, sera *C*D^a*MN*. 31. *lacking T; placed after* 32 *in IK;* (son) soi *R*. 32. Ausi *R*, Aucire *T*, Ausis D^a; guerres *IK*. 33. (non es) nom es *CR;* (greu) mors D^a. 34. (Tant) Si *I*. 35. (Q'ieu) Que *C*D^a*MNRT;* (aman) amat *T*. 36. Dons *C;* (qu'il) quels *CT;* (no) noi *R*.

V. 37. Al reys ques filhs de b. p. *R;* (de) del D^a*IKNT*. 38. (Q'es) E *R;* bos e belhs *CRT;* eissaman *A*. 39. (Car) Que *CNRT*, E *M;* ben sap *IK*. 40. Chansso ten uai *R;* chanso *CNT*. 41. (q'el) quil D^a. 42. Totz autres reys *R;* autre rey *C;* et enansa *R*, ez enanansa *M*. 43. (sera) seray *R*, degra *M*. 44. (Si cum) Co *T;* (cabals) reyals *CMN*, lials *RT*.

VI. *lacking CMT*. 46. (Seign' En) Senher *EIKNR*. 48. carns D^a*IKR*. 49. Las saluas D^a*EIKN*.

TRANSLATION

I. Since I do not dare to disclose nor tell my faithful thoughts to her whose lover I am she would do a great act of pity if only, with her eyes or by speaking, she would show me some semblances by which I might grow bolder in my prayers. For if she only knew my woes, never would I seek anything else of her.

II. The lover who loves faithfully is free from great distress when he dares to tell his misfortunes to her whom he loves; for, if my Lady knew at least the torment which she makes me suffer, my daily task would be lighter. Because she does not know my woes, I die an unloved lover.

III. Fair Lady, of noble lineage, I am yours without reserve, more truly so than the slave who is bought and sold, since I do not wish to escape during my life. For my heart has offered itself to the point of her lance. Love, since I can in no wise be faithless or false, I pray your mercy, that I may be saved.

IV. Without any doubt, you have more power over me than the Old Man (of the Mountain) over the race of Assassins, who are so obedient to him that they go to slay his deadly enemies, though they be even beyond France. That is a small thing: so much more am I loyal to you that I slay myself for your love. Therefore I do much more than they do.

V. To the good King, son of a good father, go your way, Song, into Aragon, as a present to him, since he is both good and fair; for he can speak well and do better. He shines far above other kings, and increases his fame; wherefore my song will be excellent, as he is wont to be—and I likewise.

VI. My Lord Gaston, your fame honors Gascony likewise. As salt preserves flesh, you preserve it from the worst misfortunes.

NOTES

Ten MSS: *ACDᵃEIKMNRT*. The relations of the MSS are very confused. Even *Dᵃ*, which is normally very close to *IK*, agrees in one important variant (8) with the other MSS, against *AEIK;* on the whole, *Dᵃ* seems closest to *N* (23, 26). The group *CMT* is clearly indicated in lines 25–27 (where *C* has supplied a line to fill out the number), and also in 5 and in the fact that VI is lacking. Although *AEIK* stand together in 8, as we have seen, in 27 *DᵃIKN* stand against *AER* on the one hand, and *CMT* on the other. The position of *R* is very doubtful. It seems best not to try to construct a stemma.

Base: *A*.

15. *Midonz*. Pleonastic subject, after *il* in line 14.

22. *no·m vuoill*. I do not wish myself, to possess myself, to escape from your possession. It might perhaps be preferable to read *non*, with the majority of the MSS, and interpret the line as referring back to the preceding *estraire:* "I am yours without drawing back, which I do not wish (to do) as long as I live." But this seems strained.

23. *mos cors*. Another case of the unfortunate confusion in Provençal between "heart" and "body." Here, the former.

29. For this figure of the Assassins, see poem 24, line 13.

35. *aman*. This repetition of the rime word (9) is unusual for Aimeric.

36. *il*, the Assassins.

43. *sera*. The *eu* in 45 must be taken as an afterthought; the subject of *sera* is *mos chans*.

43

I. Pus ma belha mal' amia
M'a mes de cent sospirs captal,
A for de captalier lial
Los ai cregutz quascun dia
D'un mil, per q'ueimais seria,
Sol qu'a lieys plagues, cominal,
Que los partissem per egual,
Qu'aissi·s tanh de companhia.

II. Pero, si·n vol senhoria,
Ben es dregs, quar mais pot e val,
Et hie·l port tan d'amor coral
Que no·n puesc. Neus s'ieu podia,
Son voler non desvolria
Mas sol d'aitan, non de ren al,
D'amar son fin cors natural:
Ve·us tot quan li desdiria.

III. Mas elha·m pregu' e·m castia
Que m'en lais, car pert mon jornal;
Et ieu non puesc, si Dieus me sal,
Qui donc lo cor no·m trazia
Et autre no·m n'i metia.
E mei huelh meron de tot mal;
Per que, s'en ploron, no m'en cal,
Quar percasson lur folhia.

IV. Piegz m'es que si m'aucizia.
Quan la prec ni·n suy en logual,
Elha·m respon e·m ditz aital
Que fort s'en iraisseria,
Si daveras lo dizia.
No m'en cre: peccat fai mortal;
Et si·l n'ai mostrat maint senhal,
Per que creire m'en deuria.

V. Irasca s'en o s'en ria,
Qu' era·l dic que non es venal,
Mas ver a guisa de messal,

So qu'ieu l'ai dig tota via.
No·n puesc mais quar n'a feunia,
Qu'ieu feunei per lieys atretal;
Mas ab tot so m'a plus sensal
Que nulh' autra non auria.

VI. Reys d'Arago, quascun dia
Son vostre ric fag plus cabal,
Tant gent hi sabetz metre sal
Ab solatz et ab paria.

VII. Jes me mezeis non creiria
Qu'a Monferrat ni a Moncal
Vis lo marques emperial,
S'autra vetz non lo·y vezia.

VIII. La contessa Na Maria
Tant es bona, si Dieus me sal,
Qu'autr' am mais be ni ab meinhs mal
Non sai, qui tort no·l fazia.

VARIANTS

I. 1. Pus mama la belamia *R*, Pois ma mala enemia *c;* Puois que ma bella amia *A*, Puois ma bella mia *D*. 2. Mac mes *ADIK;* (cent) mil *M;* cabal *R*. 3. fors *N*, fort *R;* captaliee *D*, cabalier *c*. 4. Los lai pueis cregutz quec dia *R;* Lai puois cregut *ADIK*, Los lai cregutz *Nc*. 5. E per so hueimais seria *M;* De nul (*corrected from* mil) a^1; (D'un) De *ADIKN;* serian *D*. 6. Razos et dreitz comunals *c;* (qu'a) cap *R;* (cominal) com mal *IK* (*corrected in later hand to* comunal *in K*). 7. (Que los) Quels *Cc;* partissen *IKN*a^1, partissam *M*. 8. Caissi tanh *IK*a^1.

II. 9. Pois sin uolla segnoria *c;* (si·n) seu a^1; (senhoria) maioria *ADIK*. 10. (quar) qe *c*. 11. Et em port lamor tant coral *c;* Et hieu ai tan a^1, Et ieu iel tant *DIK;* (coral) leial *N*a^1. 12. Qel neis si fort o non lia *c;* (puesc) vuelh *R;* (s'ieu) si *ADIKMR*. 13. (desvolria) uolria *D*, desdiria a^1*c*. 14. De nulha res mas sol daitan *R*, Mas daitant e non de ren al *c;* dan tan *I*, da tan *K*. 15. Damor a^1; (son fin) lo sieu *R*, son gent *c;* cor *IKMc*. 16. Veus tot qant endes uoldria *c;* (tot) tant *D;* desderia *I*.

III. 18. Quẽ lais *C*, Qeu men lais *c;* (pert) prec *IKN* (*corrected to* perc *in K*), pet *R;* mon *lacking R*. 19. (non) nom *D*. 20. Quil cor del cors non (nom *IK*) trazia *ADIK;* (Qui) Si a^1*c;* (no·m) non *N*a^1*c*, men *M*. 21. E un autre nom metia *M;* (no·m n'i) non ni *c*, non noi *R*, no men *A*, no mel *D*, nol me *IK*. 22. (E) Mas *ADIK*, Don *R*, *lacking* a^1; (huelh) al *N;* merom *C;* (de) del *c*. 23. E si els sen ploron *R*, E sil sem ploron *c;* ploron de no men cal *M;* (m' en) mel *N*. 24. (Quar) Quels *R*, Qil *c;* procassam *c*, percaissom *D;* (lur) ma *ADIK*.

IV. 25. (si) qui a^1; mausezia *IK*, maucia *D*. 26. (ni·n) sin *M*, en *R*, uiu a^1 (*corrected from* uin). 27. (Elha·m) Qellam *ADIK*, Qem *M*, Estam a^1; e ditz maital *DIKRc*. 28. for *M;* (s'en) se *a*[1]; iraissezia *I*. 29. Sieu *ADIK;* (daveras) dautras uetz *a*[1], adaueras *R*, dauans *N;* (lo) loill *M*, loi *NR*. 31. (mostrat) moreirat *N;* (maint) mo *C*.

V. 33. Azir sen sis uol on ria *ADIKc*. 34. Qe ben sai qe no mes uenal *c;* (Qu'era·l) Queras *R*, Que nol *C*, Que tal *N*. 35. Mas per uer dun libre messal *C*, Anz es uers cun libre missal *N*, Neus (Qe *c*) plus uer dun libre messal *a*[1]*c*, E anz es uers qon dun mesal *M*, Anz esuers si com dun messal *R;* (de) dun *D*. 36. E tot ço qeu li diçia *c;* (qu'ieu) quel *R;* (l'ai) nai *Ra*[1]. 37 No *C;* (quar) sis *ADIKc*, sil *R;* (n'a) ma *C*, nia *R*, nai *a*[1]. 38. Qi en fel soi per leys atertal *R;* (lieys) lo *D*. 39. Ab tot some a mielhs senssal *c;* (sensal) sesai *D*, lial *R*. 40. Que (Queu *IK*) qan lim diei (di *D*, dei *c*) non (nom *DIK*) auia *ADIKc;* autre *a*[1]*;* nun *a*[1], nom *MR;* auia *N*.

VI. *lacking Nc;* VII *in C*, VIII *in Ma*[1]. 41. (quascun dia) tota uia *MRa*[1]. 42. *lacking a*[1]; ric *lacking CMR;* (fag) don *ADIKR*. 43. Tant i sabetz gen (gen *lacking M*) m. s. *Ma*[1]; (Tant) Quar *C*. 44. a pariã D.

VII. *lacking ADIKNRc;* VI *in CMa*[1]. 45. me metes *M*. 46. (Qu'a) En *M*. 48. autre *a*[1]; (lo·y) lai *M*, li *a*[1].

VIII. *lacking ADIKNRc;* VII *in Ma*[1]. 50. Es tan bona *Ma*[1]. 51. (am) ab *Ma*[1]. 52. (qui) qe *a*[1].

TRANSLATION

I. After my fair and wicked love has committed to me more than one hundred sighs as a fund, like a faithful partner I have since increased them every day by a thousand. Therefore, henceforth it should be common stock, if only she willed it so, in such a way that we might share them equally, for that is the law of partnerships.

II. However, if she wants a senior partner's share, that is quite right, for she has more power and riches (than I), and I love her so sincerely that I have no power in the matter. Even if I could, I should not gainsay her will, save only in so far, and in naught else, as to love her noble and pure self. That is all that I should gainsay her.

III. But she begs and entreats me to leave off, since I lose (the fruit of) my labor. But, as God help me, I cannot, unless someone took my heart from me and put another one there instead. And my eyes are to blame for everything; therefore, if they weep, I care not at all, for they seek their own folly.

IV. It is worse for me than if she killed me. Whenever I beseech her or find an opportunity to do so, she answers and tells me merely that she would be very angry if I were sincere about it. She does not believe me; and in that she sins mortally. Indeed, I have shown her many a sign of it, for which she should believe me.

V. Let her be angry about it or let her laugh at it; since now I say to her that what I have always told her (about my love) is not false, but as true as a mass-book. I cannot help it if she does feel resentment, for I was resentful just as much on her account. Nevertheless, she has me more in her power than any other woman would ever have me.

VI. King of Aragon, every day your noble deeds grow more abundant, because you know how to season them so nicely with friendliness and good manners.

VII. I should hardly believe myself that I once saw the lordly Marquis at Montferrat or at Moncal, if I should not see him there another time.

VIII. The Countess Lady Mary is so good that, as God help me, I know no other lady with more good qualities and with fewer bad ones, unless one should wrong her.

Ten MSS: *ACDIKMNRa*^{1}*c*. Stanzas one and four are quoted in the *Breviari d'amor*, lines 28840 and 29528, respectively (variants: 5. *per qu'ieu m'ayseria*. 7. (*Que los*) *Quels*. 27. *Qu'elam*. 29. *Sieu*).

Critical edition, W. P. Shepard, in *Todd Memorial Volumes*, II, 182. Our text differs considerably from that one, which was based on *A*, rather than *C;* the change is Mr. Shepard's own, due no doubt to the fact that two of the envois do not appear in *A*. De Bartholomaeis (*Poesie storiche*, II, 32) prints stanzas I and VII in the text of *C*, as transcribed by Mahn.

The following stemma is probably the most satisfactory that can be constructed:

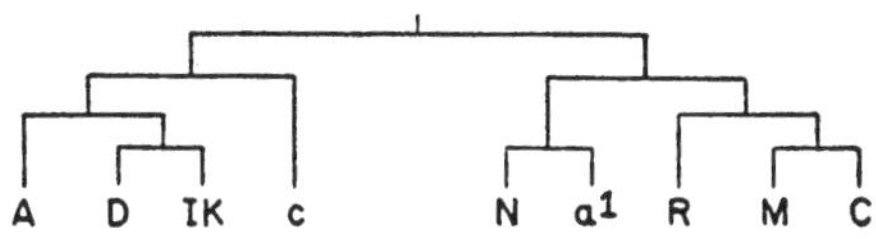

The main division rests on lines 33, 37, 40.
ADIK: 2, 4, 9, 20, 22, 24, 27, 29
DIK: 11, 40
Na^{1}: 11
CMR: 42 (ric *lacking*)
CM: 42 (*fag*)
In addition, we must admit that *a*^{1} had access to a MS like *M* for the last two envois; this seems the most likely explanation, since *Ma*^{1} have little or nothing in common up to that point.

Base: *C*.

4. Shepard: *L'ai puois cregut*.

5. Shepard: *De mil*.

6. *cominal*. The idea is of something shared equally, as explained in the next line. We translate freely "common stock," to point up the figure of an investment.

9. *senhoria*. Control, i.e., a controlling interest in the partnership.

12. *no·n puesc*. An elliptical expression, whose sense is fairly obvious. Shepard punctuates with a comma after these words and a period at the end of the line, and translates accordingly.

19–20. The sequence of tenses is loose, as often in Old Provençal and Old French.

20. Shepard: *Qui·l cor del cors no·m trazia*.

21. Shepard: *no m'en metia*.

22–24. Cf. poem 29, lines 8–11, and the note there.

22. Shepard: *Mas mei huelh*.

24. Shepard: *ma folhia*.

27. Shepard: *Quelha·m*.

29. Shepard: *S'ieu*.

33. Shepard: *Azir s'en si·s vol o·n ria*.

37. Shepard: *si·s n'a feunia*.

40. Shepard: *Que quan li·m diei non avia*.

42. Shepard: *ric don*.

43. *metre sal*. This seems to mean "season, give savor to."

47. *marques emperial*. Probably William IV of Montferrat. See the Introduction for him and for Countess Mary in the next envoi.

44

Can qe·m fezes vers ni çanço,
Eras voil far moz senes so,
C'una dona·m trob' oçaiso
  On sui esbaïz e torbaz;
Qu'ela·m prega e·m diz çastian
Que·m lais de donei e de çan,
Que trop sui vellz ad obs d'aman.
  Mas, s'ages subtilmen cerçaz
Mos aibs, no crei que m'o dixes,
Qu'a tot lo meinz lo cors i es.
E sai conoisser mals e bes
  E saviezas e foldaz,
E sai grazir e mercejar
Qui·m fai honor ni benestar
E be per be guierdonar
  E mal per mal, s'i·m soi forsaz.
Enqueras ai autre saber,
C'als bos me sai far car tener
Et als crois doptar e temer,
  Tan soi soptils e veziaz;
E sai entre·ls plus conoissenz
Solaçar ab moz avinenz,
Mas non ges a toz egalmenz,
  Que bon' es mesura en solaz.
E a bonas donas sai be
Parlar e dir ço que·s cove,
E quan dic ni respon, gar me
  De dir ço don sia encolpaz.
E se granz guerra·n sorz ni·n creis,
Pousc m'armar sols per mi mezeis
Del tot, que no'i mermi coreis.
  Pois mont a caval toz armaz;
E qan soi montaz en destrer,
Poing lo del espero e·l fer,
Tan que·l faz sallent e corser.
  E quant es be amaestraz
Et eu son armaz toz desus,
No·m par qu'Ectors ni Tideüs

Fezes doas jostas negus
  Plus tost en un besong qu'eu faz;
Qu'eu ai pertusaz manz escuz
Ab ma lansa per meiz fenduz,
E n'abat e son abatuz;
  E quant caz son tost relevaz.
E no cresaz que trop sojorn
Qu'en la batailla ades no torn
E josti meill a l'autre jorn
  Q'al premer no fezi, se·us plaz.
Et en la batalla eissamen
De las mazas fer duramen
Tals colps qe·l bruz fai espaven,
  Qan s'encontron li talabaz.
E pos de batalla be·m vai,
Que combatre posc be e sai,
Et on plus josti, plus me plai,
  Be son a tort vellz apellaz.
Mas se a cheval o de pes,
La don' ab me s'en combates,
E per batailla m'aproes,
  No·m tengra pois per forjujaz.
Messager, porta mon flabel
En la Marca lai a·N Sordel,
Qu'en faza juzamen novel
  Leial, aissi cum s'es usaz,
  Si q'en sia desencolpaz.

VARIANTS

1. Can qeu *U.* 2. Aram *U;* mot *U.* 3. Una *U;* ma trobat *U.* 4. Don *U.* 6. Qeu milais *U.* 7. Qar *U.* 8. Mas sellages *U.* 9. Mos obs *D;* qel mo dises *U.* 10. lo cor *U.* 12. saiviessa *U.* 16. si soi *U.* 17. Ancar ai *U.* 18. Cal pro *U.* 19. E al croi *U.* ***After*** 20, ***U intercalates these four verses:*** E pos annar ben e venir E afan e soiorn sofrir Els als obs caud e freid sentir Tant soi del tot ben afeitat. ***Then follow in U*** 25–28, 21–24, 29ff. 21. conoiscen *U.* 22. ab mot avinen *U.* 23. Mas non ai tot engalmen *U.* 24. Bona mesurem sollaz *U.* 25. a bona donna *U.* 27. Esseu dic o respond gard me *U.* 28. De so donneu fos encolpat *U;* dom *D.* 29. gherra sorz ni creis *U.* 30. Pos mi armar per mi esteis *U.* 31. qe nul mac coreis *U.* 32. E poi montar tot caval armat *U.* 33. Can soi armat nel destrer *U;* dester *D.* 34. Eul pong dels esperos el fer *U;* dan espero *D.* 35. Qeus faz s. *U.* 37. Qant eu sui de tot armat sus *U.* 38. Nom par qe galvain ni artus *U.* 39. iontas *U.* 40. ennun b. *U.* 41. Eu nai pertusat *U.* 42. E de ma lansa *U;* mei U. 43. Qan eu abat ni soi abatuz *U.* 44. E *lacking U.* 45. Ni non cugez qeu trop s. *U.* 47. gostri

U. 48. Qel p. *U;* fez *U.* 49. Et *lacking* *U.* 50. (las) la *U.* 51. Tal colp *U.* 52. Cant el sen contre los t. *U.* 53. (E) Donc *U;* ben *U.* 55. Com plus combat plus me plai *U.* 56. Donc soi a tort vuls encolpat *U.* 57. Seu a caval o a pes *U.* 58. La donna mes combates *U.* 59. mo aproes *D*, mesproes *U.* 60. per fort vizaz *D.* 61. fablel *U.* 62. (lai) tot *U.* 63. Qem fassa *U.* 65. Qeu sia d. *U.*

TRANSLATION

Although I have made for myself *vers* and *chansos*, now I wish to compose words without music, for a lady brings an accusation against me, by which I am amazed and troubled. She begs and tells me, in reproof, to give up lady-service and song, for I am too old to be a lover. But if she subtly had considered my character, I do not believe that she would have said that to me, for at least my heart is right there.

I can recognize good and evil, wisdom and foolishness; and I know how to show gratitude and give thanks to any one who does me honor or a favor, and repay good with good and evil with evil, if I am forced to do so. Also, I have another wisdom: I know how to make myself held dear by good people and feared and dreaded by bad ones, so subtle and clever am I. Among the knowing ones I can converse with graceful words, but not in equal measure with all, for moderation in talk is good. To good ladies I know how to speak and say what is fitting; and when I speak out or make answer, I care not to say anything for which I might be blamed.

But if a great war begins or spreads thence (from these ladies), I can arm myself alone without help with everything needful, so that I lack no belt. Then I mount my horse all armed; and when I am on my war-horse, I prick and rowel him with my spur until I force him to leap and run. When he is well mastered and I am in full armor upon him, I think that neither Hector nor Tydeus did two jousts, in case of need, quicker than I; for I have pierced and rent down the middle many shields with my lance, and I smite some down and am smitten myself. When I fall, I rise quickly; and think not that I dally long; but I always return to the battle and joust better the next day than I did the first, if you please. Also, in the battle I deal such blows with my mace that the noise of it excites terror, when the bucklers meet.

It goes well with me in battle, for I have the strength and the skill to fight well. I like it best when most I joust: so I am wrongly called old. But if the lady should fight with me on horse or on foot and should test me in battle, I should not then consider myself condemned unjustly.

Messenger, bear my *flabel* into the Marches, to Sir Sordello, that he may make a new and fair judgment of it, as he is wont to do, so that I may be freed of blame.

NOTES

Two MSS: *DU*. Critical editions by Bertoni, in *Revue des langues romanes*, XLVI, 245–249, and by De Bartholomaeis, in *Poesie storiche*, II, 80–84. Bertoni divides this poem into stanzas of four lines each; De Bartholomaeis, into stanzas of eight lines; and Maus (*Peire*

Cardenals Strophenbau, no. 78) into stanzas of twelve lines. The distribution of the rimes makes all these arrangements possible. As far as the MSS are concerned, *D* has no stanzaic division at all, but begins each verse on a new line, with a capital letter; judging by the two diplomatic editions in the *Archiv* (XXXIII, 296 and XXXV, 395), *U* has no valid division into stanzas, either (the only one indicated being a purely arbitrary splitting into groups of fourteen lines each, in XXXV, 395). We prefer to follow the MSS in this matter.

The two MSS differ rather widely, and are not copies of one original. The readings of *D* are on the whole preferable, and we have adopted it, as did Bertoni and De Bartholomaeis, as the basis for our text. Our edition differs occasionally from the two earlier ones, generally in a closer adherence to the text of *D*.

Bertoni calls this poem a sort of *vanto*. Pillet-Carstens suggest also the designation *escondig*. Aimeric himself calls it *moz senes so* (line 2) and *flabel* (or, with *U*, *fablel*, line 61). It is an appeal to Sordello to disculpate the author of his lady's accusation that he is too old to love. This is rather curious, since Sordello (like Uc de Saint Circ) makes precisely the same charge against Aimeric, as we have seen in the Introduction.

Bertoni dates the poem, with a vague reference to De Lollis's *Sordello*, "alla fine del secondo decennio del sec. XIII." But De Lollis (*op. cit.*, p.17) dates it 1227–1229, when Sordello was in Treviso. De Bartholomaeis puts it "before 1228." It must have been composed fairly late in Aimeric's life, so De Lollis's date is acceptable.

1. De Bartholomaeis: *Anc quem*. A misprint?

7. Bertoni: *Qar* (from *U*).

9. We adopt, with De Bartholomaeis, the reading of *U* (*aibs*), which seems clearly preferable to *D*'s *obs*, retained by Bertoni.

10. De Bartholomaeis: *lo cor* (from *U*).

21. At this point, De Bartholomaeis introduces the four extra verses from *U* into his text.

25. Bertoni: *bona dona* (from *U*).

29. Bertoni expands the MS *guerrā* and *nī* into *guerra·m* and *ni·m*. De Bartholomaeis: *guerra* and *ni* (from *U*).

30. De Bartholomaeis: *sol*.

33. Bertoni keeps *D*'s *dester*.

34. Bertoni adopts the reading of *U* for the whole line; De Bartholomaeis adopts *U*'s *dels esperos*. We prefer to emend *dan* to *del* (based on *U*'s reading).

35. De Bartholomaeis: *valent* for *sallent*. Why?

36. De Bartholomaeis: *bes* for *be*.

38. Bertoni (but not De Bartholomaeis) prefers *U's Galvain* and *Artus*.

42. De Bartholomaeis: *meig*.

48. De Bartholomaeis: *fezis*.

52. Bertoni derives *talabaz* from *talamacium*, given by Du Cange, and identifies it as a piece of armor, perhaps a kind of shield—OF *talevas*, Ital. *talevaccio*, etc. Levy, *PD*, "sorte de bouclier."

59. Bertoni reads *m'esproes*, with *U*. We prefer to emend *D*'s reading by dropping the *o* of *mo*, as does De Bartholomaeis.

60. De Bartholomaeis keeps the *fort vizaz* of *D*, but emends *No·m* to *Bem*.

61. De Bartholomaeis: *fablel* (with *U*).

64. De Bartholomaeis: *es* for *s'es*. Why?

45

I. Qui la vi en ditz:
Pus Dieus tan hi mes bes
E Na Beatritz,
Non hi a merces ges;
Quar tan gent noiritz
Sos guais cors cortes es
Que sera falhitz
Gauchs que non l'agues res.
Lo sieus dous esguars clars,
Corals, dels gensors flors,
Rendri' els parlars cars
Gaug, tant es doussors.
Pueys l'onratz onrars pars,
Qu'es autz pus qu'onors sors,
Platz, e·l conhdeyars, dars
No·m val tan d'alhors.
Tan diria, si·n crezia
Mon cor, de lieys chan- tan,
Qu'enemia m'en seria
La belha qu'aman blan.
Que·l valria, si·n perdia
Lieys qu'am ses enjan tan?
Qu'ie·n penria e m'amia
Destric e·l mieu dan gran.

II. Anc de nulha gen
No fon hom trobatz natz
Que tan finamen
Ames dezamatz. Fatz
Son, pus non aten
Joys, ni no·m n'es datz gratz.
Segon falhimen
Sai que sui senatz. Patz
En volgr' et acort fort,
Tan sui cossiros, blos
E ses tot deport. Tort
N'an gran sas faissos;
Qu'en luec de cofort port

El cor ambedos   sos
Huels. Ve·us lo conort!   Mort
M'an li belh respos,
Que d'amansa   ·m fes semblansa
Quan son guai cors fi   vi,
E ses lansa,   que no·m lansa
Sos huelhs ni no·m ri   ni
Vol m'onransa,   ni m'enansa,
Ans lonha de si   mi.
Ses duptansa   n'a mermansa
Sos pretz, quar m'auci   cli.

III. Pos m'a tot conquis
Qu'en re no·m biays   vays
Lieys cui sui aclis,
Ni d'al no m'apays   mais,
E quar sos pretz fis
Es dels plus verays   rays,
Volgues e sufris,
Quar for' als savays   fays,
Qu'ab lo sieu voler,   per
So que lor pezes,   des
Me luec e lezer   ver,
Sol qu'ieu la preyes.
No volgra aver   er
D'autra que·m colgues   pres
De se, ni jazer   ser-
Tan, ni que·m baizes.
S'ieu amaire   ses estraire
Li suy, ni leyals   tals,
Non puesc faire   pauc ni guaire,
Tan li sui sessals,   als.
Quar camjaire   ni trichaire
No·l sui, ni venals   fals.
M'es vejaire,   per mon paire,
Que·m n'es plus corals   mals.

IV. La belhaire   desotz l'aire
Es als bos et als   mals,
Per qu'es maire   del maltraire
L'onors e·l captals   sals.

VARIANTS

I. 1. (la vi) la ue *EMRW*, lam *Q*. 2. (Pus) Mals *R*; tans *DENa*[1], *lacking Q;* (hi) ni *a*[1], *lacking W*. 4. (hi a) ma *Q*, ies a *W*. 5. (gent) ben *Q*. 6. (guais) ien *R*. 7. (falhitz) sazitz *R*. 8. (Gauchs) Iois *Q*; (que) anc *W*; (no l') non *M*. 9. (dous) dons *a*[1]; (clars) clartz *IK*, cars *R*. 10. (dels) de *MRa*[1], del *Q*; iensers *R*. 11. (els) el *DEIKN*, als *MRa*[1], al *W*. 12. Gautz *W*, Gug *Q*. 13. Pueys *lacking D*; lontaç onraç *Q*. 14. Qes qes autç *Q*; (autz) uitz *W*. 15. El sieus can deiars dars *R*; condeiraç *Q*. 16. Non *R*; (d'alhors) doi lors *Q*. 17. deria *N*, dizia *R*; sim *I*, sieu *M*; crizia *D*. 18. cors *R*; (lieys) leu *M*. 19. Que enemia *R*; men saria *M*, men se seria *D*, men se feria *Q*. 20. *lacking C*. 21. *lacking C*; Quem *RW*; (valdria) uaria *DN*; (si·n) sim *E*, sieu *MR*; perdria *IM*. 22. (qu'am) can *D*, canz *a*[1], quieu am *W*. 23. Tan quieu auria e mamia *R*; (Qu'-ie·n) Qieu *M*, Qeill *D*, Qil *Qa*[1], Qui *IK*. 24. (e·l) al *IKM*; (mieu) syeu *W*.

II. 26. No fo trobatz hom natz *R*, Non fon atrobatz natz *W*. 29. Soi ieu car naten *R*, Suy car non laten *W*; non naten *a*[1]. 30. Iornz non nes *a*[1]; Ioi *EMQRW*; nom mes *N*, no mes *MR*, no nes *QW*. 32. (que) qieu *MR*; sena paz *D*. 34. (Tan sui) Suy en *W*; angoissos *DMN-QRWa*[1]. 35. Suy sens tot confort tort *W*; (deport) conort *R*; Tort *lacking E*. 36. *lacking E*; Nagran *CM*, Nam gran *N*; (sas) sa *CQ*, fas *a*[1]. 37. *lacking E*; Quen siec de deport *R*; Qan luec *Q*. 38. Al cor *RW*. 39. (Ve·us) ues *M*, neus *Q*; (conort) deport *R*; Mort *lacking Q*. 40. Mal sieu ien respos *R*, Ma le gentz respos *W*; Mai *Q*, Ma *a*[1]; (li) lo *NQa*[1]; (li) siei *DIKM*; belh *lacking IK*. 41. (Que) Qan *M*, Car *R*; demansa *Ra*[1], damansansa *E*; ·m *lacking DEIKNQW*; fe *Q*, ses *W*. 42. (Quan) Pus *R*; (guai) bel *W*; ui fi *C*; fi *lacking IW*. 43. Es e delansa *R*; (E) Er *MWa*[1]; (que no·m) sos huelhs *C*, que non *EW*. 44. *lacking R*; Mas a mi non ri ni *C*; Sos huelhs ni *lacking D*. 45. *lacking Ra*[1]; menassa *D*. 46. *lacking a*[1]; An *R*; si de mi *Q*, de mi si *R*. 47. (mermansa) me enansa *R*, meninanza *a*[1]. 48. (Sos pretz, quar) Car aysi *W*; (cli) eli *EKNR*, di *Da*[1].

III. *lacking W*. 49. (Pos) Si *R*. 50. Qa re *Q*, Que res *R*, Queren *a*[1]; (vais) nais *Ra*[1]. 51. (Lieys cui) Am *R*, Leis eill *DN*, Leis eli *Q*, Leis on *a*[1]. 52. Qen als *M*, E dals *R*, Qe dals *a*[1], Ni dals *IK*; mais *lacking D*. 53. Alegre cor fis *M*; E *lacking E;* pres *R*. 54. Sol qel plus uerais iais *M*; Ques *Ra*[1]; (dels) belhs *C*; (rais) bais *N*. 55. Volgra qe s. *M*; sustris *Q*. 56. (als) al *IKQRa*[1], aill *D*, *lacking M*; saluais *M*. 57. (Qu'ab) Ab *a*[1]. 58. (que lor) qa lur *M*, ca luy *R*; (des) del *Q*. 59. (luec) luee *Q*; (ver) ner *Q*, uezer *a*[1], per *R*. 60. (Sol) Tan *M*, So *N*; (qu'ieu) qe *DIKQ*; (la) lan *D*; (preyes) pres *Q*. 61. uolria *Ma*[1]; (aver) uer *D*. 62. (que·m) quen *I*; (colgues) tolgues *Q*, cogues *R*; pres *lacking CE*. 63. (jazer) iases *Q*, chazer *R*. 64. ni *lacking Q*; (que·m) quen *IM*, que *N*. 65. Sieus *DE*, Fins *MR*; (amaire) auaire *Q*; (ses) sel *a*[1]. 66. (ni) e *MNR*, *lacking D*; (tals) cals *QR*. 67. Non a faire *C*, Nom faire *E*. 68. Tan li sui selalls als *D*, Tan li on ceu fals als *Q*, Tant li soi cels als als *a*[1]; (als) sals *M*, tals *R*. 69. (Quar) Pos *Ma*[1], Ar *Q*, Que *R*; (camjaire) bausaire *M*, cam laire *a*[1], can iogare *Q*; (ni trichaire) nurichaire *a*[1]. 71. Trichaire mes ueiaire per mon paire *E*, Per mon paire mes ueiaire *R*; ues iaire *N*. (Que·m) Quen *DQ*, Qe *IKR*; (n'es) mes *IK*.

IV. *lacking MQRW*. 73. Per bellaire aug retraire *a*[1]; (La) Ta *K*. 74. (Es) Er *D*, Lei *a*[1]. 75. (Per) Ler *D*; (del) de *a*[1]. 76. (captals) chaltals *D*.

Instead of III-IV, W has the following two stanzas: Sill ques caps e guitz On uera merces es Don quieu sia ausitz Dun ioy que promes mes Cuns gentz cors grasitz Ma am plasen bres pres Don syeu suy traitz Pechatz e non fes es Cautres plasers cars ars Non pot far socors sors Magra un dous baysars pars Fora dels mellors pors Fera chantars clars Disent las lausors plors Mes aral presars cars Non say si lamors Am quem lia mi ualria Satendia aman tan E seria cortesia Sim leuges la fan gran Car sun dia ma corria Dun ioy quiel deman tan Non calria sieu moria Pueys da qui enan lan.

Donc dic ala gen Que mandon crosar ar Quieu non ay talen Ni cor de passar mar Neys sil monimen Sabia cobrar car Sella mo defen De prez non a par car Gara consin lauray ray Ponna col desir rir Am leys non faray may Am per dyeu morir Cam sin ten am fort cadena Cam pueys quieu la uic tric Damor ben am dousa pena Canc mal non sentic dic Say si mena non mestrena Con leyal amic gic Mas quispera trobar mena Daur per istar ric pic Blanc elena das mestrena Quels uostres prez ric cric.

TRANSLATION

I. Whoever has seen her says of her: If God put so many good qualities in Lady Beatrice, there is no mercy in her at all. Her graceful, courtly body is so nobly formed that no pleasure which did not include her would be complete. Her sweet, bright, cordial glance, flower of the noblest, would give pleasure to obscure words, such is its sweetness. Since her honored honor, raised higher than Honor itself, and her graciousness, are equally pleasing, no favor from another would help me much. If I should believe my own heart, I should say so much about her in my song that the fair lady whom I adore as a lover would be my enemy. What avail would it be to her, if I should lose her whom I love without guile? I should get thereby great distress of mind and great harm in my love.

II. Never was born of any people a man who loved so faithfully without being loved in return. A fool am I, since I do not anticipate any pleasure, nor is any favor given to me. And yet, following my error, I know that I am wise. I should like to have peace and a strong accord with her, I am so care-worn, poor, and without any pleasure in life. Her features wrong me, for, in place of a comforting thought, I keep in my heart both her eyes; and that is, after all, a comfort. Her fair words in answer have slain me, since she made a pretense of love when first I saw her form, gay, graceful and without a weapon; for she does not cast her eyes at me (like a lance); nor does she smile on me or wish to honor me. Rather, she holds me at a distance from her. Without doubt, her fame is lessened thereby, for she slays me, humble me.

III. Since she has overcome me entirely, in such a way that I never turn away from her to whom I am obedient nor do I ever find satisfaction elsewhere, and since her true fame is a ray of the purest, would that she would will and permit (for this would be burdensome to the evil-minded) that of her free will and to do them (the evil-minded) a despite, she would give me an occasion and a real chance merely to make a prayer to her. (If that were so,) I should not desire now to have from any other lady the heritage of being received in her bed nor of lying with her in all safety nor of being kissed. If I am her unreluctant and constant lover, I can do elsewhere little or nothing, I am so subject to her. Because I am neither inconstant nor deceitful to her, nor venal nor false, it seems to me, by my father, that my woe is the more deeply felt on that account.

IV. She is the fairest under the canopy of heaven in the eyes of the good and the bad alike. Therefore her fame is the cause of my suffering, and yet my reward is sure.

NOTES

Eleven MSS: *CDEIKMNQRWa*[1]. Critical edition by Zingarelli, *Due trovatori*, p. 65. Our edition differs from this in only a few passages, noted below. Concerning the additional stanzas in *W*, we agree with Zingarelli that they are not a part of Aimeric's poem, though they follow the same elaborate metrical system.

It seems hopeless to try to construct a stemma for this poem. The MSS fall into no constant groups, other than *IK*, which we take for granted. The nearest approach to a well-defined group is *MRa*¹ (10, 11), which frequently breaks up into all possible pairs: *MR* (21, 30, 32, 65), *Ma*¹ (61, 69), *Ra*¹ (41, 45, 54). *CE* likewise agree most of the time, though they present no striking common errors. The text evidently puzzled the copyists in several spots, and individual deviations are numerous.

Most of the MSS are defective in one way or another. For that reason, our text is of necessity somewhat eclectic; but, like Zingarelli, we follow *C* as far as possible.

This *descort* is one of Aimeric's least characteristic compositions. The numerous echo-rimes and the short lines lead him into tortured expressions quite unlike his usual style, which is comparatively easy and natural. And as a result, the meaning is occasionally doubtful.

11. *cars*. We take this to be used here has in *rims cars:* unusual, therefore difficult of comprehension. Much of the present poem could be so described.

13. *pars*. We take this with *Platz, e·l conhdeyars*, in line 15, although the construction is awkward.

18. *chantan*. The internal rime breaks up the word.

21. Zingarelli : *Quem valria s'ieu perdia*, with *R*. We interpret the passage: What would it avail Lady Beatrice if I lost on her account the one whom I love?

23. Zingarelli: *Qu'ieu penria*, which does not alter the sense. We understand *e* to mean *en*, which appears in some MSS.

36. Zingarelli: *N'a gran sa faissos*, with *C*. The meaning is in any case the same. It seems preferable not to take *agran* as a verb-form.

43–44. Zingarelli: *E ses lansa sos huelhs lansa, Mas a mi non ri, ni*. But this is an isolated reading in *C*, and, though slightly more comprehensible, is probably wrong. We take *E ses lansa* to mean little more than "unarmed," an expression which is explained thus: For she does not cast (like a lance) her eyes at me.

63–64. *sertan*. The end-rime divides the word (as the internal rime does in line 18); this is the only instance of such a liberty in Aimeric.

75. *maire*, "mother," and therefore "source, cause."

46

I. Qui sofrir s'en pogues,
Bon fora c'om s'estes
Que ja puois non blasmes
So que lauzat agues.
Pero ses tot pro dan
E ses sojorn affan
E ses ajuda fais
Volria eu portar mais
Que desonor sofrir,
Don no·m pogues cobrir
Ni m'en auses vengar.
Non o poiria far:
E si a pro venganssa
Qui·s part de falsa amanssa.

II. Sui m'en partitz? Non ges!
Anz m'en soven ades,
De lieis, tant m'estai pres
Del cor so qu'a mespres.
Si sui partitz d'aitan
C'a tot lo meins penssan
Mespretz sos faitz savais;
Car una on creis e nais
Bes plus c'om non pot dir
La·m fai desabellir
E de mon cor loignar,
E si·m fai tant amar
C'anc en plus greu balanssa
Non fo Andrieus de Franssa.

III. C'aissi cum sers o pres
Sui sieus liges confes.
Et anc nuills hom c'ames
Tant leu non fo conques;
C'al traire de son gan,
Sa bella man baisan,
M'intret tant aquel bais
Qe·l cor del cors mi trais
Al retorn d'un sospir,

Per qe·l viure e·l morir
Mi fai ensems mesclar.
Et hom no·is pot gardar
Ni cobrir de sa lanssa
D'Amor, pois dreich la lanssa.

IV. E non er ni non es,
Ni cuich c'om anc trobes
En dompna c'anc nasques
Ses totz mals tantz de bes.
Per q'ades, on q'ieu m'an,
Humils e mercejan
Li sui, fis e verais,
Si q'en ren non biais;
E s'ieu ab gen servir
Ni sofren, ab blandir,
No·i puosc merce trobar,
Ja no·is deu hom fiar
Mais en bella semblanssa
Ses peing o ses fianssa.

V. Dompna, s'aisi·us preses
Cum mi pres, ni·us forsses
Amors, ni mercejes,
Si cum sol far merces,
Vos m'agratz fin talan.
No·m tengatz en soan,
Si tot m'ai lo pel sais,
Qe·l cors es fres e gais;
E sai bos faitz grazir
Et honramens chausir
E so qe·is taing celar.
E sol d'aqest penssar
Mi fessetz perdonanssa;
Anc d'als no·us fi pesanssa.

VI. La reina ses par
De Tolosa sap far
E dir so don s'enanssa
Totz jorns e creis s'onranssa.

VII. L'enfan pot hom lauzar
Castellan, cui Dieus gar,
C'om el mon de s'enfanssa
Tant dreich vas Pretz no·is lanssa.

I. 1. Si suffrir sem p. *Q*. 2. (Bon) Dregz *C*, Ben *D^c FaIKNPQc*; com estes *R*. 3. (non) nom *D*. 4. (lauzat) blasmat *B*. 5. Pero pro ses tot dan *M*, Pero sens tot prodon *P*. 6. (sojorn) sciom *P*. 8. Volgra porta mais *P*; (eu) en *D^c*, *lacking B*; (mais) dan *Q*. 9. (Que) Qi *Q*. 10. Dom no *D*; (cobrir) partir *J*. 11. Ni nom nauses uengar *A*, Ni non mauses u. *M*, Nim ausas u. *P*. 12. (Non o) Ieu no *C*, Ninol *M*, Ho no *N*, Non *c*, Ni no *P*, Ne no *D^c*. 13. (pro) ia *Fa*. 14. Quisi part *Fa*, Qi part *M*; aymansa *R*.

II. (V *in C*). 15. partir *c*. 16. Anc *Q*, Cans *R*; (m'en) mi *CIKMNQRc*. 17. (m'estai pres) nestai p. *K*, mensta p. *D*, mes (mi *Q*) apres *NQ*. 18. (Del) De *R*; (so qu'a mespres) so que ma espres *A*, so que ma pres *BJM*, que ma perpres *C*. 19. Partitz si soi *R*; (Si) Sim *CP*, Sin *N*; (sui) cõ *Q*. 20. Qe tot lo mens (mos *P*) prezan *PR*; Qe totz *c*; pessam *D*. 21. (Mespretz) Membri *CM*, Menç pres *Q*, Mens pretz *R*, *lacking P*; son faiz saluais *P*. 22. Qar una creis o nais *P*, El fron men creis em nais *R*; (Car una on) Qun autram *CIKM*, Cun autron *N*, Cun autra *Q*; (on) en *c*; (e) em *R*. 23. El bes com *R*; (Bes) De *C*, Bel *N*, Bellas *P*, Pretz *M*; (c'om) con *N*. 24. Jam *PQ*; fan *R*. 26. E sai (si *Q*) tan ben amar *IKNQ*, Aisi mes pres damar *R*; (E si·m fai) Et a mi *C*, E leis mi *M*. 27. Qant *P*; (greu) gran *C*. 28. (fo) so *c*; fo nandrieus *or* fon andrieus *IKMNQR*; audreis *P*.

III. (II *in C*, IV *in M*). 29. Pero de tal so pres *R*; Aissi *CJMPc*; o pres *lacking P*. 30. Francx e fis e cofes *R*; liegers *J*. 31. *lacking J;* Canc negus homs cames *R*; (Et) Ni *M*, Qe *c*; hom *lacking D*. 32. Non fo plus (tan *JPc*) leu conques *CIJKMNPQRc*, Tan no fo leu c. *D*. 33. Quel traire de son gay *R*. 34. (Sa bella) Sa blanca *CM*, Semblan ca *R*, La b. *P*; (man) ma *C*. 35. Intret *IKNQR*, Memblet *M*; aquela bais *N*. 36. (mi) men *IKP*. 37. recor *P*; (d'un) del *CIKMQR*. 38. Si que uiure murir *CM*; (viure e·l) uoirel *D*, uiure *Q*. 39. Mi fai *lacking P*; (ensems) en ses *P*, esser *c*; mesclatz *c*. 40. (no·is) non *Q*; garar *R*. 42. pois qe dreit lansa *P*, pois tan for la lança *c*, tan d. la l. *R*; (pois) per *Q*.

IV. (III *in CM*). 43. Ja non er *CIKMNQR*, E ia ner *P*, Non er *D*, E ia non er *c*. 44. Ni non cug qom t. *M*, Se tut qat com t. *P*, Ni aig camas t. *Q*; (cuich) crey *R*; (anc) mais *CIKN*. 45. qanc mais nasques *Q*; (c'anc) tanc *P*. 46. Qasembles tan de bes *P*, Cestors malç talç de bes *Q*, Ses tot mal canc de bes *R*; tan *Mc*. 47. Per qe des er enan *P*, E pero on qieu an *M*, Pero ues on quieu an *C*; (on) hom *c*; (q'ieu) qe *Q*; (m'an) an *IK*, uan *NQ*. 48. Humil *CP*. 49. (Li) Sil *C*. 50. (q'en) que *CQc*; (ren) men *Q*, res *R*; nom *CR*. 51. Si ab ien seruir *P*; sofrir *R*. 52. Suffren ni *CIKN*, Silfren ni *Q*, Suffren et *MPR*; Ni *lacking D*; (ab) a *DIKP*. 53. (No·i) Non *M*. 54. No si deu hom f. *R*, Ja mais nom uuelh f. *CM*; (Ja) Ra *Q*; (deu) de *P*. 55. (Mais) Plus *CM*; (semblanssa) fianza *P*. 56. (peing o) gaie *M*, pech o *Q*; (fianssa) fermanza *IKNPQRc*.

V. (IV *in C*). 57. se sif preses *P*, sa uos p. *Q*. 58. Con pres mi nieus forces *R*; (Cum mi) Come *IKQ*, cu mi *c*; (pres) preses *D*. 59. (ni) nius *M*, en *IKNP*, e *CR*; (mercejes) malmenes *M*, pueis intres *R*, merceios *D*. 60. El uostre cors merces *R*; fal *D*. 62. (No·m) Nim *M*, Non *Qc*; tengratz *CMR*. 63. (m'ai) ai *MP*; los pells s. *M*, lols pels s. *c*, lo pesais P. 64. Qel es et frech e g. *Q*; (es) ay *P*; fresc *CNc*, fresch *P*, frescs *M*, frecs *DIJKR*; iais *R*. 65. ben fag (faiz *c*)*IKNQR c*, bel faiz *P*. 66. E a honor qausir *P*, E leaumen gauçir *Q*, E noblamen chauzir *R*, Et honradament chauzir *c*; honramen *CIKMN*. 67. (qe·is) que *IKQ*; (taing) qay *P*. 68. (E sol d'aquest) De sol aquel *IKNQ*, De sol aquest *CMR*, Sol qe daqest *P*, E sol de cest *BDc*, E sol daisest *J*; pezar *M*, peçar *Q*, penar *P*. 70. El uostre cors nom mostres pus pezansa *R*; (Anc d'als) Quanc mais *CIKMNQc*; (no·us) nolh *CJ*; (fi) fes *M*, fitz *c*, *lacking P*; (pesanssa) perdonança *Q*.

VI. *lacking DR*. 71. A ragina *P*; (ses par) qeus par *Q*, sap far *c*. 72. (De Tolosa) Elienors *CIKNQ*, Elienor *J*; (sap far) ses par *c*. 73. (so) co *N*; dunc *P*. 74. (Totz jorns) Sos pretz *Pc*, Tot iorn *CJM*; (s'onranssa) se'rasa *Q*.

VII. *lacking DIJKMNQR*. 77. Que nulhs hom de senfansa C; (el) del *c*. 78. (no·is) non *Cc*.

TRANSLATION

I. If one could restrain oneself, it would be good to refrain from blaming what one had praised. Therefore, I would rather endure loss without profit, woe without joy, and a burden without help, than suffer a dishonor which I could not hide and which I should not dare to avenge. I could not do that; and yet he has a worthy vengeance who quits a false love.

II. Have I quitted her? By no means! Rather, I bear her constantly in mind, her fault is so near my heart. And yet I have quitted her, in so far at least that in thought I scorn her wicked deeds, since another (love), in which are born and grow more good qualities than one can say, makes her (my first love) now unpleasing to me and drives her far from my heart; and it also makes me love so much that Andrew of France was never in a more grievous state of indecision.

III. For, like a serf or a prisoner, I am her avowed vassal; and never was any man who loved overcome more easily; for, when I kissed her beautiful hand as I drew off her glove, that kiss penetrated me so far that it drew the heart from my body with an exhaled sigh, so that she makes life and death mingle together in me. And no man can guard himself from the lance of Love, since he hurls it straight.

IV. Never will there be, nor is there now, nor do I think that one ever found in any lady who was ever born so many good qualities without any faults. Therefore, wherever I go, I am humble, thankful, and true to her, so that I stray from her not at all. And if I cannot find mercy in her, by means of courteous service, suffering and flattery, never should anyone trust henceforth, without some pledge or guarantee, in a fair exterior.

V. Lady, if Love had seized you and had laid violent hands on you, as he seized me, and if he had shown pity, as he is wont to do, you would have had a gracious feeling towards me. Scorn me not, even though my hair is gray, for my heart is young and gay; and I can give thanks for benefits and discern what is honorable and conceal what should be hidden. Would that you might pardon me for that single thought! I never did aught else to offend you.

VI. The peerless Queen of Toulouse knows how to act and to speak in such a manner that her honor is exalted and increased always.

VII. One can rightly praise the Infante of Castile, whom God guard, since no man as young as he strives so diligently for worth and honor.

NOTES

Fifteen MSS: *ABCDD*[c]*FaIJKMNPQRc*. Only the first stanza appears in *D*[c] and *Fa*. A few fairly constant groups may be distinguished. *IKN* agree consistently throughout, and are often joined by one or more of *CMQR* (22, 43, 52, 68). Likewise, *ABD* agree with some regularity. Lines 22, 52 and 68 would suggest a major division into *ABDJc* and *CIKMNQR*, with the position of *P* somewhat doubtful. But in the important variant of line 72, the division is rather: *ABMPc* versus *CIJKNQ* (lacking *DR*). At least one common mistake (74) would place *Pc* together. In view of the conflicting evidence, a stemma is out of the question.

Critical edition by W. P. Shepard in *Todd Memorial Volumes*, II, 186. Our edition differs from this in only a few places, which are indicated below; but our orthography is not that of *C*.

Base: *A*.

13. *si a*. Shepard reads *sia* (subjunctive of *esser*).

18. Shepard: *so que m'a pres* (with *BJM*). We follow the majority of the MSS: *so qu'a mespres* "the wrong that she did."

28. The lost romance, *Andrieus de Fransa,* enjoyed a great popularity among the troubadours. Aimeric refers to it again in 49, line 30. See Gaston Paris in *Romania,* XVIII, 473, and Birch-Hirschfeld, *Ueber die den provenzalischen Troubadours bekannten epischen Stoffe,* pp. 82–84.

38–39. Cf. Folquet de Marseille (ed. Stronski, IX, 3): *Quar viure·m faitz e morir mesclamen.*

41–42. For the redoubled possessive, *sa lanssa d'Amor,* see Bertoni, *Trovatori d'Italia,* p. 559, and Tobler, *Vermischte Beiträge,* II, 78; also poem 8, line 6.

62–64. Poem 44 is devoted to a similar defense against an accusation that the poet is old. But, as that poem was composed in Italy, and the present one probably in Spain (see the envois), I can hardly agree with Mr. Shepard's remark, in his earlier edition, that both may have been addressed to the same lady.

71–72. The "Queen of Toulouse" is, as we have seen in the Introduction, Eleanor, daughter of Alfonso II of Aragon, and wife of Raymond VI of Toulouse. Since her name was Eleanor, it is hard to know which reading is correct, the one we have adopted or that which calls her *Elienor.*

47

I. Ses mon apleich non vau ni ses ma lima,
Ab que fabreich motz et aplan e lim,
Car ieu non veich d'obra sotil e prima
De nuilla leich plus sotil ni plus prim,
Ni plus adreich obrier en cara rima
Ni plus pesseich sos digz ni mieills los rim.
Mas el destreich d'Amor, tant no m'escrim,
Sui, fe que·us deich, e no m'en val escrima.

II. Si per merce fetz Amors apercebre
La bella que mos precs non apercep
Que deignes me per servidor recebre,
Mout feira be, e faill car no·m recep.
Non sai per que m'auci ni·m vol decebre,
Que bona fe l'ai on plus mi decep.
Non a en se merce, si no·n soisep;
Mas orguoill cre, que no·n li cal soisebre.

III. Ben es d'amor voja e de merce sema.
Las! per q'ieu plor? que·l cor m'a de joi sem;
Que no·m socor, anz si loigna e s'estrema
De mi, c'aillor vol qe·m mut e m'estrem.
Non a paor, ni tant ni cant non trema,
De la dolor don ieu fremisc e trem,
Per q'ai major mal e·m par que plus crem,
Car de l'ardor que m'art ella non crema.

IV. Tant doussamen mi ven nafrar e poigner
Q'ieu non o sen, ni no sai ab qe·m poing;
Puois ses onguen mi sap garir et oigner
Ab un plazen esgart: ve·us ab que m'oing;
Que fai mon sen ab ma voluntat joigner,
Que d'un talen los trob qe·ls lia e·ls joing,
Per qu'eu corren venc vas lieis don mi loing,
Tant promet len e fai de loignor loigner.

V. Senes manjar, dompna, ·m poiriatz paiser
Ab gen parlar, qe·l cortes digz mi pais,

C'ab esqivar   mi tornatz en iraisser,
  Per c'om blasmar   no·m deu s'ieu m'en irais.
Neis l'engraissar   en pert; q'ieu fora graisser.
  Per autr' afar   no·m fail la carns ni·l grais;
  E s'ab prejar   en vos Merces no nais,
Fora·m, so·m par,   mieils que fossetz a naisser.

VI. Ab doutz esgar   sap sos vezedors paiser
  Et ab honrar   N'Emilla, cui jois pais,
  C'Onor ten car   e Pretz, c'ab lieis renais,
E Dompnejar   soffr' e·l fa mort renaisser.

VARIANTS

I. 1. Ses mos apleitz *R*, Senç mon apselg *c*; (ni) e *R*; ma lina *I*, mal lima *P*. 2. A qe P; aplam *U*, aplanc *R*, plan *P*. 3. (Car ieu non) Queu non *DIKPQUc*, Quieu non hi *CNR*; (veich) uieng *D*; (e) ni *CIKNPQRUc*. 4. (plus . . . plus) tan . . . tan *C*; subti *P*. 5. *lacking I*; (obrier) obrar *CRU*; (en) ni *Q*, e *D*. 6. (pesseich) speg *P*, sprereg *c*, plech *U*, pesses *R*; (digz) dig *IK*, motz *PUc*; (mieills) plus *R*; (rim) lim *R*. 7. (el) ab *P*; destre *N*; damor non nos crim *D*; d'Amor *lacking c*; (m'escrim) nescrim *IKPc*. 8. Soiz so qeus deg *P*, Son que feus dreg *IK*; (Sui) Que *R*, Per *U*; que (qel *P*, res *R*) no me ual *CPRUc*.

II. 9. mercem *C*, merces *U*; fezes amors percebre *ADIKNQ*; (fetz) fos *P*. 10. (La) A la *R*; (precs) prez *P*; non apercebr *P*, non percep *R*, non na perceub *U*. 11. doignes *D*, degues *N*; mes *IK*. 12. Molto fera fol qar non receub *U*; be *lacking c*; cor nom recebr *P*, ca non percep *Q*; non *A*. 13. ni *Q*; mi uol aisi decebre *R*. 14. Que per ma fe *C*; Qen *U*; (l'ai) ai *Uc*, iai *P*; (on) eu *U*; ma deceb *D*; decebr *P*. 15. Non a merce ab se ni non soyssep *C*, Non a merce per qe no mi soisep *R*; (a) ai *Uc*; si nol i soisebr *P*; (soisep) sonrceub *U*, sox be *c*. 16. Mos orgoils *D*; cre *lacking D*; qe non qal qe sen soi sebre *P*, qe nol calha s. *R*, (li) len *C*, lor *U*, lol *c*.

III. 17. (d'amor) amors *R*; uoia de m. s. *DIKN*, uueia de merce e sema *R*, uog o de m.s. *c*, nueia de m. s. *Q*; (sema) e uia *P*. 18. La *P*; per qe *CQRUc*; quela ma de ioi sem *A*; cor *lacking D*; (m'a) mai *Uc*, mor *P*; (joi) ior *IK*. 19. Si nõ socor *IK*; non *U*; salloing *P*; se *lacking Uc*; e *lacking c*. 20. uol qeu mande mescrem *P*; (qe·m) quen *I*, qeu *U*. 21. Don nai *U*; ni quan *lacking P*; non *lacking C*. 22. (la) ma *AD*; (don) que *R*, dom *D*. 23. mal e pus far que c. *R*, mal enqer qe plus trem *U*; (e·m) e *C*; par *lacking P*. 24. Qar de la dolor *Uc*, Qar la dolor *P*; qi mord *U*, quieu ai *CR*.

IV. *lacking P*. 25. (mi) men *D*; uenc *Uc*; (nafrar) afar *Q*. 26. Qe *QRU*; (o) ai *CR*; (ab) a *U*; (qe·m) qe *c*. 27. (oigner) ongre *D*. 28. Queu non o sen ab un p. e. *D*; uei *U*. 29. Quem *CR*; (mon sen) ma ley *R*; (ab) e *CR*, a *Uc*; hongier *D*. 30. Qi *Q*, Qa *U*; las trob a qel iung *U*, las trob qels lie noing *c*; lo trop *Q*, los prec truep *R*; (e·ls) el *DIK*. 31. (venc) ueing *U*, ueng *c*, tenc *N*. 32. Tan mi promet len *Uc*; (len) leu *R*; (de loignor) del onor *R*, de langor *U*; (loigner) loing *Q*.

V. *lacking P*. 33. dõnã podias *D*, d. me podes *IK*; ·m *lacking c*; podiatz *A*. 34. dig *C*. 35. Cabels chiuar *Q*, Cabusquiar *D*, Qab es quiar *U*; ira issir *D*. 36. non deu *Uc*; (s'ieu) se *CQR*; (m'en irais) mirais *R*. 37. lingrassar *Uc*, les graisar *Q*, la graysa *R*; (en) em *Uc*; (q'ieu fora) quem feira *C*, qeum f. *U*, qeun f. *c*. 38. (no·m) non *U*; la carn *CNRUc*, lan car *Q*; (ni·l) el *U*. 39. (E s'ab prejar) E sapchatz si *R*; preia *I*, peiar *c*. 40. son par *DI*; qeu fossez *Uc*.

VI. *lacking P*. 41. esgars *R*; los uencedors *R*, so foçedors *Q*, senz uenzedor *Uc*. 42. E ab emar *Q*; onrat *U*; (N'Emilla) la bela *R*, ma dona *C*, ne nulla *Q*. 43. (qu'ab) ab *R*. 44. Ab bels captiens quen aysi fai renaiser *R*; soste e fai r. *C*; (e·l) er *U*; (fa) sa *A*; enaisser *ADQ*.

TRANSLATION

I. I do not go about without my plane and my file, with which I fabricate words and plane and file them, for I see no subtle and delicate work of any sort subtler or more delicate (than mine), nor a more skillful worker in precious rimes, nor one who breaks up his words more, nor who rimes them better (than I). But, by the faith I owe you, I am so (caught) in the stress of Love that struggling avails me not, however much I struggle.

II. If of his mercy Love should make to heed the Fair One who heeds not my prayers, so that she deigned to accept me as her servant, he would do exceedingly well. But she errs since she does not accept me. I know not why she slays me and wishes to deceive me, for I keep good faith to her, even when she deceives me most. She has no mercy in her, unless she borrow some; but she trusts in pride, so that she cares not about borrowing any.

III. In truth, she is void of love and empty of mercy. Alas! why do I weep? Because she has emptied my heart of joy; since she helps me not, but rather moves away and betakes herself far from me, for she wills that I go hence and betake myself elsewhere. She has no fear, nor does she tremble at all from the pain which makes me shudder and tremble, wherefore my woe is greater and I seem to burn the more, because she does not burn with the ardent desire which burns me.

IV. So softly she comes to wound and pierce me that I do not feel it, nor do I know with what she pierces me. Then, without any ointment, she can cure and anoint me with a loving glance: Behold! she anoints me with that in such a way that she makes reason and desire unite, for I find them of one mind which binds and unites them. Therefore, I come toward her hastily, toward her from whom I remove myself, for she makes such smooth promises and makes one depart from farther away (brings one back from a distance?).

V. Without food, Lady, you could feed me with a gentle speech, for the courteous word feeds me; but by your reserve you turn me to wrath, wherefore no one should blame me if I am wroth. I even lose fat on that account, for I should (otherwise) be fatter. Flesh and fat forsake me for nothing else. And if Pity be not born in you with my prayer, better were it, I think, that you were still unborn.

VI. My Lady, whom Joy feeds, knows how to feed those who look on her with a sweet glance and with honorable demeanor, for she holds dear Honor and Worth, which is reborn in her, and she upholds Lady-service and resurrects it when dead.

NOTES

Eleven MSS: *ACDIKNPQRUc*. Critical edition by W. P. Shepard, in *Speculum*, II, 304. Our text differs only slightly from this one, but we have followed the orthography of the base MS (*A*) rather than that of *C*.

In general, the relations of the MSS are fairly clear. The following stemma indicates them:

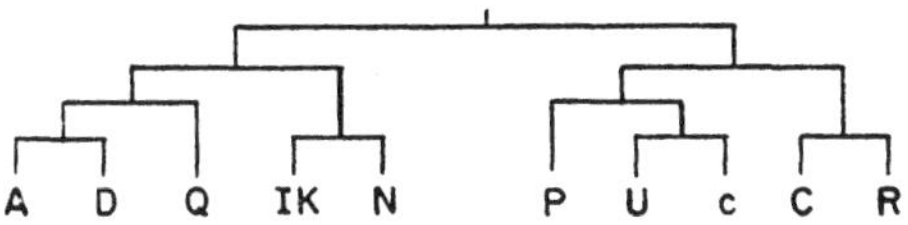

For the main division, lines 8 and 9.
ADQ: 44
AD: 3, 22
PUc: 6
Uc: 14, 19, 24, 25, 32, etc.
CR: 15, 24, 26, 29
The position of *Q* is not very certain, as it often has readings all its own. That of *N* is even more doubtful, though it does seem clearly to belong with the group *ADIKQ*. In the absence of more positive testimony, we place it with *IK* largely because of the order of poems in the MSS, which indicates a very similar source.

This poem is more conventional than 25 in its use of derivative rimes, which go in pairs: *lima, lim,* etc. The eight identical internal rimes in each stanza are, however, noteworthy. It might be pointed out that De Bartholomaeis, who prints the first eleven and a half lines and the envoi (*Poesie storiche,* II, 34; text of *A*), counts each of our lines as two, which, in view of the extra rimes, is legitimate.

3. *d'obra.* This construction, partitive *de* after negative verbs, is very rare in Provençal. Cf., however, Bernart de Ventadorn (ed. Appel), 31, 45: *non ai de sen per un efan.*

9. De Bartholomaeis: *fezes Amors percebre* (with *ADIKNQ*). This reading, though otherwise preferable, seems excluded by the system of derivative rimes; and the next line clearly has *apercep,* not *percep.* One could conceivably read there *non, a! percep*; but this would be something of a strain. Shepard: *merce·m* (with *C*).

18. Shepard: *per que plor* (with *CQRUc*).

21–22. Appel (in Levy, *SW,* VIII, 426) doubts the existence of a verb *tremar* in Provençal. He was apparently unacquainted with this passage, which confirms Jeanroy's interpretation of a line in William of Aquitaine (poem 10, line 15 in Jeanroy's edition). The existence of *tremar,* which I (Mr. Shepard) explain as a contamination-form from *tremer* and *tremblar,* must now be recognized.

31–32. The most difficult passage in this song. The reading *de loignor loigner* seems assured by the agreement of the majority of the MSS. I (Mr. Shepard) believe that Aimeric has coined the verb *loigner* (ordinarily *loignar*) for the rime's sake. The expression *loigner de loignor* I take as a conceit ("go far from farther") meaning "come nearer," quite in keeping with the affected taste of the whole piece. (I am not too happy with this explanation, but can offer nothing better. F.M.C.)

33. Here, the sense demands the reading *poiriatz,* rather than the *podiatz* or *podes* of *ADIK.* The distribution of these variants makes us question somewhat the position of *N* and *Q* in our stemma.

36. Shepard: *si m'en yrays* (with *C*).

44. *mort.* Omitted by mistake in Shepard's earlier edition.

48

I. S'ieu hanc chantiei alegres ni jauzens,
Er chantarai marritz ez ab tristor,
Que totz mos gaugz torn' en dol ez en plor,
Per qu'ieu suy tristz e mos chans es dolens,
Quar lo melher marques e·l plus valens
E·l plus honratz e·l plus fis ses falsura
. . . .
Es mortz, lo pros marques d'Est e·l prezans;
Ez en sa mort mor Pretz e Joys e Chans.

II. Ges lo marques non es mortz solamens;
Que·l melher coms qu'anc fos de sa ricor
Es mortz ab lui, que·ns dobla la dolor
E·l dan, don ja non er restauramens,
Tan gran perda hi fai lo remanens.
Segle caitiu e de falsa natura,
Soven es traitz aquelh qu'ab vos s'atura,
Quar qui plus fai ni ditz vostres comans,
Aisselh n'es plus enjanatz mil aitans.

III. Las! qui sabra mais tan entieiramens
Far ad autrui honramens ni honor?
Ni qui aura ja mais tan fin' amor
Ves sos amix ni ves sos bevolens?
Ni on sera mais tan d'esenhamens
Cum el marques fo? Per que Pretz pejura.
Ni qui sabra ja mais tan ben dar cura
De totas gens? Que·ls privatz e·ls estrans
Sabia tener amics et agradans.

IV. Ges enquera no puesc serrar mas dens
Qu'ieu del comte non digua sa lauzor.
De totz bos aips foron sieu li melhor,
Que gen parlars e dous aculhimens
E largueza e fors' ez ardimens
E guays solatz e beutatz fin' e pura
Foron ab lui. Ai, las! tan gran fraitura
N'aurem huei mais dels dos amics amans
. . . .

V. Trop es lo dols angoichos e cozens,
Que Valors pren el marques, mo senhor,
Qu'elh era caps de Pretz e de Valor
E flors e frugz de totz bos complimens
E mayestre d'onors e d'onramens.
Las! qui pot dir la gran dezaventura
Ni·l dol ni·l dan ni la descofitura
Qu'avem preza, don es la perd' e·l dans
Remas ab nos anguoissos e pezans.

VI. Senher verays Jhesus omnipotens,
Reys dreituriers, humils, ples de doussor,
Salvaire Crist, cuy claman peccador,
Als dos baros, Senher, siatz guirens,
Qu'en lor era Merces e Chauzimens
E Lialtatz ab fiansa segura.
Per so devetz, Senher Dieus, per dreitura,
A quasqun d'elhs esser vers perdonans,
Que quasqus fo fis e ses totz enjans.

VII. Lo plang fenisc ab dol ez ab rancura,
Quar de dol mou ez ab dolor s'atura,
E per so deu ab dol fenir mos chans,
Que·l mielhs del mon s'es perdutz en un lans.

VARIANTS

I. 3. tot *R*. 4. tritz *R*. 5. valen *R*. 6. onrat *R*; fi *R*. 7. *lacking CR*. 9. mor *lacking in R, then added above the line*.

II. 13. dans *C*. 16. (aquelh) aysel *R*. 17. dis *R*. 18. (n'es) es *R*.

III. 22. bes volens *R*. 24. (que) cuy *R*. 26. tota *R*; estranhs *CR*.

IV. 31. Quel *R*; el dos *R*. 32. largeze forse a. *R*. 33. guay *CR*. 36. *lacking CR*.

V. 38. Quel *R*; elh *C*. 40. flor *C*. 41. E maystre donor *R*.

VI. 47. (humils) senher *R*. 48. qui *C*. 54. fos fis *R*.

VII. 55. fenis *C*. 56. (ab) en *R*. 58. perdut *R*.

TRANSLATION

I. If ever I sang joyously and gladsome, now I shall sing afflicted and with sadness, since all my joy turns into woe and weeping, wherefore I am sad and my song is mournful; for the best Marquis, the worthiest, the most honored, the truest without falsehood . . . is dead, the noble Marquis of Este, the praiseworthy; and in his death die Worth and Joy and Song.

II. The Marquis has not died alone, since the best Count who ever was of his nobility is dead with him, which doubles our grief and our loss, which can never be made good, so great is the loss which those left behind suffer in them. False and evil World, he who abides in you is often betrayed, for he who says and does most your commands is deceived a thousand times the more.

III. Alas! who will now be able to do, so wholeheartedly, honor and respect to others? And who will now have such true love for his friends and well-wishers? And in whom will be found such good manners as there were in the Marquis? Therefore, Glory declines. And who will now care so well for all manner of folk? For he knew how to keep by him intimates and strangers as friends and agreeable acquaintances.

IV. I can now with difficulty lock my teeth to keep from uttering praise of the Count. The best of all good qualities were his, for noble words and sweet hospitality and generosity and strength and bravery and pleasant companionship and a true, genuine beauty were in him. Alas! we shall henceforth miss very much the two loving friends. . . .

V. Too painful and afflicting is the grief which Glory suffers for the Marquis, since he was the chief of Fame and Worth, the flower and fruit of all good deeds, and the master of Honor and Repute. Alas! who can utter the great misfortune, the grief, the loss and the discomfiture we have undergone? The loss and the affliction have remained with us, the grieving and the afflicted.

VI. Omnipotent Jesus, true Lord, righteous King, humble and full of pity, sovereign Christ to whom sinners pray, protect, Lord, the two barons, for Mercy and Pity were in them, and Loyalty and real Faith. Therefore, Lord God, you should rightly pardon truly each of them, since each was loyal and without deceit.

VII. I end my *planh* with grief and bitterness, for it begins from grief and abides in grief; and for that my song should end with grief, since the best in the world has disappeared in a single instant.

NOTES

Two MSS: *CR*. The variants are mostly not significant, and the two versions come from closely related sources. Base: *C*. Critical edition (based apparently on *C*, but with a number of emendations from *R*) in De Bartholomaeis, *Poesie storiche*, I, 186–189.

A *planh* on the death of Azzo VI of Este and the Count of San Bonifazio. See poem 30 (another *planh* on the same two deaths), and the comment and references there.

7. Verse lacking in both MSS.

14. *lo remanens*. That which is (those who are) left behind in the world.

16. *traitz*. One syllable; *traire* for *traïr* is common. It is hard to see exactly what Aimeric means by lines 15–18; their connection with what precedes and what follows is loose.

24. De Bartholomaeis puts the question mark at the end of the line, and refers *que* to the *marques*.

26. De Bartholomaeis puts the question mark at the end of line 27, and supplies after *totas gens* the words "come faceva lui." This strains the syntax somewhat.

27. *Sabia*. This word should have three syllables, but can count for only two here. The only similar instance that we have found in Aimeric is poem 25, line 40.

36. Verse lacking in both MSS.

37–45. De Bartholomaeis says that this stanza is lacking in *C*. He is mistaken; both MSS have it.

47. De Bartholomaeis reads (with *R*) *senher ples de doussor*.

56. De Bartholomaeis: *de dolor;* probably a slip of the pen; *C* has *ab*, and *R* has *en*.

49

I. S'ieu tan ben non ames
De cor ab ferm atur,
Ja no·m fora tan dur
Si Amors me malmenes;
Mas quar sui del tot sieus,
Mielhs que d'autrui ni mieus,
M'es plus greu quar m'auci;
E fai o, so·us afi,
A ley de mal senhor,
Que·l sieu serv l'an pejor
Ez ab menhs de merce,
On plus li fan de be.

II. Tot m'a tornat cofes
E de clar en escur
E volpilh de segur,
Quan que m'asegures,
Q'un gienh que·m semblet lieus
Ladonc, qu'era m'es grieus,
Mi fetz, ab que·m tray
Al prim qu'ieu Midons vi,
Don miei huelh trichador
An camjat ris per plor,
E si mals lor en ve,
Lor en blasmon, non me.

III. Quar m'es del cor tan pres,
Sai be que desmezur;
Mas son cors fresc e pur
Fora dregz qu'en blasmes,
Qu'es blancs aissi cum nieus,
Qu'ieu, ges plus que N'Andrieus,
Non ai poder de mi;
E blasme·n atressi
Sos huelhs e sa color
E sobre tot Amor,
E quar aissi·s capte
Cum se tanh ni·s cove.

IV. Mas ves mi tot ades
A·l cor plus fort de mur;
Ez ieu suefr' ez endur,
Cum hom tristz ez engres,
Tan vey qu'es mos gaugz brieus.
Pero, plus que romieus,
Sai ni lai no·m desvi,
Ans tenh lo dreg cami,
Cum s'anav' a Santor;
Ez on plus vas lieys cor,
E plus m'en lonh ancse,
Per que·l cors pro no·m te.

V. Al rey que ten em pes
Valor, on que pejur,
T'en vai em bon aür,
Chans, que, s'elh no regnes,
Remazutz fora·l trieus
De Pretz, mas no vol Dieus
Qu'en Araguo·s cambi,
Qu'elh mezeis lo chauzi
Entre·ls bos per melhor.
Per so, qui fai lauzor
Del valen rei, dese
Ditz quascus: Be·us en cre.

VI. Lo pron Guaston sal Dieus
De Biarn, qu'ieu sui sieus
Per totz temps, so·us afi,
Ez elh mieus atressi,
A guiza de senhor,
Quar fa de gran major
Son pretz, e no·s recre,
Que·l mielhs met sobre·l be.

VARIANTS

I. 4. me *lacking D*. 8. E pren men sous (seus *D*) afi *ADR*. 9. Car man bon seruidor *R*. 10. Que siei seru lant p. *A*, Que sei ome p. *D*, Que sei ser aun (seru an *IK*) p. *EIK*, Vezem de mal senhor *R*; ser *C*. 11. Cal sieus a mens merce *R*. 12. plu *C*, fant *A*.

II. 14. escur *DR*. 15. uolpilhs *R*. 16. (Quan) Ans *R*. 17. Cus ris me semblet sieus *R*; Eus genz *D*; giens *K*; (que·m) que *C*, quen *DD*[c]*I*. 18. Cadoncx era mot greus *R*; Adoncs *D*[c]; qeras *D*. 19. fe *R*. 20. (qu'ieu) que *D*[c]*R*; midon *D*. 21. (trichador) trahidor *ADD*[c]*R*. 22. Aun *E*; rir *D*. 23. mal *DIK*. 24. blasme en *D*, blasmen *A*; (non) a *D*.

III. 25. (del) al *R*; (tan) plus *ADR*. 26. quem *ER*. 27. Del sieu cors gent e pur *R*; (Mas) E *D*; cor *C*. 28. Taisera (Tayseram *R*) qen (quem *R*) blasmes *ADR*. *Verses* 30–36 *and* 42–48 *are interverted in ADR*. 30. Et ieu plus que nandreus (andreus *D*) *ADR*; nardreus *I*. 31. (de) en *AD*. 33. (Sos) Sor *C*. 35. Car enaissis (enaissi *D*) chapte *AD*; Car aysi nos capte *R*. 36. (Cum) Cous *D*; (se tanh) sataing *AD*; (ni·s) es *R*.

IV. 37. (ades) ases *E*. 38. (de) dun *AD*, que *E*; pus fort durmir *R*. 39. sobre et endur *E*, sofretz endur *IK*, suefrendur *R*. 40. hom *lacking E*; trist *CD*, fel *R*. 41. Vey (Neis *D*) que mos g. es brieus *ADR*; (qu'es) que *IK*. 42. (Pero) Et eu *ADR*; (que) cuns *ADEIKR*. 43. desfi *D*. 44. tenc *EIKR*, sec *AD*; dreit *E*; (lo) mon *R*. 47. Plus (Mays *R*) mi loigna de se *ADR*; (m'en) me *IK*. 48. cor *E*.

V. 49. A tei *D*. 50. Bon pretz cal (cals *A*) queis (que *R*) p. *ADR*; qi qes periur *H*; peior *IK*. 52. Chansos qui dels non es *R*; (que) car *IK*; (no) na *D*. 53. Romasutz *IK*. 54. (no) nol *A*. 56. (Qu'elh) Qi *H*; meteus *R*. 57. (Entre·ls) En *H*; (bos) pros *R*; pel *AH*. 58. E qand (canç *D*) ieu dic (fatz *H*) lauzor *ADH*, Per so car a lauzor *R*. 59. Del bon rei nin dic be *ADH*; (Del) De *R*. 60. Tuit dizon beu en cre *H*.

VI. *lacking D*. 61. pro *R*, pros *E*. 62. biaurn *I*.

TRANSLATION

I. If I did not love so well with constant, heart-felt effort, it would not be hard for me even though Love mistreat me. But, since I am all his, more than mine or another's, it grieves me the more that he slays me; and I assure you that he does so, like unto the evil master whose servants find him worst and least merciful when they serve him best.

II. He makes me insolvent and changes me from light into darkness, from safety into cowardly fear, however I may assure myself; for a trick, which then seemed trifling but which now is grievous, he played on me, with which he betrayed me, the first time that I saw my Lady. Therefore my deceitful eyes have exchanged laughter for tears; and if ill comes upon them for that, let them blame themselves for it, not me.

III. I know well that I do what is unfitting when I keep her so close to my heart; but it would be right to blame for it her fair, pure body, white as snow, since I have no power over myself, no more than Sir Andrew; and blame also her eyes and her complexion and, above all else, Love, because she conducts herself as is fitting and proper.

IV. She has toward me a heart harder than a wall; and I suffer and endure like a sad, unhappy man. I see that my joy is short-lived. Yet I stray not to one side or the other, but keep to the straight road, like a pilgrim, as if I were going to the Holy Sepulchre. The more I hasten toward her, the more she keeps away from me, so that my haste avails me not.

V. To the King who upholds Valor, wherever it may degenerate, go your way in good luck, Song; for, if he did not reign, the road to Fame would have been blocked. But God does not wish that there should be change in Aragon, since He Himself chose him (the King) as best among the good. Therefore, whoever praises the valiant King, everyone at once says: I believe you truly.

VI. God save the worthy Gaston of Béarn, for I am his man forever, I assure you, and he mine likewise, after the manner of a lord, for he makes his fame greater and is never recreant, for he puts the better above the good.

Ten MSS: *ACDD^{c}EHIKR* and *Sg*. D^c contains only the second stanza, *H* only the fifth; this fifth stanza in *H* was listed erroneously by Bartsch as number 5 of Aimeric's poems. We were not able to utilize *Sg* for our edition. Critical edition by Adolf Kolsen in *Zeitschrift für französische Sprache und Literatur*, 56 (1932), pp. 436–440. The orthography is occasionally different from ours, but the text is not substantially different. Stemma:

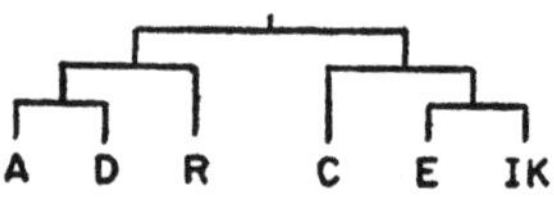

The main division (*ADR—CEIK*) rests on vv. 8, 21, 25, 28, 41, 47, 50, and especially on the position of vv. 30–36 and 42–48. Evidently two rather different versions of the poem were current. For the smaller groups:
AD: 31, 44, 58–59,
EIK: 10
Both D^c and *H* seem to belong with *ADR*, but they contain so few lines that it is hard to place them more exactly.

Our text is based on *C*.

10. *l'an pejor*. I have not found any use of *aver* very close to this; Levy and Raynouard have nothing at all similar. The meaning seems clear enough: they have him worse, they have in him a worse master.

25. *m'es del cor tan pres*. Compare the expression *tant m'estai pres del cor* (46, lines 17–18).

30. *Andrieus de Fransa* also appears in 46, lines 27–28; see note there. Judging by these similarities (cf. the preceding note), and by the fact that both poems are based on a six-syllable line, rare in Aimeric, one suspects that poems 46 and 49 were written at about the same time; both were certainly composed in Spain.

45. *Santor*. The Holy Sepulcher (*sanctum sanctorum*).

50

I. Si cum l'arbres que, per sobrecargar,
Frang se meteys e pert son frug e se,
Ai perduda ma belha dona e me
E mon entier sen frag, per sobramar.
Pero, sitot mi suy apoderatz,
Anc jorn no fi mon dan ad escien;
Enans cug far tot so que fatz ab sen,
Mas ar conosc que trop sobra·l foudatz.

II. E non es bo qu'om sia tan senatz
Que a sazo no sega son talen;
E si no·i ha de quasqu mesclamen,
Non es bona sola l'una mitatz.
Quar be·s deve hom, per sobresaber,
Nescis, e·n vai maintas vetz folhejan,
Per que s'eschai qu'om an en loc mesclan
Sens ab foudatz, qui o sap retener.

III. Las! qu'ieu non ai me mezeis en poder,
Ans vau mo mal enqueren e cerquan;
E vuelh trop mais perdre e far mon dan
Ab vos, dona, qu'ab autra conquerer;
Qu'ades cug far ab aquest dan mon pro
E que savis ab aquesta folhor;
Pero, a ley de fi fol amador,
M'avetz ades, on piegz mi faigz, plus bo.

IV. No sai nulh "oc" per qu'ieu des vostre "no,"
Per que soven tornon mei ris en plor;
Et ieu cum folhs ai gaug de ma dolor
E de ma mort, quan vey vostra faisso.
Quo·l bazalesc qu'ab joy s'anet aucir,
Quant el miralh se remiret e·s vi,
Tot atressi etz vos miralhs de mi,
Que m'aucietz quan vos vei ni·us remir.

V. A vos no·n cal quan me vezetz morir;
Abans o faitz de mi tot enaissi

Cum de l'enfan qu'ab un maraboti
Fai hom del plor laissar e departir,
E pueys quant es tornatz en alegrier
Et hom l'estrai so que·l donet e·l tol,
Et el adoncs plora e fai maior dol
Dos aitans plus que non fetz de premier.

VI. Reys Castellas, ges vostre pretz no col
De melhurar, c'uey val pro mais que hier.

VARIANTS

I. 1. Aisi con *GOQc*; lalbres *ABDIK*, lalbre *JRf*. 2. (son) lo *R*; e se *lacking I*. 3. *lacking I*; Aissi ai ieu perdut ma domna e me *M*; Ai eu perdut *ABDJOPRScf*, Ai perdut a^1, Ai eu perduda *GQ*; (ma) un a^1; belle *f*; (domn') madona *Q*. 4. (E mon entier sen frag) E mon enten son fraig a^1, E mos engeins (geniz *D*) si fraing (ses fraitz *J*) *ABDJ*, E mon enter se fraing *PS*, *lacking I*; (frag) fraing *cf*, frac *Q*. 5. (mi) men *GIKNQ*a^1; despoderatz *C*. 6. (fi) si *Q*; ab ensien *IKN*. 7. *lacking c;* (Enans) Anceis *ABDJ*, Anz en *GIKNQ*a^1*f*, Anz me *M*, E non *R*; (so que) qant eu a^1, so quen *N*, so quei *IK*, qan qe *M*, zo quant *PS*. 8. (sobra·l) pueial *R*.

II. 9. (E) Mas *M*; (bo) ben *Sc*; (tan) trop *ABDGIJKMQR*a^1*f*, tot *OP*, totz *N*; (tan senatz) asennaz *c*. 10. Mas a sazo sega hom son t. *M*; a (*lacking N*) sazos *ABDGJNQRf*; (no) na *R*; segual so talenç *Q*; talan *G*. 11. E si a luec non fa hom m. *M*; Car si *R*; (no·i a) nõ ia *IK;* chascus *GR*. 12. sola la una *N*, una sola *R*; miltatz *O*. 13. Car ben es hom per trop s. *f*; Ben esdeuen *ABM*, Que be esdeuen *D*, Car be saue *R*; (be·s) be *GIKNOPQS*a^1*c*. 14. (e·n) e *R*; (vai) uen *O*; (maintas) moutas *C*. 15. Pes qe *c*; ques sesquai *f*; (qu'om an en) con auen *Q*, com aia en *c*; (en) a *Rf*, *lacking I*; locs *IKNR*, lou *OPS*, luey *f*. 16. Sen *ABDGIKMNOQR*a^1*f*; (ab) e *M*, a *Q*; foudat *ABIJKNR*a^1*f*; qui o sap gen retener *DPS*, quil sap gen r. *GIKNOQ*a^1*cf*, quils sap gen r. *AB*, quiu sap gen r. *J*, qis uol gen captener *M*.

III. 17. Lais *DFaQ*, Sas *O*; quieu mezeis non ai mi em p. *f*; (qu'ieu) qui *Q*; me *lacking* a^1; en pode *P*. 18. Anc *N*, An *D*; (mal) dan *ABDJM*; qeren *QS*; enquere escarcan *f*; cenquan *C*. 19. Per queu uoill mais *GQf*, Et eu uoil mais *FaIKN*; Eu uoilh *B*; perdre faire *N*. 20. Adab uos *O*; (qu'ab) que *CR*a^1. 21. (Qu'ades) Cancse *ABDJO*, Canc sen a^1, Car eu *GPQScf*, Car mi *M*; (cug) tuic *O*; (aquest) qest *c*; (ab) en *ABDJMO*. 22. (ab) en *ABDJ*; (aquesta) qesta *IKc*. 23. (fi fol) fol fin *ABDFaIKMNR*a^1, fol fui *Gf*, fol sui *Q*. 24. Mauez a hom despeis mi faz plus bo *O*; Manetz ades *P*; (ades) totz temps *IK*, tosteps *N*; on plus mi faitz mal plus bo *J*; fa *c*, fai *P*; (bo) be *D*.

IV. 25. (No) Io *O*; des lo uostre a^1; ("no") nom *N*. 26. (Per que) Pero *ABDFaGIJKMNOPQS*a^1*cf*; torna mon (mos *Fa*, mons *IK*) ris *FaGIKNQf*; (mei) meis a^1. 27. El sieu a^1; (gaug) ioi *ABDGJQ*. 28. Cant ieu remir uostra gaia faizon a^1; (vey) mir (*corrected from* uir *N*) *GIKNOPQRScf*; uostras faysos *R*, uostras faisso *f*. 29. (Quo·l) Con *N*; bazales *C*, basalencs *ABD*, baselisc *GQ*, baselesc *NP*, basalisc *FaO*, bazeli *J*, balaric *R*, baicelis a^1, basalecs *c*, baisalics *f*; ioie sanet a ocire *c*, ioi sanet a ocir *P*; sane D, sanec *O*; auzire *f*. 30. Cal el mirals *O*; (el) al *f*; (e·s vi) esesui *Q*. 31. (atressi) eissamen *FaGIKNQf*, enaissi *M*; miralh *CGIKNOPQRSc*; (de) a *BDFaIJKMNOPRScf*, ab *GQ*, e a^1. 32. Qui *D*, Et *S*; (ni·us) eus *MR*, ni uos a^1; (remir) ui *O*.

V. 33. E nous en (an *D*) cal *ABDGIJKMNPScf*, E no uos cal *O*, E uos non cal *Q*; (quan) ca *G*. 34. Enans *JM*; a faitz *N*, en fai *O*; (enaissi) atressi *ABDJMRa*[1]. 35. (de) a *Mf*; qu' *lacking Q*; morabeti *C*, marabuti *DO*, marabutin *IK*, marapoti *f*. 36. Fay hom laysar del (de *a*[1]) plor e d. *Ra*[1]; (laissar) sebrar *ABDJ*, desebrar *M*; (del) de *IKMNQa*[1]; (departir) partir *M*. 37. *lacking O* (*vv.* 12–28 *of poem* 29 *follow without a break*); lalegrier *a*[1]. 38. *lacking O*; (l'estrai) illestrai *M*; so quel la dat el tol *f*; (tol) tal *N*. 39. *lacking O*; Mais nes iratz ez ha mil tans de dol *C*, Adoncs plora e mena maior dol *M*; maier *S*. 40. *lacking O*; (Dos aitans plus) E plora mais *C*, Mil a. p. *DGJMQcf*, Mil tant plus fort *PS*, Pus per un cent *Ra*[1]; (fetz) fey *R*.

VI. *lacking DGJMOQRa*[1]*f*. 41. (Reys Castellas) Tiriaca *ABK*, Triaca *I*, Triacha *N*, Bel castellan *PS*; (col) cal *Nc*, tol *PS*. 42. (val pro) ualetz *AB*; pro *lacking IK*; (pro mais) mais plus *N*.

TRANSLATION

I. Like the overloaded tree which breaks and loses its fruit and itself, I have lost my fair lady and myself and have broken down my sense, by overmuch loving. However, although I am overcome, never did I wittingly do harm to myself. Rather, I think that I do all that I do with sense; but now I recognize that folly overcomes it.

II. It is not well for a man to be so sensible that at times he cannot follow his desire; and, if there is not a mixture of the two (sense and folly), one half alone is not good, for one becomes an imbecile by too much knowledge and goes about many a time acting foolishly. Therefore it is fitting that one should mix, sometimes, sense with folly, if one can remember that (precept).

III. Alas! I cannot control myself, but go searching and seeking my own harm, and prefer by far to suffer loss and bring about my own hurt with you, Lady, than to prevail with another; for I always think to profit by this hurt and to act wisely by this folly. But, following the example of the faithful, foolish lover, you hold me the better when you treat me worse.

IV. I know no "yea" for which I would give your "nay", on account of which my laughs often turn into weeping; and I, like a madman, feel joy from my grief and my death, when I see your face. Like the basilisk which went joyfully to its death when it was reflected in the mirror and saw itself, even so are you my mirror, for you slay me when I see you and look upon you.

V. You care not when you see me die. Rather, you treat me as one does the child whom one causes to cease and put aside his crying with a penny; and then, when he has turned to rejoicing and one takes back and deprives him of what one had given him, then he cries twice as hard and has twice as much sorrow as he did at first.

VI. King of Castile, may your fame not cease to grow, which is far more renowned today than yesterday.

NOTES

Twenty-one MSS: *ABCDFaGIJKMNOPQRSa*[1]*bcfg*. Of these, *Fa* contains only stanzas three and four, *O* only lines 1–36, and *b* (which we have not consulted) only four lines. MS *g* (which we have likewise not consulted) attributes the poem to Uc Brunec. Barbieri quotes the first four lines (ed. Tiraboschi, p. 112. Variants: 3. *Ai ieu perdut; done e me*. 4. *mos engenhs ses fraitz*. These are apparently the lines appearing in *b*, upon which Barbieri drew).

Critical edition in Bartsch-Koschwitz, *Chrestomathie*, col. 177; variants are not given for all the MSS. Their text is somewhat eclectic, based primarily on *AB*; it differs, therefore, from ours in a number of lines, which will be noted below.

The following partial stemmas seem relatively certain:

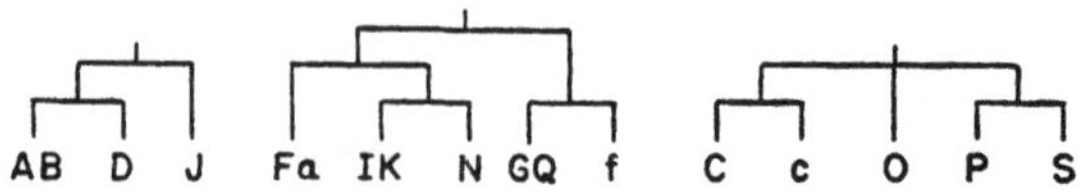

ABDJ: 4, 7, 22, 36
ABD: 29
AB: 16
FaGIKNQf: 26, 31
FaIKN: 19
IKN: 6

GQf: 19
GQ: 3
COPSc: 7 (-*c*), 41 (-*O*)
Cc: 41
PS: 7, 40, 41

The position of *MRa*¹ is rather doubtful; *M* seems to have something in common with *ABDJ* (28, 34), and *Ra*¹, which often go together (36, 40), seem fairly close to *C* (20, 33); but these relations are not constant. It seems impossible to construct a stemma that will show the relative positions of all the MSS.

Base: *C* (which we have emended several times when it stands entirely alone).

This is probably the most famous of Aimeric's poems, being the one which Dante singled out for highest praise. The thought is not original, but the song rises above the common level because of several effective metaphors and by a general ease and naturalness that are all too rare in Old Provençal.

3. Bartsch-Koschwitz: *Ai eu perdut.*

4. B-K: *mos engenhs se franh.*

7. B-K: *Anceis*; in earlier editions, Bartsch reads *Enans.*

9. B-K: *trop.*

10. B-K: *a sazos.*

11–12. That is, there must be a mixture of sense and folly (or *talen*); one alone is not good.

13. B-K: *Ben esdeven*; in earlier editions, Bartsch reads *Car ben deven.*

15–16. *Dulce est desipere in loco* (Horace, *Odes*, IV, 12, 28).

16. B-K: *quils sap gen.* Reading *o*, we must refer it to the general idea of mixing folly and sense; *retener*, consequently, will not mean "hold in check," but rather "bear in mind," a common meaning of the word.

21. B-K: *en* (for *ab*).

23. B-K: *fol fin.*

25. Compare the very similar expression in poem 38, line 29: *No sai nulh gaug per qu'ieu des ma dolor.*

26. B-K: *Pero.*

31. B-K: *a mi.*

33. B-K: *E no·us en cal.*

39–40. For these two lines, we reject the isolated reading of *C*, and follow the text of *A*, which is substantially that of nearly all the MSS.

41. *Reys Castellas.* This reading has rather poor MS support, for it occurs as we print it only in *Cc*; *PS* have something similar, but it will be noted that these four MSS belong to one group. The reading *Tiriaca* (which Bartsch-Koschwitz adopt) may therefore be preferable, although the person designated would then be quite unknown. It is difficult, incidentally, to see how either of these two readings could possibly have been taken for the other. As for the word *col*, Levy (*SW*, I, 279) quotes only one example (from Arnaut Daniel) of *colar* meaning "ablassen."

51

I. Sitot m'es grieus l'afans
Que·m fai Amors suffrir,
Ja no cujetz que·m vir
Mos pessatz ni mos chans
Ni mos entendemens,
Tant ai de conoissensa,
De lai on mos cors es,
Aissi ab ferm talan;
Que l'amoros semblan
Que·m fes Midons m'a pres,
Per qu'ieu li·m ren ab francha bevolensa.

II. Francx ez humilians,
Volontos de servir,
Li serai ses mentir
Al temps de totz mos ans;
Qu'aisi·l sui bevolens
Qu'en res no·i fas falhensa.
Doncs, si eu li disses,
Cum l'autr' amador fan,
Quo·l sui fis ses enjan,
Vengra m'en ja nulhs bes?
No sai, quar sol del pensar ai temensa.

III. Pero mals quant es grans
No pot ges leu guerir,
Quan hom non l'auza dir.
Per qu'ieu serai preyans
Merce dels falhimens,
Sol quar anc fi parvensa
Qu'en lieys mon cor agues?
O yeu! Per que? Quar tan
Val qu'ira·s remembran
Ben leu cum ye·m sui mes
En sos poders senes tota tenensa.

IV. Lo sieus guays cors prezans,
Francs ab dous aculhir,
Se sap tan gent aizir
En totz faitz benestans
Que no·i qual mai ni menhs,
Quar tan azaut comensa
E fenis totas res
Qu'om non lo torn' a dan;
E si·l quier merceyan
S'amor, tem que li pes;
Tenrai m'en doncs paguatz ab l'entendensa.

V. Mas entre dos amans
Deu esser, ses mentir,
Quant hom lo pot chauzir,
Us fizels drogomans,
Azautz e conoyssens,
Que saubes far valensa,
Qu'ab plazens ditz cortes
Sos bes dir' e celan,
E·ls bes traisses enan
E ja mals no·y caubes,
Quar en mans locs val belha captenensa.

VI. Al pros comte prezan,
Mo seynhor, dic e man
Que, s·ieu poder agues
Si cum ai lo talan, bel fera captenensa.

VARIANTS

I. 1. lafan *R*. 3. (no) nous *R*; (que·m) ques *R*. 10. fei *R*. 11. li men ren *R*.

II. 12. Franc *C*. 15. (ans) sens *R*. 18. E doncx sieu *R*. 21. nulh *R*. 22. (del) de *R*.

III. 23. mal *CR*. 25. Ca *R*. 26. quien *R*. 30. (O) E *R*. 32. co men soi mes *R*. 33. poders se senes *R*; temensa *CR*.

IV. 34. Lo sieu guay *CR*; prezan *R*. 35. Franc *CR*; dos *R*. 37. benestan *R*. 43. (pes) pe *R*. 44. ab sol la entendensa *C*, ab entendensa *R*.

V. 49. azaut *C*. 51. Cap *R*; plazen *C*. 52. Sõ bel d. *R*. 53. trassios *R*; enan *lacking R* (*space left blank*). 55. Quan *C*.

VI. 57. Mos senher *R*. 59. (fera) fora *R*.

TRANSLATION

I. Although the suffering is grievous which Love makes me bear, think not that I turn (elsewhere) my thoughts or my songs or my affection, so much gratitude have I toward her where my heart is, with such faithful longing. The loving glance which my Lady cast at me has captured me, and therefore I surrender myself to her with sincere good-will.

II. Sincere and humble, desirous of serving, I shall be toward her always, without lying, for I am so in love with her that in nothing do I fail. So, if I told her, as other lovers do, how truly faithful I am to her, would any good come to me from that? I know not—since I am frightened merely by the thought of it.

III. However, any sickness, when it is great, cannot easily be cured when one does not dare to tell about it. Why shall I beg mercy for my mistakes, only because I once disclosed that I had set my heart upon her? Yes! Why? Because she is so noble that she will easily remember how I placed myself in her power without any holding back.

IV. Her gay, stately, noble body, with her sweet courtesy, can so finely adapt itself to all praiseworthy actions that it has need of nothing more or nothing less, for it begins and ends all things so cleverly that one never speaks ill of it; and if I beg and implore her love, I fear that it may vex her; I shall therefore be satisfied merely with my feeling of love.

V. Between two lovers there should be, truly, if one can find him, a faithful, skilled and wise interpreter, who would know how to be helpful; for with pleasing, courtly words he would talk, in secret, of her good qualities and would publish them abroad; and there would be no bad qualities found in her, for in many a place a fair bearing helps.

VI. To the worthy and honored Count, my Lord, I speak and send this message, that, if I had the power as I have the will, I should make a fine display.

NOTES

Two MSS: *CR*. The two versions are closely related, although the scribe of *R* apparently had some difficulty in reading the text he was copying (vv. 15, 53). Other variants in *R* may be due to the same reason, or to this scribe's habitual carelessness. We have chosen *C* as base.

33. *tenensa*. We have rejected the *temensa* of the MSS, since it occurs in the rime in line 22; the emendation is an obvious one.

56. We have discussed in the Introduction the possibility that this count, otherwise unidentified, is Raymond VI of Toulouse; notice that Aimeric calls him *mo seynhor*.

52

I. Totz hom qui so blasma que deu lauzar
Lauz' atressi aiso que deu blasmar;
Ez hieu o dic per so quar es Amors
Forjutjada per nescis jutjadors
Que no sabon adreit mostrar per que;
Mas er es temps que ditz hom de mal be,
Ez atressi que de ben ditz hom mal,
Per que lor digz non es conditz de sal.

II. Estranhamen se deuria pensar
Selh qu'autrui vol reprenden vergonhar,
Qu'ieu ai vist manhs repres reprendedors
E manhs baissatz qu'estre cujavan sors;
Per que selh deu qui repren guardar se
Qu'om no puesca lui repenre de re,
Qu'abans deu hom se meteys far leyal
Qu'altruy apel traidor ni venal.

III. A manhs homes aug Amor acuzar
Ez el maldir d'Amor asotilar,
Que cavaliers ai vistz e trobadors
Que de baissatz fes altz e d'altz aussors,
Tant eslaissatz que non tenion fre
De dir d'Amor tot mal senes merce,
Aissi cum es de tracion mortal;
E selh qu'a faitz de nien fan aital.

IV. Mas ges adreg non o pot hom proar,
Qu'Amors fai ben tot aisso que deu far,
Qu'en amairitz intr' ez en amadors
Don nays ez ieys cortezi' e valors
E tot aisso qu'en verai pretz perte.
Non es de plus tengud' Amors, so cre.
Doncs, pus lo ben lor mostra ez ilh fan al,
Quar la·n blasman fan peccat crimenal.

V. Per Crist, menton, segon so qu'a mi par,
Que non es reys que puesca ben guardar

Son regisme totz sols ses valedors,
Des qu'el troba sos vassals traïdors.
Doncs, pus Amors fai tot so que cove
E silh qu'a faitz li porton mala fe,
Dic qu'om deu dir d'els per dreg natural
So qu'ilh an dig d'Amor, si Dieus me sal!

VI. Una domna sai que no troba par
Que de beutat puesc' ab lieys parejar;
E sa beutatz es entre las gensors
Genser aissi com entre fuelhas flors.
Hieu am lieys trop, mas elha petit me,
Mas ades n'ai un conort que·m reve,
Qu'al meynhs s'ilh tot del sobreplus no·m val,
Tan n'ai d'onor que ben cobri·l captal.

VII. Quar conoys plus dels autres e mante
Sen e saber e tot so qu'es de be,
L'Emperaire que sobre·ls valens val
Conoichera s'ieu dic ben o dic mal.

VARIANTS

I. 1. (qui so) caiso *GIKNOQUc*; so lausa que deu blasmar *f*; brasma *c*. 2. Lais a. *c*, Blasm a. *f*, Lanza ausi *O*; aco *ABDIKNR*, aço *Q*; (blasmar) lauzar *f*. 3. Et ieu dic o *ABDIKNRf*, Ez eu dic zo *O*, Eu dic *Uc*, Et eo dic *Q*; amor *I*. 4. Fors iutgada *GQR*, For iugat *IK*. 5. (adreit) ades *R*; (mostrar) iutgar *A*. 6. Mas er es temps qun dizon del be mal *O*; (es) el *U*, al *c*, *lacking B*; (ditz hom) dizon *Qf*; del *BN*; mal de be *R*. 7. *lacking O*; que diz hom (dizon *f*) de ben mal *Uf*; del *ABDGIKNQ*. 8. (que) quel *A*; (conditz) condutz *DR*, codiç *N*, diz *U*.

II. 9. E franchamen *CR*, Astruingnament *O*; sen deuria apensar *O*; deuriom *C*. 10. (vol) uoln *Q*; reprende (repende *G*) v. *GOQ*, reprendre et v. *BDUc*, reprendre et enseignar *A*, reprende v. *f*. 11. Car yeu ay uist aut mans reprendedors *R*; (Qu'ieu) Se *O*; nai *OUc*; ai ia uist *C*, ai ço uist *OQ*; maint *OQU*, mail *c*, *lacking C*; (repres) pres *Q*, *lacking N*. 12. maint *GOQU*; baissar *O*; (estre) esser *DD*^{c}*IK*; cuidaua *N*; (sors) sus *c*. 13. Per qal sel deu gardar qi repren si *c*; Per caisel deu *ABDGIKNOQ*, Per que deu cel *f*; reprendre *O*; (se) be *U*. 14. Si qom no pusca *c*; repenre lui *R*; (de) en *NR* (en re *added later, above the line, in N*). 15. Quenans *ABDFaIKNOf*, Car ans *R*; (deu hom) deuen *c*; leia *D*. 16. Caitrui *D*; (apel) tener *U*, per *c*; triccador *U*.

III. 17. (manhs) tanz *U*, motz *f*; amors *R*. 18. (Ez el) El lo *f*; maldig *ABDIKNORUcf*; damors *R*. 19. caualer *GOQ*; uist *DGIKNOQRUcf*; (e trobadors) en t. *I*, et raubadors *Q*. 20. bassetz *ABDGIKNOQRc*, bas *U*. 21. Tant es lassatz chascus que non ten fre *AB*; elaissatz *f*; (non) nõ y *f*; tenian so fre *N*, ten poi sufre *U*, ten piu fren *c*. 23. de traitor *Uc*. 24. Acel qa (qai *Q*) fait de nien atretal *GQ*; E selhs *ACDIKf*, Aicil *U*, Acil *c*; (faitz) fuiz *O*; (nien) men *Uc*; (fan) fun *O*.

IV. 25. (o) lo *GQ*, lom *U*, lon *c*; (pot hom) podon *ABDIKNOQ*, pod hom *U*, podom *Gf*. 26. Camor fai zo ben totz qe deu far *O*; (aisso) aco *ABDIKNR*. 27. Car de maritz intret en aymadors *R*; Qentramairitz *B*; entra en *OUc*, intres en *C*. 28. Don (Dom *DN*) nais domneis c. e v. *ABDIKNORf*, Donnais doncs c. e v. *Uc*. 29. (aisso) aco *ABDIKNR*; (qu'en) qu'a *ABDIKNOR*, qe *Uc*; uerais pretz *IKNO*. 30. Non es del (de *Q*) plus amors crezenz (creçut *Q*) zo cre *GQ*; (de) del *Uc*; plus negus damors *O*. 31. Doncs pois lor mostra ben *AB*; lur o mostra silh fan als *R*; (al) mal *Uf*. 32. (Quar) Ni *f*; (la·n) la *Cf*, ben *O*; (la·n blasman) ambas man *U*, amb las mans *c*, lan blasmat *R*; pechat fant *B*; (fan) fai *U*, fun *O*; criminals *R*.

V. 33. (Per Crist, menton) De Crist m. *O*, Per quieu en dic *Cf*; Crist *lacking c, though a space is left blank*; menton *lacking Q*; (qu'a mi) que men *IK*, que me *Ucf*. 34. (Que) Coi *A*, Cuoi *B*, Cui *D*, Cuei *NR*, Qa *U*, Co *c*; non es res *U*, no ne rens *c*; que ben puosca garrar *IK*. 35. reingnesmes *U*, regnesme *GQc*; (sols) sals *D*; ballidors *GQUc*. 36. (Des) Pus *Rf*, Deus *Uc*; (qu'el) que *ABDGNOQRf*, qi *Uc*; son uasal *U*; trichadors *f*. 37. (Amors) adors *U*, aors *c*; (fai) fui *O*; (que) ques *GQUcf*, quel *IKNOR*. 38. E cels *DNf*; (qu'a faitz) cafartz *O*; (li) lor *Q*; porta *c*, a fait *U*. 39. per dreg dels natural *R*. 40. Sa *D*; (qu'ilh) quel *CO*, quels *f*; (dig) faich *ABDIKNR*.

VI. *lacking f*. 42. bontat *O*; (ab) a *GNQU*; (parejar) prezar *Uc*. 43. es *lacking N*. 44. Genser *lacking Uc*, Gensers *R*; cum es entre f. la flors *U*; entre las fuelhas *R*, entre foilla *c*. 45. Et ieu am la (la am *IK*) trop (mot *R*) et ill petit me *ABDIKNORUc*. 46. (n'ai) uai *U*; (que·m) qe *c*. 47. (Qu'al) Cul *O*; (s'ilh) si *ABDIKNORUc*; (del) de *GQRUc*; sobre toç *Q*; non *GNQ*. 48. Tant ai *R*, Nai tant *IK*; (d'onor) de ioi *ABDIKNR*, donors *GQUc*; (cobri·l) coble los *c*, trobi *R*.

VII. 49. del *D*. 50. (Sen) Chant *R*; tot cant es *RU*; toz *G*. 51. (sobre·ls) sobre *DQU*, sobrel *G*, sobreç *N*, sobre le *c*; ualen *Uc*. 52. Conoiserai *N*; dic o ben o mal *IK*, dic ben o mal *O*.

TRANSLATION

I. Every man who blames what he should praise praises likewise what he should blame. I say this because Love is condemned by foolish judges who do not know how to show cleverly wherefore. Now is the time when one speaks good of evil and likewise evil of good: wherefore their saying is not seasoned with salt.

II. He who wishes to shame another by his blame should think about it seriously; for I have seen many blamers blamed and many cast down who thought themselves exalted. Therefore he who blames should take care that no one can blame him for anything, for a man should first make himself loyal before calling another treacherous or disloyal.

III. I hear many men accuse Love and in subtle wise speak ill of him;—but I have also seen knights and troubadours whom he raised high from a lowly state and from high to higher still, so unrestrained that they used no check in speaking ill of Love without any pity, so that it is a case of mortal treason; and those whom he has raised up from nothing act thus!

IV. But one cannot prove that rightly; for Love does well whatever he should do, since he enters into ladies loved and into their lovers, from which act courtesy and valor and everything that pertains to true worth are born and come forth. Love is not obliged to do more, I believe. Therefore, since he shows them the good and they do otherwise, when they blame him for it they commit a mortal sin.

V. By Christ! They lie, as it seems to me, for there is no king who can guard his kingdom all alone without helpers, after he finds out that his vassals are traitors. Therefore, since Love does well everything that is fitting, and those whom he has made are faithless to him, I say that one should, by the law of nature, say of them what they have said of Love—so God help me!

VI. I know a lady who finds no peer who can compare with her in beauty. Her beauty is noblest among the noble, like the flower among the leaves. I love her much: she loves me little; but I have always a comfortable thought which pleases me—that at least, even if she does not help me to a surplus, I have so much honor from her that I get back my capital.

VII. Because he knows more than the others and upholds wisdom and knowledge and everything good, the Emperor, who is worthy over the worthy, will know whether I speak well or ill.

NOTES

Sixteen MSS: *ABCDD^{c}FaGIKNOQRUcf*. Both *D^c* and *Fa* contain only the second stanza. De Bartholomaeis (*Poesie storiche*, II, 167) prints stanzas I and VII, after Mahn's reading of *C*. The following stemma represents fairly well the relationships of the MSS:

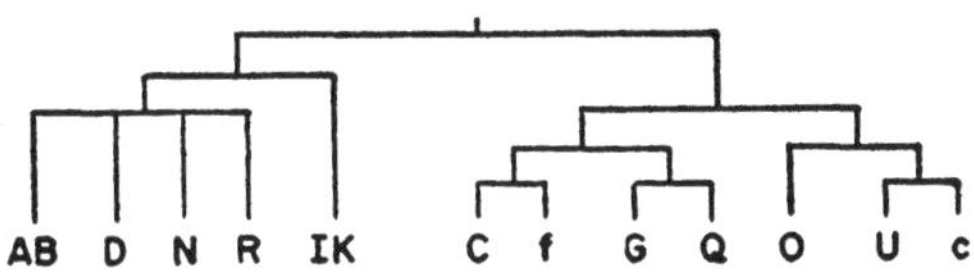

The main division is based on lines 40, 48.

IK: 33, 34, etc.
ABDNR: 34

Cf: 32, 33.
CGQ(f): 28, 45, 46
GQ: 24, 30
OUc: 11, 27
Uc: 23, 32, 34, etc.

The exact position of *DNR* is hard to determine, since they seem to have no constant affiliations among themselves; nor does any one of them seem notably closer than the others to *AB*. We have not tried to place *D^c* and *Fa*, as they contain too little to judge by; but they appear to belong with *ABDIKNR*. There are many deviations from the groupings indicated in this stemma, but mostly of a sort (e.g., 37) that can be explained as coincidence or as the result of independent correcting of the text in hand. The common mistake of *CR* in 9 (*E franchamen* for *Estranhamen*) is due to an easy substitution of a more obvious word for a less obvious one.

Base: *C*.

For the subject of the poem, see the introductory note on number 40. Many of the expressions here are similar to those in 40 and 17.

13–14. Cnyrim, *Sprichwörter*, no. 593.

26. Cf. the thought of poem 15, likewise addressed to Frederick II.

48. *captal*. Aimeric makes use of commercial terms in a number of poems. Compare the first stanza of 43.

53

"US JOIS NOVELS, COMPLITZ DE GRANS BEUTATZ"

The poem appearing under this number in Bartsch and Pillet-Carstens is only a part of the poem of Daude de Pradas *Ben aj' amors, car anc me fetz cauzir* (124, 6). See the part of the Introduction dealing with attributions, and my article in *Modern Language Notes*, May, 1949, p. 333. Since the poem has been edited critically, apart from the two MSS versions which bear the name of Aimeric, by Mr. A. H. Schutz, in his edition of Daude (*Bibliothèque méridionale*, number 22, 1933), we will not reproduce the full text here. But we give in an appendix a separate critical edition of the version attributed to Aimeric.

APPENDIX

We have denied to Aimeric two poems (31, 53) previously attributed to him. For our reasons, see the section of the Introduction which deals with attributions. In order that the poems may be easily accessible, we print them here. We have already given a critical edition of 31 in *Romance Philology*, II, 83; so we simply give the text of the poem here, without variants. The other (53) is, as we have seen, part of a poem by Daude de Pradas. We have published, in *Modern Language Notes*, May, 1949, p. 333, a set of variants indicating how the version ascribed to Aimeric differs from the critical text of Mr. Schutz, as printed in his edition of Daude. The version printed here is the text of *C* (uncorrected), with variants from *R*; these are the two MSS which give the poem to Aimeric.

31

(text of *A*)

I. Lanqan chanton li auzeil en primier,
E son partit d'invern e del tempier,
E·il prat son vert, blanc, e vermeill e blau,
E clar li riu contra·l doutz temps soau,—
Adoncs estau d'amor en cossirier,
De fin talan leial e dreiturier,
Cum s'ieu l'agues fina e naturau.

II. Fals amador mi fant gran destorbier,
Car son janglos, enojos, mal parlier;
Mas ieu pero tenc la dreita carrau
E vauc avan suavet et a frau.
Qu'eu l'auzi dir en un ver reprovier:
Per trop parlar creisson maint encombrier;
Per qu'eu m'en cel a tot homen carnau.

III. Eu sui amics. Ja celar non o quier;
E m'amia non sabran lausengier.
Quan ben i pens, totz esbahitz n'estau.
Del ric penssar mos coratges s'esgau.
Dieu e midonz mi rend per preisonier.
De sa preison ja mais issir non quier,
Car l'ai plevit l'ostatge per aitau.

IV. Fresca color plus que flors de rosier,
Richa faisso, ma don' al cors leugier,
Ben puosc jurar Dieu e Sain Nicholau:
Vostra beutatz ten de totas la clau.
Prezar si pot plus d'autre cavallier
Cui vos volretz aver per soudadier.
Adorar pot lo rei esperitau.

V. No·m meravill si m'en ai desirier
Qu'eu la tengues en chambra o en vergier.
Anc Dieus non fetz sa par ni atretau.
Eu non dic trop ni non la sobrelau:
L'uoill mi mostron don la vei voluntier.
No·n cuich esser tengutz per messongier
En esta cort ni en autra leiau.

VI. Dompna, merce del vostre carcerier!
Si m'aiut Dieus qu'er m'a mout gran mestier
Que me donetz un messatgier corau
Qe·m sapcha dir de vos cossi·us estau.
Autre thesaur non vos deman ni·us qier,
Mas, s'a vos platz, un vostre latinier;
Qe ben parlar no·us puosc, maint' hora i vau.

VII. Doussa terra on vi midonz l'autrier,
Jhesus la gart de mal e d'encombrier.
Q'ieu me restrai, car ades no·i estau.
E n'ai lo cor fals et irat e brau;
Car s'ieu estes lonc lieis un an plenier,
No·m tenria totz l'ans un jorn entier.
Eu voill morir en l'ora q'ieu m'en vau.

VIII. Salamos, ten lo vers per dreiturier!
A garentis en trac Peire Rotgier,
Q'el conois ben si li mot son cabau.
Si·l sos es bons, midonz ador e lau.

53

(text of *C*)

I. Us joys novelhs complitz de grans beutatz,
Guay, amoros, cuende e de bon grat,

On es fis pretz valens e melhurat,
M'a si conquist no puesc pensar d'alhor;
Que no vau tan vas autra part
Qu'ades mon cor non an lai e mey huelh,
E s'ieu aisso lur vedi ni lur tuelh,
Ja fin' Amor no m'en fassa jauzir.

II. Gaug e plazer m'en ve on plus m'en duelh.
Be sui paguatz quan m'en ve a fugir,
Quar trop vuelh mais per lieys cui am languir
Qu'autra·m des so don ylh me fay erguelh;
E ges no vuelh per res aver conquist
Belha domna que leu m'agues joy dat,
Quar non es joys si non l'adutz Honors,
Ni es Honors si non l'adutz Amors.

III. S'Amors o vol e·m fai merce Secors,
Ieu serai tost gueritz de mas dolors
E del maltrag on ai tostz temps estat;
Mas si·m destrenh Amors e·m fier e·m bat
Que tot quan pes me sembla d'autre fuelh.
Per fols m'en tenc quar ja vuelh ni dezir
So que no·m pot ni no·m deu avenir,
E non per tal qu'ieu remanc tals cum suelh.

IV. Ges de Midons no·m pot Razos partir,
Qu'ie·m clam per Dieu o per humilitat;
E si merce tra de lieys sa ricors,
Ieu fas de sai de Merce mon capduelh;
Ez ylh no·n pert son pretz ni sa valors,
Si Chauzimens li daura son erguelh,
Que·l dieus d'amor o a per dreg jutjat
Que domna deu son amic enriquir.

V. D'esser clamans mi desviest e·m despuelh,
E grazirai si·m denha neys aucir
Amors, que m'es capdels, tors e palays
Totz jorns, ez er de pensamens honratz.
De joy novelh me ten be per paguatz,
Quar no l'enguana de re·l miradors.
Tostz temps la vuelh amar ez obezir
E car tener: qui·s vuelha, s'en janguelh!

2. e *lacking*. 4. (d'alhor) alhors. 12. (des) de. 14. que magues leu ioy dat. 22. (m'en) me. 26. (o) e. 29. valor. 30. (erguelh) escuelh. 31. (dieus d'amor) drech damors. 36. (ez er) e ser. 37. Del.

This is evidently a very faulty text. One line (5) lacks two syllables, and the rimes are often false: either because a flectional -s is added or omitted, or because the order of words is changed (35), or because a substitution of words has destroyed the rime (13). But a glance at Mr. Schutz's text will show where the mistake lies; and since our only purpose in printing this version is for comparison with that text, we do not feel obliged to indicate the correct forms here.

INDEX OF PROPER NAMES

In this table, the spellings are regularized somewhat, and all names are given in the oblique case.

GLOSSARY

Words that do not appear in Levy's *Petit dictionnaire*, or whose use by Aimeric calls for some comment; for fuller explanation, see the note on the poem and line where the word occurs.

A

abelhit (22, 20), pleasing.
agensar (20, 36), to be pleasing (used without an object).
apel (36, 6), a call (as in poker?).

B

bar (19, 46), valiant (used with a proper name).

C

car (45, 11), unusual, difficult of comprehension.
colar (50, 41), to cease.
color (32, 30), color (*masculine gender*).
cominal (43, 6), shared equally.
contracorre (4, 23), discredit.
cor. ab cor que (37, 27), in order that, so that.
cors (19, 38; 22, 32), person; *mos cors*, I.

D

delir (18, 25) destroy.
desai (23, 18); is this a mistake for a word corresponding to Old French *dehet* (*ait*) "cursed be"?
desbevolensa (20, 10) displeasure, ill-will.
desfazendat (19, 13), idler, non-participant (?).
devire (20, 37), reveal.
doussezir (7, 46; 20, 7), sweeten.

E

enfoletir (se) (20, 31), lose one's mind.
engardar (15, 29; 38, 14), to protect.
engrestara (7a, 4), a kind of flask.
entrecimamen (6, 46), entanglement, confused reasoning.
error (39, 26), error (*masculine gender*).

F

fablel, flabel (44, 61), kind of poem.

G

gaire. anz de gaire (35, 11) before long.

J

joncada (9, 1), a kind of cheese.
jorn. lo jorn (29, 12) every day?

L

laisar. lays m'o (30, 6), I leave off, I say no more.
langor (13, 6), languor.
loigner (47, 32), is this equivalent to *lonhar*? See the note.

M

malgignos (19, 29), disloyal?
matreseiar (6, 53), knock down.

P

partir razos (6, 3), to debate subjects, choose alternatives.
plai. trobar plai (10, 13), to pick a quarrel.

R

razo (19, 1) alternative in a debate; see *partir*, above.
razonar. se razonar per (6, 44) acknowledge oneself to be.
refre (18, 40), a check, curb (?).
revidador (36, 9), one who bids higher than another.
revit (36, 8), a bid made above another bid.

S

sabor. aver sabor de (19, 23), desire, crave.
sade (11, 20), pleasant, delightful.
sal, salt. *metre sal* (43, 43), season, give savor to.
sal. esser sals (28, 20), to be paid for, rewarded.

senhoria (43, 9), control, a controlling interest.
sentir (17, 45), to be gifted in perception (?).

T

talabaz (44, 52), a shield.
temor (19, 24), fear (*masculine gender*?).
tirador (32, 23), leech, blood-sucker?
to (34, 16), musical mode (?).
tremar (47, 21–22), tremble.

V

vet (13, 39), *membrum virile*.